# Star Trek
# FAQ

Series Editor: Robert Rodriguez

# Star Trek FAQ

## Everything Left to Know About the First Voyages of the Starship Enterprise

Mark Clark

**APPLAUSE**
**THEATRE & CINEMA BOOKS**
An Imprint of Hal Leonard Corporation

Published in 2012 by Applause Theatre & Cinema Books
An Imprint of Hal Leonard Corporation
7777 West Bluemound Road
Milwaukee, WI 53213

Trade Book Division Editorial Offices
33 Plymouth St., Montclair, NJ 07042

The FAQ series was conceived by Robert Rodriguez and developed with Stuart Shea.

STAR TREK trademarks and related logos are owned by CBS Studios Inc.

All photos are vintage publicity stills from the author's collection, except as noted.

Printed in the United States of America

Book design by Snow Creative Services

Library of Congress Cataloging-in-Publication Data

Clark, Mark, 1966–
    Star trek FAQ : everything left to know about the first voyages of the Starship Enterprise / by Mark Clark.
        p. cm.
    Includes bibliographical references and index.
1. Star trek (Television program)—Miscellanea. I. Title.
    PN1992.77.S73C525 2012
    791.45'72—dc23
                                                            2012002348

ISBN 978-1-55783-792-9

www.applausebooks.com

For Vanessa, my favorite Trekaholic

# Contents

## These Are the Voyages: On the Screen, 1966–69

## Prime Directives: Social Commentary and Recurring Themes

## That Which Survives: *Star Trek* in the 1970s

## On the Edge of Forever: The Legacy of *Star Trek*

# Foreword

So much has been written and said about *Star Trek* in all of its various shapes and forms and incarnations that it may be time to declare some kind of moratorium. Perhaps congressional action is necessary to protect the environment.

At the last *Trek* convention I attended, several dealers had huge tables of nothing but *Star Trek* books. Six TV series and eleven movies have generated hundreds of production diaries, tell-all memoirs, novels, spin-offs, anthologies, comics, quote books, dictionaries, encyclopedias, dissertations, deconstructions, psychoanalyses, metaphorical interpretations, and ride-along tie-ins of all kinds.

In addition to that, there have been thousands of articles, reviews, essays, studies, and even college-level courses. There have been hundreds of conventions and thousands of panel discussions. There are an uncountable number of websites about *Trek*, about all the various aspects of its production and all the people connected to it. There are websites on how to build costumes and props and sets and how to create CGI models of all the different starships. There are hundreds of videos of parodies and dozens of professional-level fan productions.

Maybe it's time to call in the EPA. A new *Star Trek* movie or TV series will cause whole forests to be plowed under, cause the sea level to rise, and deplete the oxygen levels of this planet. I fear for the future of humanity!

Okay, and maybe I had too much coffee this morning, too.

The important thing here is that a lot has been said about *Star Trek* and a lot of the stuff said about *Star Trek* has been like a game of Russian telephone. You know the game. You get a long line of people, and the first person whispers a phrase into the second person's ear. The second person whispers to the third, and the phrase gets passed from one person to the next, all the way down the line, until it gets to the last person. And what originally started out as *"We hold these truths to be self evident—"* comes back as *"Behold! Ruth sees an elephant!"*

It's been more than forty-five years since the first episode of *Star Trek* aired (September 8, 1966. NBC, 8:30 p.m.). Looking back is like looking through the wrong end of a telescope. Every day that passes, the image gets a little smaller, a little more distant. The facts become a little more blurred. The details get fuzzed. People make up things to explain what they don't know for sure. Whole mythologies grow and take on a life of their own in books and essays and websites and blogs. You are justified in being skeptical.

You hold in your hands the latest iteration. And I encourage you to bring skepticism to this effort as well. Fortunately, Mark Clark has done a great deal of research, and there's a lot more evidence here and a lot less elephant.

This is not the last word on *Star Trek*. I doubt we'll ever get the last word, but as words go, this is a good collection of them, and it will serve as a useful reference for anyone needing a good overview on the production of the first *Star Trek* TV series, the one that started it all. You'll see that for yourself, once you dive in.

But there's something else that needs to be said here, something much more important than any collection of facts, no matter how skillful the collection—*Star Trek* may have begun as a television show, but it has become something enormously greater than that. It has become a defining piece of American culture.

As a TV series, *Star Trek* was an occasionally clumsy, almost quaint vision of the future—but it also served as a running commentary on twentieth-century society. The '60s were a time of enormous cultural upheaval—a new generation was coming of age, the Cold War was threatening to heat up, a long-simmering civil rights struggle had finally come to a boil, the nation was entangled in a terrible war in Vietnam, drug use had become pandemic, and the sexual revolution was beginning to change the way men and women regarded each other. And those things were just the tip of the iceberg.

American television, always courageously avoiding any kind of controversy that might upset the viewers, stepped up to the challenge of the times and gave us seriously thought-provoking entertainment like *Bewitched, I Dream of Jeannie, Gilligan's Island, The Beverly Hillbillies, Petticoat Junction, Green Acres, The Flying Nun*, and *Mr. Ed*.

Meanwhile, over at the Desilu lot, there was this barely noticed little show that took place in some distant future and on far-off planets, so it wasn't really about *us*, was it? It was just more of that "sci-fi stuff." It had a spaceship and a guy with pointy ears and pretty women in revealing costumes. You didn't have to take it seriously, did you? And it wasn't pulling an enormous rating, so the network wasn't paying very close attention to it.

So . . . Gene Roddenberry, Gene L. Coon, D. C. Fontana, and about fifty other authors took advantage of that freedom to write stories about mutual assured destruction, the insanities of war, overpopulation, racial madness, drug use, brainwashing, cults, cultural meddling, hippie dropouts, sexual identity, and even our fundamental relationship with God. (Oh, and one odd little comedy about an invasive species in a closed ecology.)

Nobody else on television was tackling such enormous subjects. Few other shows were challenging the audience to actually *think* about things. Indeed, the great disgrace of the American television industry of the '60s was just how much the studios, the networks, and the producers underestimated their audiences.

*Star Trek* was a subversive show. It challenged the audience to think about things. Its episodes were easily digestible morality plays—the crew of the starship challenged the circumstances and were challenged in turn. They juggled logic against emotion before taking action—and always, always, they learned something in the process.

I believe this is the primary reason why *Star Trek* has had such a profound effect on its audience. Just as the crew of the *Enterprise* were challenged each week, so was the audience itself challenged to consider the morality and the ethics of the issue. *Star Trek* not only appealed to the intelligence of its audience, it *demanded* that its audience apply its intelligence.

Today, any science fiction show can have spectacular effects. Most do, depending on the size of the budget. Back in the '60s, there wasn't a lot of budget and therefore there wasn't a lot of eye candy, so the authors of the episodes had to plan their stories within much stricter limits. This turned out to be a virtue. The episodes were about the people and the ideas they were up against, not the monsters, not the effects, not the gimmick of the week. So the resolution of the situation had to come from the characters, not the double-talk generator.

And this is why *Star Trek* was a *very* subversive show. It represented a whole different context in American television. Most American television is focused inward. It's about people struggling with the circumstances of today—as if such problems are so big that they are unsolvable unless you have some kind of super power. And if that isn't enough to make you feel helpless, every eleven minutes the story gets interrupted so the advertiser can tell you that you smell bad.

But *Star Trek* said, "Hey, all the problems of today—we're going to solve them. We're going to get better, we're going to get healthier and happier and smarter and we're going to be a better species. We're going to be rational and compassionate and big enough to challenge the universe. The future is going to be great. We're going to the stars."

*Star Trek* wasn't just an optimistic vision of the future—it was a profound shift in how we thought about ourselves and our participation in that future. And it was more than that—it was one of the ways we designed and built the future we wanted to live in.

*Star Trek* showed us a world where doors slid open as we approached, where we had small flip-open communicators that let us talk to anyone in the world, where we had wall-size screens and video communication, silver discs that stored hellabytes of data, universal translators, medical beds, desktop computers, tablets that gave us instant access to information, supercomputers that understood speech, and a lot of other technologies we're still designing and building.

And all of this connected with an audience hungry for possibility—that essential human desire to imagine and create and leave the world a better place than before. Audiences didn't just watch *Star Trek*—they were moved, touched, and inspired. They saw a world in which they wanted to live.

Today, *Star Trek* has evolved into an industry, a franchise, a merchandising brand—the executives in charge cannot help but see it as a marketing device, a way to sell things, a way to generate profits.

But just like the audiences of the past, the audiences of today still see *Star Trek* as something much more.

Audiences see *Star Trek* as a promise. It stands as one of the better possibilities of the futures before us—it's a vision of a world that works for all of us, with no one and nothing left out.

And that's why this book is worth your time—it's not just a history of the most enduring television show ever, it's an acknowledgment of the passion of those who created it, as well as the enthusiasm of the audience that still loves it today.

*David Gerrold*

David Gerrold is a prolific author and screenwriter best known for writing the classic *Star Trek* episode "The Trouble with Tribbles." His 1994 novelette *The Martian Child* won the Hugo and Nebula awards and was the basis for a 2007 movie of the same title.

# Acknowledgments

Thanks and praise to:

Rob Rodriguez, who invited me to make this voyage, and whose excellent *Fab Four FAQ* served as my template.

David Hogan, who suggested I contact Rob, and whose *Three Stooges FAQ* is an eye-gouging, ear-yanking, skull-rattling must-read.

Bryan Senn, my onetime coauthor, whose peerless proof-reading skills and stalwart friendship are deeply appreciated.

The Reverend Julie Fisher, whose keen insights were invaluable.

Ron and Margaret Borst, Kip Colegrove, David Harnack, Mark Miller, Ted Okuda, and Cricket Park, whose enthusiasm for and support of this project meant more than they know.

Bookseller Lisa Meier (iwc_2004 on eBay) and the proprietors of Trace and Trev's Twisted Toys, who provided rare images.

Preston Hewis of East Bank Images, who lovingly photographed some of the memorabilia pictured in this book.

Marybeth Keating of Applause Books, who was always there when I needed help.

David Gerrold, whose books and teleplays provided inspiration.

The cast, crew, and writers of *Star Trek*, whose work only improved as I studied it more and more closely.

And, most of all, to my wife, whose sacrifices made this book possible and whose suggestions made it stronger.

May you all live long and prosper.

*Mark Clark*
*Mentor on the Lake, Ohio 2011*

# Introduction

# Tomorrow Is Yesterday

The first book about *Star Trek* appeared in 1968, while the series was still on the air. Since then, *Trek* books have multiplied like tribbles.

Numerous histories have been published, along with biographies and autobiographies of the show's cast and creative leadership. Other volumes have explored the physics, biology, computer science, and philosophy behind the program, among other topics. Many authors have attempted to analyze the appeal and cultural impact of the series. The show has also been the subject of countless magazine and newspaper articles, fanzines, and websites.

So why write another book about *Star Trek*? The answer to that question is twofold.

## What *Star Trek* Is, and What It Isn't

Primarily, *Star Trek FAQ* exists for the same reason as all those other books—because *Star Trek* is a work of profound influence and ongoing fascination.

Few (if any) television programs have had greater impact on the real world than *Star Trek*. Generations of scientists, engineers, physicians, and writers, among countless others, were inspired by Spock or Scotty or Dr. McCoy or Gene Roddenberry. Uhura and Sulu reinforced young African and Asian Americans' self-confidence and helped them feel empowered to pursue their dreams. *Star Trek* also altered the course of science fiction and popular culture by changing perceptions of SF. Once dismissed as juvenile drivel, the genre is now the stuff of blockbuster movies, smash TV shows, and best-selling novels, as well as university curriculums and museum exhibits.

*Star Trek*, which once struggled to survive from one season to the next, has become immortal—and, beyond that, inescapable. The series, and the multimedia franchise that grew from it, is now woven inextricably into the fabric of America and the world. The show's vocabulary ("warp speed," "beam me up," "set for stun") has become our own. The era of the communicator-like flip phone may have passed, but cutting-edge computer and medical technology continues to imitate *Trek*.

The classic *Trek* series also serves as a window into our past. As a film historian, I have specialized in writing about horror and science fiction productions because these works provide unique insights into their times and into the emotional state of their audiences. It's always illuminating to revisit previous generations' visions of the future. The anxieties and aspirations of every era run deep in its popular entertainments, but often bubble to the surface in works of fantasy. This is especially true of *Star Trek*, which creator-producer Roddenberry intended from the start to serve as a vehicle for social commentary.

However, *Star Trek* is not a relic, not some ancient artifact looked upon reverently but seldom actively engaged. While some elements of the show (miniskirts, go-go boots, and beehive hairdos, for instance) now seem dated, *Trek*'s overarching dramatic concerns (such as the search for harmony between cultures and for greater understanding of what it means to be human) are evergreen. As a result, *Star Trek* still seems vital, even timely. The other essential element in the ongoing appeal and relevance of *Star Trek* is its radical optimism. Roddenberry's vision of a future where the ancient evils of war, poverty, and racism have been replaced by peace, prosperity, and brotherhood comforted its audience during the turbulent 1960s and continues to reassure viewers today. In the four decades since *Star Trek* left the air, our world has made only incremental progress toward the future Roddenberry imagined. Until his vision becomes a reality—something that, sadly, is unlikely to happen any sooner than the twenty-third century—*Star Trek* will continue to serve as a beacon of hope.

## What This Book Isn't, and What It Is

The other reason I've written *Star Trek FAQ* is precisely *because* there are so many other *Trek* books already out there. The sheer, dizzying multitude of *Trek* literature can be daunting for casual fans—that silent legion of viewers who love *Star Trek* but don't speak Klingonese or go to the grocery store wearing Vulcan ears and a Starfleet uniform (not that there's anything wrong with that). These fans don't regularly attend conventions and may not consider themselves "Trekkies" or "Trekkers" (terms I have, for the most part, eschewed in the writing of this book), and they don't have time to sift through the mountain of *Trek*-related works at the local bookstore or library. Yet their patronage of *Star Trek* TV series and movies has made the franchise a cultural touchstone. *Star Trek FAQ* is aimed primarily at this audience, distilling the overwhelming volume of *Trek* scholarship into easily consumable sips.

However, I'm confident that diehards who purchase every new *Star Trek* book that reaches the market (may the Great Bird of the Galaxy bless your immortal souls) will find items of interest in *Star Trek FAQ*. While researching this manuscript, I spent eight months fishing into the nooks and crannies of *Trek* lore for revealing yet underreported stories and illuminating minutiae. Applause Books' unique *FAQ* format enables me to combine this material with more familiar elements of the *Star Trek* story in unconventional ways, smashing them together in the literary equivalent of a supercollider to produce fresh insights. I'm convinced you'll find the results exhilarating whether this is the first *Star Trek* book you've read or the fiftieth.

*Star Trek FAQ* is not an episode guide, nor is it a compendium of fictional "facts." It doesn't provide in-depth analysis of every installment, and it won't reveal how the *Enterprise*'s deflector shields work. There are numerous other resources for that type of information. As a starting place, I recommend *The Star Trek Encyclopedia* by Michael and Denise Okuda and Debbie Mirek, or the indispensable, fan-operated Memory Alpha website.

*Star Trek FAQ* is primarily a historical account, with some analysis and criticism to provide perspective. It chronicles producer Gene Roddenberry's struggle to bring *Star Trek* to television, the ingenuity and dedication demonstrated by the program's creators and cast throughout its production, the events that led to the series' premature demise, and those behind its unlikely resurrection. It also reveals how *Star Trek* affected the lives of its cast and crew—mostly for the worse, at least initially.

This is one of the most dramatic narratives in the history of film and television—and it's a love story. The series was sustained throughout its production by the passion of its producers, writers, technicians, artisans, and actors, and later revived by the adoration of its uncommonly empowered fans, who refused to let the program drift into memory. Instead, they kept it alive in reruns, by writing their own stories, through the purchase of all manner of *Trek*-themed merchandise, and by bombarding Paramount Pictures with letters until the studio finally bowed to the will of Trekdom. No fan community ever exerted such a profound pull on the direction of a media franchise or displayed more intense devotion.

While it's perfectly acceptable to read this book front to back, *Star Trek FAQ* has been designed for nonlinear consumption. Each chapter functions independently. Although this inevitably results in some duplication of information between sections, I have tried to minimize repetition. So feel free to flip around. For instance, if you're interested in Leonard Nimoy (and what *Trek* fan isn't?), you could start by reading chapters 5, 27, 16, 37, and 42, which (respectively) detail the actor's work prior to *Star Trek*, his performance as Spock, his conflicts with Roddenberry and with costar William Shatner during the show's production, his career in the years immediately after *Trek*, and the impact of the series on his personal life.

I have described this book as a distillation. This includes information from numerous books, magazine and newspaper articles, and electronic media (websites, documentaries, DVD audio commentaries, etc.). In most cases, what I've written was corroborated with multiple sources including memoirs by, published interviews with, and biographies of, the show's cast and creative brain trust. I have provided specific attribution for direct quotes and for data obtained from unique sources. A comprehensive bibliography is included, and I hope readers will use it as a gateway to a wealth of other *Star Trek* knowledge. It's impossible to include every fascinating story or amusing anecdote about this program in any single book—or even a pair of books.

*Star Trek FAQ* begins in 1921 with the birth of Gene Roddenberry and concludes in 1978 with the announcement that *Star Trek* would return as a feature film. The companion volume *Star Trek FAQ 2.0*, coming in 2013, will explore the full flowering of the franchise in the 1980s and '90s, when theatrical blockbusters like *The Wrath of Khan* and *The Voyage Home* along with sequel series including *The Next Generation* helped *Star Trek* reach the pinnacle of its popularity and cultural influence. If you enjoy this volume, I hope you'll return for the sequel.

# All Our Yesterdays

## The Prehistory of *Star Trek*

# Great Bird of the Galaxy

## The Pre-*Trek* Adventures of Gene Roddenberry

ate in life, Gene Roddenberry purposefully conflated his identity with that of his most famous creation. "I am *Star Trek*," he often said. This was true enough for the series' famously ardent fans, and Roddenberry reaped significant rewards from the association. Even though he lost control of the *Trek* movie franchise after its first entry and became a mere figurehead on *Star Trek: The Next Generation* after its first few seasons, Paramount Pictures continued to pay Roddenberry as a consultant because it knew fans would reject any *Trek* missing the franchise creator's seal of approval. Nevertheless, defining Roddenberry by *Star Trek* grossly oversimplifies the man himself. He was a complex and sometimes contradictory figure who can't be summed up in any single title.

Bob Justman came closer than anyone else to capturing the expansive Roddenberry. During *Star Trek*'s first season, associate producer Justman wrote a production memo that jokingly referred to his boss as "the Great Bird of the Galaxy." Roddenberry liked the poetic nickname, and in later years *Trek* fans adopted it as a term of affection for the creator of their beloved franchise. Some went even further, referring to him as "Goddenberry." Although far from divine, Roddenberry was everything else his worshipful fans imagined him to be—a highly intelligent, restlessly creative dynamo whose vision of a utopian future free from war, poverty, and discrimination continues to inspire millions. But he was other things, too, which fans might prefer to overlook—an unrepentant philanderer and an opportunistic egotist reluctant to give credit when due, and even more reluctant to share the monetary rewards of his success. These tendencies led to numerous personal and professional rifts during the production of the classic *Star Trek* series, conflicts that only escalated in later years when the financial stakes were higher.

Like many great storytellers, Roddenberry frequently took creative license with his own recollections. For biographers and historians, this is not only a vexing trait but also a puzzling one, considering how colorful his life truly was. If ever a story could stand on its own merits, it was Roddenberry's. Even before

A dashing, young Gene Roddenberry posed for this publicity still during production of his first TV series, *The Lieutenant* (1963–64).

he seized upon the idea that would become *Star Trek*, he had already piled up several lifetimes worth of drama as a decorated war veteran, a commercial pilot (and plane crash survivor), a Los Angeles police officer, and an award-winning screenwriter and television producer.

## Let That Be Your Last Battlefield (Early life and military career, 1921–45)

Eugene Wesley Roddenberry was born August 19, 1921, in El Paso, Texas, but moved to Southern California when he was barely a year old. His father, Eugene Edward Roddenberry ("Big Gene" to his family), joined the Los Angeles police force as a beat cop. "Little Gene" was a bright but introverted child who sometimes felt ill at ease in his own home, chafing under the Southern Baptist instruction of his mother, Caroline Goleman Roddenberry, and Big Gene's vocal racism. Although from all accounts he was a good father, the elder Roddenberry commonly referred to African Americans as "niggers" and Jews as "kikes." Young Gene escaped his discomfort by reading pulp magazines (he was especially fond of Edgar Rice Burroughs's John Carter of Mars yarns and E. E. "Doc" Smith's Skylark series), listening to radio shows (including *The Lone Ranger* and *The Shadow*), and going to the movies (where the *Flash Gordon* serials were favorites). Despite an I.Q. tested in the 99.9th percentile, young Gene made pedestrian grades in high school, where he remained aloof from most of his classmates.

Roddenberry finally emerged from his shell after entering Los Angeles City College in 1939. He was pursuing a criminal justice degree with the intent of following in his father's footsteps when he began dating Eileen Rexroat, who would later become the first Mrs. Gene Roddenberry. During his second year at LACC, Gene discovered a second love as well—flying. He joined the Civilian Pilot Training Program, an Army Air Corps–sponsored initiative that offered young men no-cost flight instruction. Roddenberry displayed great aptitude and earned his pilot's license at age nineteen. Following graduation in 1941, he put his law enforcement career on hold and joined the Air Corps. Six months later the Japanese attacked Pearl Harbor, and the United States entered World War II.

During the war, Gene piloted reconnaissance and bombing missions, usually in a B-17 Flying Fortress, with the 394th Bombing Squadron, while stationed in Hawaii, Fiji, Guadalcanal and elsewhere in the Pacific theater. Roddenberry claimed to have flown 89 missions, although that number is not verifiable. His planes were often fired upon by antiaircraft guns or attacked by Japanese fighters, but Roddenberry maintained that the most terrifying flight of his career was a recon mission that took his B-17 directly into a typhoon. Blinded by wind and rain, the low-flying plane was nearly smashed by the massive, roiling waves. On August 25, 1943, Roddenberry was attempting to take off from a makeshift airfield on the tiny island of Espiritu Santu when his Flying Fortress crashed, killing two crewmen. An official investigation blamed the accident on mechanical breakdown. A month later, Gene's unit rotated home, and Roddenberry spent the rest of the war stateside. He was awarded the Distinguished Flying Cross and the Air Medal before leaving what was by then known as the Army Air Force in 1945.

## Wink of an Eye (Commercial pilot, 1945–48)

After leaving the service, still infatuated with flying, Roddenberry moved to New Jersey and took a job as a commercial pilot for Pan American World Airways. During his off-hours, Gene (who for years had dabbled at writing poems and songs) took a pair of extension classes in creative writing from Columbia University. But his aviation career was a source of constant worry for Eileen, who feared for her husband's safety on the long international flights he was routinely assigned by Pan Am—copiloting routes from New York to Johannesburg, South Africa, and to Calcutta, India. Her concerns proved valid in June 1947. Gene was "deadheading" (a pilot flying as a passenger) on Pan Am flight 121 from Karachi, India, to Istanbul, Turkey, when the aircraft suffered an engine fire and crash-landed in the Syrian desert.

Gene survived the crash because, at the request of Captain Joe Hart, he left the flight deck to calm the panicked passengers in the plane's nearly full cabin and prepare them for the landing attempt. It was about 1:45 a.m. on a moon-less night in the pitch-black desert. On impact, the plane's fuselage was torn in two and a wing was sheared off. Jet fuel spilled and the wreckage was quickly engulfed in flames. Fourteen people died in the crash, including Captain Hart and his copilot. But Roddenberry and two flight attendants helped the other sixteen passengers escape the burning aircraft, collecting first-aid supplies and an inflatable life raft, which was used as a temporary shelter.

Even though he suffered two broken ribs and assorted bruises and cuts during the crash, Roddenberry worked through the night administering first aid to the survivors, some of whom had suffered severe burns. Fortunately, the plane had crashed near the village of Mayadin, Syria. Shortly after sunrise, local villagers descended on the scene, robbing the survivors (and the dead) of their valuables before the Syrian Army arrived to secure the crash site. (At least that's the official version of events. In his memoir *Beam Me Up, Scotty*, James Doohan recounts another version of the story. As Roddenberry told the tale to Doohan, the survivors were rescued by a gay Arab sheik who made sexual advances toward Roddenberry. Roddenberry demurred, but feared his refusal would threaten the lives of the survivors. This colorful story may be indicative of the Great Bird's penchant for embellishing his personal history.) Even after the rescue, however, the ordeal wasn't over for Roddenberry. He was detained in Damascus for weeks while the Syrian government undertook a slow-moving investigation of the crash. Even after he returned home, he had to testify at a safety inquiry held by the Civil Aeronautics Board in New York, who gave Roddenberry a commendation for his actions related to the crash.

## Where His Old Man Had Gone Before (L.A. cop, 1949–56)

Just nine months after he returned from Syria, the Roddenberrys' first child, Darleen, was born. With a growing family came increasing pressure from Eileen to give up aviation. Roddenberry resigned from Pan Am in May 1948 and moved back to Los Angeles. At age twenty-eight he belatedly took up his law enforcement career, joining the L.A. police force. Initially, he was assigned to direct traffic at the intersection of Fifth and Broadway. Roddenberry's father walked a beat his entire career. But with keen intelligence and a previously untapped writing ability, Gene rose quickly through the ranks. After just sixteen months on the force, he secured a cushy position writing press releases and speeches for Police Chief Bill Parker. In retrospect, this may seem like an odd pairing, but the bleeding-heart liberal Roddenberry admired and respected the staunchly conservative Parker, who cleaned up a corruption-plagued department and desegregated the force. Roddenberry befriended another young officer, Wilber Clingan, whom he would later immortalize by naming an alien species—the Klingons—in his honor (retaining the pronunciation of Clingan's name but changing the spelling).

In his eagerness to burnish the image of law enforcement personnel in general and L.A. cops in particular, Chief Parker made common cause with Jack Webb, producer and star of the seminal police drama *Dragnet*. Webb's TV show portrayed the LAPD as a clean-cut, efficient, professional organization. In exchange, Parker's department supplied Webb with real cases on which to base episodes. This is why *Dragnet* always ended with the announcement that "the story you have just heard is true. Only the names have been changed to protect the innocent." Roddenberry helped find these stories for Webb and his writers. This wasn't part of Roddenberry's official duties; he was paid $100 per story by *Dragnet* for supplying a one-page treatment based on actual events (usually splitting the fee with the officer involved in the case). In 1953, after selling several stories, and later watching the shows based on his submissions, Roddenberry decided he wanted a hand in the far more lucrative business of writing complete screenplays. Part of his motivation was his enlarging family. Gene and Eileen would welcome a second daughter, Dawn, in 1954. By then he had been contacted by Stanley Sheldon, a former captain in the LAPD Public Information office now working with Ziv Television Productions, who asked Roddenberry if he would be interested in serving as technical advisor for a new syndicated program called *Mr. District Attorney*. Although still employed as a police officer, Roddenberry's television career was underway.

## The Squire of Hollywood (Screenwriter and TV producer, 1957–64)

Roddenberry quickly graduated from technical advisor to full-fledged screenwriter, providing teleplays for *Mr. District Attorney* and other Ziv-produced series, such as *Highway Patrol*, under the pseudonym Robert Wesley. By 1956, police Sergeant Gene Roddenberry was pulling in more money from television than from law enforcement, and after seven years of service he resigned his post with the LAPD. Over the next several years, Roddenberry's profile—and his income—increased dramatically. Now writing under his own name, he eventually left Ziv, whose shows were syndicated to stations across the U.S. for broadcast in non-prime-time slots, and began writing for major network programs such as *Dr. Kildare*, *The Virginian*, *Have Gun—Will Travel*, and corporate-sponsored dramatic anthologies, including *Chevron Hall of Stars*, the *Kaiser Aluminum Hour*, and *The DuPont Show*. For his *Have Gun* script "Helen of Abiginian," Roddenberry won a Writers Guild of America award in 1958. In this offbeat episode, bounty hunter Paladin (Richard Boone) retrieves an Armenian dancer who tries to elope with a passing cowboy. Paladin collects a $1,000 reward from the girl's father, allays the man's concerns about his daughter's marriage, and plays cupid when the prospective groom gets cold feet.

Despite the accolades and paychecks that were rolling in, Roddenberry began to grow frustrated. Like many scriptwriters, he often was unhappy with the way his work was translated to the screen. And he recognized that the real money lay in creating the series, not in writing the episodes. In 1960, he landed a high-paying gig ($100,000 per year plus profit participation) with Screen Gems Television generating concepts for development. In less than eighteen months with Screen Gems, Roddenberry provided ideas, outlines, and in some cases full pilot screenplays for nearly a dozen proposed series, including two—the war drama *APO 923* and *Defiance County*, about a small-town D.A.—for which unsold pilots were produced. Even though the financial rewards of Gene's endeavors were significant, and despite her gratitude that he was no longer piloting, Eileen Roddenberry was increasingly unhappy with the direction of her husband's career. She was uncomfortable with the late nights and socializing that were part and parcel of the Hollywood lifestyle, and she worried about Gene's relationships with the young actresses he came into contact with. Once again, her concerns were validated as Roddenberry, dissatisfied with Eileen, indulged in trysts with several ingénues and launched a full-fledged, long-term affair with a young actress who would eventually become his second wife.

Marital issues aside, Roddenberry's fortunes continued their rapid ascent. After leaving Screen Gems, working for Arena Productions in partnership with Metro-Goldwyn-Mayer, he created his first successful pilot, which sold in 1962. NBC picked up Roddenberry's peacetime military drama *The Lieutenant*, starring Gary Lockwood as the titular Marine Corps officer, and future Man from U.N.C.L.E. Robert Vaughn as Lockwood's superior. Each week Lt. William Tiberius Rice (Lockwood) helped recruits, active-duty personnel, and even retired marines meet the personal challenges that accompany military service. To reduce costs and increase realism, *The Lieutenant* was shot at Camp Pendleton, the West Coast training facility for the U.S. Marines, and carried a seal of approval from the Corps. However, Roddenberry was frustrated with restrictions placed on him by the Marines, who nixed any story idea that portrayed servicemen in an unfavorable light. Despite generally favorable reviews, the show ran just one season, 1963–64. Appearing Saturdays from 7:30 to 8:30, *The Lieutenant* was outperformed in the Nielsen ratings by *The Jackie Gleason Show* on

CBS and the folk music program *Hootenanny* on ABC. The changing political climate, with escalating American involvement in the Vietnamese civil war, may have also played a part in NBC's decision to scuttle the series. During its short run, however, Roddenberry worked with key personnel who would serve him well in future endeavors, including director Marc Daniels, screenwriters Gene Coon and Dorothy Fontana, casting director Joe D'Agosta, and actors Leonard Nimoy, Nichelle Nichols, Walter Koenig, and Majel Barrett.

By the time NBC had decommissioned *The Lieutenant*, Roddenberry already had two more series concepts typed up. One of these was a straightforward cop show then called *Assignment 100* but later retitled *Police Story* (not to be confused with the Joseph Wambaugh series of the same name that ran from 1973 to 1977). The other was an ambitious proposal for a weekly science fiction program chronicling the spacefaring adventures of Captain Robert T. April and the crew of the starship *Yorktown*. A few details still needed to be refined, but *Star Trek* was on the drawing board. Its journey from page to screen, however, would prove far longer and more convoluted than Roddenberry (or anyone else) could have possibly imagined.

# Space Seeds

## Credited and Uncredited Influences on the Creation of *Star Trek*

S*tar Trek* did not spring forth fully formed from the mind of producer-creator Gene Roddenberry like some golden egg laid by the Great Bird of the Galaxy. Many elements now considered essential to the mythology and appeal of the franchise did not originate with Roddenberry at all, but were introduced later by screenwriters'such as Gene L. Coon (who invented the Klingons and the Prime Directive), and Theodore Sturgeon and Dorothy Fontana (who developed the coolly logical Vulcan culture in episodes such as "Amok Time" and "Journey to Babel"). Roddenberry himself stressed this, although he struggled to verbalize the creative process that led him to create the series. "I don't say that *Star Trek* was created in an instant," the producer told interviewer Yvonne Fern in her book *Gene Roddenberry: The Last Conversation.* "No, it evolved. And a good many people contributed to its evolution. But overall the idea came rather—well, it just came!"

Yes, but where did it come from?

Contrary to popular belief, few of Roddenberry's ideas for *Star Trek* were truly new or innovative. Like most creative breakthroughs, *Trek* was a synthesis of familiar elements, recognizable blocks assembled in an exciting new configuration. *Star Trek* stood apart due to the diversity of Roddenberry's sources of inspiration, the seamlessness with which he melded those influences, and his unifying vision of a promising future for the human race. Here are the most prominent component parts that Roddenberry used in creating *Star Trek*, many of which he acknowledged during his lifetime and some of which he did not:

### *Gulliver's Travels* (1726) by Jonathan Swift

One of the immortal works of English literature, Irishman Jonathan Swift's *Gulliver's Travels* (or, to use the novel's formal title, *Travels Into Several Remote Nations of the World by Captain Lemuel Gulliver*) is at once a delightful fantasy-adventure, a witty parody of the popular traveler's narratives of the early eighteenth century, and a scathing satire of the eighteenth-century English government and Anglican church. The book is divided into four parts, each chronicling a fantastic voyage by Gulliver and each making its own satirical point. The first of these—in which Gulliver is shipwrecked on the island of Lilliput and taken prisoner by its inhabitants, who are one-twelfth his size—remains perennially popular with young readers and is often abridged for a juvenile audience. Gulliver, after single-handedly capturing the entire navy of the rival kingdom of Blefuscu, becomes a favorite of the Lilliputian court (enabling Swift to lampoon the excesses of the court of King George I). Subtle and multilayered, *Gulliver's Travels* seems to grow throughout the reader's lifetime, revealing new insights and implications as its audience become more sophisticated.

From the outset, Roddenberry wanted *Star Trek*, like *Gulliver's Travels*, to function as both fanciful adventure and social commentary. As an ardent political progressive working in the relatively conservative realm of 1960s network television, Roddenberry understood that, like Swift, he would have to disguise his themes in fantasy. While he may have lacked Swift's feathery touch, Roddenberry's program offered thinly veiled statements about the Vietnam War ("A Private Little War"), prejudice ("Balance of Terror"), and segregation ("Let That Be Your Last Battlefield"), among other sensitive topics. "Censorship was so bad that if he could take things and switch them around and maybe paint somebody green and perhaps put weird outfits on them and so forth, he could get some of his ideas across," said his widow, Majel Barrett Roddenberry, in an interview featured on the *Star Trek: The Motion Picture* DVD. "He got lots of ideas through and that's how *Star Trek* was born."

In fact, while spitballing ideas with Desilu executive Herb Solow in 1964 during development of the treatment for *Star Trek*'s original pilot, Roddenberry briefly considered changing the name of the starship's leader to Captain Gulliver and retitling the program *Gulliver's Travels*. Fortunately, according to executive Herb Solow (in his book *Star Trek: The Inside Story*, coauthored with Bob Justman), cooler heads prevailed, and the show's original title was restored—although a dozen other captain's names were considered before Roddenberry finally settled on James T. Kirk.

## The Horatio Hornblower Novels (1937–62) by C. S. Forester

Not only did the captain's name change, but so did his personality. Roddenberry's original model for Kirk was Horatio Hornblower, the brooding hero of C. S. Forester's seafaring adventure yarns, set during the Napoleonic Wars. Introduced in *The Happy Return*, a 1937 tale known in the U.S. as *Beat to Quarters*, Hornblower starred in eleven novels and three short stories, becoming far and away the most famous creation of Cairo-born English novelist Cecil Louis Troughton Smith, who adopted the pen name C. S. Forester. Captain Hornblower is quiet and introspective, vexed by self-doubt and seasickness. Acutely aware of his responsibilities to his ship and its crew, command weighs on him heavily. When readers first meet Hornblower, on page four of *Beat to Quarters*, he is silently pacing the deck. "Up and down, up and down . . . he was entirely lost in thought."

THE MOST AMAZING AD-
VENTURES IN THE MOST
ASTOUNDING SERIAL !
Flash Gordon thunders into life on the screen,
conquering new worlds, destroying death-deal-
ing planets in the most fantastic episodes ever
conceived and filmed !

Universal Presents
BUSTER CRABBE
as
FLASH
GORDON

with JEAN ROGERS as Dale Arden, Charles
Middleton as Emperor Ming, Priscilla
Lawson as Lura, Frank Shannon as
Dr. Zarkov, John Lisbon as Vultan...
From Alex Raymond's Famous News-
paper Strip, Syndicated by King Fea-
tures. A Universal Picture. Directed
by Frederick Stephanie.        2A

Pressbook ad for the 1936 serial *Flash Gordon*, a childhood
favorite of Gene Roddenberry.

Such a character may seem oceans away from William Shatner's energetic, swashbuckling Captain Kirk. Yet in his original outline for the series, created to help him sell *Star Trek* to prospective production studios, Roddenberry describes his starship captain (then named Robert T. April) as "a space-age Captain Horatio Hornblower. . . . A strong, complex personality, he is capable of action and decision which can verge on the heroic—and at the same time lives in a continual battle with self-doubt and the loneliness of command." The parallel is most apparent in the series' original, rejected pilot, "The Cage," which features Jeffrey Hunter as the pensive Captain Christopher Pike. In a strongly Hornbloweresque scene, Pike reveals to his ship's chief surgeon that he is considering resigning his commission: "I'm tired of being responsible for 203 lives," Pike says. "Tired of deciding which mission is too risky and which isn't . . . who lives—and who dies." In the second *Trek* pilot, "Where No Man Has Gone Before," Kirk broods, Hornblower-like, over how to deal with Lieutenant Commander Gary Mitchell (Gary Lockwood), who has gained superhuman tele-kinetic powers. As Spock matter-of-factly lays out the options for neutralizing the increasingly dangerous Mitchell, Kirk turns away and stares into space—clearly agonizing over a decision that pits the life of a friend and trusted crew member against the safety of his ship. As the series progressed and Shatner's more upbeat, confident take on the character took hold, such moments became increasingly rare.

Ultimately, the most enduring vestige of Roddenberry's Hornblower fascination lies in the nautical jargon used aboard the starship *Enterprise*. Seeking ways to both enhance realism and help viewers unaccustomed to science fiction become acclimated quickly, Roddenberry and his writers adopted naval terminology: The *Enterprise* (always referred to in the feminine) had decks, not floors; there was no right or left, only port and starboard; no front and back, only fore and aft. Kirk kept a "captain's log." He and his crew were members of Star*fleet*. This approach worked beautifully, bringing a note of casual verisimilitude to the dialogue while making the futuristic setting seem familiar.

## Flash Gordon (1934–43) by Alex Raymond

One of the inspirations Roddenberry frequently credited for *Star Trek* was *Flash Gordon*. Cartoonist Alex Raymond's seminal space opera remains one of the best-loved and most influential works in the history of science fiction. Virtually every spacefaring sci-fi adventure owes a debt to Raymond's creation, which began as a newspaper comic strip, became one of the great movie serials and was later adapted for radio, comic books, novels, TV, and feature films.

*Flash Gordon* debuted on January 7, 1934. Raymond created the strip to compete with illustrator Dick Calkins's futuristic *Buck Rogers*, which had premiered five years earlier. Thanks to Raymond's wildly imaginative scenarios and beautifully rendered artwork, *Flash Gordon* eventually eclipsed *Buck Rogers* in terms of circulation and fan interest, although today casual fans sometimes confuse the two characters. Flash Gordon is an athletic Yale graduate and polo enthusiast who accidentally becomes embroiled in an interplanetary war between Earth and the planet Mongo, ruled by Ming the Merciless. Flash and his companions (girlfriend Dale Arden and eccentric scientist Dr. Hans Zarkov) are kidnapped and taken to Mongo, where they escape and have numerous adventures foiling Ming's plans to conquer Earth. On Mongo, our heroes are befriended by Prince Thun of the Lion Men and travel to the forest kingdom of Arboria, the ice kingdom of Frigia, the jungle kingdom of Tropica, the undersea kingdom of the Shark Men, and the flying city of the Hawkmen. Eventually, after spending years on Mongo, Flash and his friends would defeat Ming and go on to new adventures on other alien worlds. By then, however, *Flash Gordon* had found a second life on motion picture screens.

Universal Pictures' thirteen-chapter serial *Flash Gordon* (1936), starring former Olympic swimmer Charles "Buster" Crabbe in the title role, followed the plot of Raymond's strip with reasonable fidelity. The serial proved extremely successful and spawned two sequels, *Flash Gordon's Trip to Mars* (1938) and *Flash*

*Gordon Conquers the Universe* (1940), all headlined by Crabbe. Despite their low-budget production values and badly dated costumes and visual effects, the *Flash Gordon* serials feature some of the most iconic imagery in all of science fiction cinema, including their smoke-belching rocket ships and spark-spewing ray guns. Roddenberry was a fan of both the serials, which were syndicated and reran on television into the 1970s, as well as the comic strip, which continued under the direction of various writers and artists until 2003.

The influence of *Flash Gordon* on *Star Trek* becomes most apparent when the *Enterprise* squares off against the evil galactic empires of the Klingons and Romulans in episodes such as "Errand of Mercy" and "The *Enterprise* Incident," or when Kirk battles alien monsters in rock-'em, sock-'em yarns like "Arena" (featuring the Gorn, a giant lizard) and "A Private Little War" (with the Mugato, a horn-headed white gorilla). But the underlying concept of space travelers venturing to new worlds, meeting strange creatures (some friendly, others hostile), getting into various predicaments and often having to slug their way out is straight out of *Flash Gordon*. In the 1990s, the *Star Trek* franchise paid tribute to the legacy of *Flash Gordon* by having helmsman Tom Paris and ensign Harry Kim play out the adventures of the fictional character "Captain Proton" (in black and white, no less) on the holodeck of the starship *Voyager*. These seriocomic episodes were designed to emulate the look and feel of the classic *Flash Gordon* serials of the 1930s, right down to the cheesy costumes and antiquated special effects.

## Pulp Magazine Covers (1920s–50s)

As a boy, Roddenberry enjoyed all the diversions youngsters of his generation embraced—not only movies and comic strips but also radio serials (especially *The Lone Ranger* and *The Shadow*) and especially pulp magazines (so called because they were printed on cheap, rough paper with ragged edges). In recollections quoted in David Alexander's biography of Roddenberry, *Star Trek Creator*, Roddenberry's boyhood friend Ray Johnson remembers the future Great Bird reading *Amazing Stories* and *Astounding Science Fiction* for hours on end, becoming so engrossed in the tales that he lost all awareness of the world around him. And Dean Scurr, a high school classmate of Roddenberry's, recalls young Gene habitually reading science fiction in class, hiding magazines behind his textbook so he appeared to be studying.

Science fiction was born in the pulps—the term was coined by *Amazing Stories* publisher Hugo Gernsback—and esteemed authors such as Isaac Asimov, Ray Bradbury, Arthur C. Clarke, and Robert A. Heinlein launched their careers there. Nevertheless, most pulp fiction was clumsy and formulaic, catering to the assembly line–like needs of critically disreputable magazines churning out 128 pages of content per month. To entice prospective buyers to plunk down their dime for the latest issue, publishers relied largely on eye-catching, sometimes lurid painted cover illustrations. Artist Frank R. Paul's dramatic artwork, usually featuring elegant spaceships or grotesque monsters, helped sell *Amazing Stories* and other pulps from the late 1920s through the early 1950s. His bold and imaginative illustrations were as pivotal as the work of any writer in helping the fledgling sci-fi genre find an audience. Accordingly, when the first World Science Fiction Convention met in New York in 1939, rather than an author, Paul was chosen as the Guest of Honor. The work of artist Earle K. Bergey, which often featured scantily clad buxom women, also proved popular and influential. Illustrators Leo Morey, Howard V. Brown, Alex Schomburg, and, later, Frank Kelly Freas also left a mark on the genre with striking cover art.

In the 1960s, when Roddenberry was preparing to shoot the first *Star Trek* pilot, he drew inspiration from pulp cover images. Screenwriter Samuel Peeples, an avid collector of sci-fi pulps, reports that Roddenberry asked to photograph the covers of several magazines from his extensive collection. Later, Roddenberry passed along the photos to art director Matt Jefferies, who designed the *Enterprise* and other *Star Trek* spacecraft. Among the images Roddenberry gave Jefferies was Frank R. Paul's cover for the October 1953 issue of *Science Fiction Plus*, edited by Hugo Gernsback, featuring a spaceship with many design similarities to the *Enterprise*, including two cylindrical rocket engines separated from the main body of the craft by long struts. Roddenberry also provided pulp covers, including those by Earle K. Bergey, as guidelines for production designer Bill Theiss, who designed futuristic (and usually skimpy) costumes for *Star Trek*'s female guest stars.

## Space Cadet (1948) by Robert A. Heinlein

One of the most obvious antecedents of *Star Trek* was *Space Cadet*, an early novel published by Robert A. Heinlein, later revered as "the dean of science fiction writers." Like his contemporaries Isaac Asimov and Arthur C. Clarke, Heinlein rose through the ranks of editor John W. Campbell's *Astounding Science Fiction* magazine, which published many of Heinlein's short stories and serialized some of his novels. Heinlein helped raise the genre's standards in terms of both scientific plausibility and literary merit. He won numerous Hugo and Nebula awards over the years, and in 1974 was given the first Grand Master Award for lifetime achievement from the Science Fiction Writers of America.

Roddenberry may have been influenced by Heinlein's "future history" stories, which were interrelated tales that bolstered believability by taking place at various points along a single imaginary timeline stretching from the middle of the twentieth century to the early twenty-third century. During *Star Trek*'s three-season run on NBC, Roddenberry worked with script supervisors including Dorothy Fontana to assure that the details of his program's "historical background" remained consistent. In the decades since, the writers and producers of various *Trek* series and movies have protected Roddenberry's Heinlein-like commitment to continuity, keeping the sprawling *Star Trek* mythos remarkably coherent and logical. On a broader level, the social and political themes expressed on *Star Trek* often ran along lines similar to Heinlein's libertarian humanism. Heinlein was especially strong in his rejection of segregation or racism of any sort, a theme that recurs frequently in *Star Trek*. (In this aspect, Roddenberry may also have been inspired by the work of Eric Frank Russell, whose tales about the crew of the starship *Marathon* were among the first sci-fi stories to feature African American characters without racial stereotyping.)

Clearly, however, Roddenberry drew from *Space Cadet*, one of Heinlein's early "juvenile" novels. Although aimed at young readers, these action-packed books featuring youthful protagonists never compromised Heinlein's high standards for scientific accuracy or polished word craft, and remain among his most enduringly popular works. *Space Cadet* follows teenager Matthew Dodson as he struggles through the arduous training required to join the Interplanetary Patrol, and chronicles his first adventures as a novice Patrolman. The similarities between *Space Cadet* and *Star Trek* are numerous. Among the most striking: *Space Cadet*'s Solar Federation, like *Star Trek*'s United Federation of Planets, is a utopian meritocracy (and, informally, both are referred to as simply "the Federation"). The Interplanetary Patrol, like Starfleet, is a precision-tuned military organization of high moral character on a peaceful mission (to protect the well-being of humans and other beings throughout the solar system). Like Starfleet, its membership includes persons of all races and nationalities, including off-worlders. And coincidentally (or not), Matthew Dodson and James T. Kirk both hail from Iowa. These commonalities were thrown into sharp relief by producer J. J. Abrams's 2009 motion picture *Star Trek*, which "rebooted" the franchise by taking the story back to Kirk's days as a cadet at Starfleet Academy.

*Note:* Although Roddenberry insisted Starfleet was "paramilitary" rather than military, the organization's naval nomenclature and iconography, along with Captain Kirk's tendency to refer to himself as "a soldier," makes this distinction difficult to support.

## The Voyage of the Space Beagle (1950) by A. E. van Vogt

Another of the inspirations Roddenberry readily acknowledged for *Star Trek* was *The Voyage of the Space Beagle*, a glittering gem of sci-fi adventure from Canadian author Alfred Elton van Vogt. Van Vogt was yet another of the many authors discovered by John W. Campbell and frequently published in *Astounding Science Fiction* during the 1930s and '40s. Van Vogt's punchy prose and lightning-paced, thought-provoking plots, often involving journeys through space or time, were extremely popular and inspired later writers, including Harlan Ellison and Philip K. Dick. *The Voyage of the Space Beagle*, like many of van Vogt's novels, was what the author called a "fix up," cobbled together by linking four previously published short stories: "Black Destroyer" (1938), "Discord in Scarlet" (1939), "M33 in Andromeda" (1943), and "War of Nerves" (1950). Despite its ungainly, episodic structure, *The Voyage of the Space Beagle* remains a thrilling read. The *Beagle* (named in honor of Charles Darwin's ship, the *H.M.S. Beagle*) is an Earth

An early edition of Robert A. Heinlein's 1948 novel *Space Cadet*, which Roddenberry often named as a primary inspiration for *Star Trek*.          *Photo courtesy of Lisa Meier*

spacecraft inhabited by hundreds of scientists on a decades-long mission of galactic exploration. The explorers encounter several sentient extraterrestrial species, most of them hostile, including the Courl, a race of pantherlike carnivores with tentacles sprouting from their shoulders; the birdlike, telepathic Riim; the Ixtl, last survivor of an ancient race, which invades the ship and lays its eggs in several members of the Beagle's crew; and Anabis, a noncorporeal consciousness that feeds on the deaths of other living beings. Even casual viewers of *Star Trek* will immediately recognize parallels between the exploits of the starship *Enterprise* and those of the *Beagle*. For instance, how many times did Kirk and Spock encounter beings made of "pure energy"?

To enhance *Star Trek*'s credibility within the science fiction community (he badly wanted the series to be taken seriously by the genre's fans and professionals), Roddenberry recruited prominent sci-fi authors to write episodes. Many of the luminaries he drafted into service for *Star Trek* contributed outstanding shows: Harlan Ellison wrote "The City on the Edge of Forever," widely regarded as the series' single best episode; Theodore Sturgeon penned "Amok Time," the first story to delve deeply into the Vulcan culture; and horror specialist Robert Bloch delivered the characteristically creepy "Wolf in the Fold" (about an Anabis-like noncorporeal being that feeds on fear). However, not every author Roddenberry approached could adjust to the specialized demands of writing for TV. Van Vogt, although among the first writers Roddenberry tapped to work for *Trek*, was one of those who never managed to develop a satisfactory treatment. Nevertheless, his influence on the series remains significant.

## Childhood's End (1953) by Arthur C. Clarke

The development of First Officer Spock was even more labored and convoluted than that of Captain Kirk. The unflappably logical half-Vulcan science officer played by Leonard Nimoy bears very little similarity to Roddenberry's original vision of the character. It's possible that Spock—at least in his nascent form—may owe his existence in part to British author Arthur C. Clarke's acclaimed novel *Childhood's End*. Clarke wrote several Hugo and Nebula Award–winning novels, but remains best known as the coauthor of the screenplay for director Stanley Kubrick's masterpiece *2001: A Space Odyssey* (1968). *Childhood's End*, the third of Clarke's fifteen novels, was expanded from an earlier short story, "Guardian Angel" (1950). At the height of the Cold War, with Eastern and Western powers vying to land the first rocket on the moon, a race of benevolent extraterrestrials arrives on Earth, promising to bring peace and prosperity—but refusing to reveal themselves until fifty years have elapsed. Once the aliens, known as the Overlords, finally emerge, it becomes obvious why they have been in hiding for five decades. Red-faced bipeds with horns, spaded tails and leathery wings, they resemble Earth's mythological demons. Humankind's association of their physical appearance with satanic evil is written off as vestigial evidence of an unsuccessful prehistoric encounter between humans and the Overlords. But a few human skeptics remain wary of their benefactors . . .

Roddenberry was well-acquainted with *Childhood's End* (he discusses the novel in some depth with author Yvonne Fern in her interview book *Gene Roddenberry: The Last Conversation*) and appears to have been fascinated by the idea of friendly aliens who are devilish in appearance. In his original outline for *Star Trek*, Roddenberry describes Spock as "almost frightening—a face so heavy lidded and satanic you might expect him to have a forked tail. . . . Half-Martian, he has a slightly reddish complexion and semipointed ears. But—strangely—Mr. Spock's temperament is in dramatic contrast to his satanic look." This Spock was not detached and clinical, but warm and amiable, with "an almost catlike curiosity over anything the slightest [bit] 'alien.'" In makeup tests for the first *Trek* pilot, "The Cage," Nimoy was painted red. The face paint was discarded after tests showed that, viewed in black and white, the red Spock came out looking like an African American satyr. (Even though *Star Trek* was broadcast in color, in 1966 most Americans still had black-and-white TVs.)

Roddenberry's insistence on Spock's demonic appearance—especially the pointed ears—nearly derailed the entire project. The network's sales staff feared that the character would make the series tough to market in the Bible Belt and warned that some affiliates might decline to broadcast the show. (These anxieties proved baseless.) A photo of Spock included in NBC's advance promotional booklet for *Star Trek* was airbrushed to smooth out Spock's pointed ears and reshape his eyebrows. Earlier, when it granted Roddenberry the extraordinary opportunity to shoot a second pilot, NBC requested several changes to the program—including the elimination of Mr. Spock. Roddenberry steadfastly refused, preferring to abandon *Star Trek* altogether rather than go forward without this key character. All this despite the fact that in "The Cage" Spock was so thinly written he had no discernible personality. Apparently Roddenberry was simply fixated on the Clarkean conceit of a kindly "devil."

## Forbidden Planet (1956)

The impact of *Forbidden Planet* on *Star Trek* is undeniable but perhaps overstated.

The 1950s rang in the first heyday of science fiction cinema with the release of classics such as *The Thing from Another World*, *The Day the Earth Stood Still* (both 1951), *War of the Worlds* (1953), and scores of other sci-fi hits. Even in its day, however, *Forbidden Planet* was something special—not simply an earthbound monster movie dressed up in science fictional trappings, but thoughtful, spacefaring speculative fiction produced on a lavish scale by a major studio. The story, loosely based on William Shakespeare's *The Tempest*, sends Commander John J. Adams (played by Leslie Nielsen—yes, *that* Leslie Nielsen) and his United Planets space cruiser to Altair IV to investigate what happened to a group of colonists who attempted to settle the planet twenty years earlier. Adams learns that during the early days of the colony a mysterious unseen creature killed most

Roddenberry screened *Forbidden Planet* (1956) for his creative team during preproduction of the first *Star Trek* pilot, but the film's influence on the series has been overstated.

of the settlers and destroyed their spaceship. Altair IV—in the dim past home to a mighty, superscientific race known as the Krell—is now inhabited only by the colonists' reclusive former leader Dr. Morbius (Walter Pidgeon), his beautiful nineteen-year-old daughter (Anne Francis), and their mechanical manservant Robbie the Robot. Then the invisible monster, unheard from for twenty years, returns and begins killing members of Adams's crew . . .

Roddenberry freely credited *Forbidden Planet* as an inspiration for *Star Trek*, which is hardly surprising. It was thought-provoking, thrill-packed sci-fi adventure, complete with spaceships, robots, laser guns, aliens, and monsters—everything he (and most other sci-fi fans) loved. Moreover, Metro-Goldwyn-Mayer, the studio that made *The Wizard of Oz* and *Gone with the Wind*, brought the full power of its spectacular production capabilities to bear on the project, and it shows—especially in the picture's sometimes breathtaking production design and Oscar-nominated visual effects. *Forbidden Planet* offered something *Star Trek* could aspire to.

There are marked similarities between *Star Trek* and *Forbidden Planet*. For example, like *Trek*, *Forbidden Planet* involves a peace-loving interstellar military organization in service of an interplanetary government and features a tough-minded captain who's chummy with the ship's physician. The movie's plot proves similar to that of several *Star Trek* episodes, including the first ever broadcast, "The Man Trap" (featuring the reclusive Professor Crater and the shape-shifting Salt Vampire).

Nevertheless, Roddenberry did not—as detractors have sometimes claimed—simply change *Forbidden Planet*'s character names and uniform colors to create *Star Trek*. Most elements shared by *Forbidden Planet* and *Star Trek* originate not with the film but in sci-fi literature, like Heinlein's *Space Cadet*. And key components in *Star Trek*'s appeal—such as its interracial crew, including a prominent nonhuman—are absent from *Forbidden Planet*. It's true that Roddenberry screened *Forbidden Planet* during preproduction of the first *Star Trek* pilot (in a memo, he even suggested trying to buy a print or acquire frame enlargements from the film), but he did so for the benefit of art director Matt Jefferies and his production design team, who were creating sets, props, and models for the show. Ultimately, the *Enterprise*, its interiors, and Starfleet-issue equipment bore little resemblance to their counterparts in *Forbidden Planet*. (Producer Irwin Allen's rival TV series *Lost in Space*, a simplistic program seldom compared to the cerebral *Forbidden Planet*, displays just as many significant commonalities with the film, including its saucer-shaped Jupiter 2 spacecraft—very similar to *Planet*'s C57-D cruiser both in exterior design and interior layout—and the presence of a show-stealing Robot.)

## Wagon Train (1957–65)

While pitching *Star Trek* to prospective production studios and, later, to broadcast networks, Roddenberry invariably referred to his project as "*Wagon Train* to the stars." There are indeed basic conceptual similarities between the two programs. TV's *Wagon Train*, inspired by director John Ford's 1950 Western *Wagonmaster*, followed the exploits of wagon master Seth Adams (Ward Bond) as he and his trail-hardened assistants led tenderfoot settlers from Missouri to California, becoming embroiled in complications of all sorts during stops along the way. (When Bond died in the middle of the show's fourth season, his character was replaced without explanation by wagon master Christopher Hale, played by John McIntire.) Like the starship *Enterprise*, the wagon train often would approach a settlement, send out a search party, and run into trouble, a quandary that usually forced the wagon master or his fellow travelers to wrestle with some moral issue. As with *Trek*, many episodes featured a recognizable guest star (among the luminaries who appeared during *Wagon Train*'s 284-episode run were Bette Davis, Peter Lorre, and Lou Costello). Inevitably the dilemma would be resolved by the end of the show, and the train would trundle off to its next adventure, in much the same manner that Captain Kirk and company would leave orbit and warp away into the unknown. All this suggests that *Wagon Train* may have provided Roddenberry with a structural template upon which to build his science fiction idea. That's certainly possible.

However, it's equally likely that Roddenberry simply used the *Wagon Train* parallels as shorthand to help him explain *Star Trek* to dubious executives who knew nothing of, and cared less about, science fiction. His actual inspiration could have been something entirely different. (The basic narrative structure of *The Voyage of the Space Beagle*, as well as *Gulliver's Travels*, is much the same as both *Trek* and *Wagon Train*.) Roddenberry later admitted that he, somewhat dis-ingenuously, tried to pass off *Star Trek* as an outer space version of cowboys and Indians. His attempt to equate *Star Trek* with Westerns was carefully calculated. Not only did television bosses understand Westerns better than sci-fi, Westerns were bankable commodities in the 1950s and '60s.

During the 1958–59 season, for example, half of TV's twenty-eight best-rated shows were Westerns, including the top four programs (No. 1 *Gunsmoke*, followed by *Wagon Train*, *Have Gun—Will Travel*, and *The Rifleman*). And Roddenberry's choice of *Wagon Train* as *Trek*'s Old West counterpart was particularly well considered. The venerable series ran for eight seasons, as long as any TV Western except *Gunsmoke*, *Bonanza*, and *The Virginian*. It spent half of that time in the Nielsen Top 10 and was the top-rated program for the 1961–62 season. However, the tactic of "disguising" *Star Trek* as a Western nearly backfired. When Roddenberry delivered "The Cage," *Star Trek*'s original pilot, it bore few similari-ties to *Wagon Train* or any other Western ever made. Executives felt misled and rejected "The Cage." Fortunately, Roddenberry was given a second chance, and *Star Trek* took flight.

# 3

# The High Command

## Executives Who Played Pivotal Roles in the *Star Trek* Story

lthough creator-producer Gene Roddenberry envisioned *Star Trek* vividly, preparing a sixteen-page outline that described the program's setting and characters in meticulous detail, and even provided thumbnail story ideas, the concept continued to evolve as it journeyed from scenario to screen. Along the way, a handful of studio executives and network programmers changed the course of the series' development, some through their support of the program and others by their lack of interest in it. If any of these behind-the-scenes power brokers had reached a different decision, *Star Trek* might have emerged as a very different show—if it emerged at all.

### Norman Felton

Roddenberry's first attempt to sell *Star Trek* was unsuccessful but instructive. Norman Felton (whose Arena Productions developed Roddenberry's first series, *The Lieutenant,* in conjunction with Metro-Goldwyn-Mayer) not only rejected *Trek* but provided a litany of reasons why the idea would never work—complaints Roddenberry would hear time and again from other executives. Felton and his working-class parents had emigrated from London to Cleveland, Ohio, in 1929. The then-sixteen-year-old Felton found work driving a delivery truck but dreamed of becoming a playwright. Seven years later he won the Rockefeller Fellowship in Playwriting, which allowed him to attend the University of Iowa, where he earned a bachelor's degree in 1940 and a master's the following year. After college Felton hired on with NBC radio in Chicago. With the dawn of television, he moved to New York to pursue opportunities in the new medium and won his first Emmy Award in 1952 for directing an episode of *Robert Montgomery Presents.* After forming Arena Productions, he created the highly rated medical drama *Dr. Kildare,* which ran from 1961 to '66. At the time Roddenberry pitched *Star Trek* to Felton, the producer was on the cusp of his greatest success, launching *The Man from U.N.C.L.E.,* which ran from 1964 to '68, earned Felton a second Emmy, and spawned the short-lived *Girl from U.N.C.L.E.* spin-off.

Roddenberry approached Felton even before *The Lieutenant* was officially canceled, but Felton became the first of several executives to pass on *Star Trek.*

He was concerned about the production demands and potential costs of the show, which from the beginning Roddenberry pictured as an hour-long, full-color program. Felton also questioned whether adult audiences would embrace an outer space adventure series. While the sci-fi anthology *The Twilight Zone* had met with success, as of 1964 the only shows with spaceships, ray guns, and other elements that featured prominently in Roddenberry's proposal were kiddie fare like *Captain Video*, *Space Patrol*, and *Rocky Jones, Space Ranger*. Many other executives, Roddenberry would soon learn, shared Felton's trepidation. Had Felton backed Roddenberry's idea, *Star Trek* might have had a much quicker route to the screen, but it wouldn't be the *Star Trek* we know today, which was shaped by the input of Herb Solow at Desilu and the demands of executives at NBC.

As it happened, *Star Trek* and Norman Felton parted ways and followed different trajectories. Although he worked through the 1970s, none of the series Felton produced following *The Man from U.N.C.L.E.* survived more than a season. He is a past president of the Producers Guild of America, which bestows the Norman Felton Award annually to the year's Outstanding Producer of Episodic Television Drama.

## Herb Solow (and Oscar Katz)

The well-connected Roddenberry continued to shop *Star Trek* around town, earning rejections from MGM's Alan Courtney and other executives before Oscar Katz and Herb Solow at Desilu Productions finally expressed interest in the proposal. Katz, the Executive in Charge of Production for Desilu, and Solow, his assistant, were tasked with finding worthwhile investments for the studio's meager development funds, money supplied primarily by CBS as part of Desilu owner Lucille Ball's contract for *The Lucy Show*. When Katz, a former vice president at CBS, left Desilu in 1965, Solow ascended to the position of Executive in Charge of Production.

Solow, a graduate of Dartmouth College, began his career as a talent agent and later served as head of daytime production at CBS and later NBC, where he made contacts that proved beneficial to *Star Trek*. One of the first projects Solow convinced Katz to gamble on was *Star Trek*. (Katz and Solow also used Desilu's resources to help Bruce Geller develop *Mission: Impossible*. Later, Solow worked with Richard Levinson and William Link to create the long-running detective series *Mannix*.) In his book, Solow admits that he signed Roddenberry to a script development deal without even reading the complete sixteen-page prospectus for the series.

Although Solow recognized all the same potential pitfalls for the series that had scared off Felton, Courtney, and others, he also saw *Star Trek* as cutting-edge television and a potential breakout hit. One of the most important things Solow did was to solidify Lucille Ball's support for *Star Trek*, despite objections from skittish Desilu board members. Then he worked alongside Roddenberry to try to sell the series to the networks. In this effort, Solow's enduring friendships with programming heads at NBC proved invaluable. He remained intimately involved with *Trek* throughout its first two seasons, often running interference for Roddenberry with NBC's programmers and Standards and Practices department (the censors). Solow's position became untenable in 1968 after Ball sold Desilu to industrial conglomerate Gulf + Western, which turned the studio into a division of Paramount Pictures. Solow left prior to *Trek*'s third season for a vice presidency at Metro-Goldwyn-Mayer. In 1973, he left that post to enter independent film and TV production but met with limited success. He and former *Trek* associate producer Bob Justman cowrote the definitive account of the series' production, *Inside Star Trek: The Real Story* (1996). Solow's wife, Yvonne Fern, wrote the in-depth interview book *Gene Roddenberry: The Last Conversation* (1994).

## Lucille Ball

The unsung hero in the *Star Trek* saga is Lucille Ball. While she wasn't directly involved in the development, casting, or day-to-day production of the show, nothing happened at Desilu without Lucy's blessing, and *Star Trek* was an extremely ambitious project for her production company.

Ball, born in Jamestown, New York, in 1911, began modeling and acting in her late teens but struggled to find (and keep) theatrical roles until she signed on as an RKO Radio Pictures contract player in 1933. Working for RKO and later for MGM, the vivacious redhead appeared in scores of B-budget programmers—musicals, melodramas, noir films, and comedies—but failed to achieve major stardom. That changed when she and her first husband, Desi Arnaz, developed *I Love Lucy*. The legendary sitcom, chronicling the antics of dizzy housewife Lucy Ricardo (Ball) and her Cuban bandleader husband Ricky (Arnaz), ran on CBS from 1951 to '57, never finishing lower than third in the Nielsen ratings and earning five Emmy Awards (with seventeen other nominations). The show was succeeded by *The Lucy-Desi Comedy Hour*, a series of occasional specials that appeared on CBS until 1960. These programs made Ball the most famous and perhaps most beloved woman in television history.

Together Ball and Arnaz founded Desilu, which produced *I Love Lucy* and other hits like *The Untouchables*. But Ball and Arnaz divorced shortly after *The Lucy-Desi Comedy Hour* left the air, and Ball borrowed heavily to buy out her ex-husband's interest in the company. Without Arnaz's business savvy, the studio's fortunes declined. By 1964, the only Desilu series in production was *The Lucy Show*, a simplistic sitcom that relied on Ball's star power to overcome shopworn storylines. Most of the studio's soundstages were rented out to other production companies (*The Andy Griffith Show* and *The Dick Van Dyke Show*, among many other programs, were shot there). *Star Trek* represented a major investment of resources for the cash-strapped company. Initially, networks were skeptical that Desilu could meet the production demands of an hour-long weekly series that required extensive visual effects and specialized wardrobe and set designs. Some members of Desilu's board of directors shared those concerns and warned

Lucille Ball and Desi Arnaz pose outside the gates of Desilu Productions during their *I Love Lucy* heyday. After the couple divorced, Ball purchased the studio and, as president and CEO of Desilu, green-lighted the development of *Star Trek*.

Ball that the venture was too risky. Nevertheless, Ball threw her support behind Solow and *Star Trek*. Now it was up to Solow and Roddenberry to find a network willing to get on board.

## James T. Aubrey Jr.

The colorful, controversial James T. Aubrey Jr. entered the *Star Trek* story shortly afterward, when, as president of CBS, he offered Roddenberry the opportunity to pitch *Star Trek*. Aubrey, the son of a successful advertising executive, grew up in an affluent Chicago suburb and attended Princeton University. After serving in the Air Force during World War II (he was Jimmy Stewart's flying instructor), Aubrey found work on the sales staff of a CBS television station in Los Angeles and began his rapid ascent of the corporate ladder. Working in ever-higher capacities in the production and programming departments at CBS and briefly at ABC, Aubrey helped develop hit series, including *Have Gun—Will Travel*, *Maverick*, and *The Donna Reed Show*. He took over as president of CBS in late 1959 when his predecessor, Louis G. Cowan, resigned in the wake of the quiz show rigging scandal involving *The $64,000 Question*. As president, Aubrey introduced long-running, highly profitable shows such as *Gilligan's Island*, *The Beverly Hillbillies*, and *The Andy Griffith Show*. Despite his tremendous success, the arrogant, dictatorial Aubrey was not well liked. Some of his network's biggest stars couldn't stand him. These included Lucille Ball, who habitually referred to Aubrey as "that S.O.B."

After his *Star Trek* pitch to CBS, Roddenberry joined the ranks of those who despised the executive. Aubrey and members of his staff grilled Roddenberry for nearly two hours (an extraordinarily long time for a pitch meeting), only to later notify the producer that CBS was passing on *Star Trek* because the network had already scheduled another sci-fi drama, producer Irwin Allen's *Lost in Space*. Roddenberry was livid and feared that ideas he had laid out for Aubrey and his staff (including strategies for controlling costs and other details) would be used to benefit the rival series. However, Aubrey probably took the meeting with Roddenberry not to steal the producer's plans but to placate Ball, who remained the face of his network.

It's interesting to speculate what the results might have looked like had Aubrey taken on *Star Trek* instead of *Lost in Space*. CBS was more generous with production funds than NBC (both *Lost in Space* and the Desilu-produced *Mission: Impossible* had higher per-episode budgets than *Star Trek*), and Roddenberry and his writers often felt constrained by cost limitations. However, CBS pressured the producers of *Lost in Space* to steer that series toward camp following the meteoric success of ABC's *Batman* in 1966. Such an approach was anathema to the *Star Trek* creative team, who to a person disdained the juvenile *Lost in Space* as substandard sci-fi.

In early 1965, a few months before the second *Star Trek* pilot was shot, Aubrey was fired by CBS amid allegations that the executive was taking kickbacks from producers in exchange for scheduling their shows. In 1969, after a few nonproductive years as an independent producer, he assumed control of the flagging MGM studio. In typically iron-fisted fashion, he restructured the company, canceling projects and firing personnel mercilessly. Within a year, Aubrey had returned the studio to profitability and reduced its debt by $27 million. He resigned from MGM in 1973 and spent the final years of his career as an independent producer of (mostly forgettable) TV movies.

## Grant Tinker

In its final, broadcast form *Star Trek* represents a compromise between Roddenberry's soaring vision of a utopian future and Grant Tinker's Midas-touch instinct for attracting viewers.

Grant Tinker, born in Stamford, Connecticut, in 1926, first joined NBC in 1949 as an executive trainee fresh out of Dartmouth. He left just two years later to pursue opportunities in independent production (he would help develop *The Dick Van Dyke Show*, among other programs), but returned to the Peacock Network for two far more productive tenures. The first of these was during the early 1960s, when he served as NBC's chief West Coast programming executive. It was in this capacity that Tinker and his associates, Jerry Stanley and Mort Werner, accepted then rejected and finally purchased *Star Trek*.

Roddenberry and Solow first met with the NBC brain trust in May 1964. Tinker was intrigued by the creative possibilities of the concept but less enthusiastic about its commercial potential and, given the daunting scale of the production, dubious of Desilu's ability to deliver a credible product. He warily agreed to order the development of a script, but it took several more meetings before Tinker was confident enough to approve "The Cage," *Star Trek*'s unusually ambitious and extravagant original pilot. Although "The Cage" proved that Desilu was up to the technical challenges of the series, executives were dissatisfied with other aspects of the show. "The Cage" was rejected. But rather than abandoning the project altogether, Tinker and Werner took the extraordinary step of ordering a second pilot, while stipulating major changes to the cast and characters that they believed would make the show more appealing to a wide audience.

Tinker's development savvy—already demonstrated when he green-lighted smashes *Bonanza*, *I Spy*, and *The Man from U.N.C.L.E.* for NBC—would be affirmed in the years ahead. After leaving NBC in 1970, he cofounded MTM Enterprises with his second wife, actress Mary Tyler Moore. MTM scored a long series of hits during the 1970s, including highly rated sitcoms such as *The Mary Tyler Moore Show*, *The Bob Newhart Show*, and *WKRP in Cincinnati*, as well as critically acclaimed dramas *Hill Street Blues*, *St. Elsewhere*, and *Lou Grant*. Following his divorce from Moore in 1981, Tinker returned to NBC as CEO. He took the then-last-place network to the top of the ratings with a combination of now-iconic sitcoms (*The Cosby Show*, *Cheers*, *Family Ties*) and lighthearted action shows (*The A-Team*, *Remington Steele*, *Miami Vice*). He left NBC following its sale to General Electric in 1986, but his efforts set the stage for the network's "Must See TV" dominance in the 1990s. It was, to say the least, an impressive rise. Yet during those same years, *Star Trek* would make an even more astonishing ascent, rising phoenixlike from the ash heap of network cancellation to become a cultural touchstone and a multimillion-dollar revenue engine.

# 4

# Caged

## Revealing Differences Between *Star Trek* and Its Unaired Pilot

T he original *Star Trek* pilot was imaginatively written, inventively designed, and elaborately produced. It was also a dud.

Despite the best efforts of creator-producer Gene Roddenberry and Desilu production chief Herb Solow, NBC passed on "The Cage," an unusually ambitious and polished pilot filmed at a princely cost of nearly $616,000 (nearly $4.5 million in inflation-adjusted dollars), including $164,000 in overruns, which Desilu was forced to absorb. For decades afterward, Roddenberry derided the network for rejecting "The Cage," mocking one executive's assessment that the pilot was "too cerebral." But Roddenberry's bitterness belied the reality that he had played a game of bait-and-switch with NBC. He sold network executives on *Star Trek* by comparing the series to Westerns like the popular *Wagon Train*. "I said, 'Look fellas, it's little more than a Western,'" Roddenberry explained in an interview featured on the *Star Trek: The Original Series Season One* DVD collection. "'They have space ships instead of horses, zap guns instead of six-shooters, but it'll be familiar.'" Then he delivered "The Cage," which is nothing at all like *Wagon Train* or any other Western ever made. "They didn't get what they had asked for or agreed upon, and they were naturally very upset," Roddenberry admitted.

NBC programming heads Grant Tinker, Jerry Stanley, and Mort Werner had other concerns as well. While the executives were dazzled by the show's production values (they were knocked out by its sets, costumes, and special effects), they were far less impressed with the dramatic possibilities of the characters and with the performances of the cast. Also, they were troubled by the sexual content of the pilot story (especially the appearance of a scantily clad, green-skinned Orion slave girl): If *Star Trek* was always this racy, potential censorship issues loomed.

A quick recap of "The Cage" may be in order. Responding to a distress signal, a landing party from the starship *Enterprise*, led by Captain Christopher Pike, beams down to Talos IV, where a survey vessel crashed eighteen years earlier. Pike is captured by the planet's wily natives, bubble-headed telepaths capable of reading minds and thought-casting powerful illusions. They try to entice the captain into mating with Vina, a lovely young Earth woman, in hopes of breeding a race of slaves. Vina proves unable to seduce Pike (even when, with telepathic help, she assumes the appearance of the aforementioned Orion), so the Talosians kidnap Pike's all-business female first officer, called simply Number One, and his more amorously inclined yeoman, J. M. Colt, to serve as other potential mates. Yet still the captain resists. Pike overpowers one of his captors, but the aliens respond by taking mental control of the *Enterprise.* It appears to be a stalemate until the Talosians read the ship's databanks and surmise that humans are "too violent" to make good slaves. The Earthlings are released—except for Vina, who it's revealed was severely injured in the long-ago crash, her broken body crudely reconstructed by the Talosians. "They had never seen a woman before," the misshapen Vina explains. She chooses to remain on Talos, where she can maintain her illusion of youth and beauty.

By the standards of 1960s television, this was a strikingly fresh and compelling yarn, one that would eventually make an excellent *Star Trek* episode (actually, two). Nevertheless, it's fortunate for *Trek* fans that NBC rejected "The Cage." Had the network accepted this pilot, *Star Trek* would have been a very different program—and, in all likelihood, a far less successful one. Despite the pilot's undeniable strengths, most of the elements that made *Star Trek* so persistently popular are absent from "The Cage." Here's a rundown of telling contrasts between this original pilot and the final program:

## Captain Pike

Christopher Pike (played by Jeffrey Hunter), although brave and capable, tends toward melancholy, beset by self-doubt and recriminations. Distraught over the deaths of two crewmen on a recent away mission, and weary of the burdens of command, he considers resigning his commission with Starfleet. Hunter, best remembered for his portrayals of John Wayne's sidekick Martin Pawley in *The Searchers* (1956) and Jesus in *King of Kings* (1961), delivers a thoughtful, sensitive performance. His take on the character hews closely to Roddenberry's original conception of the starship captain as a spacefaring Horatio Hornblower, but it stands in stark contrast with William Shatner's confident, swashbuckling James T. Kirk. Hunter's brooding Pike strikes a more downbeat note for "The Cage" than is characteristic of the finished *Star Trek.* When the ebullient Shatner signed on to replace Hunter, Roddenberry was forced to reimagine the character. The high-spirited panache Shatner brought to his role helped brighten the tone of the entire show.

## Mr. Spock

Although Spock (Leonard Nimoy) is featured in "The Cage," he is hardly the coolly logical, emotionless Vulcan that would eventually become a television sensation. He flashes a broad grin when he encounters singing alien plants on the surface of Talos and, later, whirls and cries out in alarm when Number One and Yeoman Colt are beamed to the planet's surface by the Talosians. As with Captain Pike, this Spock conforms closely to Roddenberry's original vision of the character. The creator-producer's initial outline for the series describes Spock as gentle-hearted, with "a quiet temperament in dramatic contrast with his satanic look. . . . His primary weakness is an almost catlike curiosity over anything the slightest [bit] 'alien.'" In "The Cage," however, the role is so thinly written that Spock is barely a character at all. The Vulcan second lieutenant is a bystander to the plot (even Yeoman Colt plays a more active role) and remains distinguishable from the rest of the crew only by Nimoy's prosthetic ears. It's hardly surprising that NBC executives, after receiving damning research from the network's sales department regarding the character's demonic appearance, wanted Spock eliminated; his presence adds little to the pilot. Ultimately, of course, Spock (and Nimoy) remained, becoming the only crew member from "The Cage" to stay on board with *Star Trek*. But along the way the character would undergo an even more profound alteration than the switch from captains Pike to Kirk.

## "Number One"

In "The Cage" it's the nameless female first officer, referred to simply as "Number One" (and played by Majel Barrett), that possesses an expressionless, emotionless demeanor. This is troublesome for a couple of reasons. First of all, there's no logical reason for her to behave this way. (Even the Talosians

In addition to a different captain (Christopher Pike, right, played by Jeffrey Hunter), "The Cage" also featured a very different Mr. Spock, at least in terms of personality.

dismiss her icy exterior as "largely a pretense.") And secondly, although other characters in "The Cage" describe Number One as machinelike and unfeeling, Barrett doesn't consistently play the part that way. She clearly seems embarrassed when the Talosians expose her hidden fantasies about Captain Pike, and again when, in the episode's closing minutes, Yeoman Colt asks Pike which of the three women the captain would have chosen as his mate. At other points Barrett displays worry, frustration, and relief. But since the actress is *trying* to seem cool and unemotional, she comes off flat, showing none of the warmth and likeability she would later bring to her recurring role as Nurse Chapel, or to her *Next Generation* appearances as Lwaxana Troi. Although Roddenberry later charged that NBC wanted Number One eliminated from the show because the network was uncomfortable with a woman being second-in-command on a starship, Desilu production chief Herb Solow clarifies that the network actually encouraged the casting of women and minorities. "They just didn't want Majel," Solow writes in his book *Inside Star Trek*. Despite his personal attachment to Barrett, with whom he was having an extramarital affair, Roddenberry reluctantly eliminated Number One from the crew. With *Star Trek*'s second pilot he would conflate the character with Mr. Spock, elevating the Vulcan to first officer (granting him a far more prominent role in the storylines) and lending him the cool, unemotional personality originally intended for Number One. The rest would be television history.

## Other Characters and Actors

Another striking feature of "The Cage" is that, aside from Number One, the *Enterprise* bridge crew is composed entirely of white men. There are no equivalents for Lieutenant Uhura (Nichelle Nichols) and Lieutenant Sulu (George Takei), or even any Scottish or Russian accents to be heard. In short, there's nothing like the multinational rainbow coalition that served Captain Kirk, no at-a-glance depiction of a human future free of racism and xenophobia. This aspect of the show ranks among *Star Trek*'s most inspirational and widely admired features, and its absence greatly diminishes "The Cage."

Yet there are further weaknesses among the pilot's characters and cast. Dr. Phillip Boyce (John Hoyt) and Yeoman Colt (Laurel Goodwin) pale in comparison to their later counterparts, Dr. Leonard "Bones" McCoy (DeForest Kelley) and Yeoman Janice Rand (Grant Lee Whitney). Although Hoyt and Goodwin are serviceable in their roles, both characters are hackneyed stereotypes. The folksy charm of McCoy, in particular, is sorely missed. Navigator Jose Tyler (who, despite his Latino first name, is played by the decidedly Anglo-looking Peter Duryea) has no discernible personality whatsoever, and Duryea's performance is cringe-inducing. Perhaps most damaging of all, this ensemble demonstrates no inkling of the chemistry that quickly developed among Shatner, Nimoy, and Kelley as Kirk, Spock, and McCoy. The only cast members who seem to have any rapport are Hunter and guest star Susan Oliver as Vina. Week in and week out, the Shatner-Nimoy-Kelley team's unique blend of personalities and performance styles gave fans something dynamic to watch, even when the plots were less than scintillating. It's difficult to imagine the Hunter-Barrett-Hoyt trio spawning such devotion.

## Sets, Costumes, and Lighting Design

"The Cage" seems far more somber than the later *Trek*, and not just because of Captain Pike's dour personality. This is due in part to the pilot's drab sets, costumes, and lighting. Captain Kirk's *Enterprise* is a bright, color-splashed place. Its gleaming hallways are dotted with red, blue, and yellow instrument panels. Turbolift doors are painted red, as are the helm and the rail around the bridge. The captain's cabin features a number of homey touches, including paintings, a sculpture, and even a potted plant. Male crew members sport their now-iconic gold, blue, and red tunics, while female crew members wear similarly colored miniskirt-length dresses (with go-go boots, no less). Even though it was shot on the same sets, Captain Pike's *Enterprise* could hardly be more dissimilar. The *Enterprise* of "The Cage" is nearly monochromatic, full of blank gray walls. Turbolift doors are pale blue, barely distinguishable from gray, and the helm and bridge rail are painted black. The captain's cabin is far more Spartan; its only visible amenity is a built-in shelf full of severe-looking books. As with most of the rest of the ship, its walls are unadorned. There are no red tunics in use aboard this *Enterprise*, only pale blue and gold (and even those colors are covered with charcoal gray jackets when the crew leaves the ship). Typically the lighting of future *Star Trek* episodes would be bright, designed to "pop" red objects, and sometimes employ purple, green, and blue gels to evocative effect. However, "The Cage" is flatly lit, underscoring the sterile, militaristic look of the sets and costumes. These are subtle differences, but they add up. And in sum, the *Enterprise* of "The Cage" seems like a far less inviting place to spend a five-year mission, or even a three-season run.

## Differences in "Treknology"

In "The Cage," Pike and his landing party are armed with lasers, not "phasers." The *Enterprise* utilizes "hyperdrive" engines that warp time (not space), with rockets (rather than "impulse engines") for backup propulsion. The ship avoids space debris with a "meteorite beam" rather than the familiar deflector screen. These variations may or may not seem minor, depending on how emotionally invested you are in the show's imaginary technology. But taken as a whole, they suggest a less innovative and cohesive set of science fictional concepts than those employed by the finished program. While it took a while for all the details to coalesce, *Star Trek*'s casual employment of consistent futuristic technical jargon lent its stories an essential measure of believability. Its ideas seemed fresh, and its verbiage was unique. The use of Buck Rogers words like "laser" and "rocket"

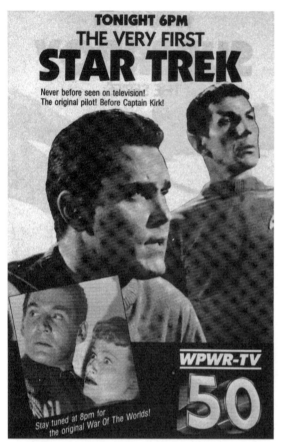

TONIGHT 6PM
THE VERY FIRST
STAR TREK

Never before seen on television!
The original pilot! Before Captain Kirk!

WPWR-TV
50

Stay tuned at 8pm for
the original War Of The Worlds!

*TV Guide* advertisement for the long-delayed broadcast of *Star Trek*'s rejected original pilot, "The Cage." The adventure finally aired October 15, 1988, twenty-four years after it was filmed.

in "The Cage" makes the twenty-third century sound more like the 1930s. It doesn't help matters that the props created for this pilot—especially the cylindrical "lasers" and chunky communicators—are clumsy-looking compared to those developed for the later series.

Roddenberry and Solow had secured production funds for "The Cage" from NBC with the understanding that, if it were rejected, the pilot could be aired as a fill-in Movie of the Week. *Star Trek* was saved from that ignominious fate when network executives took the extraordinary step of requesting a second pilot. Eventually, all but nine minutes of "The Cage" would be used in the two-part episode "The Menagerie," joined with a newly created framing sequence.

Roddenberry remained proud of "The Cage" and often showed a black-and-white 16 mm print of the show at *Star Trek* conventions and other public appearances. Unfortunately, the original negative of "The Cage" was cut up when "The Menagerie" was produced, and for many years the only extant complete version of the series' first pilot was Roddenberry's battered black-and-white print. Early home video releases of "The Cage" combined 16 mm black-and-white footage with the color 35 mm footage used in "The Menagerie." Then, in 1987, the original negative trims from "The Cage" were discovered in a Los Angeles film vault, and a painstaking restoration was undertaken. The complete, full-color version of the original *Star Trek* pilot finally aired in 1988 as part of a television special, *The Star Trek Saga: From One Generation to Another*, hosted by Patrick Stewart. Along with the seventy-nine original episodes, "The Cage" was digitally remastered in high definition, with new computer-generated visual effects, for release on Blu-ray in 2006.

# 5

# Spock's Brain

## Notable Pre-*Trek* Appearances by Leonard Nimoy

In retrospect, it may seem as if Leonard Nimoy was destined to play Spock. It was kismet. Or perhaps, as a visitor to the *Star Trek* set once suggested to the actor, he was chosen by extraterrestrials to "house the alien entity known as Spock." (Nimoy recounts this anecdote in his autobiography, *I Am Spock.*) However it happened, it is now impossible for most of us to think of Nimoy without thinking of Spock, or vice-versa. But the two weren't always synonymous, and Nimoy played a wide variety of roles (albeit in relative obscurity) on film, television, and the stage before donning his now-famous *Trek* uniform—and ears.

Nimoy was born March 26, 1931 (just four days after his future costar, William Shatner) and raised in a working class, mostly Italian-American Boston neighborhood, where his Yiddish-speaking Orthodox Jewish family made him an outsider. In *I Am Spock*, Nimoy recalls seeing the Charles Laughton version of *The Hunchback of Notre Dame* as an eight-year-old and identifying with the gruesome-looking but gentle-hearted Quasimodo, a righteous outcast. *The Hunchback* ignited Nimoy's ambition to become an actor and, later, provided inspiration for his most famous role. "The seed that would become Spock was planted," Nimoy wrote in his memoir.

### Kid Monk Baroni (1952)

After appearing in a few New England theatrical productions, Nimoy moved to Los Angeles in 1951 to pursue film and television parts. A year later he landed the title role in *Kid Monk Baroni*, a low-budget boxing melodrama that Nimoy has called "my big break." Considering that almost no one saw the movie and the actor earned very little salary, the point may be debatable. But certainly *Kid Monk Baroni* offered Nimoy, just twenty years old when this picture was shot, a plum role and gave him a calling card that led to additional work.

Nimoy plays a young delinquent named Paul Baroni, nicknamed "Monk" because of his apelike face (disfigured at birth by the clumsy use of forceps). The nickname takes on a dual meaning when Paul is taken under the wing of

Father Callahan (Richard Rober), who teaches the young man how to box. Paul becomes a faithful churchgoer and even sings in the choir. But when he accidentally wounds the kindly priest, Paul flees and launches a professional boxing career, taking special pleasure in destroying the faces of "pretty boy" opponents in the ring. Then his manager (played by Bruce Cabot, star of the 1933 *King Kong*) gets Paul involved with the mob. Eventually, "Kid Monk" Baroni decides to have plastic surgery and give up boxing, but these plans go awry.

Although fourth-billed (with a special "Introducing" credit), Nimoy dominates this picture. He's on-screen nearly every second, and he's very effective, giving a sympathetic and naturalistic performance. In many respects, Paul Baroni is a dream role: Nimoy plays high drama and low comedy, romances two women, and does actorly things like speak with an accent and appear under disfiguring makeup. Nimoy saw his character as a latter-day Quasimodo, he stated in a DVD audio commentary for the film.

Unfortunately, Nimoy's work remains by far the most appealing aspect of *Kid Monk Baroni*, which suffers from threadbare production values (Nimoy's "monk-face" makeup is particularly crude), tin-eared dialogue, and uneven performances from the rest of the cast (which also includes Jack Larson, soon to play Jimmy Olsen on *The Adventures of Superman* TV show). Despite Nimoy's fine work, *Kid Monk Baroni* functions on the level typical of its producer, Jack Broder, the cut-rate mogul behind cinematic gems such as *Bride of the Gorilla* (1951) and the immortal *Bela Lugosi Meets a Brooklyn Gorilla* (1952). Not surprisingly, the picture sank like a stone at the box office. For his efforts Nimoy earned about $400 and got to take home two cheap suits from the film's wardrobe. The actor was left to grind out the next thirteen years taking small roles in movies and television, while also working theatrically and, later, as an acting instructor (his future clients would include teen idol Fabian). Nimoy's next few film roles show how little immediate benefit the actor reaped from *Kid Monk Baroni*. He played Narab, a stock henchman (but, notably, Nimoy's first turn playing an extraterrestrial) in the twelve-chapter serial *Zombies of the Stratosphere* (1952), appeared in redface as Chief Black Hawk in the Poverty Row oater *Old Overland Trail* (1953), and took uncredited bits as a football player in *Francis Goes to College* (1952) and as a nameless sergeant battling giant irradiated ants in *Them!* (1954).

## *M Squad* Episode "The Fire Makers" (1959)

Nimoy soldiered through Hollywood's trenches, playing thankless roles in B-movies like *The Brain Eaters* (1958) and dozens of TV shows. During this era, perhaps due to his 6-foot-1 height and somewhat exotic looks (especially when sporting a mustache), he was frequently cast as a criminal. On *Dragnet* ("The Big Boys," 1954) he was an armed robber and car thief; on *Highway Patrol* ("Blood Money," 1958) he was the mastermind of a protection racket; on *Sea Hunt* ("Dead Man's Cove," 1959) he played a man who murders his wife and tries to make it look like a diving accident; on *Perry Mason* ("The Case of the Shoplifter's

Shoe," 1963) he was a hit-and-run driver who kills a kleptomaniac; and so on. But a special place must be reserved in Nimoy's personal rogues' gallery for Ben Blacker, the shameless arsonist, murderer, and all-around rat bastard he portrayed in "The Fire Makers," a 1959 episode of *M Squad*. Playing the vilest character of his career, Nimoy delivered a wildly enjoyable performance.

Ben and his brother Harry (James Coburn) are partners in an arson-for-hire racket employed by unscrupulous business owners who want to torch their own stores or factories to collect insurance benefits. During their latest job, Ben clubbed a luckless security guard over the head and left the old man to burn to death in the fire. Now, unsatisfied with his cut of the profits, Ben conspires to have his brother blamed for the murder, knowing that Harry will hide Ben's involvement in the crime out of family loyalty. When Lieutenant Frank Ballinger (series star Lee Marvin) begins to suspect Ben is mixed up in the arson business, Ben tries to kill the detective with a firebomb.

Cast alongside future star Coburn and screen legend Marvin, Nimoy steals the episode with his bravura portrayal of the preening, volatile, and probably sociopathic Ben, who brags to his girlfriend about his plans to sell out his big brother, then panics as soon as the cops

Leonard Nimoy made his first appearance as an extraterrestrial in the 1952 Republic serial *Zombies of the Stratosphere.*

begin to unravel his dunderheaded "master plan." His mercurial, jittery performance recalls the over-the-top villainy of cult favorite Tim Carey, a character actor who made a career out of playing fidgety lunatics during the 1950s and '60s, when he made brief but memorable appearances in classics such as *The Wild One* (1950) and *The Killing* (1956) as well as numerous B-budget Westerns and noir films. Nimoy returned to *M Squad*, a gritty police procedural set in Chicago (and subject of the later parody *Police Squad*), for a smaller, less flashy role in the 1960 episode "Badge for a Coward." Again, he played the bad guy (a cop-killing stickup man), but a far less entertaining one.

## *Combat!* Episode "The Wounded Don't Cry" (1963)

When he wasn't playing the heavy, Nimoy sometimes found himself in roles with subtly Spock-like qualities. That was the case with "The Wounded Don't Cry," a 1963 episode of the war drama *Combat!*, in which Nimoy appears as Newman, an unusually sympathetic, sensitive soldier who pleads for humane treatment of wounded German POWs. The bilingual Newman translates for Sgt. Chip Saunders (star Vic Morrow) after the platoon captures a Nazi aid station. The story's primary conflict falls between Saunders and Bauer (Carl Boehm), a German doctor who wants to retrieve a supply of plasma from a truck damaged in an Allied air raid. Without the plasma, the wounded Germans will die. Saunders doesn't think the doctor (or his patients) can be trusted, but Newman argues for helping the wounded. "Sorry I can't show hate for guys who are dying or see a plot in every act of mercy," Nimoy sneers. Then Newman is gravely injured when two wounded SS officers try to escape. Suddenly his survival also depends on acquiring the plasma, and Saunders reluctantly agrees to allow Bauer to recover the supply—but insists on accompanying the doctor.

Nimoy's role is small (he spends the final three-quarters of the episode unconscious or off-camera) but pivotal, and his endearing, heartfelt performance remains memorable despite its brevity. The actor seems remarkably at home as Newman, a man set apart from his comrades-in-arms by his ability to speak German and because he views the war through a different moral lens. Like Spock, he's an outsider who is also an important member of the team and a person of high intelligence and personal integrity. Nimoy returned to *Combat!* in 1965 for a thankless role (again as a translator, but this time in a tiny, underwritten part with no distinct personality) in "The Raider."

## *The Outer Limits* Episode "I, Robot" (1964)

Had he not been cast in *Star Trek*, science fiction fans would probably remember Nimoy primarily for his supporting role in this classic episode of the fabled 1960s sci-fi anthology series. "I, Robot," based on an Otto Binder short story (not the Isaac Asimov book of the same title), tells the story of Adam Link, an android put on trial for the murder of its creator. Small-town authorities consider Adam "an engine of destruction" and want to destroy the "tin man." But Nina Link (Marianna Hill), daughter of the deceased inventor, lures celebrated civil rights lawyer Thurman Cutler (Howard Da Silva) out of retirement to defend the robot. Nimoy plays street-savvy St. Louis newspaperman Judson Ellis. At first Ellis is skeptical of the entire business, assuming the affair is "a hoax" or "a gimmick" and referring to Adam as a "living eggbeater." But ultimately he becomes convinced that Adam contains a nearly human consciousness—and that the robot is innocent.

While it's a secondary part, Ellis sets the entire plot in motion by suggesting Nina contact Cutler, and, through his wry commentary on the proceedings, serves as the episode's conscience. Nimoy is in top form as the glib, jaded reporter whose sense of fairness and justice is reawakened during the trial. He invests his character with intelligence and compassion that triumphs over the occasionally creaky dialogue ("You may end up a skele-tin man, but I'm gonna make you famous," he promises Adam).

"I, Robot" emerged as one of the most popular and memorable episodes of the brilliant but short-lived original *Outer Limits* series, which ran on ABC just a season and a half from 1963 to 1965. The show was revived by production company MGM in 1995, enjoying a five-season run on the Showtime network and two more seasons on the Sci Fi Channel. During its inaugural season, the new *Outer Limits* remade "I, Robot," with Nimoy taking over the starring role as crusading attorney Thurman Cutler. As Cutler, Nimoy supplied another fine performance. The Judson Ellis character was written out of the remake. Nimoy had appeared on *The Outer Limits* earlier in 1964, with a faceless bit part in "Production and Decay of Strange Particles," an episode about invaders from subatomic space. The actor made a similarly forgettable appearance on the most celebrated of all science fiction-fantasy anthologies, *The Twilight Zone*, playing a nondescript infantryman in the antiwar parable "A Quality of Mercy" in 1961.

## *The Man from U.N.C.L.E.* Episode "The Project Strigas Affair" (1964)

It was here, not on the bridge of the *Enterprise*, that Nimoy and Shatner first crossed paths, guest starring in an episode of this seriocomic spy series. Shatner, whose career was far more advanced than Nimoy's at this point, enjoyed better billing and is seen to greater advantage in "The Project Strigas Affair," but Nimoy's sly comic performance nevertheless proves a winner. He plays Vladeck, the ambitious aide to a rabble-rousing Balkan ambassador who poses a potential threat to the international community. Secret agents Napoleon Solo (Robert Vaughn) and Illya Kuryakin (David McCallum) are assigned to discredit Ambassador Kurasov (played by Werner Klemperer, best remembered as *Hogan's Heroes*' Colonel Klink). Shatner portrays a likeable young chemist who agrees to help Solo and Kuryakin. U.N.C.L.E. (short for United Network Command for Law and Enforcement) schemes to turn Kurasov into a laughingstock. But Vladeck plays his cards wisely and winds up benefiting from the ignominious downfall of his imperious, condescending boss.

Shatner and Nimoy have one brief scene together (Shatner, drunk at a party, puts his arm around Nimoy and calls him "Calvin Coolidge"). There is no hint of the camaraderie that would later make Kirk and Spock such an appealing team. Indeed, Shatner didn't even remember that he had worked with Nimoy before he signed on for the second *Star Trek* pilot, "Where No Man Has Gone Before," a year later. Most of Nimoy's scenes are with Klemperer, with whom he has a prickly comedic rapport. If Nimoy doesn't quite steal the show, he remains a vital participant in most of the episode's best moments. Although *The*

Nimoy slogged through a variety of thankless roles prior to *Star Trek*, including an ignominious appearance as Chief Black Hawk in *Old Overland Trail* (1953).

*Man from U.N.C.L.E.* later descended into self-parody and camp, "The Project
Strigas Affair" was made during the show's more straightforward first season and
remains a credible spy-fi adventure. "Strigas" was the fifth episode of the series to
air. Too bad Nimoy wasn't cast in the show's second episode, "The Vulcan Affair."

## *The Lieutenant* Episode "In the Highest Tradition" (1964)

Nimoy's appearance on *The Lieutenant* remains, without a doubt, the most
important of his early career—not for the performance he delivered on-screen
(although it was very good) but for the contacts he made on the set. *The
Lieutenant*, a peacetime military drama, ran on NBC for just one season, 1963–64,
and was soon forgotten. The series remains notable for only one reason: It was
the first weekly program created and produced by Gene Roddenberry. "In the
Highest Tradition," while hardly great television, remains a fascinating artifact
due to its many *Star Trek* connections.

Nimoy guest stars as Gregg Sanders, a Hollywood producer-director plan-
ning a movie about a World War II battle that took the lives of six marines, all of
whom won Medals of Honor. His assistant is played by Majel Barrett, the future
Nurse Chapel (and second Mrs. Gene Roddenberry). The episode was directed
by Marc Daniels, who would helm fifteen *Star Trek* episodes, including the classics
"Space Seed," "Mirror, Mirror," and "The Doomsday Machine." The primary

focus of the story is the way preparations for the film alter the life of retired Lt. Peter Bonney (Andrew Duggan), the former commanding officer of the six fallen marines, and create headaches for *The Lieutenant*'s nominal protagonist, Lieutenant Bill Rice (played by Gary Lockwood, who would guest star in "Where No Man Has Gone Before").

All the episode's finest moments belong to Nimoy's Sanders, whose unshakeable faith in himself and his project, and his uncanny ability to instantly translate Bonney's complex, real-life memories and emotions into facile action-movie clichés, is equally admirable and laughable. Like so many of Nimoy's best performances, Sanders is a character with inner conflicts and surprising depths, a man who understands he's treading a fine line between honoring the fallen marines and exploiting them. The show was produced in late 1963 and aired February 29, 1964. As far as Nimoy knew, it was just another job. He continued plugging away in numerous other television roles, including appearances on *Get Smart* and *Gunsmoke*. Nimoy guest starred opposite DeForest Kelley in an episode of *The Virginian* titled "Man of Violence" (1965). Appropriately enough, Kelley played a doctor and Nimoy his patient.

Meanwhile, budding screenwriter Dorothy Fontana was working as Roddenberry's production secretary on *The Lieutenant*. In April 1964, while awaiting word from NBC on whether or not *The Lieutenant* would be renewed, Roddenberry handed Fontana the outline for a proposed new series called *Star Trek* and asked her for her thoughts. She took it home, read it, and, as she recounts in her introduction to the book *Star Trek: The Original Series 365*, the next day asked Roddenberry: "'Who's going to play Spock?' Gene slid a photo across his desk. It was of Leonard Nimoy."

The actor's career was about to shift into high gear. Or rather, warp speed.

# 6

# The Man Who Would Be Captain

## Memorable Pre-*Trek* Roles for William Shatner

While most *Star Trek* cast members came to the program without a great deal of on-screen experience or audience recognition, William Shatner already had assembled an impressive résumé, playing small roles in big movies, big roles in small movies, and earning acclaim for his performances on stage and television. He had proven himself adept with both high drama and low comedy. And even though two previous TV series starring Shatner quickly fizzled, the actor had become familiar to viewers through his frequent guest appearances on dozens of other programs. The camera liked Shatner's face, and producers liked his professionalism and work ethic.

Although he usually played WASPy Americans, Shatner was Jewish, born in Quebec on March 22, 1931, the son of Joseph Shatner, a Central European haberdasher who had immigrated to Canada and founded a modestly successful company that manufactured inexpensive suits. Joseph wanted young Bill to take over the family business and was appalled when his son took up a theatrical career instead. Nevertheless, Joseph Shatner instilled in his son an abiding commitment to an honest day's labor. Such dedication would serve the actor well throughout his career, even though it failed to translate into wealth and fame prior to *Star Trek*.

### *Henry V* in Stratford, Ontario (1954)

An actor's career is a series of chain reactions, with one good performance opening up new opportunities (or a bad one closing them off), solid work in those subsequent roles leading to further opportunities, and so on. For William Shatner, a single performance as Henry V provided the initial thrust that launched his professional career.

After leaving his father's haberdashery (where he had worked packing suits), Shatner joined the Canadian National Repertory Theatre in Ottawa (where he earned thirty-one dollars per week), summering at the Mountain Playhouse back home in Montreal. A few years later, at age twenty-three, he joined the prestigious Stratford Festival in Ontario for three seasons, beginning in 1954. As one of a half-dozen young actors in the company, he was initially assigned minor parts, such as the Duke of Gloucester, his role in the company's 1954 production of Shakespeare's *King Henry V*. However, Shatner was also selected to understudy star Christopher Plummer—although he had no expectation he would actually be called upon to replace Plummer. Nevertheless, Plummer was struck down by a kidney stone, and Shatner was asked to fill in on short notice. Owing to a brief rehearsal schedule, there had been no understudy's run-through. At this distance, since the performance was not filmed, we must rely on the actor's recollection of the event in his autobiography *Up Till Now*. According to Shatner, things went "inexplicably" well until the very end, when he momentarily went blank but managed to cover his panic until the final lines of the play came back to him.

It wasn't quite the Hollywood cliché—"You're going out there a nobody, but you're coming back a star!"—but his surprisingly well-received performance as Henry V proved to be Shatner's first big break. It impressed festival director Tyrone Guthrie, who cast the actor in a leading role in his production of Christopher Marlowe's *Tamburlaine the Great*. After a successful Canadian run, Guthrie moved *Tamburlaine* to Broadway, where Shatner made his debut on the Great White Way. And that, in turn, led to further opportunities.

## Ranger Bob on *Howdy Doody* (1954)

Although Shatner elected to return to Stratford for two more seasons, his work in *Tamburlaine the Great* attracted several offers for additional, off-season work in film and television, including his first recurring role on a TV series—as Ranger Bob on the beloved NBC children's program *Howdy Doody*. From December 1947 through September 1960, ventriloquist "Buffalo" Bob Smith costarred with the wooden-headed Howdy Doody and a clown named Clarabelle (originally played by Bob Keeshan, the future Captain Kangaroo) on this Western-themed show, shot in front of a live audience of kids who actively participated in the program (even singing the theme song) from the "peanut gallery." Although it's cherished by baby boomers who grew up with the program, *Howdy Doody* isn't fondly remembered by Shatner. As a young actor with big ambitions—to say nothing of ego—he was frustrated playing a subservient role to a freckle-faced marionette and a clown who communicated by honking a horn rather than speaking. He soon quit *Howdy Doody*. It was an ignominious beginning to one of the great careers in television history. Who could have foreseen that Shatner would eventually star in four successful series—*Star Trek*, *T. J. Hooker*, *Rescue 911*, and *Boston Legal*—spanning more than four decades in the industry?

## Westinghouse Studio One: Episodes "The Defenders, Parts 1 and 2" (1957)

At first, Shatner enjoyed most of his TV successes on the corporate-sponsored weekly dramatic programs that were staples of the medium's Golden Age, including the *Goodyear Television Playhouse*, *Playhouse 90*, *Kraft Television Theatre*, the *Hallmark Hall of Fame*, and the *U.S. Steel Hour*. One of the most popular of these programs was *Westinghouse Studio One*. In 1957, Ralph Bellamy and Shatner costarred as a father-and-son legal team in a two-part *Studio One* courtroom drama titled "The Defenders." By resorting to courtroom theatrics, Shatner's character loses his father's respect but wins the case, saving a young man (played by Steve McQueen) falsely accused of murder. The show earned rave reviews and high ratings, so CBS decided to develop it as an ongoing series. Shatner and Bellamy were offered the leads, but both turned it down. *The Defenders* went on to a successful four-season run with E. G. Marshall and a young Robert Reed (future patriarch of *The Brady Bunch*) as the father-and-son lawyers.

Around this same time, Shatner also turned down a studio contract offer from Metro-Goldwyn-Mayer and (perhaps surprisingly, given the actor's later success as a pitchman) numerous commercials. He wanted to pursue more glamorous roles on Broadway—and landed one as the male lead in the romance *The World of Suzie Wong*, which opened in 1958 and ran for fourteen months. Starring in the title role was the French-Vietnamese actress France Nuyen, who would later appear as the titular alien princess in the *Star Trek* episode "Elaan of Troyius." Shatner earned kind notices (as well as $750 per week), but *Suzie Wong* turned out to be his only Broadway hit.

Meanwhile, financial pressures were mounting. Shatner had married actress Gloria Rand in 1956, and Leslie, the first of the couple's three daughters, arrived in 1958 (followed by Lisabeth in 1960 and Melanie in 1964). Shatner returned to television to pay the bills but without the advantage of an ongoing series to provide a reliable paycheck. He became an in-demand guest star, appearing on shows ranging from *Alfred Hitchcock Presents* to *Route 66* to *Gunsmoke* to *Dr. Kildare*. Ironically, one of the shows Shatner worked on most frequently was *The Defenders*, where he made five appearances from 1963 to '65, usually playing either a defendant or a prosecutor.

## Thriller Episode "The Hungry Glass" (1961)

The wide variety of TV roles he played during this period helped Shatner both hone his craft and display his abilities. Viewers who know him only as Captain Kirk may be surprised at the range and finesse Shatner displayed in these diverse and often challenging parts. "The Hungry Glass," an episode of the anthology series *Thriller*, provides a case in point.

NBC's *Thriller*, hosted by the great Boris Karloff, ran for just two seasons (it was clobbered in the ratings by CBS's *The Red Skelton Show*) but produced some excellent episodes, picking up creative steam midway through its first season when the show transitioned from Hitchcockian crime-suspense stories to full-tilt, blood-curdling, supernatural horror. First aired January 3, 1961, "The Hungry Glass" was one of the earliest of these new-breed *Thriller* episodes. In it, newlyweds Gil and Marsha Thrasher (Shatner and Joanna Heyes) buy a haunted mansion, where the vengeful spirit of a vain old woman lives on in the house's mirrors and other reflective surfaces, luring unsuspecting visitors to their deaths. Shatner's performance is carefully calibrated: At first he exudes cool confidence, laughing off "local superstition"; then he lets the character's self-assurance slowly crumble as Gil comes to believe evil spirits are indeed at work; finally, for the story's frantic climax, he uncorks a full-blown, Shatnerian freak-out. The actor is especially effective in those scenes where Gil tries to hide his growing fears from his wife. Overall, "The Hungry Glass" is a satisfyingly spooky show, and one that helped set the tone for what would follow for *Thriller*'s next season and a half. This was more like what viewers wanted from a show hosted by horror icon Karloff. Ratings improved enough over the rest of the season to earn the show a renewal.

Shatner was quickly invited back and costarred in the final episode of *Thriller*'s first season, "The Grim Reaper." Unfortunately, both the episode and Shatner's role proved far less memorable than his first outing. This time around, he was cast as the doting nephew of a kooky mystery author who buys a cursed painting. Written by Robert Bloch from a story by Harold Lawlor, the screenplay builds to an E.C. Comics-style "surprise" ending that's not very surprising. Shatner does what he can, but his character is one-dimensional and his dialogue at times insipid. Coincidentally, in both of his *Thriller* appearances Shatner appeared alongside future castaways from *Gilligan's Island*. Russell Johnson, aka the Professor, plays the real estate agent who sells the Thrashers the haunted house in "The Hungry Glass," and Natalie Schafer, best remembered as Lovey Howell, plays the dotty novelist in "The Grim Reaper."

## *Judgment at Nuremberg* (1961)

By the late 1950s, Shatner was hearing the same line over and over again. "At that point in my career it seemed like every phone call I got from a movie director or a TV producer or an agent began with the statement, 'Bill, honestly this [fill in the blank] is the one that's going to make you a star,'" Shatner wrote in *Up Till Now*. The first of Shatner's supposedly star-making roles arrived in 1958, when he was cast opposite Yul Brynner, Richard Basehart, and Lee J. Cobb in director Richard Brooks's high-profile adaptation of Dostoyevsky's *The Brothers Karamazov*. Shatner played the youngest brother, Alexi (even though the actor later admitted that he couldn't make heads nor tails of the book). Despite an ample budget, a fine cast, and an impressive literary pedigree, Brooks's film was an artistic and commercial disappointment and did nothing to advance Shatner's career.

A few years later came *Judgment at Nuremberg*, an important "message picture"—a courtroom drama about the Nazi war crimes trials—with a star-studded cast, directed by the respected Stanley Kramer (*Inherit the Wind, On the Beach*, etc.). Shatner was offered the role of a young army lawyer. His agent assured him this was the picture that would finally make him a star, but the actor also believed the project would keep the memory of the Holocaust alive to serve as a warning against similar atrocities. *Judgment at Nuremberg* was a box-office hit and a critical triumph. It racked up eleven Academy Award nominations and took home two Oscars, including Maximilian Schell as Best Actor. Spencer Tracy was also nominated as Best Actor, and Montgomery Clift and Judy Garland earned Supporting Actor and Actress nominations. Burt Lancaster, Richard Widmark, and Marlene Dietrich contributed memorable supporting performances. Lost in the shuffle, however, was Shatner. Although by his mere presence the actor brought some warmth and charm to his role, Captain Harrison Byers is a colorless, do-nothing character. He's the guy who swears in the aging stars playing the witnesses in the trial, so they can give spectacular performances while Shatner sits at a table wearing a headset and scribbling in a notepad. His most dramatic dialogue is, "Raise your right hand." Still, Shatner enjoyed making *Judgment at Nuremberg*. It was a noble endeavor, and it gave the young actor a chance to work alongside performers he had idolized, especially Tracy.

## The Intruder (1962)

Nobody thought *The Intruder* would make Shatner a star, and it didn't. But it should have.

Shatner is simply sensational as Adam Cramer, a carpetbagging demagogue who travels to a sleepy Southern town to inflame white resentment over the desegregation of the fictional Caxton High School. He hopes to stir up the locals' fear and loathing and manufacture a racial incident that will discredit desegregation laws and the civil rights movement in general. The quick-witted, silver-tongued Cramer is reprehensible but riveting as he dupes and race-baits the white citizenry (including members of the Ku Klux Klan) into homicidal violence, including a church bombing. Along the way, he also seduces the depressed wife of a traveling salesman and the teenage daughter of the local newspaper editor. Ultimately, however, Cramer's machinations spin out of control, and he is undone by his own dark ambitions. The entire film turns on Shatner's subtle, oily portrayal of Cramer. His performance that suggests if he hadn't later become a starship captain, Shatner might have made an excellent Ferengi.

Produced and directed by Roger Corman and written by frequent *Twilight Zone* scribe Charles Beaumont, *The Intruder* remains a powerful viewing experience, uncommonly frank and uncompromising for its era. (For instance, whites use the word "nigger" with now-shocking casualness and frequency.) But the picture was a bit *too* powerful in its day. Although it won a special citation at the Venice Film Festival and performed well in other international exhibitions, Corman had great difficulty distributing *The Intruder* in the U.S. The drive-ins and exploitation houses that played his usual B-movies wouldn't touch it, and Corman did not yet have the critical cachet to earn many art house bookings. Naturally, the film was virtually impossible to sell in the South. As a result *The Intruder* became the first (and for many years only) Corman production to lose money.

It's a wonder the film was made at all. Shatner's and Corman's autobiographies both feature jaw-dropping stories about the movie's production. Shot on location in Mississippi County, southeast Missouri, *The Intruder* required careful subterfuge (few locals saw the real script or had any idea what the film was truly about). Despite these precautions, however, enough of the story leaked to agitate area bigots, and the cast and crew operated under constant threat of physical violence. The film's provocative cross-burning scene was the last footage shot—afterward, the entire company packed up and drove hundreds of miles north, where they could sleep safely. Despite the fact that it lost money, Corman routinely names *The Intruder* as his personal favorite among the nearly 400 films he has produced. Shatner is also justifiably proud of the picture. But since nobody saw it, it did little for his career.

## *The Twilight Zone* Episode "Nightmare at 20,000 Feet" (1963)

William Shatner first entered *The Twilight Zone* on November 18, 1960, with the broadcast of "Nick of Time," an episode about a honeymooning couple whose car breaks down in small-town Ohio. While waiting for repairs, Don (Shatner) and Pat (Patricia Breslin) drop into a local diner for lunch and discover a penny fortune-telling machine in their booth. The newlyweds are amazed to discover that the mechanical "Mystic Seer" actually *can* predict the future. Superstitious Don, who carries a rabbit's foot and a four-leaf clover keychain, quickly becomes fascinated, even fixated, on the machine, but Pat fears it—and the influence it's exerting on her husband. "Nick of Time," broadcast the week after one of the *Zone*'s best-remembered episodes ("In the Eye of the Beholder") midway through the show's second season, is a subtle, thought-provoking yarn written by the famed Richard Matheson. Shatner and Breslin both give warm, endearing performances as the just-married couple discovering each other's strengths and weaknesses and learning how to forge their path together. All in all, it's a very good show.

But Shatner was seen to far greater advantage when he returned to the series for "Nightmare at 20,000 Feet," revered as one of the greatest (not to mention scariest) of all *Zone* episodes. Broadcast October 11, 1963, during the series' fifth season, the story—again by Matheson—features Shatner as Bob Wilson, a high-strung salesman flying home to his family after recovering at a sanitarium from a nervous breakdown. As the plane flies through the stormy night sky, Wilson spots a furry little man—a gremlin—on the wing, attempting to sabotage the

In this publicity still, William Shatner hams it up with the gremlin that tormented him during the classic *Twilight Zone* episode "Nightmare at 20,000 Feet."

engine. But since the creature hides whenever anyone other than Wilson looks out the window, no one believes him. Instead, they assume the salesman's mind is going again. Increasingly agitated and frightened, Wilson decides he must defeat the gremlin himself, even if doing so lands him back in the sanitarium. "Nightmare at 20,000 Feet" is twenty-five minutes of perfectly constructed white-knuckle suspense. Matheson, adapting from his own short story, improves upon the original by giving Wilson a wife and other characters to talk to, externalizing the character's thought process. But Shatner's face registers all the emotion necessary to convince viewers of the terror of the scenario—disbelief, fear, frustration, anger, despair, and finally determination and relief. It's a masterful performance, among the finest of his career.

One of the best loved of all *Twilight Zone* episodes, "Nightmare at 20,000 Feet" was also among the four classic episodes recreated for the 1993 big-screen *Twilight Zone: The Movie*, with John Lithgow in the Bob Wilson role. Years later, when Shatner took on a recurring featured role in Lithgow's sitcom, *3rd Rock from the Sun*, about a family of aliens living incognito among humankind, the show's writers couldn't resist an inside joke based on the two actors' *Twilight Zone* connection. In his first *3rd Rock* scene, Shatner, playing Lithgow's boss (known as the Big Giant Head), has just arrived from "out of town." Lithgow asks if he had a good flight. "It was horrible," Shatner replies. "I looked out and saw something on the wing of the plane." Lithgow, incredulous, exclaims, "The *same thing* happened to me!"

## *The Outer Limits*: Episode "Cold Hands, Warm Heart" (1964)

Shatner delivered another tour de force performance in *The Outer Limits* episode "Cold Hands, Warm Heart." Astronaut Jefferson Barton (Shatner) returns to a hero's welcome after becoming the first man to orbit the planet Venus. But he's puzzled by an eight-minute blackout he suffered while orbiting the planet and plagued by strange nightmares and an inability to keep warm (even with the furnace turned up to eighty-five, he wears a sweater and gulps down hot coffee). Since he's supposed to pilot an upcoming mission to Mars (prophetically titled Project Vulcan), he tries to hide his condition from both military doctors and his beloved wife (Geraldine Brooks). But then his hands begin turning into scaly claws . . .

Many critics and fans consider *The Outer Limits* the best science fiction TV show ever made, but it was not financially successful at the time. "Cold Hands, Warm Heart" was the second episode broadcast during the program's second season, but only fifteen more would air before ABC cancelled the series, which at the time suffered in frequent comparisons with CBS' *The Twilight Zone*. While only forty-nine episodes of *The Outer Limits* were produced, most of those are now treasured as classics. "Cold Hands, Warm Heart" isn't one of the series' finest episodes—like the offbeat "Zanti Misfits," about a gang of ant-like alien criminals, or writer Harlan Ellison's hard-hitting "Soldier," which inspired director James Cameron's *The Terminator*—but it's a solid entry and one that, like "The Hungry Glass" and "Nightmare at 20,000 Feet," depends entirely on the actor's performance to carry the tale. The script offered Shatner several well-written romantic interludes in addition to the suspenseful, at times even horrific, primary story line.

## *For the People* (1965)

Eight years after he declined to star in *The Defenders*, Shatner accepted the lead in another weekly courtroom drama, producer Herb Brodkin's *For the People*. Shatner starred as Assistant District Attorney David Koster, an ambitious young prosecutor trying to balance his passion for his job against the demands of his marriage to a free-thinking professional viola player, Phyllis (Jessica Walter). The cast also featured Howard Da Silva as Koster's boss and Anthony Celeste as police detective Frank Malloy. The show—which in certain respects anticipated the long-running NBC series *Law & Order*—was praised by critics but lasted just thirteen episodes because CBS slotted it opposite the top-rated program on television, ABC's Western powerhouse *Bonanza*. "Test patterns had better time spots," Shatner wrote in his autobiography. "*For the People* never had a chance."

But at least it was picked up by the network, which was more than could be said for the first series in which Shatner agreed to star. In 1963, he had played the title role in the two-hour pilot film *Alexander the Great*. Envisioned by producer Selig J. Seligman (who had created the hit series *Combat!*) as a weekly costume drama based on the adventures of one of history's fabled military commanders, the show promised lots of horseback chase sequences, sword fights, and scantily clad women. Shot in Utah on a tiny budget, the telefilm was directed by Phil Karlson (whose filmography includes the noir gem *Kansas City Confidential* [1955] and the later cult classic *Walking Tall* [1973]) and costarred John Cassavetes, Joseph Cotten, Simon Oakland, and a pre-*Batman* Adam West. Despite this astounding cast, Seligman was unable to find a taker for his unusual series. *Alexander the Great* belatedly aired as a movie-of-the-week in January 1968.

In retrospect, the failure of his two previous TV shows was a disguised blessing. If CBS had given *For the People* a more favorable time slot, Shatner may not

Magazine ad for Shatner's short-lived legal drama *For the People*, in which he played a young prosecuting attorney with a complicated personal life.

have been available when *Star Trek* producer-creator Gene Roddenberry went looking for replacement starship captains in the spring of 1965. Then fans may have been stuck with someone like Jack Lord as Captain Kirk. But that's another chapter.

## Incubus (1966)

In most respects, writer-director Leslie Stevens's *Incubus* is a fairly typical low-budget horror film. In fact, with an overtly symbolic, Bergmanesque storyline and cinematographer Conrad Hall's German Expressionist-influenced lighting schemes, it's smarter and better crafted than most other movies of its stripe. But that's not why *Incubus* is remembered. It's famous—or perhaps infamous—because Stevens shot the film in Esperanto, the "global language" invented by Russian philologist L. L. Zamenhof. In 1887, Zamenhof published the first textbook for Esperanto, which he hoped would eventually serve as a universal second language and help promote understanding between people from different nations and ethnic backgrounds. Stevens, creator of *The Outer Limits*, shared Zamenhof's idealism and wanted to promote use of the language.

*Incubus* is the story of a demon named Kia (Allyson Ames), a succubus who lures sinners to their doom and claims their souls for Satan. But she's bored with preying on the weak-willed and black-hearted. Looking for a greater challenge, she decides to try to seduce and destroy the saintly Marc (Shatner), a devoutly Christian war hero. To her surprise, Marc falls in love with her, refusing a simple tryst and insisting on a church wedding; the story becomes a battle of wills between Marc's pure love and Kia's inveterate evil.

When William Shatner signed to play the lead in the film, he didn't know it would be shot in Esperanto. The script was written in English, so the actor naturally assumed it would be performed in that language. Nevertheless, Stevens won Shatner over with his enthusiasm for the idea of shooting in Esperanto. Since none of the cast spoke Esperanto, they were all shipped out for an intensive, two-week training on the language and its proper pronunciation (despite which, the same words are pronounced completely differently by various members of the cast). Stevens directed in Esperanto, or tried to. Shatner first saw the film at an international film festival, where it was subtitled in Italian. Since he didn't speak Italian, and had long since forgotten his limited Esperanto, he found the experience incomprehensible. So did most other viewers wherever the film was shown—which wasn't many places. *Incubus* played a few film festivals in the U.S. and received general release only in France.

Filmed in May 1965, after the cancellation of *The Outer Limits*, *Incubus* wasn't issued anywhere until 1966. By then, Shatner had taken on a new role, the one that really would (eventually) make him a star: Captain James T. Kirk of the starship *Enterprise*.

# 7

# Spectre of the Gun

## Memorable Pre-*Trek* Roles for DeForest Kelley

ackson DeForest Kelley was the son of the Reverend Ernest Kelley, an itinerant Southern Baptist minister. Born January 20, 1920, DeForest Kelley spent his youth in Northern and Central Georgia, moving from town to town and church to church every few years (and sometimes more often) along with his older brother, his mother, and his stern father, whose fire-and-brimstone sermons often railed against the evils of smoking, drinking, dancing, and moviegoing. Despite his father's dim view of show business, however, young DeForest—who was blessed with a fine voice—sang not only in the church choir but on WSB, an AM radio station in Atlanta. It was his first taste of stardom. As a teenager, Kelley began to rebel against his father's strict rule. In 1939, now yearning for a career in theater, he bolted for California, where he moved in with an uncle in Long Beach. Kelley soon joined the Long Beach Community Playhouse, where he quickly rose through the ranks and into leading roles. Along with a handful of other Community Playhouse performers, Kelley also acted in local radio dramas. His assured performances, unique delivery, and chiseled good looks soon attracted the attention of Hollywood talent scouts. Over the next five years, he earned interviews and screen tests with several studios, and in 1942 narrowly missed out on the star-making role of hit man Philip Raven in *This Gun for Hire* (instead, the part went to another then-unknown, Alan Ladd). Independent producer Walter Wanger was prepared to offer Kelley a contract in 1943, but just when success seemed within reach, World War II intervened. Kelley was drafted.

Appropriately enough, given the actor's later relations with extraterrestrials, Kelley spent most of his military career in Roswell, New Mexico. Because of his experience in radio, Kelley was assigned to the Army Signal Corps and worked as an air traffic controller at an Air Corps training base. In his off-duty hours, the actor continued to pursue his theatrical ambitions, participating in morale-boosting camp revues and radio programs. He was so impressive in these appearances that in January 1945 he was transferred to the First Motion Picture Unit in Hollywood—also known as Camp Roach, since it was based at the Hal Roach Studios. There, Kelley worked behind the scenes and sometimes on camera making military training films such as *How to Act if Captured*. More importantly, he rubbed elbows with Hollywood royalty and befriended other rising stars including George Reeves. Kelley—known simply as "De" (pronounced "Dee") to his friends—was always well liked by his coworkers, who described him as kind and courteous, with a warm sense of humor and talent much larger than his ego. Kelley's personal life was blissfully uneventful, consumed mostly by evenings at home with his wife Carolyn, a former Community Playhouse costar he married in 1945 and remained devoted to until his death 54 years later. After the war, in February 1946, Kelley finally received the offer he had been waiting for. Paramount—who had chosen Alan Ladd over him for *This Gun for Hire*—signed Kelley to a modest multiyear contract, which paid $150 per week for the first year, increasing to $200 per week the following year, with forty weeks guaranteed annually. But Kelley's struggles were far from over. For the next twenty years, stardom remained elusive and financial security tenuous.

## *Fear in the Night* (1947)

Kelley made his motion picture debut, and played his only starring movie role, in this offbeat, low-budget film noir.

The first of five quirky features directed by B-movie screenwriter Maxwell Shane (whose previous writing credits included *The Mummy's Hand* [1944]), *Fear in the Night* features Kelley as mild-mannered bank teller Vincent Grayson, who dreams he has committed a murder and then comes to believe his nightmare may be true. In the dream, he kills someone he doesn't know in a place he thinks he's never been. To help solve the mystery, Grayson turns to his brother-in-law Cliff (Paul Kelly), a cop. But as evidence piles up against Grayson (who finds himself in possession of a key and a button, evidence from the crime scene), Cliff suspects his brother-in-law may be using him to establish an insanity defense.

*Fear in the Night* (not to be confused with a 1972 Hammer Films thriller of the same title) was adapted from a Cornell Woolrich short story. It's a far-fetched yarn, turning on several unlikely plot devices including a preposterous hypnotism angle. The tale is told in over-the-top fashion by Shane, who tricks out the picture with all sorts of flashy gimmicks (superimposing the dead man's face on a close-up of Kelley's eyes, for instance). Despite all the directorial flash, however, the movie's primary strength is Kelley. He supplies an earnest, at times intense performance far better than this undistinguished vehicle deserves. The actor's innate likeability shines through, yet he also suggests a capacity for violence that keeps viewers guessing whether or not Grayson could really be the killer. Kelley also provides voice-over narration throughout the film (much of it distorted by heavy reverb, in another distracting style choice by Shane). Viewers will notice that the actor's Georgia drawl, utilized so effectively in his later Westerns and on *Star Trek*, is virtually absent here. Kelley had worked hard to eradicate his accent, only to find it useful again later in his career. Shane adapted the same Woolrich story again, with marginally better results, under its

DeForest Kelley (left) thought he was on his way to stardom when he was assigned the lead in the low-budget noir thriller *Fear in the Night* (1947), opposite Paul Kelly. But this turned out to be his only starring role in a feature film.

original title *Nightmare* in 1956. That version featured Kevin McCarthy as Grayson and Edward G. Robinson as the brother-in-law cop.

*Fear in the Night* was issued on the bottom half of a double bill and performed well in some markets, but did little to advance Kelley's prospects. Paramount next assigned Kelley parts in a pair of short subjects and a thankless role in *Variety Girl* (1947). In that picture (which Kelley despised), he plays one of the characters featured in the framing scenes that link what is essentially a musical-comedy revue built around cameos by headline stars such as Bob Hope and Bing Crosby. The studio seemed unsure what to do with Kelley, who showed promise but wasn't a typical leading man. After loaning him out for appearances in two religious shorts, Paramount dropped him in 1948.

The next nine years were the toughest of Kelley's career. While he landed a trickle of minor film and television roles, the Kelleys subsisted on Carolyn's salary as a secretary. The actor was often very effective in his tiny parts. In the Edward G. Robinson melodrama *Illegal* (1955), Kelley had a small but unforgettable role as an innocent man convicted of, and executed for, the murder of his wife. The actor's work in this ten-minute sequence, which opens the film, is heart-wrenching. "I didn't kill her, I loved her!" he pleads with the prison chaplain on his way to the electric chair. But even such outstanding moments failed to earn Kelley larger parts. Also during this period, the future "Bones" McCoy made his first foray into sci-fi with three appearances on *Science Fiction Theatre*, coincidentally playing doctors in the episodes "Survival in Box Canyon" (1955) and "Y.O.R.D." (1956).

## *You Are There!* Episode "The Gunfight at the O.K. Corral" (1955) and *Gunfight at the O.K. Corral* (1957)

During these lean years Kelley received much-needed support from another Long Island Community Theatre alum, Barney Girard, then working as casting director for *You Are There*, a CBS educational series starring newsman Walter Cronkite and featuring reenactments of famous historical events. Cronkite anchored the program, which integrated mock news reports and interviews "from the scene" of events like the destruction of the airship *Hindenburg*, the Salem witch trials, and Abraham Lincoln's Gettysburg Address. *You Are There* began as a radio program in 1947, moved to TV in 1953, and continued until 1957 (and was briefly revived as Saturday morning programming for the 1971–72 season).

Girard helped Kelley land roles in nine *You Are There* episodes from May 1953 through January 1956, including a pivotal part as Ike Clanton in the "The Gunfight at the O.K. Corral" episode broadcast November 6, 1955. It was Kelley's first appearance as a Western villain, and he was stunningly effective. The actor's friends and family were taken aback by how frightening their gentle-natured friend seemed as Clanton. More importantly, Kelley's performance wowed producer Hal Wallis, who watched the show while preparing a big-budget, star-studded feature film version of the story. Almost immediately, Wallis began trying to cast Kelley to play Ike Clanton in *The Gunfight at the O.K. Corral* (1957), directed by John Sturges and costarring Burt Lancaster as Wyatt Earp and Kirk Douglas as Doc Holliday. But while Wallis twisted the arms of Sturges and casting director Paul Nathan to consider Kelley for the part, Kelley obliviously signed on to appear in the RKO B-Western *Tension at Table Rock* (1956). By the time Wallis was able to offer the Clanton role to Kelley, Kelley couldn't accept because the shooting of the Clanton scenes conflicted with the filming of *Tension at Table Rock*. Instead, Kelley took the small role of Morgan Earp, one of Wyatt's big brothers, in *Gunfight at O.K. Corral*.

Left with less than ten minutes of screen time and few lines, Kelley had very little to do in Wallis's *O.K. Corral* but did it beautifully. The actor has a brief speech in which Morgan "says his piece" about his younger brother riding with the notorious killer Holliday (Morgan's against it), but is most impressive simply sitting with Lancaster and John Hudson (playing Virgil Earp) as the Earp brothers brood through the wee hours as their showdown with the Clantons approaches at dawn. Simply sitting in a chair and staring into space, Kelley's face becomes a portrait of anxiety and determination; you can almost see the gears turning in Morgan's head as he contemplates the recent murder of his younger brother and his own possible impending demise. Minutes later, Kelley cuts an iconic figure walking, with a six-gun strapped to his hip, to the O.K. Corral alongside Lancaster, Douglas, and Hudson. The actor had discovered his métier.

A dozen years later, Kelley made a third appearance at the O.K. Corral in the *Star Trek* episode *Spectre of the Gun*, in which Kirk, Spock, McCoy, Scotty, and Chekov find themselves trapped at the famous gunfight—standing in for the villainous Clantons. The episode was created, in part, as a nod to Kelley's former fame as a Western villain. Sturges asked Kelley to reprise his role as Morgan Earp in the director's *Hour of the Gun* (1967), but Kelley had to decline due to his commitments to *Star Trek*.

## Warlock (1959)

*Gunfight at the O.K. Corral* opened the floodgates to a steady stream of film and television roles, usually as second-gun-to-the-left badmen. While this wasn't the career Kelley had envisioned for himself, he nevertheless enjoyed the first flush period of his working life. Carolyn quit her secretarial job to handle her husband's fan mail and track his residuals. Kelley played a Confederate cavalry officer in the lavish Civil War epic *Raintree County* (1957, starring Montgomery Clift and Elizabeth Taylor), portrayed one of Richard Widmark's henchmen in Sturges's *The Law and Jake Wade* (1957), and appeared on more than a dozen TV series (mostly Westerns) during the two years that followed *Gunfight*.

Occasionally, these black-hat roles offered Kelley room to demonstrate the wider range of his ability. One such part was Curley Burne, henchman of crooked cattle baron Abe McQuown (Tom Drake) in director Edward Dmytryk's *Warlock*. In this unusually morally and psychologically complex Western, merchants from the town of Warlock, Utah, tired of having their stores shot up by McQuown's rowdy cowboys, and frustrated by the ineffectiveness of the local constabulary, hire gunman Clay Blaisedell (Henry Fonda) to bring order. Blaisedell arrives with his fawning, club-footed man Friday (Anthony Quinn) in tow, but the duo soon run afoul of the local deputy (Richard Widmark) and alienate many of the townsfolk Blaisedell has sworn to protect.

The story, adapted from a novel by Oakley Hall, is told in shades of gray, without clearly defined good guys and bad guys. That includes Curley, a minor but integral character brought to vivid life by Kelley. He emanates a rare blend of charm and menace during an early scene in which Curley taunts Blaisedell about the marshal's gold-handled Colt pistols, luring the lawman into a barroom gunfight. Curley is outdrawn, but Blaisedell doesn't fire. "Ooo-wee!" Kelley hoots, seeming more amused than scared by the incident. Curley tips his hat to Blaisedell on his way out of the saloon. Later, he proudly shows Blaisedell wanted posters he's drawn up, offering a reward for the marshal's capture. Kelley flashes a broad "Bones" McCoy grin as Curley points out the poster's "excellent lettering and spelling." Ultimately, Curley's dormant sense of honor, reawakened by Blaisedell, leads him to turn the tables on McQuown and force a fair fight between the deputy and his back-shooting boss. These scenes feature Kelley at his best, making his character's churning emotions apparent through subtle but telling changes in his posture and tone of voice. It's a fine, authentic performance—one of many in this rich but often overlooked Western epic. Shot in color and Cinemascope with three A-list stars, the costly *Warlock* wasn't the smash 20th Century-Fox was hoping for. Perhaps as a result, the picture remains underrated. Kelley always counted it as one of his best movies.

## *The Virginian* Episode "Man of Violence" (1963)

The venerable *Virginian* ran on NBC for nine seasons, from 1962 to 1971, making it the third-longest-tenured of all TV Westerns, trailing only *Gunsmoke* (twenty seasons) and *Bonanza* (fourteen seasons). *The Virginian* was also the first Western to run in a ninety-minute time slot, making each weekly installment the equivalent of a made-for-TV movie. Kelley appeared on the show twice in 1963, but the first of those episodes, "Man of Violence," was by far the more memorable for a couple of reasons. "Man of Violence" marked Kelley's first work with Leonard Nimoy—with Kelley playing a doctor and Nimoy his patient, no less. Perhaps more importantly, the show gave Kelley a meaty supporting role that enabled him to flex his muscles to a greater extent than any of his big-screen parts.

In "Man of Violence," ranch hand Trampas (Doug McClure) sets out to avenge the murder of his uncle and gets caught up in a scheme to smuggle gold out of Apache territory. Kelley plays Dr. Belden, an alcoholic cavalry surgeon trying to save the life of a man named Wismer (Nimoy), one of the gunmen who murdered Trampas's uncle. When he learns that Wismer and his partner Judson (William Bryan) have discovered gold, an unscrupulous trader named McGoff (Michael Pate) kills Wismer and steals his treasure map. Trampas joins McGoff on his expedition into Apache territory, telling McGoff he can have the gold, but he (Trampas) wants Judson. Shortly after entering Indian land, however, they find Dr. Belden, drunk and forlorn. Distraught because he thinks his drunken negligence led to Wismer's death, Belden has decided to commit suicide by letting the Apaches kill him rather than face a court-martial. "Maybe I thought it was the easy way out," Belden says. "I always take the easy way out."

Not only is Kelley a very convincing drunk, but he seems genuinely distraught and bitter. Yet, over the course of the adventure, Belden's spirits rally. He warns Trampas against pursuing the destructive path of hate. When Trampas asks who the doctor ever hated, he replies simply, "Myself." Eventually the doctor redeems himself, not only learning about Wismer's true fate but saving Trampas's life along the way. Kelley is superb throughout, portraying a man whose self-loathing is exceeded only by his devotion to his medical oath. Coincidentally, the teleplay for "Man of Violence" was written by John D. F. Black, who would serve as an associate producer on *Star Trek* during the show's first season.

## 333 Montgomery (1964)

There was at least one producer in Hollywood who believed Kelley was capable of playing something other than the interchangeable Western badmen that constrained his creativity but supplied his meal ticket. That producer was Gene Roddenberry, who gave Kelley the starring role in *333 Montgomery*, a failed television pilot that eventually aired as an episode of *Alcoa Theatre.*

Produced by Columbia's Screen Gems subsidiary, the prospective series was based on the memoirs of celebrated San Francisco defense attorney Jake Ehrlich and starred Kelley as the crusading Jake Brittin, who agrees to defend Frank Piper (Steve Peck), a philandering lowlife who admits he fired three fatal shots into the husband of his married lover. Based on Piper's version of events, however, Brittin believes the gunman was lured into the killing by the victim's wife and is guilty of only manslaughter, not capital murder.

Roddenberry built *333 Montgomery* entirely around Kelley; the actor is either on-screen or heard through voice-over narration during every scene. Brittin is a passionate and learned man who quotes the classical poets and is prone to soliloquies (looking out of his office windows, he sees the Bay Bridge to one side and Alcatraz on the other, a dichotomy that to him sums up "the alpha and omega of man's possibilities"). The crafty attorney employs shameless courtroom theatrics to play on the jury's sympathy and suckers the police into helping him discover new, exculpatory evidence. Brittin's closing argument is soaring, flowery, and politically charged—questioning the morality of capital punishment. The jury finds Piper guilty of manslaughter, not murder, saving the man's life. But afterward, Brittin refuses to shake his client's hand. Kelley's performance is slick and confident throughout, brimming with vigor and moral conviction.

Kelley, who traveled to San Francisco and met with Ehrlich to prepare for *333 Montgomery*, took this opportunity very seriously, and it shows. Kelley seems energized by the chance to trade in his Stetson for a snap-brim fedora and reestablish himself as a dramatic lead. Interestingly, Jake Brittin in key respects anticipates Leonard McCoy. Although "Bones" would never quote Ovid, both he and Brittin are professional men, passionate about their work and guided by a strong moral compass. In their distinct ways, both try to save lives. Like many of Roddenberry's early projects, however, *333 Montgomery* proved too unorthodox and perhaps too progressive for its era. *Perry Mason* this wasn't. Ultimately, network executives decided that audiences weren't ready for a show about a lawyer who helps admitted killers escape the gas chamber. Although the pilot failed to sell, Roddenberry kept Kelley in mind for future projects.

## Apache Uprising (1965)

Of all Kelley's Western outlaws, none were more reprehensible—or more colorful—than Toby Jack Saunders, the craven, trigger-happy sidewinder he played in *Apache Uprising*. The film itself isn't anything special, just one in a string of low-budget oaters that Paramount producer A. C. Lyles made in the 1950s and '60s with aging Western stars who could be hired on the cheap. The story, adapted by Max Lamb and Harry Sanford from their book *Way Station*, cobbles together familiar elements from earlier, better pictures like *Stagecoach* (1939), *Broken Arrow*, (1950) and *Rawhide* (1951). Kelley's performance provides the only real point of interest, but it's very interesting indeed.

Toby Jack is a belligerent, underhanded, antisocial creep who, despite his status as an underling to primary bad guy Vance Bruckner (John Russell), seems to be the only truly dangerous character in the story. Bruckner hires Toby Jack and a second accomplice to help him rob a stagecoach when it stops at a way station. The trio plot to steal a payroll from the coach and cover their tracks by killing all the witnesses, including the driver (Lon Chaney Jr.), the guard (star Rory Calhoun), all the passengers, and any bystanders at the station. But their planned bloodbath is compromised when the Comanche stage an untimely uprising.

"Killing's about the easiest thing there is," Toby Jack says when Bruckner explains the plan. Kelley plays Toby Jack as a seething cauldron of pent-up rage and plain meanness. He's constantly spoiling for a fight, but loses both of the scraps he gets into—only to try to exact revenge by shooting, stabbing, or

In this shocking scene from *Apache Uprising* (1965), outlaw Toby Jack Saunders (Kelley) guns down unarmed comedy relief sidekick Arthur Hunnicutt (that's him on the barroom floor). Toby Jack was the most despicable of Kelley's many Western villains; he gave Kelley nightmares.

clubbing his opponent in the back. In the film's most shocking moment, he guns down the story's comedy relief, an unarmed old man played by perpetual sidekick Arthur Hunnicutt. *Apache Uprising* loses most of its steam when Toby Jack takes an arrow to the chest with fifteen minutes left in the eighty-seven-minute picture. Considered in contrast to the lovable "Bones" McCoy, Kelley's spellbinding portrayal of Toby Jack Saunders demonstrates the full extent of the actor's range. One tribute to his work here is that, according to biographer Terry Lee Rioux, of all his Western villains the only one that ever troubled Kelley, that gave him nightmares, was Toby Jack.

## Police Story (1965)

In 1965, Roddenberry had two TV series in development. One was *Star Trek*, the other was *Police Story*, a crime drama inspired by his tenure with the LAPD. From the outset, the producer had wanted Kelley to play the chief medical officer of his starship. But he also wanted Kelley in a recurring role as the coroner in *Police Story*, and—at least initially—the crime drama won. The thirty-minute *Police Story* pilot—which was produced in the same time frame as the second *Trek* pilot, "Where No Man Has Gone Before"—starred Steve Ihnat as Captain James Paige, who led a team of special detectives who reported directly to the chief of police and handled complex, high-profile cases. The regular cast also featured Rafer Johnson and Grace Lee Whitney. Unlike the other movies and TV shows mentioned in this chapter, which are readily available on DVD or streaming from sites such as Netflix or YouTube, Roddenberry's *Police Story* could not be located and seems to have vanished from the face of the Earth. Whatever the show's merits, however, it failed to sell. When *Star Trek* was picked up and *Police Story* was not, Roddenberry quickly moved Kelley (along with Whitney) from one program to the other. Kelley replaced Paul Fix, who had portrayed Dr. Piper in "Where No Man Has Gone Before." Along with William Shatner and Leonard Nimoy, Kelley was about to undertake a role that, for better or worse, would redefine his career.

# 8

# Report to the Bridge

## The Pre-*Trek* Careers of Majel Barrett, James Doohan, Nichelle Nichols, George Takei, Grace Lee Whitney, and Walter Koenig

T he six performers who, along with William Shatner, Leonard Nimoy, and DeForest Kelley, played recurring characters on *Star Trek* took widely varied, sometimes danger-filled paths into show business. Their stories are as distinct as their *Star Trek* characters (Nurse Chapel, Engineer Scott, Lieutenant Uhura, Helmsman Sulu, Yeoman Rand, and Ensign Chekov), and often more dramatic than anything they were asked to play on television. Nichelle Nichols, who began her performing career as a dancer, not only faced racism but ran afoul of the mob. Grace Lee Whitney, who began her career as a singer, battled alcoholism and other personal demons. James Doohan fought the Nazis in France and was maimed during the conflict. George Takei and Walter Koenig took to acting as a refuge, to help them cope with traumatic childhoods. Yet, while they came from different places and took divergent routes, for Doohan, Nichols, Takei, Whitney, Koenig, and Majel Barrett, all roads led to the starship *Enterprise*—and immortality.

### Majel Barrett

The future Nurse Chapel, born Majel Leigh Hudec on February 23, 1932, began acting classes at age ten. She regularly appeared in plays at Shaker Heights High School in her hometown of Cleveland, Ohio, and earned a degree in theater arts from the University of Miami in Coral Gables, Florida. Yet she never seriously considered making acting her career until she flunked out of law school in the mid-1950s. Then she moved to New York, where, as Majel Barrett, she landed a few minor theatrical roles, including a nine-month stint with the touring company of *The Solid Gold Cadillac* as it traveled across the Southwest and California. She moved to Hollywood in the late 1950s to break into film and television, but her pre-*Star Trek* résumé included only a half-dozen bits and uncredited walk-ons in feature films, plus minor supporting parts in seven television series.

Fortunately, however, one of those TV shows was producer Gene Roddenberry's *The Lieutenant*, where Barrett appeared opposite Leonard

Lovely young Majel Barrett vamps it up in this glamorous publicity still.

Nimoy. The statuesque, thirty-two-year-old actress soon began a torrid affair with the married Roddenberry, and in 1964, Roddenberry cast her as First Officer "Number One" in the original *Star Trek* pilot, "The Cage." That pilot was rejected, and, at the request of NBC, the Number One character was eliminated from the show. But after a second pilot, "Where No Man Has Gone Before" (1965), earned a green light from the network, Roddenberry created the recurring role of Nurse Chapel for Barrett. She and Nimoy were the first actors cast by Roddenberry for *Star Trek*, and the only ones to appear in both "The Cage" and the subsequent series.

During the show's first season, Roddenberry began sharing an apartment near the Desilu Productions studio with Barrett, who he would marry shortly following *Star Trek*'s cancellation and the final dissolution of his first marriage. Roddenberry also asked Barrett to provide the voice of the *Enterprise* computer, and the actress continued to supply computer voices for every *Star Trek* film and TV series until her death, from leukemia, in 2008. Barrett also appeared as Lwaxana Troi in several episodes of *Star Trek: The Next Generation*.

## James Doohan

Like William Shatner, James Doohan was Canadian, born in Vancouver, British Columbia on March 3, 1930, and raised in Sarnia, Ontario. Like Gene Roddenberry, Doohan was a World War II veteran, a decorated member of the Royal Canadian Artillery who stormed Normandy's Juno Beach on D-Day. As Doohan returned to camp a few nights later, a jumpy sentry shot off his right middle finger (which is why Scotty's right hand is almost never in frame on *Star Trek*). Doohan was struck by a total of six bullets that night but survived, took pilot training, and served through 1945 as an army flyer. After the war, Doohan, who had joined the army in part to escape from his abusive, alcoholic father, returned to Canada. Since he had always possessed a fine singing voice and natural gift for imitating accents, Doohan decided to pursue a career in radio. He began taking voice and acting lessons and landed his first Canadian Broadcasting Corporation appearance in January 1946.

Over the next dozen years, he would appear on thousands of CBC radio broadcasts and hundreds of CBC television programs, nearly all of them live (and almost none of them preserved today). Among his many roles during this era were parts on the seminal science fiction programs *Tales of Tomorrow* and *Space Command*, as well as a short tenure as Timber Tom on the Canadian version of the children's program *Howdy Doody*. (Coincidentally, Shatner had briefly appeared in the similar role of Buffalo Bob on the American version of the show.) Doohan split time between Toronto, where he worked for the CBC, and New York, where he studied acting, appeared in plays, and formed long-lasting friendships with fellow actors including Leslie Nielsen. Doohan's personal life was troubled—in his memoir *Beam Me Up, Scotty*, he describes his first marriage as loveless and bitter—but his career was booming, and in the late 1950s, he moved to Los Angeles to pursue higher-profile film and television work.

Aided by his flair for accents, Doohan quickly established himself as a versatile character actor, landing roles on dozens of television series including *The Twilight Zone, The Outer Limits*, and *Voyage to the Bottom of the Sea*. In 1964, his marriage finally disintegrated. Doohan left his wife, the former Janet Young, and their four children and moved in with his pal Nielsen. But the work kept coming, and in '64 and '65 alone he racked up seventeen film and television appearances. One of those was as Chief Engineer Montgomery Scott in the second *Star Trek* pilot, "Where No Man Has Gone Before."

## George Takei

Like Roddenberry and Doohan, George Takei's life was shaped by World War II—but in a very different way. Takei, born April 20, 1937, and his Japanese American family was interned, forcibly removed from their Los Angeles home and shipped to Arkansas and, later, Oregon, spending the duration of the war in camps encircled in barbed wire and patrolled by armed guards. Takei's parents were declared "disloyals" when they refused to provide "friendly" responses to a pair of questions on a form all adult internees were required to complete. His mother, the former Fumiko Emily Nakamura, a native-born American, was stripped of her citizenship, and his father, Takekuma Norman Takei, faced possible deportation. After the war, a protracted legal battle averted Takekuma's deportation and eventually restored Fumiko's citizenship.

As a result of these troubles, young George struggled with ambivalent feelings about his homeland. He challenged his father when Takekuma began studying to earn American citizenship in the early 1950s, following passage of the landmark Immigration and Naturalization Act of 1952, which allowed Asian Americans to become nationalized citizens (previously, they had been barred). "But America has treated us so badly," Takei, in his autobiography *To the Stars*, recalls asking his father. "What made you decide to become a citizen of a country like this?" His father's answer—"My choice is to help America be what it claims it is"—helped Takei move beyond his anger and resentment over his family's internment and instilled in him a sense of civic duty that he has carried ever since.

After graduating from high school, Takei briefly attended the University of California at Berkeley with the intent of becoming an architect. But he secretly dreamed of becoming an actor and, after winning his father's grudging permission, transferred from Berkeley to UCLA to study theater. By the time he graduated from UCLA in 1960, Takei had earned honors for his performances in student plays (twice named Best Supporting Actor at the school) and had earned small roles on the television series *Playhouse 90* and *Perry Mason*. His first big-screen acting assignment was looping English dialogue for the American release of the Japanese giant monster movie *Rodan* in 1957. He briefly studied in England before returning to Los Angeles, where he landed a steady stream of small stage, film and TV roles, including bit parts on *The Twilight Zone* and *Voyage to the Bottom of the Sea*.

When he interviewed with Roddenberry in 1965 for a spot in "Where No Man Has Gone Before," Takei was ecstatic about the role of Lieutenant Sulu— and not just because it meant steady, good-paying work. He was inspired by Roddenberry's vision of a multiethnic starship crew as the avatar of a postracial future for the human species and excited by the opportunity to play a heroic Asian character. "This was unbelievable," Takei wrote in *To the Stars*. "This project was a quantum leap ahead of anything on the air, the role, a real trailblazer. And this was really happening to me! . . . I was lightheaded." It was the kind of role he didn't even dare dream about during his boyhood.

## Nichelle Nichols

Although her pre-*Trek* résumé included few film or television roles, Nichelle Nichols was a triple-threat (singer-dancer-actor) professional with more show business experience than most of the show's other cast members.

Born Grace Nichols on December 28, 1932, in the Chicagoland exurb of Robbins, Illinois, Nichols studied both ballet and Afro-Cuban dance as an adolescent and landed her first professional dancing gig at age fourteen. Four years later, she married dancer Foster Johnson, giving birth to a son, Kyle, in 1951. The marriage failed, but Nichols's career continued to ascend. Now working primarily as a singer, she toured with Duke Ellington and Lionel Hampton and made hundreds of nightclub appearances across the United States and Europe throughout the 1950s, including one that led to an uncomfortable entanglement with a Milwaukee crime boss and a Canadian gig that ended in an attempted rape. Tiring of life on the road and yearning to spend more time with her son, Nichols moved to Los Angeles in the late 1950s to try to find film and television work.

Her first screen appearance—an uncredited role in the chorus of director Otto Preminger's 1959 adaptation of *Porgy and Bess*—proved very important, as the actress explains in her autobiography, *Beyond Uhura.* "This was the break I'd been waiting for, though not because it brought me sudden fame," she writes. Working alongside African American stars including Sidney Poitier, Dorothy Dandridge, Pearl Bailey, and Sammy Davis Jr. "opened doors for me that I might have otherwise been knocking on for years."

While several theatrical roles followed, five years elapsed before Nichols stepped in front of the cameras again. When she did, in 1964, it was for her first television appearance, in an episode of Roddenberry's *The Lieutenant.* Nichols played the wife of Ernest Cameron (Don Marshall), a young black Marine assigned to the same unit as a white racist (played by Dennis Hopper) who, along with a gang of other bigots, once beat

According to its accompanying text, this stylish publicity photo was intended to promote "Nichelle Nichols, Torch Singer."

Cameron nearly to death. When Lt. Bill Rice (Gary Lockwood, the show's star), learns of the two men's personal history, he asks why the attack occurred. "I was just another nigger who didn't know his place," Cameron explains. This excellent episode, titled "To Set It Right," was directed by Vincent McEveety, who would later helm six installments of *Star Trek*, including the classic "Balance of Terror."

Nichols and Roddenberry struck up a friendship, which blossomed into a romance until Nichols learned that the married Roddenberry was also having an affair with Majel Barrett. "I could not be the other woman to the other woman,"

Nichols writes in *Beyond Uhura*. The romance ended but the friendship continued, and Roddenberry added Nichols to the cast of *Star Trek* once the show had been green-lighted by NBC. Roddenberry not only created the character of Lieutenant Uhura specifically for her, but asked Nichols to collaborate in writing the character's detailed backstory, although little of this material made it into *Star Trek*'s teleplays.

## Grace Lee Whitney

A young-looking thirty-six when she won the role of Yeoman Janice Rand on *Star Trek*, Grace Lee Whitney already had nearly twenty years of experience as a model, actress, and vocalist. Born April 1, 1930, in Ann Arbor, Michigan, as Mary Ann Chase, she was renamed Grace Lee by her adoptive parents, the Whitneys. She began her show business career as a teenage jazz vocalist, opening nightclub dates for established artists such as Billie Holiday and touring with various groups including Spike Jones and His Other Orchestra (the zany bandleader's noncomedic ensemble). Modeling jobs and minor theatrical roles eventually followed, including a small part in comedian Phil Silvers's revue *Top Banana* (she reprised her role in the 1954 film adaptation of the show). Whitney fell in love with the show's snare drum player, converted to Judaism, and married him. The couple moved to Los Angeles in the late 1950s, and over the next eight years, she landed bit parts in director Billy Wilder's *Some Like It Hot* (1959)—she appears alongside Marilyn Monroe, Tony Curtis, and Jack Lemmon in the famous "upper berth" scene—and *Irma La Douce* (1963), along with guest spots on more than two dozen TV series, including *The Outer Limits* and *Batman*.

In 1963, she appeared in an episode of Gene Roddenberry's *The Lieutenant*. Roddenberry was impressed and offered her a major role in his 1964 pilot *Police Story*. When that show failed to sell, he brought two members of its cast—DeForest Kelley and Whitney—on board with *Star Trek*. Whitney, wearing Yeoman Rand's blonde beehive wig and red minidress, was featured prominently in initial publicity for the program, yet the character appeared in just eight episodes before Whitney left the show under controversial circumstances midway through Season One (see Chapter 10, "Ahead, Warp Factor One"). In her autobiography, *The Longest Trek*, Whitney writes that her dismissal from the show exacerbated alcohol and other substance abuse issues she had been struggling with for decades. Although her tenure was the shortest among the cast, she would be fondly remembered by fans of the show and would make a belated return to *Star Trek*, again as Rand, in the first, third, fourth, and sixth installments of the feature film series, as well as in episodes of *Star Trek: Voyager* ("Flashback," 1996) and the fan-created Internet series *Star Trek: The New Voyages* ("Of Gods and Men," 2007).

# Walter Koenig

Even though he affected the phoniest-sounding Russian accent in Hollywood, Walter Koenig was of authentic Russian Jewish heritage. In 1915, his grandparents and their four children emigrated from Lithuania to Chicago, where Koenig was born September 14, 1936. In his autobiography *Warped Factors*, Koenig, a self-identified "neurotic," writes that he spent most of his childhood feeling lonely and scared. His father's radical political beliefs (he was an ardent communist) placed the family's financial security and even physical safety in jeopardy during the McCarthyist Red Scare era of the 1950s. No wonder Koenig began seeing a psychologist in elementary school. However, he discovered during the summer between second and third grade, while appearing in a play at a socialist summer camp, that he enjoyed acting and was good at it. Entering the persona of a character freed him from his own anxieties.

He spent two years at tiny Grinnell College in Grinnell, Iowa, as a pre-med student. Then, after his father died suddenly of a heart attack, Koenig decided to pursue his true love and transferred to UCLA and entered its theater arts program. After graduation in 1958, he earned an invitation to continue his education at the prestigious Neighborhood Playhouse in New York City, where his classmates included James Caan and a half-dozen other up-and-comers who went on to prominent careers in film and television and on Broadway. Koenig moved back to Los Angeles after completing the two-year Neighborhood Playhouse program but struggled to find consistent employment, in part due to his diminutive stature (at five-foot-six, he was never considered leading man material). He made twenty-two mostly minor, sometimes uncredited, film and TV appearances over the course of the next six years.

In 1964, he landed a memorable role as a tough-talking juvenile delinquent in the *Alfred Hitchcock Presents* episode "Memo from Purgatory" (coincidentally directed by Joseph Pevney, who would later helm fourteen *Star Trek*s). And he had a featured role in an episode of Gene Roddenberry's *The Lieutenant*, but, unlike many *Star Trek* cast members, *The Lieutenant* was not the actor's pivotal pre-*Trek* assignment. For Koenig, that part was Alexi, a troubled Russian exchange student the actor portrayed in "The Boy Without a Country," a 1963 installment of the high school melodrama *Mr. Novak*. In that episode, Koenig appeared along with actor Joe D'Agosta. Four years later, D'Agosta was working as the casting director on *Star Trek* when Roddenberry decided to add a young, good-looking, mop-topped officer to his bridge crew—someone along the lines of Davy Jones from *The Monkees*—in an effort to attract more teenage viewers. When it was decided that the character would be Russian instead of British, D'Agosta thought of Koenig, who was about the same size as Jones, looked a bit like the singer, and had proven he could play a Russian on *Mr. Novak*. Koenig auditioned and won the part, joining the show at the beginning of its second season.

# *Enterprise* Incidents

## Behind the Scenes, 1965–69

# 9

# Alternative Factors

## Roads Not Taken to the Second
## *Star Trek* Pilot

n July 1965, *Star Trek* boldly went where no show had gone before: back
into pilot.

Ordinarily, when a series fails to sell, the project is consigned to obliv-
ion. But NBC executives were impressed enough with "The Cage," *Star Trek's*
rejected original telefilm, that they took the unprecedented step of ordering
a second pilot rather than abandoning the concept. While this presented an
extraordinary second chance, producer Gene Roddenberry and his creative
team understood this was also the series' *final* chance. After investing $450,000 in
"The Cage" (Desilu Productions kicked in an extra $164,000 to cover overruns),
NBC agreed to sink another $300,000 in a second, as yet untitled, pilot, making
this an extremely expensive do-over. If the network remained unsatisfied with
this second attempt, *Star Trek* would be scrapped and NBC would write off a
princely three quarters of a million dollars in development funds ($5.4 million
in inflation-adjusted figures).

With its money on the line, the network demanded major changes to the
cast, characters, and overall tone of the show. To meet NBC's expectations,
Roddenberry would have to reshape and, in some aspects, reimagine the program. Along the way, he and his team would have to choose wisely from various
options as they made pivotal decisions regarding the show's content and cast.
The *Star Trek* story might have had a very different ending if this second pilot
had been "The Omega Glory," starring Jack Lord as Captain January, leader of a
Spock-less starship *Enterprise.* Here are the key issues Roddenberry and company
faced at this delicate stage of the program's development, the decisions they
made, and the alternatives they discarded.

### Rejected Teleplays

The first order of business was to devise a storyline for the second pilot. NBC
wanted a show that packed more action than "The Cage," which executives
considered too static and "cerebral." They also wanted Roddenberry to tone
down the sexual content of the show. Three potential pilot teleplays were written, which Roddenberry supplied to NBC for consideration.

From those, the network selected screenwriter Samuel Peeples's **"Where No Man Has Gone Before."** In this episode, *Enterprise* helmsman Gary Mitchell accidentally gains superhuman telepathic and telekinetic abilities after the ship encounters a mysterious energy barrier at the edge of the galaxy. Mitchell, a Starfleet Academy classmate of Kirk's, becomes imperious and unstable as his powers increase, posing a danger to the *Enterprise*. Forced to choose between his ship and his friend, and acting on advice from Spock, Kirk decides to strand Mitchell on a distant planet—but Mitchell, whose powers are now approaching the godlike, resists. Appropriately, since Roddenberry had sold NBC on *Star Trek* by describing the show as an outer space Western, at the time Peeples was best known as the author of several popular Western novels, written under the pen name Brad Ward. His teleplay "Where No Man Has Gone Before" featured a tension-packed scenario, rich in both interpersonal drama and bare-knuckled action scenes. It proved to be an ideal choice for a pilot episode.

The other two teleplays Roddenberry sent to NBC might not have worked so well. They were:

**"The Omega Glory"**—Captain Kirk, Mr. Spock, and Dr. McCoy beam down to Omega IV, a planet reduced to barbarism by a centuries-old war between factions known as the "Kahms" and the "Yangs." The situation is complicated by the presence of Captain Ronald Tracey of the starship *Exeter*, who, after being stranded on the planet, has provided military aid to the Kahms in blatant violation of the Prime Directive. Kirk eventually realizes that Omega IV is a parallel Earth and that the ancient conflict is the Cold War between East (the name "Kahms" derived from Communists) and West ("Yangs" = Yankees). Although written by Roddenberry himself, this remains one of the most improbable and heavy-handed of all *Star Trek* stories. Not only was "The Omega Glory" passed over as a potential pilot, but it lingered on the shelf until late in Season Two, even though the show remained desperate for usable teleplays throughout its first season. It finally aired March 1, 1968.

**"Mudd's Women"**—This humorous episode features Harcourt Fenton Mudd, an interstellar con man who provides gorgeous wives to lonely space settlers— until Kirk discovers that Mudd's women owe their beauty thanks to regular doses of an illegal drug. Written by Stephen Kandel from a story by Roddenberry, "Mudd's Women" would become a fan favorite. It introduced the recurring character of Harry Mudd (played by Roger C. Carmel), a likeable scoundrel who would exasperate the *Enterprise* crew in two classic *Trek* episodes and an installment of the animated series. Nevertheless, the story was too lighthearted and too racy to satisfy NBC as a pilot. Instead, it became the second regular episode of the show produced and the sixth one to air, running October 13, 1966.

## Captains Who Abandoned Ship

While Roddenberry struggled to develop a teleplay that would meet NBC's demands, *Star Trek* was dealt another serious blow: Jeffrey Hunter wanted out.

Hunter, who had starred in "The Cage" as Captain Christopher Pike, was under contract to appear in the series if the original pilot sold but not to appear in the unforeseen second pilot. The actor was unhappy with "The Cage" and ambivalent about moving out of feature films and into a full-time job on television. The show's leadership had no recourse other than to let him go, leaving *Star Trek* without a star. Selecting Hunter had been a long and arduous process.

In 1977, Bantam Books adapted *Star Trek*'s second pilot, "Where No Man Has Gone Before," as a comic book–like "Fotonovel."

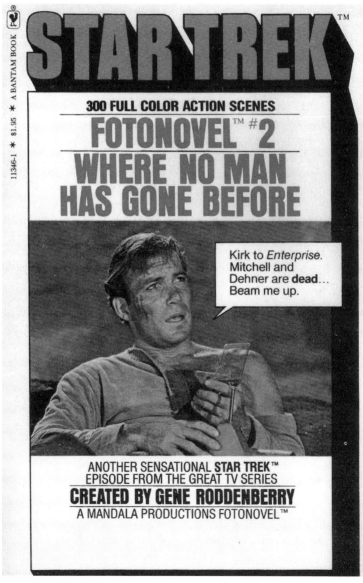

Among the forty names submitted for the role by one casting consultant were Hunter, Lloyd Bridges, Nick Adams, Cameron Mitchell, Peter Graves, Rod Taylor, Sterling Hayden, Robert Stack, George Segal, Jack Lord, and William Shatner. This list was eventually whittled down to a group of five that included James Coburn in addition to Hunter. NBC asked Roddenberry to consider Patrick McGoohan and Mel Ferrer, but neither were serious candidates. Now, with Hunter out of the picture, Roddenberry, Desilu production chief Herb Solow, and casting director Joe D'Agosta went back to their forty-name original list and reconsidered their options.

The team settled on Jack Lord as their top choice. Lord (the stage name of actor John Joseph Patrick Ryan) had appeared in more than a dozen films and guest starred on scores of television series but, in 1965, was best recognized for his turn as CIA agent Felix Leiter in the first James Bond film, *Dr. No* (1962). Roddenberry offered the captaincy of the starship *Enterprise* to Lord but balked when the actor asked to produce as well as star and demanded an astronomical 50 percent profit participation in the program. Roddenberry moved on, and so did Lord. In 1968, the actor agreed to star in TV's *Hawaii Five-O*, which ran for twelve seasons and 279 episodes (200 more than *Trek*). For appearing as Detective Steve McGarrett—whose signature catchphrase "Book 'em, Danno" quickly entered the popular vernacular—Lord received one-third profit participation. When series creator Leonard Freeman died in 1974, Lord took over as executive producer and gained complete creative control over the series.

After scratching Lord's name off his list, Roddenberry turned to a Canadian actor with a résumé not dissimilar to Lord's—William Shatner. Shatner was stinging from the midseason cancellation of his first television series, the courtroom drama *For the People*. Despite the failure of that program, Shatner remained recognizable to TV viewers as a frequent guest star on other shows—by 1965, he had racked up appearances on forty-five television series, some on multiple occasions, not counting appearances on stage and in feature films. Casting director D'Agosta told Roddenberry biographer David Alexander that in 1965 Shatner "had the same thrust going for him that Clint Eastwood and Steve McQueen did." Clearly, Shatner would be the show's star (or so he thought), and his agent negotiated a star's contract. Shatner received a salary of $5,000 per week plus 20 percent of that salary for the first five reruns of each episode, as well as 20 percent profit participation. He was an inspired choice to play *Trek*'s new starship captain. His zesty, upbeat approach to the role helped supply the energy boost NBC felt the program needed.

## Discarded Names for the Captain of the *Enterprise*

With Shatner stepping in for Hunter, Roddenberry felt the character needed a new name. Already the captain's name had changed multiple times. In his initial proposal, Roddenberry had named the captain Robert T. April. For a while he considered the names Captain Winter or even Captain Gulliver. In "The Cage,"

Hunter had portrayed Captain Christopher Pike. A memo Roddenberry sent to the Desilu research department sought legal clearance for fifteen possible new names for the captain of the *Enterprise*. According to the list, reprinted in Herb Solow and Robert Justman's *Inside Star Trek*, the ship might have been led by any of the following captains: January, Flagg, Drake, Christopher, Thorpe, Richard, Patrick, Raintree, Boone, Hudson, Timber, Hamilton, Hannibal, Neville, or (last on the list) Kirk. As an afterthought, Roddenberry scrawled a sixteenth name, "North," at the bottom of the list in all-capital letters. Roddenberry finally chose "Kirk" simply because he liked the sound of the name. This was another good call. Somehow, Captain Kirk rolls off the tongue better than Captain Timber or Captain Neville.

## Decommissioned and Short-Tenured Crew Members

Not only was Captain Pike replaced for the second *Star Trek* pilot, but so was nearly his entire crew. Ironically, although the network was satisfied with Hunter, it wanted most of the other roles recast. John Hoyt as Dr. Boyce, Laurel Goodwin as Yeoman Colt and Peter Duryea as Lieutenant Tyler were out. NBC also demanded that two characters—First Officer Number One (played by Majel Barrett) and Second Lieutenant Mr. Spock (Leonard Nimoy)—be eliminated entirely. NBC's marketing research indicated that Spock's satanic appearance might make the program difficult to sell in the Bible belt. Roddenberry reluctantly agreed to eliminate Number One but, despite intense pressure to meet the network's demands, refused to jettison the Vulcan, making it clear that there would be no *Star Trek* without Spock. The presence of a nonhuman crew member was integral to the concept of the show, he argued. Eventually, NBC acquiesced and the character remained on board.

However, First Officer Spock of "Where No Man Has Gone Before" would be very different from the smiling, curious second lieutenant Spock of "The Cage." Roddenberry not only promoted the Vulcan to second-in-command (giving him a more prominent role in storylines) but gave him Number One's cool, computer-like personality as well. Curiously, since NBC objected primarily to the character's physical appearance, Roddenberry never entertained the possibility of changing Nimoy's makeup to something less threatening. Retaining Spock would prove to be perhaps the best of all the choices Roddenberry made at this time. The (admittedly limited) success *Star Trek* enjoyed during its original network run grew in large part from the audience's fascination with Mr. Spock and the logic-driven Vulcan culture.

Careful consideration was given to the show's guest stars, since helmsman Gary Mitchell and psychologist Elizabeth Dehner were the most prominent characters in Peeples's teleplay other than Kirk and Spock. Roddenberry brought in Gary Lockwood, star of his first series, *The Lieutenant*, to appear as the doomed Mitchell. To play Dr. Dehner, he hired Sally Kellerman, who would earn an Oscar nomination as Best Supporting Actress for her performance as Margaret "Hot

Lips" Houlihan in director Robert Altman's 1970 blockbuster *M\*A\*S\*H*. Both Lockwood and Kellerman contributed excellent performances to "Where No Man Has Gone Before," even though they were forced to perform in painful, silver-colored hard contact lenses.

With Lockwood and Kellerman on board, all that remained was filling out the rest of Captain Kirk's crew. Perhaps emboldened by a memo from NBC programming chief Mort Werner encouraging Roddenberry to hire minority (especially "negro") actors (another document reprinted in *Inside Star Trek*), the Great Bird of the Galaxy this time selected an ethnically diverse bridge crew for the starship *Enterprise*, including Japanese American George Takei as physicist (not yet helmsman) Sulu and African American Lloyd Haynes as communications specialist Alden. Both of these parts were newly created for the pilot, as was a third role: chief engineer Montgomery Scott, played by Canadian James Doohan. Fresh-faced ingénue Andrea Dromm signed on to play Yeoman Smith, while Hollywood veteran Paul Fix was hired to play Dr. Piper.

While Takei and Doohan would become forever identified with Sulu and Scotty, none of the other cast members stuck. Once the series finally received the green light, *Star Trek* underwent another round of recasting. Haynes, given virtually nothing to do in "Where No Man Has Gone Before," was replaced by Nichelle Nichols as Lieutenant Uhura. Haynes went on to costar in writer-producer James L. Brooks's acclaimed comedy-drama series *Room 222* from 1969 to 1974. Dromm, who enjoyed a meteoric rise to fame playing a perky flight attendant in an airline commercial, left no impression whatsoever as Yeoman Smith. Grace Lee Whitney was hired to step in as Yeoman Janice Rand, while Dromm landed only one more screen role, in the forgettable Troy Donahue comedy-mystery *Come Spy with Me* (1967). Fix's gruff Dr. Piper was overshadowed in "Where No Man Has Gone Before" by Kellerman's Dr. Dehner. He was replaced by DeForest Kelley as Dr. Leonard "Bones" McCoy. Fix's career, which began in the silent era, continued into the early 1980s. He played supporting roles in well over a hundred movies and TV shows, appearing most memorably as Judge Taylor in *To Kill a Mockingbird* (1962).

## The Jettisoned Original Version

The second *Star Trek* pilot went into production July 20, 1965, and wrapped eight days later, one day over schedule and $30,000 over budget (once again, Desilu made up the difference). But postproduction dragged on for ten months, partly due to delays in completing its special visual effects and partly because Roddenberry was also finishing the *Police Story* pilot. NBC finally received "Where No Man Has Gone Before" in January 1966. It took a month for the network to render its verdict. Despite a disastrous test screening, NBC decided to move forward with *Star Trek* and informed Desilu that the program would appear on the network's fall schedule. Even though half the *Enterprise* crew was subsequently replaced, and even though the show's costumes and props were

"Where No Man Has Gone Before" guest starred Gary Lockwood, who had played the title role in Gene Roddenberry's previous series, *The Lieutenant*. A few years later, Lockwood would portray astronaut Frank Poole, who is murdered by the HAL-9000 computer in *2001: A Space Odyssey*.

more like those from "The Cage" than those seen in later episodes, "Where No Man Has Gone Before" was considered usable as a regular installment of the series. It became the third episode broadcast, airing on September 22, 1966.

However, the broadcast version differed noticeably from the pilot approved by NBC executives. The original version of "Where No Man Has Gone Before" had a unique title sequence, different musical cues, and featured on-screen titles designed to follow commercial breaks (announcing "Act I," "Act II," and so on) in the style popularized by producer Quinn Martin with hits like *The Fugitive*. The original "Where No Man Has Gone Before" also included nearly five minutes of additional footage that had to be trimmed to get the episode to the then-standard fifty-minute broadcast length (allowing time for commercials). For many years this original version was believed lost, but a print surfaced in Germany in 2009 and was included as a bonus feature on *Star Trek: The Original Series—Season Three* Blu-ray collection. As of this writing (in the fall of 2011), it has never aired on television. However, it was shown at the WorldCon science fiction convention in Cleveland, Ohio, in September 1966, where Roddenberry first unveiled his soon-to-premiere series to genre fans and insiders. It earned a standing ovation.

# 10

# Ahead, Warp Factor One

## Laying the Foundation

F rom the very beginning, *Star Trek* was a remarkable program, daring in both format and content. But it took a while for the show's writing and production capabilities to catch up with its ambitions, and for the cast to get a handle on their characters. Throughout its first season, despite many intimidating obstacles, the series slowly came together. During the spring, summer, and fall of 1966, creator-producer Gene Roddenberry assembled a gifted team of writers, directors, technicians, and artisans. Once everyone was in place, the show ascended to a new level of excellence. Along the way, the building blocks of *Star Trek* mythology fell into place. In the end, the zealous efforts of the show's cast and crew were rewarded with an Emmy nomination for Best Dramatic Series and, most importantly, a renewal by NBC. The following milestones mark the series' first-season maturation.

### April 27, 1966: Dorothy Fontana Submits Her Treatment for "Charlie X"

Initially, the biggest problem facing Roddenberry, associate producer Bob Justman, and script consultant John D. F. Black was a dearth of filmable stories. *Star Trek* was unattractive to most established screenwriters, who had little interest in science fiction and who feared the offbeat show wouldn't survive long enough for their teleplays to be produced, or to earn additional royalties through reruns. To fill this creative void, and to shore up the program's sci-fi credentials, Roddenberry invited high-profile authors such as Theodore Sturgeon, Harlan Ellison, Robert Bloch, Richard Matheson, Jerry Sohl, Jerome Bixby, and George Clayton Johnson to write for the show. A handful of these luminaries (including Ellison, Bloch, and Matheson) had experience writing for TV, but most did not, and turning their ideas into episodes often required long and arduous rewrites. Some SF authors invited to write for *Trek*, including the legendary A. E. van Vogt, never devised a workable concept at all.

Fledgling screenwriter Dorothy Fontana was working as Roddenberry's secretary when he asked her to pen the *Star Trek* Writers Guide (commonly referred to as the show's "Bible"), which summarized the series' characters, setting, and core concepts for prospective screenwriters. Impressed by her work, Roddenberry assigned Fontana to develop a script based on his outline for a story called "Charlie Is God." Fontana's treatment, retitled "Charlie X," marked her first contribution to a *Trek* teleplay. Three drafts later, the script was ready to shoot. "Charlie X," filmed July 12–19 and aired September 14, emerged as one of the best of the show's early installments. Under the gender-neutral byline D. C. Fontana, she went on to write nine more episodes, including the landmarks "Journey to Babel" and "The *Enterprise* Incident." When Black left the show midway through Season One, Fontana took over as story editor, a position she retained until the conclusion of Season Two. In that capacity she provided uncredited polishes on twenty-six teleplays. Fontana, whose tenure as story editor coincided with the show's creative peak, became a mainstay of *Star Trek*'s original incarnation, as well as of the later animated series and the first season of *The Next Generation*.

## May 24, 1966: Shooting of "The Corbomite Maneuver" Begins, with DeForest Kelley, Nichelle Nichols, and Grace Lee Whitney

"The Corbomite Maneuver," the first regular episode of the series produced, also featured the debuts of DeForest Kelley as Dr. McCoy, Nichelle Nichols as Lieutenant Uhura, and Grace Lee Whitney as Yeoman Rand.

Roddenberry transferred Kelley to the *Enterprise* when another pilot, *Police Story*, failed to sell. It was the producer's second failed attempt to create a series for Kelley, following the stillborn legal drama *333 Montgomery* in 1964. The actor's fine work as Leonard "Bones" McCoy rewarded Roddenberry's loyalty. Kelley's warmth, humor, and compassion helped humanize *Star Trek*, making the show seem almost homey despite all the futuristic gadgetry and alien settings. And his rapport with costars William Shatner and Leonard Nimoy provided the secret ingredient in the Kirk-Spock-McCoy chemistry. Kelley excelled in both McCoy's sympathetic heart-to-hearts with Kirk and his (usually) comedic verbal jousts with Spock. Writers enjoyed writing for Kelley and gave his character little quirks (like the doctor's loathing of the transporter device) that were fun to play and further endeared McCoy to audiences. Although Kelley's contract didn't guarantee him work in every episode, McCoy failed to appear in just three installments throughout the next three seasons: "What Are Little Girls Made Of?" "The Menagerie, Part II," and "Errand of Mercy."

At first, Nichols, a former guest star on Roddenberry's *The Lieutenant* (and an ex-girlfriend of the producer), was given nothing much to do other than sit in a chair on the bridge and announce, "Hailing frequencies open, Captain." Eventually, however, writers began to flesh out Uhura and occasionally gave Nichols the opportunity to demonstrate her lovely singing voice. Even when her role seemed robotic and thankless, however, Nichols—by her mere presence—delivered a powerful statement. *Star Trek* premiered in the thick of African Americans' struggle for civil rights. The sight of a black woman in a leadership position on the flagship of the Federation inspired numberless young people of color.

Whitney, another *Police Story* refugee, was featured prominently in the show's early publicity. A sexy female yeoman had been part of Roddenberry's original outline for *Star Trek*, and other young, blonde, female yeomen had appeared in the two pilots. Yet Janice Rand failed to develop as a character. Whitney left the show under controversial circumstances four months later, after appearing in just eight episodes.

"The Corbomite Maneuver" also remains notable as the first episode with George Takei's Lieutenant Sulu at the helm of the *Enterprise*. Takei had appeared in the second pilot, "Where No Man Has Gone Before," but Sulu had a less prominent assignment as a blue-shirted physicist. Designer Bill Theiss's iconic "redshirt" uniforms also debut here, although the gold-blue-red color designations (correlating to command, science, and operational functions) was not yet established, as evidenced by Uhura's appearance in a gold minidress rather than her usual red.

## June 3–13, 1966: Cyclorama Introduced During Production of "Mudd's Women"

"Mudd's Women," the second episode produced for Season One, marked several firsts, including Roger C. Carmel's bow as planet-hopping flimflam artist Harry Mudd. Also making its first appearance in this episode was the soundstage cyclorama that, with strategic employment of red and yellow gels, created the pink-orange sky of planet Rigel XII. Production designer Matt Jefferies and cinematographer Jerry Finnerman reused the cyclorama, lit with gels of various colors, to generate skies for all the many planets Captain Kirk and crew visited—except those rare adventures shot on location. The cyclorama was typical of Jefferies's elegant and ingenious solutions, which helped maximize the show's modest construction budget. Except for the bridge, every *Enterprise* set pulled double or triple duty: the briefing room was redressed for use as the commissary, the recreation room, and numerous other spaces; the engine room doubled as the shuttle bay; and the same cabin set was shared by everyone—Kirk, Spock, and passengers alike.

## June 23: Marc Daniels Begins Directing "The Man Trap"

Marc Daniels directed more episodes of *Star Trek* than anyone else—fifteen in all, including classics like "Space Seed," "The Doomsday Machine," and "Mirror, Mirror." But his most important contribution to the show's success may have occurred while the cameras were turned off. During the shooting of "The Man Trap," Daniels set up a folding table adjacent to the soundstage. While sets were dressed and lights were rigged, he sat at the table with the cast and ran lines for the upcoming scenes. As a result, actors' performances improved and filming required fewer takes. Daniels, coincidentally, was scheduled to helm the next episode as well, so the table—and the read-throughs—remained in place throughout production of "The Naked Time," from July 1 through July 11. By the time Larry Dobkin arrived to direct "Charlie X" on July 12, the show's "table rehearsals" had become a fixture. They would continue until the final episode, "Turnabout Intruder," which wrapped on January 9, 1969. Directors came and went, but the cast remained committed to working together between setups rather than retreating to their dressing rooms, as was common on most series. Guest stars were also expected to participate. These informal rehearsals were especially important during the show's first season because revised pages arrived on the set daily. Roddenberry often worked until the wee hours of the morning, sometimes pulling amphetamine-powered all-nighters, polishing dialogue or reworking scenes. His efforts, combined with the dedication of the cast and directors like Daniels, resulted in a better written, more convincingly performed, and more efficiently produced program.

## July 1–11, 1966: Nurse Chapel Debuts in "The Naked Time"

"The Naked Time," written by John D. F. Black and directed by Marc Daniels, was another key early episode. By introducing Majel Barrett as Christine Chapel, it completed the show's legendary cast of characters. Roddenberry, who was carrying on an affair with Barrett, had been searching for an opportunity to bring the actress back aboard the *Enterprise* ever since her "Number One" character was axed (by network demand) following "The Cage." He created Chapel for her, but the nurse's presence was as big a boon to DeForest Kelley as to Barrett. Nurse Chapel provided a colleague for Dr. McCoy to share scenes with as writers continued to expand Kelley's role. Although hired as a supporting player, Kelley was rapidly becoming the show's third lead.

"The Naked Time," the seventh episode produced and the fourth one broadcast, became the first story to focus on the show's supporting characters. In it, the crew of the *Enterprise* falls prey to an alien infection that compels them to act out repressed feelings and desires: Sulu takes up a fencing foil and bounces around like one of the Three Musketeers; Spock hides away and cries. "The Naked Time" not only introduces Chapel but establishes the nurse's unrequited romantic interest in Spock. The character would continue to serve as an on-again, off-again source of sexual tension for the Vulcan. This episode, along with Richard Matheson's "The Enemy Within," served as guideposts for future screenwriters as they fleshed out the personalities and backstories of the *Enterprise* crew.

Chapel also featured conspicuously in her next appearance, "What Are Little Girls Made Of?," but soon fell into line with the rest of the supporting characters, stepping forward only occasionally for isolated moments during "Journey to Babel," "Return to Tomorrow," and a handful of other installments.

Adding Majel Barrett to the cast as Nurse Chapel provided DeForest Kelley with a counterpart to share scenes with. This, in turn, helped writers expand Dr. McCoy from a supporting character to the show's third lead.

## Late August 1966: Welcome Aboard, Gene Coon

Gene L. Coon, who replaced Roddenberry as the show's line producer three months into its maiden voyage, was exactly what *Star Trek* needed. He was a capable producer whose steady hand ensured that the series didn't miss a beat in production efficiency, while enabling Roddenberry to focus more on story development. Coon also wrote or cowrote eight episodes during his tenure as producer, including the classics "The Devil in the Dark," "Space Seed," and "Errand of Mercy," and is credited with introducing the Klingons, the Prime Directive, the villainous Khan Noonien Singh and warp drive inventor Zefram Cochrane, among other building blocks of *Trek* mythology. Perhaps best of all, given the program's continued stress to meet its airdates, Coon was also an astonishingly fast writer. Reportedly, he penned "The Devil in the Dark" from start to finish in four days. He also mentored young writers like David Gerrold, who he encouraged and guided through the creation of "The Trouble with Tribbles." In all, Coon oversaw the production of thirty-one episodes, including many of the series' finest installments. With his arrival, the final piece of the creative puzzle clicked into place.

## September, 1966: The Curious Case of Janice Rand

Whitney's Yeoman Rand made her final appearance in "The Conscience of the King," the show's thirteenth episode, produced in late September. Her last scene is a brief, nonspeaking walk-on. Rand would not be seen again for the remainder of the series and her departure would never be explained or even mentioned. The character was eliminated because, although Janice Rand was created to provide a source of romantic tension for Captain Kirk, writers believed that her presence was cramping Kirk's Playboy-of-the-Galaxy style with the bevy of beautiful babes who beamed aboard each week. At least that's always been the official version of events, and it's a reasonable explanation.

However, the truth behind the departure of Grace Lee Whitney may be more complex. In her autobiography *The Longest Trek*, Whitney claims that on August 26, 1966, after the Friday night cast party for the previous episode ("Miri"), someone she refers to only as "The Executive"—but whom she describes as tall and "a womanizer"—sexually assaulted her in a Desilu meeting room following a bungled seduction attempt. She believes she was removed from the show as a result of this incident. In his book *Star Trek Memories*, Shatner provides Whitney's account of the alleged assault but also reports that the actress's behavior on the set had become erratic due to heavy drinking. In *The Longest Trek*, Whitney acknowledges being an alcoholic and diet pill addict during her tenure on the show but denies that this affected her performance. Her termination from *Star Trek* sent Whitney into a tailspin of addiction and other self-destructive behavior, but she gained sobriety in the 1980s and made cameo appearances as Rand in four of the *Star Trek* feature films (*Star Trek: The Motion Picture*, *The Search for Spock*, *The Voyage Home*, and *The Undiscovered Country*).

## October 11–18: New Footage Created for "The Menagerie"

Despite the best efforts of the show's writers, cast and crew, meeting airdates remained a week-to-week battle for *Star Trek*. To buy desperately needed breathing room in the production schedule, Roddenberry and his team decided to shoot new footage that could be combined with scenes from the scrapped original pilot, "The Cage," to create a two-part epic. This would enable the program to fill two airdates but would require less than a week of original production. The plan meant scuttling Roddenberry's original idea of expanding "The Cage" to feature length (by shooting the crash of the starship *Columbia* on Talos IV) and issuing the picture theatrically. The plan also presented some tricky writing problems, given the presence of Leonard Nimoy as a very different Spock in "The Cage" and Majel Barrett as both the brunette "Number One" and the blonde Nurse Chapel. The clever solution—having Spock commandeer the *Enterprise* to transport the grievously injured Captain Pike to Talos IV—was conceived by John D. F. Black, but his teleplay was heavily rewritten by Roddenberry, who received sole writing credit for the episode. Ace director Marc Daniels was engaged to shoot the new footage, which was skillfully integrated with judiciously edited material from "The Cage" to form "The Menagerie."

The resulting two-part episode won a Hugo Award at the 1966 WorldCon and remains one of the series' most enduringly popular tales. But the most important

*TV Guide* ad for a special two-hour syndicated broadcast of "The Menagerie, Parts I and II" from the 1970s. This two-part adventure, which provided desperately needed breathing room in the show's production schedule, remains one the series' most beloved stories.

thing about this landmark adventure was that it alleviated some of the pressure on the *Trek* creative team. With a couple of fortuitous programming changes by NBC (*Star Trek* was preempted twice during its first season—for a Jack Benny holiday special Thanksgiving week and again for a Ringling Brothers Circus special in March) and one strategically deployed rerun ("What Are Little Girls Made Of?" was repeated December 22, just eight weeks after its initial broadcast), *Star Trek* met the remainder of its Season One airdates.

With increased flexibility in terms of deadlines and budgets came a significant uptick in quality. "The Menagerie, Parts I and II" aired November 17 and 24, 1966. Nearly all the thirteen episodes that followed during Season One were outstanding. This lineup of classics includes "Shore Leave," "The Squire of Gothos," "Arena," "Tomorrow Is Yesterday," "Return of the Archons," "Space Seed," "This Side of Paradise," "The Devil in the Dark," "Errand of Mercy," and "The City on the Edge of Forever."

## September 8, 1966: *Star Trek* Premieres with "The Man Trap"

By the time *Star Trek* made its broadcast debut, several episodes had been completed. Which one to air first was a matter of considerable debate. "The Corbomite Maneuver," the first episode produced, would have served as an ideal introduction but was nixed by NBC because it took place entirely aboard the *Enterprise*; the network preferred stories that involved travel to alien planets. "Charlie X" was ruled out for the same reason. Justman argued for "The Naked Time," but it was also a "ship show" rather than a "planet show." The second pilot, "Where No Man Has Gone Before," was problematic because it didn't include key cast members such as Kelley. And everyone agreed the comedic "Mudd's Women" would give viewers a misleading impression of the series' tone. Finally, NBC settled on "The Man Trap," a rip-snorting sci-fi adventure complete with a murderous monster, the "Salt Vampire" of planet M-113.

*Star Trek*'s premiere earned middling ratings and unenthusiastic reviews. *Weekly Variety*'s critic ventured that the show was "better suited to the Saturday morning kidvid bloc" than prime time. NBC continued to air episodes in a haphazard order that made it difficult for viewers to follow the development of the show's characters and its emerging mythology. "Charlie X," produced eighth, aired second, followed by "Where No Man Has Gone Before" and "The Naked Time." Although made first, "The Corbomite Maneuver" was broadcast tenth. When the show was syndicated in the 1970s, episodes were typically sequenced in production order.

## February 2, 1967: Production Wraps on "Errand of Mercy"

This episode, written by Gene Coon and directed by John Newland, remains best known as the adventure that introduced the Klingons. But it's also notable as the last episode in which Spock is referred to as a "Vulcanian." Moving forward, persons from the planet Vulcan were referred to simply as Vulcans. Despite some nagging "Vulcanian"-like anomalies—in "Mudd's Women," for instance, the *Enterprise* engines rely on lithium (not dilithium) crystals—the show's mythology had begun to cohere.

Although no one imagined that generations of fans would devote themselves to studying such minutiae, writers and producers nevertheless strived to ensure the continuity of the show's setting, characters, and technology, meticulously crafting an integrated "future history" from week to week, teleplay by teleplay. By now, most of the foundational elements of the *Star Trek* universe were present, including the United Federation of Planets (named in "A Taste of Armageddon") and its two main adversaries, the Romulans (introduced in "Balance of Terror") and the Klingons. Also established:

- The names Starfleet and Starfleet Command entered the *Trek* lexicon with "Court Martial." This episode also featured the *Enterprise*'s first trip to a star base.
- The frequently ignored Prime Directive was first explained in "The Return of the Archons."
- The Vulcan neck pinch was first seen in "The Enemy Within," and the mind meld was first witnessed in "Dagger of the Mind."

The show's early publicity photos (including this one) seemed to suggest that the stars of *Star Trek* would be William Shatner, Leonard Nimoy, and Grace Lee Whitney. Nevertheless, Whitney was released midway through Season One, after appearing in just eight episodes.

- The Eugenics Wars and other future-historical events were introduced in "The Conscience of the King" and "Space Seed."
- Photon torpedoes enter the arsenal of the *Enterprise* with "Arena."
- The shuttlecraft and shuttle bay both debut with "The Galileo Seven." (All the show's shuttlecraft effects footage originates here, by the way. Whenever shuttles are seen in future episodes, it's through the use of stock shots from *The Galileo Seven*, sometimes matted into different backgrounds.)

## March 9, 1967: "The Devil in the Dark" Airs

"The Devil in the Dark" remains notable in its own right for many reasons. It's a terrific episode, with Kirk and Spock facing what seems to be a bloodthirsty monster, but which turns out to be a loving mother simply trying to protect her offspring. William Shatner considers this, along with "The City on the Edge of Forever," the show's high point, a sentiment shared by many fans. But the original broadcast of "The Devil in the Dark" had additional significance. As the end credits rolled, NBC made a voice-over announcement that *Star Trek* would return for a second season. This unprecedented, on-air renewal commitment ended a months-long letter-writing campaign in support of the program surreptitiously organized by Roddenberry and involving prominent science fiction authors, led by Harlan Ellison. On more than one level, it was a moment of triumph.

## April 6, 1967: "The City on the Edge of Forever" Airs

And this installment marked another victory. Produced in February 1967, at great expense ($245,316, more than any episode other than the show's two pilots) and after numerous painstaking rewrites (which sparked a decades-long feud between Roddenberry and screenwriter Ellison), "The City on the Edge of Forever" became the show's most popular adventure and a television landmark. Among other accolades, this episode went on to win a Hugo Award for Best Dramatic Presentation.

## June 4, 1967: The Emmy Awards

By the time the Emmys rolled around, Roddenberry and his team had already thrown themselves headlong into story development and preproduction for Season Two. But the show's brain trust took time out to attend the ceremony because *Star Trek* was nominated in five categories including Outstanding Dramatic Series and Outstanding Performance by an Actor in a Supporting Role in a Drama (Leonard Nimoy). Unfortunately, *Trek* was shut out. Another rookie series from Desilu, producer Bruce Geller's *Mission: Impossible*, was named Outstanding Dramatic Series. Nimoy lost to Eli Wallach for his work in the TV movie *The Poppy Is Also a Flower*. (At the time, supporting performers in TV movies and series competed in the same category.)

Nevertheless, *Star Trek*'s first season must be considered an astounding success. Despite unique production problems, oppressive budget restrictions, and incessant network needling, the show had proven critics wrong and built a loyal following. Out of imagination and elbow grease, long workdays and sleepless nights, Roddenberry, Coon, Fontana, Jefferies, Daniels, the cast, and the rest of the *Star Trek* team laid the foundation for a towering monument—the greatest franchise in science fiction history.

# Engineering Department

## The Screenwriters of *Star Trek*

he starship *Enterprise* is powered by the controlled interaction of matter and antimatter. But *Star Trek*, like all television programs, was fueled by screenwriting. Without high-quality teleplays, *Trek* might have flamed out like so many other quickly cancelled series. Luckily, at least during its first two seasons, the show's writers supplied a steady stream of scripts that managed to present sometimes complex science fiction concepts in understandable ways, to flesh out the show's diverse cast of characters, and to include all the action and dramatic tension necessary to hold viewers' attention for sixty minutes. During Season One, the show's writing staff worked Scotty-like last-minute miracles on many occasions, barely meeting deadlines to avoid missing airdates. Working under incredible pressure, these gifted men and women created on the fly a remarkably elaborate, cohesive mythology now cherished by generations of viewers.

Here's a rundown of some of the series' most important writers and their contributions to the *Star Trek* legacy.

### Gene Roddenberry

During its first two seasons, *Star Trek* creator and producer Gene Roddenberry also served as the series' most important writer. Although few teleplays bore his name (and some of those that did, like "The Omega Glory," were unimpressive), Roddenberry personally rewrote or polished, usually without credit, virtually every episode that aired during the 1966–67 and '67–68 seasons. Many writers complained bitterly about Roddenberry's extensive reworking of their scripts, but the Great Bird of the Galaxy made certain every episode conformed to his vision for the show, taking special care to protect consistency of characterization and continuity of the tricky technical details that were the bane of many would-be *Trek* writers. As a former Writers Guild of America award winner and lifelong sci-fi fan, Roddenberry was uniquely positioned to ensure each episode hit all the beats necessary for television drama and also functioned credibly as science fiction. The importance of his rewrites is best demonstrated by the precipitous decline in quality *Trek* suffered during its final season, when Roddenberry abandoned his meticulous oversight of the scripts. The episodes broadcast during Season Three proved wildly uneven, offering some superb shows ("The *Enterprise* Incident," "Spectre of the Gun") and some dreadful ones ("Spock's Brain," "The Way to Eden"), with occasional jarring lapses in characterization and technical jargon.

## Gene L. Coon

Aside from Roddenberry, the writer who most influenced *Star Trek* mythology was Gene L. Coon, who also served as line producer for *Star Trek* during most of its first two seasons. Like Roddenberry, Coon was a World War II veteran who saw action in the Pacific theater and also a respected television professional. Coon's prior credits included scripts for dozens of series—including twenty-four episodes of *Wagon Train*, one of Roddenberry's often-cited inspirations for *Star Trek*—and production work on *The Wild, Wild West*. Coon's *Trek* scripts defined the Prime Directive (in episodes like "Bread and Circuses") and introduced the Klingons (in "Errand of Mercy"), warp drive pioneer Zefram Cochrane (in "Metamorphosis"), and genetically engineered superman Khan Noonien Singh (in "Space Seed"). He received screen credit on ten *Star Trek* teleplays, and in his capacity as producer provided uncredited polishes to numerous other scripts.

Coon was a well-liked member of the *Star Trek* team whose sense of humor shined through in his episode "A Piece of the Action." He also guided young screenwriter David Gerrold through the creation of "The Trouble with Tribbles." When Coon left *Star Trek* in the middle of its second season due to personal issues, Roddenberry told associate producer Bob Justman, "We'll have to find someone else to take his place, but no one will ever be able to fill his shoes," according to Justman and Herb Solow's book *Inside Star Trek*. After his departure, Coon contributed occasional scripts to the show under the pseudonym Lee Cronin. Later he produced the short-lived espionage series *It Takes a Thief*, starring Robert Wagner and Fred Astaire, and wrote for another dozen TV shows. He died of lung cancer in 1973. One of his last jobs was cowriting *The Questor Tapes*, one of Roddenberry's failed post-*Trek* projects.

## D. C. Fontana

Dorothy Catherine Fontana penned several landmark *Star Trek* scripts and also served as the series' story editor. In her editorial capacity, Fontana was second only to Roddenberry as Defender of the Flame and Keeper of the Continuity. She wrote the show's first "Bible," which explained *Trek*'s characters, settings, and core concepts for prospective writers. Not only did Fontana serve as watchdog for the show's rapidly growing mythology, but she created major elements of the *Trek* mythos herself in watershed teleplays such as "Tomorrow Is Yesterday," the show's first time-travel story; "The *Enterprise* Incident," which explored

Romulan culture and involved "cloaking" technology; and "Journey to Babel," which introduced Spock's parents, Sarek (Mark Lenard) and Amanda (Jane Wyatt), along with the blue-skinned Andorian and porcine Tellarite species. In all, Fontana (sometimes working under the pseudonym Michael Richards) had a hand in writing thirty-six of the show's seventy-nine episodes, including many uncredited polishes.

Later, Fontana served as associate producer on the *Star Trek* animated series and wrote the cartoon episode "Yesteryear" (the only animated installment with story elements considered "canonical"); contributed scripts to *Star Trek: The Next Generation* (including the series pilot, "Encounter at Farpoint") and *Star Trek: Deep Space Nine;* and created scenarios for three *Trek* video games. Roddenberry employed Fontana as production secretary on his first series, *The Lieutenant*, and for many years counted her among his most trusted allies. The two eventually had a falling-out, precipitating Fontana's mid–Season One departure from *The Next Generation.* Despite her close affiliation with *Trek*, Fontana has contributed stories or screenplays for dozens of other television series, both live-action and animated, across many genres, including *The Waltons, Dallas,* and *Babylon 5.* As of 2011, she was teaching screenwriting for the American Film Institute in Los Angeles. The fictional science fiction writer K. C. Hunter, played by Nana Visitor in the *Deep Space Nine* episode "Far Beyond the Stars," was created to honor Fontana.

## Jerome Bixby

Roddenberry desperately wanted *Star Trek* to have credibility within the community of science fiction fandom. So he invited several respected sci-fi authors to write for the series. Some, such as A. E. van Vogt, were unable to adjust to the specialized demands of writing for television. Jerome Bixby, however, flourished, supplying three complete teleplays ("Requiem for Methuselah," "Day of the Dove," and "Mirror, Mirror") and sharing credit for "By Any Other Name" with Fontana. With "Mirror, Mirror," Bixby introduced the idea of a parallel "Mirror Universe" containing evil alter egos of the *Enterprise* crew (including a scar-faced Lieutenant Sulu, who tries to advance his career by assassinating Captain Kirk, and a malevolent, goateed Mr. Spock). The concept proved so popular it was revived by *Deep Space Nine* and *Star Trek: Enterprise.* The Mirror Universe also has been explored by writers of numerous *Trek* novels and comic books.

While not as a big a name as Theodore Sturgeon, Harlan Ellison or other high-profile authors who wrote for *Star Trek*, Bixby's credentials within the world of literary SF were impeccable. He had written scores of science fiction short stories and was a former editor of the pulp magazine *Planet Stories*, which published early work by genre legends such as Ray Bradbury and Philip K. Dick. Unlike many authors Roddenberry engaged for *Trek*, Bixby had experience writing scripts, having penned three screenplays, including the cult classic *It! The*

*Terror from Beyond Space* (1958). One of Bixby's short stories served as the basis for the eerie *Twilight Zone* episode "It's a Good Life," featuring a spoiled young boy with godlike mental powers, which was remade for the 1993 *Twilight Zone* feature film. Another Bixby story, cowritten with Otto Klement, provided the scenario for the 1966 movie *The Fantastic Voyage*, about a miniaturized submarine that travels through a human body. Bixby passed away in 1998.

## Theodore Sturgeon

Ted Sturgeon, renowned for his gripping short stories and novellas, was one of the first authors Roddenberry contacted about working for *Trek*. Although only two of his scripts were produced ("Shore Leave" and "Amok Time"), both are fan favorites. "Amok Time" was the first episode to explore Vulcan culture, introducing the concept of Pon Farr (the Vulcan mating cycle) and the customary valediction "Live long and prosper." Much of the franchise's elaborate Vulcan mythology originates with or is extrapolated from this episode. Like Bixby, Sturgeon had limited screenwriting experience, having penned teleplays for the short-lived *Tales of Tomorrow* TV series (1950–51). In 1974, his novella "Killdozer" served as the basis for a well-remembered made-for-TV movie of the same title, and in 1986, two of his stories were adapted for episodes of the revived *Twilight Zone*. Sturgeon, who died in 1985, is also remembered for "Sturgeon's Law" ("Ninety percent of SF is crud, but 90 percent of everything is crud") and for the personal credo that guided his fiction: "Ask the next question." The Theodore Sturgeon Award, a juried prize issued by the Center for the Study of Science Fiction at the University of Kansas, has been awarded annually since 1987 for the year's best science fiction short story.

## Robert Bloch

In 1960, director Alfred Hitchcock and screenwriter Joseph Stefano turned Robert Bloch's novel *Psycho* into one of the greatest box-office hits of the decade. Bloch, a prolific author of horror and horror-tinged science fiction short stories and novels, parlayed the phenomenal success of *Psycho* into new opportunities, penning dozens of screenplays and teleplays and optioning many of his short stories for use in film or television. The three *Star Trek* episodes written by Bloch ("Wolf in the Fold," "Catspaw," and "What Are Little Girls Made Of?") are characteristically dark, even Halloweenish. "Wolf in the Fold," which integrated ideas from Bloch's short story "Yours Truly, Jack the Ripper," pitted Captain Kirk and his crew against Jack the Ripper—or rather a fear-devouring, noncorporeal life force that had previously inhabited the human host known as Jack the Ripper. Bloch, who as a young man befriended and was greatly influenced by legendary horror author H. P. Lovecraft, received the Hugo, Bram Stoker, and World Fantasy Awards during his sixty-year career. He died of cancer in 1994 at age seventy-seven.

## Margaret Armen

Like Robert Bloch, Margaret Armen wrote three *Star Trek* episodes, all in a common style. But while Bloch penned *Star Trek* horror yarns, Armen wrote spacefaring romances. She was a workaday screenwriter whose other credits included dozens of Westerns (*The Rifleman*, *The Big Valley*), detective shows (*The Mod Squad*, *Barnaby Jones*) and other programs (*The Bionic Woman*, *Marcus Welby M.D.*). Her *Star Trek* scripts included "The Paradise Syndrome," in which an amnesia-struck Captain Kirk (aka "Kirok"), left on a primitive planet, goes native and marries the beautiful young Miramanee (Sabrina Scharf); "The Gamesters of Triskelion," in which the captured Kirk romances his green-haired, silver-bikinied guard Shahna (Angelique Pettyjohn), then later knocks her unconscious; and "The Cloud Minders," which offered romantic entanglements for both Kirk and Spock. Armen also wrote two episodes of the *Star Trek* animated series, "The Ambergris Element" and "The Lorelei Signal," as well as a teleplay for the scuttled *Star Trek: Phase II* series in the late 1970s. She passed away in 2003 at age eighty-two.

## Stephen Kandel

Stephen Kandel was a remarkably productive screenwriter with more than seventy produced teleplays to his credit during a career that stretched from 1956 to 1990. His work included multiple episodes of highly rated programs including *Batman*, *I Spy*, *Mission: Impossible*, and *MacGyver*, for which he wrote a whopping seventeen episodes. But in the realm of *Star Trek*, the versatile Kandel served a specialized function: He was the unofficial biographer of scoundrel Harry Mudd, guest star in two well-remembered lighthearted episodes, "Mudd's Women" and "I, Mudd."

"Mudd's Women," the sixth episode broadcast, was among the clutch of stories considered for development as the second pilot episode for the series. Kandel's teleplay, based on a story by Roddenberry, introduced the character of Harcourt Fenton Mudd (played by Roger C. Carmel), a notorious interstellar con man whose current business is supplying beautiful "wives" to residents of remote settlements. Subsequent investigation reveals that the women owe their good looks to an illegal drug, and although the miners elect to go through with the marriages as planned, Mudd is placed under arrest. Undaunted, Mudd returned for the Season Two sequel "I, Mudd," which found him the master of a race of curvaceous female androids. Kandel authored a third appearance for the character in the animated series episode "Mudd's Passion." (Kandel also wrote the unrelated episode "Jihad" for the cartoon program.)

Kandel's two Mudd teleplays were novelized by writer J. A. Lawrence and published under the title *Mudd's Angels* in 1978. Yet another revival was planned for the character on *Star Trek: The Next Generation*. The concept was for Mudd to awaken from cryogenic sleep to fluster Captain Jean-Luc Picard as he had

Captain Kirk a generation earlier, but the scenario was heavily revised (and Mudd written out) when Carmel died in 1986. However, the greedy, amoral, yet comically appealing Mudd may have served as a forerunner of the Ferengi, a species introduced on *Next Gen* and featured prominently on *Deep Space Nine*.

## Harlan Ellison

Acclaimed author Harlan Ellison wrote only one *Star Trek* episode, but it was the one most fans consider the best of them all, "The City on the Edge of Forever." The reason Ellison wrote only one *Trek* episode is because he was incensed over Roddenberry's changes to his original teleplay. Ellison labored over the script for months, writing and rewriting at Roddenberry's request, before turning in what he thought would be the final product. Nevertheless, Roddenberry oversaw major changes to the scenario. (For more about "The City on the Edge of Forever" and the Roddenberry-Ellison feud, see Chapter 16, "Private Little Wars.")

The prickly Ellison, who once described himself as "the most contentious person on Earth," remains renowned for his hard-hitting speculative fiction, for which he has received eleven Hugo Awards, six Bram Stoker Awards, four Nebula Awards, and two World Fantasy Awards, among other laurels. He edited the groundbreaking anthology *Dangerous Visions* (1967), which collected thirty-three stories considered too politically controversial or sexually explicit for publication in mainstream science fiction magazines. Ellison began writing for the screen in 1953 and has been honored by the Writers Guild four times. His other notable teleplays include two classic episodes of *The Outer Limits*—the Writers Guild Award–winning "Demon with a Glass Hand" and "Soldier," which director James Cameron acknowledges as the inspiration for *The Terminator.*

## David Gerrold

David Gerrold was a twenty-two-year-old aspiring screenwriter whose first produced teleplay became a classic. With guidance from Coon, he penned "The Trouble with Tribbles," a seriocomic episode about rapidly multiplying, Klingon-averse, trilling alien fur balls that became one of the most beloved of all *Star Trek* episodes. Coon rejected the first four *Trek* scenarios Gerrold proposed, but kept encouraging the talented and ambitious young writer. Finally Coon accepted a story Gerrold originally titled "The Fuzzies." Gerrold managed to sell just one more scenario to *Trek*, which was developed by Margaret Armen into the episode "The Cloud Minders." Later, however, Gerrold penned two installments of the animated series, including the sequel "More Tribbles, More Troubles." He submitted the outline for a *Next Generation* teleplay dealing with homosexuality among two *Enterprise* crewmen, which was so heavily rewritten by Roddenberry that Gerrold obtained a Writers Guild injunction to prevent it from being produced. Gerrold also wrote three episodes (none of them involving tribbles) of the fan-created Internet series *Star Trek: The New Voyages*. In 1973, Gerrold published two of the first books about the history and impact of the series, *The World of Star Trek* and *The Trouble with Tribbles*, an account of the making of the episode. He has also written two *Star Trek* novels. In 1977, "The Trouble with Tribbles" was also published as a "Fotonovel," with the story told in frame enlargements. Gerrold went on to write for many other television programs, including *Babylon 5* and the 1980s revival of *The Twilight Zone*.

## Richard Matheson

Richard Matheson has written scores of short stories, novels and screenplays, many of which are now revered as classics. He is perhaps best known for his horror novel *I Am Legend*, which has been filmed (sometimes without credit to the author) at least four times, and for the fourteen teleplays he wrote for the original *Twilight Zone*. Among many other movies, Matheson penned most of director Roger Corman's Edgar Allan Poe adaptations and the teleplay for *The Night Stalker* (1972), which became the highest-rated made-for-TV movie of all time to that point. Although he wrote only one *Star Trek* episode, it was an important one. In Matheson's "The Enemy Within," a transporter malfunction accidentally creates two Captain Kirks, one pensive and compassionate, the other impulsive and violent. The fifth episode broadcast, "The Enemy Within" was the first *Trek* story to explore the inner life of Captain Kirk. It also defined the working rapport of the Kirk, Spock, and McCoy team. For this episode, Matheson created Dr. McCoy's signature line, "He's dead, Jim." Future screenwriters would adhere to the framework Matheson established here. Matheson remains active, and his stories are still frequently adapted for the screen. The 2009 film *The Box* was based on Matheson's tale "Button, Button." In 2010, he was inducted into the Science Fiction Hall of Fame.

# Equipment Locker

## Sets, Props, Costumes, Makeup, and Special Effects

The brilliant work of *Star Trek*'s screenwriters, actors, and directors would have been forfeit if not ably supported by the artisans and technicians who built the show's sets and props, designed its costumes and makeup and created its special effects. Establishing a believable futuristic milieu for the program was essential. Over the years, countless science fiction films and TV series have been ruined by hokey-looking sets and costumes, and laughable visual effects. The devoted and often ingenious efforts of unsung heroes like Matt Jefferies, William Theiss, Fred Phillips and Ed Milkis made sure that such a fate never befell *Trek*. Although the classic *Trek* series looks (charmingly) dated today—most of the show's visual effects were redone using computer animation for the series' release on HD-DVD and Blu-ray disc—it was a cutting-edge production in its day, as evidenced by the show's eight Emmy nominations in various technical categories.

*Star Trek* presented peculiar difficulties not shared by most of its competitors (the Westerns, detective shows, spy adventures, and other dramas of the era). You couldn't simply buy a Gorn suit off the rack or order a spare tricorder from the usual prop rental agencies. These items had to be individually crafted. Yet *Star Trek* was shot on the same six-day schedule as every other hour-long TV drama and on a budget only (at first) slightly higher than average ($193,000 per episode during its first season, declining to $187,500 during Season Two and a meager $178,500 for Season Three). The cast's salaries rose as the budgets decreased, putting ever-increasing pressure on the show's technical crew to do more with less.

### Sets

Designing and constructing the interior of the starship *Enterprise*, as well as the "strange new worlds" the ship explored each week, was one of many responsibilities for Walter M. (Matt) Jefferies, who served as *Star Trek*'s production designer and art director. (He shared art direction duties with Rolland Brooks for a season and then took over both roles full-time for the remainder of the series.) Like many of the show's leaders, Jefferies was a World War II veteran, a former bomber pilot who flew missions over Europe and North Africa. After the war, he hired on as a set decorator at Warner Brothers. Jefferies hired his brothers, Philip and John, to assist him on *Star Trek*. He remains best known as the designer of the revolutionary *Enterprise*, which looked nothing like any spaceship seen before on film or television, and of the ship's instantly recognizable bridge, transporter, and engine room sets. Jefferies also designed the hand phasers and Klingon battle cruiser.

More than any other individual, Jeffries created the look of the *Star Trek* universe. Some of his most memorable productions include "The Trouble with Tribbles," for which he built both the exterior and interior of Space Station K-7, and "Amok Time," which gave viewers their first (and for many years only) look at Vulcan, Mr. Spock's rugged, red desert home world. (Spock's cabin and McCoy's office also debuted with this episode.) But perhaps Jefferies's most striking creation was the eerie, surreal Western town featured in "Spectre of the Gun," with obvious facades set against a blood-red sky. In this episode, the Melkotians force Captain Kirk and his landing party to participate in a re-creation of the Gunfight at the O.K. Corral—with the Starfleet officers standing in for the doomed Clanton gang. Gene Coon's teleplay called for this episode to be filmed on location, but Season Three budgets were so tight that location shooting was no longer feasible. Jefferies devised a visually arresting yet thrifty solution. The otherworldly look of the place is explained by having the Melkotians create the fragmentary Tombstone out of "bits and pieces" from Kirk's memory and imagination.

After *Trek*, Jefferies worked on many more movies and television shows, including *Little House on the Prairie*, where he served as art director from 1974 to 1983, working on 193 (out of 204) episodes of the classic family drama. Jefferies died of congestive heart failure in 2003, following a long battle with cancer. The cylindrical, instrument-crammed crawlspaces frequently seen on all Starfleet spacecraft are referred to as "Jefferies Tubes" in his honor.

## Props

As a cost-cutting measure, all the props for *Star Trek* (and other Desilu series) were supposed to be built by the studio's in-house prop shop. As the start of shooting for the show's first season drew near, however, it became apparent that Desilu's in-house staff could not produce communicators, phasers, and other specialized equipment in the necessary quantity or time frame required to meet the schedule. So associate producer Bob Justman turned to old friend Wah Chang of Project Unlimited, a renowned maker of specialty props, monster suits, and other sci-fi accoutrements. Chang had supplied many of the props and creature prosthetics used on Justman's previous series, *The Outer Limits*, and had created the original phasers, communicators, and Talosian makeup prosthetics used in "The Cage." In short order Chang developed high-quality working models of the communicator and phaser, and designed and built the first tricorder.

The iconic Starship *Enterprise* (pictured on this 1976 Topps trading card sticker) was designed by ingenious production manager Matt Jefferies.

However, when Desilu's unionized prop makers learned Justman had gone to Project Unlimited, they filed a grievance, arguing that Chang's creations couldn't be used because Chang was not a union member. (Somehow, Chang's nonunion status hadn't come up during production of "The Cage.") To circumvent the labor issue, Justman told Desilu that the equipment in question wasn't made especially for *Star Trek*; they were original Chang creations that the associate producer had purchased for use on the show. (In his book *Inside Star Trek,* Justman refers to this gambit as "a little fib.") The purchase of prefabricated props was permissible under union rules.

Chang went on to provide a great many more "ready-made" props and equipment for *Trek*, including the Gorn suit from "Arena"; the Salt Vampire suit from "The Man Trap"; Balok, the imposing-looking alien puppet from "The Corbomite Maneuver"; the original Romulan Bird of Prey spacecraft from "Balance of Terror"; Spock's Vulcan lute, seen in several episodes; the neural parasites from "Operation—Annihilate!"; and, most famously, the tribbles. Due to budget constraints, Chang's association with *Star Trek* ended midway through Season Two. *The Outer Limits* was just one of Chang's many notable pre-*Trek* credits. He had worked extensively with producer George Pal and won an Academy Award for his contributions to *The Time Machine* (1960). Later, Chang would create the dinosaurs seen on TV's *Land of the Lost* (1974–76) before retiring from the movie business to pursue a successful career in fine art sculpture. He died in 2003 at age eighty-six.

Justman's other go-to resource for specialty equipment was Irving Feinberg, the show's Desilu-assigned prop master. Feinberg wasn't an artist like Chang, but he had a keen eye for items that could be repurposed. It was Feinberg, for instance, who found the snazzy-looking Swedish salt shakers that passed for Dr.

McCoy's diagnostic tool and laser scalpel. Feinberg, who had worked previously on Desilu's *The Untouchables*, served as prop master for all three seasons of *Star Trek*. His services became even more valuable once Chang was no longer available. Feinberg, who apparently left the industry after *Star Trek*'s cancellation, died in 1991 at age eighty-two.

## Costumes

Costume designer William Theiss undertook the unenviable task of designing flattering yet unearthly-looking costumes for the show's many guest performers from week to week, along with the even less enviable task of making sure his creations were realized on time and on budget. Toward this end he scoured fabric outlets for flashy or futuristic material that could be purchased on the cheap, and, according Herb Solow and Bob Justman in their book *Inside Star Trek*, he supervised a secret "*Star Trek* sweat shop." He reportedly rented an apartment near the studio where nonunion seamstresses often worked through the night piecing together the show's attire in blatant disregard of union rules. Theiss designed the iconic gold, blue, and red Starfleet tunics but remains best known for the revealing outfits he created for *Star Trek*'s female guest stars. Although he rarely gave interviews, Theiss's "Theory of Titillation" has been frequently quoted: "The degree to which a costume is considered sexy is directly proportional to how much it looks like it is about to fall off."

For "What Are Little Girls Made Of?," Theiss contributed two of his most famous designs. The first was the daring pantsuit worn by Sherry Jackson as Andrea, featuring a top consisting entirely of two criss-crossed strips of fabric that barely covered the actress's breasts. The second was the imposing outfit worn by Ted ("Lurch") Cassidy as the murderous android Ruk, including an oversized three-quarter-length jacket with giant shoulder pads that made the 6-foot-9 Cassidy seem truly giant. For "Is There in Truth No Beauty?," Theiss designed a jewel-covered gown for Diana Muldaur to wear as the blind Dr. Miranda Jones. This garment was lovely but also functioned believably as a cleverly camouflaged censor web that enabled Jones to "see." And for "The Cloud Minders," Theiss created widely disparate costumes that expressed at a glance the chasm between two cultures in conflict. The idle, artistically inclined dwellers of Stratos, the cloud city, wear soft, pastel-colored garments designed for beauty: The men appear in silky, elegant robes, the women in flowing skirts and bikini tops with dainty capes. Everyone's hair is carefully coiffed. The worker class "Troglytes," who labor in brutal conditions in the mines beneath the planet's surface, wear strictly utilitarian attire. Men and women both dress in grubby red and blue jumpsuits, with their shaggy, unkempt hair held back by sweaty-looking bandanas. The episode contains a lot of dialogue about the cultural gulf between the cloud-dwellers and the Troglytes, but Theiss's costumes tell viewers everything they need to know.

Roddenberry remained loyal to Theiss, who worked on the producer's only feature film, *Pretty Maids All in a Row* (1971), as well as his failed pilots *Genesis II* (1973) and *Planet Earth* (1974). In 1987, Theiss returned to serve as costume designer for *Star Trek: The Next Generation* and redesigned Starfleet's uniforms for the twenty-fourth century. He continued with *Next Gen* until his death, from AIDS, in 1992. In all, Theiss worked on 29 different movies and TV shows, including the classic films *Spartacus* (1960) and *Harold and Maude* (1971).

## Makeup

Makeup artist Fred Phillips worked hand in hand with both Theiss and the show's cinematographers (usually Jerry Finnerman) to ensure that the cast looked their best. He also created the appearance of the Vulcans, Romulans, Klingons, Orions, and other alien species featured on *Star Trek* (except for those that required full-on monster suits, like the Gorn and the Mugato). But Phillips's most important contribution to the success of *Star Trek* may have been in making sure that Spock's ears didn't look ridiculous.

Prior to the filming of the series' original pilot, "The Cage," both Phillips and Leonard Nimoy were gravely concerned about Spock's ears. The company Desilu had hired to make the ears had delivered several unacceptable attempts and seemed unable to produce the kind of detailed, natural-looking appliances that were essential to sell Spock as a dignified, intellectual character. Nimoy, already plagued by misgivings about appearing in alien makeup, feared he would become a laughingstock if he had to work with the goofy-looking, Desilu-purchased ears. But studio bean counters refused to grant Phillips the $600 it would cost to acquire the ears from a reliable alternate source. Just days before shooting on "The Cage" was set to begin, Phillips defied his superiors and ordered a freshly molded set of prosthetic ears from a friend in the makeup department at Metro-Goldwyn-Mayer. "To this day I am most grateful to Fred Phillips for saving the day and insisting on doing the job properly," Nimoy wrote in his memoir *I Am Spock*. "Fred put his own job on the line; he could have been fired for spending the money without authorization." And *Star Trek* could have bombed if the *Enterprise*'s first officer came off looking like some overgrown leprechaun.

While almost every *Star Trek* episode features excellent makeup, "Journey to Babel" remains, arguably, Phillips's greatest triumph. For this installment, he created two new alien species—the blue-skinned, antennae-topped Andorians and the furry, pig-snouted Tellarites. Of no less importance was the subtle artistry Phillips displayed in "aging" Mark Lenard, who passed as Spock's father even though the actor was less than seven years older than Nimoy. Jane Wyatt, who played Spock's mother, was twenty-one years older than Nimoy and fourteen years older than Lenard. Yet Amanda looks younger than Sarek! Phillips later devised much more extreme old age makeup for "The Deadly Years," in which the cast ages rapidly due to an alien disease.

As Andrea and Ruk from "What Are Little Girls Made Of?," Sherry Jackson and Ted Cassidy model two of costume designer William Ware Theiss's most striking creations.

Phillips was another *Outer Limits* veteran Justman brought on board to work on *Star Trek*. The makeup artist's prior credits stretched all the way back to *The Wizard of Oz* in 1939 and included more than thirty other films and TV shows, including director Roger Corman's *House of Usher* (1960), with Vincent Price, and the offbeat horror film *Incubus* (1966), shot in Esperanto and starring

William Shatner. Phillips's post-*Trek* work included twenty-seven more movies and television programs, highlighted by the classic *One Flew Over the Cuckoo's Nest* (1975). He returned to the franchise for *Star Trek: The Motion Picture* in 1979. Phillips—who had created the "classic" Klingon makeup, bronzing actors' skin and giving them Fu Manchu mustaches—invented the "modern" Klingon makeup, complete with ridged forehead, for *The Motion Picture*. (The first actor to appear in the new-look Klingon makeup was Mark Lenard.) Phillips declined an offer to work on *Star Trek II: The Wrath of Khan* due to failing eyesight. He died in 1993. Phillips's daughter Janna followed in his footsteps, working alongside her father on the first *Trek* feature film and later serving as a makeup artist during Season Two of *The Next Generation* (where she earned an Emmy nomination) and Season Three of *Deep Space Nine*.

## Special Effects

Several different special visual effects houses worked on *Star Trek*, but that wasn't the original plan. Once again Desilu had locked the program into an exclusive deal, this time with the Howard Anderson Company, which had produced visual effects for "The Cage" and "Where No Man Has Gone Before." Anderson was a well-established operation—founded in 1927, it had furnished titles and special effects for scores of movies and TV shows—and it had created outstanding visuals for *Trek*'s two pilots. For "The Cage," Anderson created the transporter "beam in/beam out" effect, which became a signature of the series. But the pilots had been produced on timelines very different from the merciless grind of an ongoing weekly series. ("Where No Man Has Gone Before" took ten months to complete.) By August 1966, with the show's September 8 premiere looming, it became clear that Anderson would be unable to produce acceptable footage in the quantity and with the speed necessary for *Trek* to meet its airdates. When the firm was unable to deliver the shots ordered for the planned title sequence Roddenberry and Justman were forced to cobble together the show's now-famous opening– with the *Enterprise* whizzing by from various angles—out of scraps and trims left over from the two pilots.

Although *Star Trek* continued to work with Anderson, Roddenberry contracted with several other visual effects shops to share the workload. These firms included Van der Veer Photo Effects, which had provided visuals for *The Outer Limits*; Cinema Research, a recently founded company whose first motion picture (*The Wizard of Mars*, a low-budget sci-fi semi-remake of *The Wizard of Oz*) didn't inspire confidence; and the Westheimer Company, a more established outfit (founded in the early 1950s) but with no science fiction experience. Overseeing and coordinating the work of these various companies was a vital task. Roddenberry hired Ed Milkis, who had worked as a film editor on *The Lieutenant*, to manage all postproduction activities, including editing, scoring, and sound effects in addition to visual effects. Milkis's work day began with a 5:30 a.m. daily conference with Justman and sometimes stretched until midnight with nightly check-ins at Anderson, Van der Veer, Cinema Research, and Westheimer. But the grueling work paid off handsomely. *Star Trek*'s visual effects earned Emmy nominations for each of the show's three seasons—although it lost three years in a row. And Milkis was promoted to associate producer for the show's third season.

Visual effects became increasingly important as the series progressed. With budgets tightening, the creative team began developing teleplays that could be shot using only regular cast members and entirely on existing sets, saving the expense of hiring guest stars and constructing new sets or shooting on location. As restrictive as this approach sounds, it produced some outstanding episodes, including "The Changeling," about a homicidal space probe; "The Immunity Syndrome." in which the *Enterprise* encounters a giant, energy-sucking space amoeba; and "The Tholian Web," in which Kirk is lost in an interdimensional rift while his ship is trapped in an energy web created by the inscrutable Tholians. Both "The Immunity Syndrome" and "The Tholian Web" earned Emmy nominations for special visual effects. "The Tholian Web" remains a fan favorite.

Milkis went on to a long and successful career producing situation comedies, enjoying his greatest triumph as executive producer of the smash hits *Happy Days* (1974–84) and *Laverne and Shirley* (1976–83). He passed away in 1996 at age sixty-five. Both the Westheimer and Anderson companies remained in operation into the 2000s. Westheimer went on to produce effects for *Star Trek IV: The Voyage Home* (1986), and Anderson created visuals for *Star Trek: Nemesis* (2002).

# Permission to Come Aboard

## Unforgettable Guest Stars

The cast of *Star Trek* was usually supplemented by visiting actors brought in to portray incidental crew members as well as the friends, enemies, and love interests Captain Kirk and company encountered from week to week. Although a handful of episodes—including "Mirror, Mirror" and "The Tholian Web," among other notable exceptions—were produced without benefit of outside talent, most featured guest stars in prominent roles and were stronger for it. This was due in part to the generally high caliber of talent that casting director Joe D'Agosta was able to bring to *Star Trek*.

D'Agosta secured the services of numerous distinguished actors who were well known to television viewers of the era. James Gregory, who guest starred in "Dagger of the Mind," had played the title role in director John Frankenheimer's classic political thriller *The Manchurian Candidate* (1962). Elisha Cook Jr., who defends Captain Kirk in "Court Martial," was a Hollywood veteran who had roughed up Humphrey Bogart in *The Maltese Falcon* (1941). And four regulars from the highly rated *Batman* TV show beamed aboard the *Enterprise*: Frank (the Riddler) Gorshin in "Let That Be Your Last Battlefield," Lee (Catwoman) Meriwether in "That Which Survives," Julie (Catwoman) Newmar in "Friday's Child," and Yvonne (Batgirl) Craig in "Whom Gods Destroy."

Other *Trek* guest stars were little recognized at the time but won distinction later. Kim Darby, who played the title role in "Miri," would ride alongside John Wayne in his Oscar-winning *True Grit* (1969). John Fiedler, who scared the wits out of the *Enterprise* crew in "Wolf in the Fold," would gain immortality as the voice of Piglet in Walt Disney's *Winnie the Pooh* cartoons. And Sally Kellerman (from "Where No Man Has Gone Before"), Michael J. Pollard ("Miri"), and Teri Garr ("Assignment: Earth") would later earn Academy Award nominations for their respective roles in *M\*A\*S\*H* (1970), *Bonnie and Clyde* (1967), and *Tootsie* (1982). A half-dozen other *Star Trek* guest stars went on to earn Emmy nominations. That esteemed group includes Diana Muldaur, twice nominated for her work as ruthless attorney Rosalind Shays on *L.A. Law*, who was so impressive in two classic *Trek* appearances ("Return to Tomorrow" and "Is There in Truth No Beauty?") that she replaced Gates McFadden as chief medical officer for a season of *The Next Generation*.

Among these gifted actors are several who, regardless of any other success they may have enjoyed, remain forever linked with *Star Trek* by the indelible performances they contributed to the series. The following actors created characters that have captured the hearts and imaginations of generations of fans.

## Michael Ansara

As Kang, the fierce yet noble Klingon commander from "Day of the Dove," actor Michael Ansara helped redefine one of *Star Trek*'s most popular alien species. The powerfully built, 6-foot-3 Ansara was a towering physical presence. More important to his role, however, was the actor's almost regal demeanor, which he developed playing Indian chiefs and Arabian princes. His Kang is a cunning warrior, but also a man of honor—in short, the type of sympathetic Klingon that would be depicted in later *Star Trek* series, beginning with *The Next Generation*. Kang served as the model for future Klingons, who were intimidating but respectable, adhering to a stringent ethical code. The character was so popular that Ansara was asked to reappear as Kang in the *Deep Space Nine* episode "Blood Oath" in 1994 and in the *Voyager* installment "Flashback" in 1996. He also played Jeyal, the husband of Lwaxana Troi (Majel Barrett-Roddenberry) in the *Deep Space Nine* adventure "The Muse" (1996).

Born in Syria in 1922, Ansara emigrated to the U.S. at age two and moved to Los Angeles ten years later. His screen career began in the late 1940s. For years, he moved between small, often uncredited, roles in major motion pictures—including director Joseph Mankiewicz's *Julius Caesar* (1953) and Cecil B. DeMille's *The Ten Commandments* (1956)—and meatier roles on television. Due to his exotic features, Ansara played a wide variety of ethnic "types," but was most frequently cast as an American Indian. He starred as Chief Cochise on the ABC Western series *Broken Arrow* from 1956 through 1959. Coincidentally, Leonard Nimoy guest starred on *Broken Arrow* in 1957. In other pre-*Trek* roles, Ansara worked with William Shatner, James Doohan, and George Takei. Ansara's other science fiction credits include Irwin Allen's movie *Voyage to the Bottom of the Sea* (1961) and episodes of *The Outer Limits*, *Lost in Space*, *Land of the Giants*, *Time Tunnel*, and *Babylon 5*. He had a recurring role as the villainous Killer Kane on *Buck Rogers in the 25th Century* (1979–81). Late in his career, he became an in-demand voice actor, and played Mr. Freeze on *Batman: The Animated Series* and related projects. From 1958 to 1974, Ansara was married to actress Barbara Eden, star of the sitcom *I Dream of Jeannie*. (The couple met on a date arranged by the 20th Century-Fox publicity department). He is now married to actress Beverly Kushida and is semiretired.

## William Campbell

Although fame, fortune, and critical acclaim eluded him, actor William Campbell made a living in film and television for more than four decades, from

1950 to 1996, before retiring and taking over as administrator of the Motion Picture Country Home in Woodland Hills, California, a retirement community for Screen Actors Guild members. During his lengthy career, the New Jersey–born Campbell appeared in more than eighty films (almost all B-movies) and television shows. He sang with Elvis Presley in *Love Me Tender* (1956) and starred in a short-lived syndicated TV series, *Cannonball* (1958–59), about cross-country truck drivers. In 1963, he starred in director Francis Ford Coppola's debut film, the low-budget chiller *Dementia 13*, and in Roger Corman's exploitation classic *The Young Racers*. But Campbell is remembered today primarily for two remarkable appearances on *Star Trek*.

During the show's first season he guest starred as the impish, apparently omnipotent Trelaine, the title character in "The Squire of Gothos." As Trelaine, Campbell delivered a delightfully swishy performance modeled, in part, after the mannerisms of pianist Liberace (whom Campbell resembled). The Trelaine character would serve as a forerunner of the Q species featured in later *Star Trek* series *The Next Generation*, *Deep Space Nine*, and *Voyager*. During the making of "The Squire of Gothos," Campbell struck up a long-lasting friendship with James Doohan. Campbell returned to *Star Trek* a season later to appear as the Klingon Captain Koloth in "The Trouble with Tribbles." Although the actor wasn't available to provide the voice of Koloth for the animated sequel "More Tribbles, More Troubles" (instead, Doohan imitated his friend's voice), Campbell reprised the character for the *Deep Space Nine* episode "Blood Oath" in 1994. He also provided the voice of Trelaine for a *Star Trek* video game in 1993. Campbell also appeared in Gene Roddenberry's only theatrical feature, *Pretty Maids All in a Row* (1971), and was a popular guest at *Star Trek* conventions in the 1980s and '90s. He passed away in 2011.

## Roger C. Carmel

During his twenty-nine-year screen career, Brooklyn native Roger C. Carmel appeared in seventy-four movies and television series, playing a wide variety of character parts. But he will be forever remembered as Harcourt Fenton Mudd, the interstellar con man who befuddled Captain Kirk and company in two *Star Trek* episodes ("Mudd's Women" and "I, Mudd"), as well as an installment of the animated series ("Mudd's Passion"). Mudd was the only recurring character outside the *Enterprise* crew featured during *Star Trek*'s original three seasons. Thanks in large part to Carmel's devilishly good comedic timing, Mudd became a great favorite of fans. The character was frequently revived by the writers of *Star Trek* novels and comic books. Although Harry Mudd was a constant source of irritation for the crew of the *Enterprise*, Carmel was well liked by the cast of *Star Trek* and became, like Campbell, a frequent guest at fan conventions in the 1980s. Nichelle Nichols writes warmly about Carmel in her autobiography, *Beyond Uhura*.

Carmel's screen career began with an uncredited bit as a stage-hand in director Sidney Lumet's 1958 feature *Stage Struck*. Carmel worked primarily on television, winning guest roles on shows including *The Alfred Hitchcock Hour, The Munsters, The Man from U.N.C.L.E.,* and *Batman* in the 1960s prior to *Star Trek*. He continued to work steadily throughout the 1970s and '80s, but obesity and poor health limited him to voice work for cartoon shows like *The Transformers* and *The Adventures of the Gummi Bears* late in his life. Had the actor been in better physical condition, Harry Mudd would have made a comeback on *Star Trek: The Next Generation*. A story was developed that would have awakened Mudd from cryogenic sleep so that he could flummox Captain Jean-Luc Picard as he once had Captain Kirk. Unfortunately, in 1986, before the plan came to fruition, Carmel died of congestive heart failure. He was fifty-four years old.

## Joan Collins

The rest of the world may know Joan Collins as Alexis Carrington from the nighttime soap opera

Roger C. Carmel's Harry Mudd episodes were so popular that they were sold as a special two-tape set during the VHS era.

*Dynasty,* which ranked among TV's most-watched programs from 1981 to '87. But *Star Trek* fans remember Collins as Edith Keeler, Captain Kirk's doomed love interest in the classic episode "The City on the Edge of Forever." Her *Star Trek* role was a departure for the actress, who was typically cast as a sex kitten. Keeler wins Kirk's heart not with her beauty, or at least not *merely* with her beauty, but with her compassion and her soaring vision of a future when war and poverty will be eradicated. It's a touching, heartfelt performance that allows Collins more range and depth in a single episode than *Dynasty* provided in six seasons. Screenwriter Harlan Ellison based Keeler on Sister Aimee Semple McPherson,

**Thursday** April 6, 1967

TV CLOSE-UP GUIDE

**7:30 (5) STAR TREK—Adventure**

## 'The City on the Edge of Forever'

COLOR Tonight's science-fiction drama is set in the past.

Under the influence of drugs, Dr. McCoy plunges through a time portal and into the New York City of the 1930's.

Joan Collins

Kirk and Spock follow him, fearing that the drugged medical officer might commit an act that will alter the course of history.

While trying to find McCoy, Kirk falls in love with Edith Keeler, a charity worker helping victims of the Depression. Kirk doesn't know exactly what McCoy is about to do, but he has learned that the doctor's actions could prove fatal to Edith.

Joseph Pevney directed from a script by Harlan Ellison. Kirk: William Shatner. Spock: Leonard Nimoy. McCoy: DeForest Kelley. Scott: James Doohan. Sulu: George Takei. (60 min.)

**Guest Cast**

Edith Keeler ........................Joan Collins
Rodent ..............................John Harmon
Policeman ...........................Hal Baylor
Galloway ............................David L. Ross

*TV Guide's* Close-Up on "The City on the Edge of Forever," previewing the episode prior to its original broadcast, highlighted Joan Collins's guest appearance.

the Pentecostal missionary who became a media sensation after founding the International Church of the Foursquare Gospel in Los Angeles in 1923.

Born in London in 1933, Collins was the daughter of talent agent Joe Collins, whose clients included actors Peter Sellers and Roger Moore and singers Shirley Bassey and Tom Jones. (Collins's sister, Jackie, is a novelist known for her racy romances, often set in Hollywood.) Joan trained at the Royal Academy of Dramatic Arts, began her screen career in the early 1950s, and had tallied more than thirty film and television credits prior to *Star Trek.* In 1954, 20th Century-Fox signed Collins because executives believed she could compete with MGM's Elizabeth Taylor. The next year, Collins appeared opposite Bette Davis in *The Virgin Queen* and starred in Howard Hawks's big-budget flop *Land of the Pharaohs.* After Fox released Collins in the early 1960s, she drifted into television, including *Batman,* where she guest starred as a villainess named the Siren. More TV and B-movie work followed her appearance on *Star Trek.* In the film *Tales from the Crypt* (1971), she was menaced by a homicidal maniac in a Santa Claus suit. And she costarred with Robert Lansing (*Star Trek*'s Gary Seven) in director Bert I. Gordon's 1977 schlock-fest *Empire of the Ants.* Collins joined the cast of *Dynasty* at the beginning of the show's second season, when the flamboyant, back-stabbing

Alexis was introduced as a rival to Krystle Carrington (Linda Evans). The show's ratings soared.

## Kathryn Hays

Without saying a word, Kathryn Hays delivered one of *Star Trek*'s most memorable guest performances in the title role of "The Empath." Playing a mute alien who learns compassion by using her empathic powers to heal first Captain Kirk and later a dying Dr. McCoy, Hays performed with otherworldly delicacy and almost balletic grace. She plays this fragile, frightened woman—who McCoy nicknames "Gem"—like a porcelain doll come to life, afraid she might be shattered at any moment. Hays's work is all the more remarkable since it's delivered entirely through pantomime. Along with a handful of other one-shot *Trek* characters, "Gem" gained an ardent cult following; she and her species have been the subject of much fan-written fiction. DeForest Kelley named "The Empath" his personal favorite *Star Trek* episode.

Born Kay Piper in Princeton, Illinois, in 1933, Hays's screen career began in 1962 and remains active. She has worked almost exclusively in television, including guest roles on *The Alfred Hitchcock Hour* and *The Man from U.N.C.L.E.* prior to her appearance on *Star Trek*. One of her earliest assignments was an episode of *Naked City* ("The Rydecker Case") written by Gene Roddenberry. She also appeared on Roddenberry's short-lived military drama *The Lieutenant* in 1963. After *Trek*, Hays costarred with Leonard Nimoy in a 1972 episode of *Rod Serling's Night Gallery*. In the 1970s, the actress found steady work on daytime soaps, appearing on *Guiding Light* in 1971 before beginning a long association with *As the World Turns*. Sporting her trademark "pixie cut" hairdo, she played the frequently married (sometimes divorced, sometimes widowed) Kim Hughes on *As the World Turns* from 1972 to 2010. Hays herself has been married three times. When "The Empath" was filmed, her husband was actor Glenn Ford, but the couple divorced in 1969.

## Mark Lenard

Of all the *Star Trek* guest stars, Mark Lenard may have been the most popular, both with fans and with producers. He made two landmark appearances—first as a nameless Romulan commander in "The Balance of Terror" and then as Spock's father, Sarek, in "Journey to Babel." Lenard was also invited back for a third appearance and considered for an even larger role.

Born Leonard Rosenson in Chicago, Illinois, in 1924, Lenard was the son of Russian-Jewish immigrants and served as a paratrooper in World War II. After the war he studied theater arts at the New School in New York and at the University of Michigan, and appeared in a handful of Broadway plays in the late 1950s. His screen career began in 1960 and included sporadic work, mostly in television, over the next thirty-three years. He continued to work regularly on the stage. Lenard brought impressive gravitas and nuance to his role as the nameless Romulan commander who engages in a cat-and-mouse battle with Captain Kirk in "Balance of Terror." His fine work won the admiration of creator-producer Gene Roddenberry and casting director Joe D'Agosta. They were so impressed, in fact, that when Leonard Nimoy and Roddenberry became embroiled in a salary dispute in the interim between Seasons One and Two, Lenard was considered as a replacement for Nimoy. After Nimoy finally came to terms, Lenard was invited back to appear as Spock's father in "Journey to Babel." His vivid, subtle performance illuminated one of the series' most complex characters. One testament to the actor's excellence is that audiences never questioned him as Spock's father, even though Lenard was only six years older than Nimoy. Roddenberry and D'Agosta asked Leonard to play Abraham Lincoln in the Season Three episode "The Savage Curtain," but the actor was unavailable.

After *Star Trek*, Lenard worked with Nimoy again in a 1970 episode of *Mission: Impossible*. He landed featured roles on the ABC series *Here Come the Brides* (1968–70), inspired by *Seven Brides for Seven Brothers*, and on CBS's short-lived *Planet of the Apes* TV series (1974), in which he played the brutal gorilla General Urko. Having portrayed a Romulan, a Vulcan, and a talking gorilla, Lenard signed on to appear as the unnamed Klingon captain featured in the opening scenes of *Star Trek: The Motion Picture* (1979). But the actor remained best known as Sarek, a role he reprised on several occasions—for the animated series episode "Yesteryear"; in the third, fourth, and sixth *Star Trek* feature films (*The Search for Spock*, 1984; *The Voyage Home*, 1986; and *The Undiscovered Country*, 1991); and in two episodes of *The Next Generation* ("Sarek" and "Unification"). In his later years, Lenard also taught acting and provided voice-over narration for commercials and documentaries. But he was unable to work during the final two years of his life as he battled bone cancer. The disease took Lenard's life in 1996 at age seventy-two.

## Celia Lovsky

Screen veteran Celia Lovsky had fewer than fifteen minutes of screen time on *Star Trek* but made every second count in her pivotal role as the legendary Vulcan leader T'Pau, who oversees Spock's ill-fated marriage in "Amok Time," one of the foundational episodes of the entire *Trek* franchise. Lovsky enriches her small role with subtle gestures and expressions that make T'Pau a fully realized character, even though her purpose is purely expository: She proudly explains her culture's ancient, Byzantine mating rituals for Captain Kirk and Dr. McCoy. The actress's thick accent and dignified bearing bring touches of the exotic and regal to T'Pau. And while Lovsky remains appropriately (for a Vulcan) aloof, she allows flickers of emotion to seep through the character's icy veneer, displaying hints of annoyance with Spock's faithless fiancée, T'Pring (Arlene Martel), and of grief when Spock appears to kill Kirk in ceremonial combat. Her superb work helps ground the episode, which was the first to explore the Vulcan culture in depth.

Lovsky, born in Austria in 1897, studied at the Austrian Royal Academy of Arts and Music before moving to Berlin to pursue film and theater roles in the 1920s. There she met and eventually married actor Peter Lorre, whom she introduced to director Fritz Lang. In 1935, following's Lorre's breakout success in Lang's *M*, Lorre and Lovsky immigrated to Hollywood. Although the couple divorced in 1945, she remained devoted to Lorre, working as his publicist and financial manager until the actor's death in 1964. As she aged, Lovsky specialized in exotic character parts in movies and television. Prior to *Star Trek*, she appeared on *Alfred Hitchcock Presents* (1959) and *The Twilight Zone* (1964), and played Lon Chaney's mother in the biopic *Man of a Thousand Faces* (1957), directed by Joseph Pevney. Pevney later directed fourteen episodes of *Star Trek*, including "Amok Time," and was instrumental in casting Lovsky as T'Pau. Lovsky's final film role was in the dystopian *Soylent Green* (1971). In all, she made more than 120 film and television appearances before her death in 1979 at age eighty-two.

## Ricardo Montalban

The distinguished Ricardo Montalban worked in film and television for nearly sixty years, piling up more than 160 screen roles, but he seldom found parts equal to his talent. *Star Trek* offered him a chance to shine as the imperious, superhuman Khan Noonien Singh, who menaced the *Enterprise* crew in the episode "Space Seed" and again on the big screen in *Star Trek II: The Wrath of Khan*. Following the shaky performance of *Star Trek: The Motion Picture*, the blockbuster success of *Wrath of Khan* assured the future of the *Trek* franchise. In "Space Seed," Montalban radiates authority and charisma as Khan seduces a female historian and out-thinks, out-fights, and out-machos Captain Kirk for most of the episode. In the end he is not so much defeated as forced to compromise. Montalban's dynamic screen presence was a source of irritation for William Shatner, who hated being upstaged. According to James Doohan, Nichelle Nichols, and Walter Koenig, Shatner held Montalban in disdain throughout the production of both "Space Seed" and *Wrath of Khan*, even though the actor was well liked by the rest of the cast and crew.

Ricardo Gonzalo Pedro Montalban y Merino was born in Mexico City in 1920 and, after appearing in a half-dozen films in his native country, moved to Hollywood in 1947. He was immediately typecast as the exotic Latin lover and romanced various starlets on the big screen for the next four years. His heartthrob status waned after 1951 when he fell off a horse while filming *Across the Wide Missouri* and suffered a grievous spinal injury that left him with a permanent limp. Throughout the 1950s, Montalban appeared in Broadway productions and supplemented his income through television guest appearances, including episodes of *Alfred Hitchcock Presents* (1960) and Gene Roddenberry's *The Lieutenant* (1964).

The once and future Khan played the kindly circus owner Armando in *Escape from the Planet of the Apes* (1971) and *Conquest of the Planet of the Apes* (1972), and earned an Emmy for his work in the miniseries *How the West Was Won* (1978). He won the leading role of Mr. Roarke on Aaron Spelling's hit *Fantasy Island* (1977–84) and later starred as the villainous Zach Powers on the *Dynasty* spin-off *The Colbys* (1985–87). He remains familiar to many viewers as the pitchman who rhapsodized about the Chrysler Cordoba and its "Corinthian leather" seats during a series of commercials made during this period. In 1993, he earned a Lifetime Achievement Award from the Screen Actors Guild. In his acceptance speech, Montalban offered the following as the five stages of an actor's career:

1.  Who is Ricardo Montalban?
2.  Get me Ricardo Montalban.
3.  Get me a Ricardo Montalban type.
4.  Get me a young Ricardo Montalban.
5.  Who is Ricardo Montalban?

Ricardo Montalban brought dignity and charisma to his role as the imperious, superhuman Kahn, one of *Star Trek*'s greatest villains.

That same year, complications from his old spinal injury left Montalban paraplegic. But the actor continued to perform voice work and occasional on-camera parts that hid his condition. He died of congestive heart failure at age eighty-eight in 2009. Montalban was a cofounder of the Nosotros Foundation, which supports Latino filmmakers. Hollywood's Ricardo Montalban Theatre is named for him.

## Robert Walker Jr.

As the endearing yet terrifying Charlie Evans, a lovesick teenage misfit with fearsome telekinetic abilities, Robert Walker Jr. delivered *Star Trek*'s earliest great guest performance. The youthful-looking Walker was twenty-six when he starred as the seventeen-year-old Charlie Evans in "Charlie X," the seventh episode produced and second one broadcast. Charlie, marooned on a remote planet as a child and raised by aliens, develops an unrequited crush on Yeoman Janice Rand (Grace Lee Whitney) and lashes out in superpowered rage when frustrated or embarrassed. In his tender scenes with Whitney, Walker seems to be nearly bursting with pent-up yearnings—physical and emotional. Charlie's frustration evidences itself in petulant, reflexive acts of violence (causing a spaceship to blow apart, "thinking" a crewman out of existence) when Charlie feels threatened or ridiculed. Walker is terrifying in these sequences, yet recaptures our sympathy in the episode's unforgettable conclusion. Charlie pleads to remain with the humans rather than return to his forlorn existence with the aliens; Walker's delivery is wrenching.

The son of two A-list Hollywood stars (Robert Walker and Jennifer Jones) and later the stepson of legendary producer David O. Selznick, Walker appeared in a few television roles as a teenager before enrolling at the Actors Studio in New York in the early 1960s. In 1963, he earned a Golden Globe as "Promising Newcomer" for his performance in actor-director Laurence Harvey's *The Ceremony*. A year later, he earned a Theatre World Award for his work in the off-Broadway productions *I Knock at the Door* and *Pictures in the Hallway*. For the rest of his career, however, his screen credits consisted primarily of low-budget films such as *Son of Blob* (1972) and TV guest appearances on shows including *The Invaders, Time Tunnel,* and *The Six Million Dollar Man*. He and his first wife, actress Ellie Wood, played minor roles in the landmark *Easy Rider* (1969). Walker is now married to actress Dawn Walker, his third wife, with whom he has a daughter and a son. Producer Ira Steven Behr offered Walker a role on *Deep Space Nine* in 1997, but the actor declined.

## William Windom

In a career that stretched from 1949 to 2006, William Windom piled up an astounding 247 screen credits, along with countless theatrical roles. But *Star Trek* aficionados remember him for his spellbinding performance as the revenge-obsessed, guilt-stricken Commodore Matt Decker in "The Doomsday Machine." Windom's edgy, pathos-laden portrayal of the haggard, half-crazed Decker, bent on destroying the giant, planet-eating superweapon that claimed the lives of his entire crew, ranks among the richest in the *Trek* canon. He made a fine Ahab for screenwriter Norman Spinrad's tale, which was modeled after *Moby Dick*.

Windom was born in New York City in 1923 and, like Mark Lenard, served as a paratrooper in World War II. After the war, he studied at the American Repertory Theatre in New York and performed Shakespeare, Ibsen, and other classical plays in various off-Broadway venues in the late 1950s and early '60s. He made his feature film debut as the prosecutor in *To Kill a Mockingbird* (1962). Windom worked with Shatner again in 1969 for a CBS Playhouse production, "Shadow Game," and reunited with Nimoy for the 1971 telefilm *Assault on the Wayne*. Windom's other sci-fi credits include two forays into *The Twilight Zone* (in 1961 and '63) and appearances on *The Bionic Woman* (1976) and *The Incredible Hulk* (1981). Windom won an Emmy Award for his portrayal of garrulous cartoonist John Monroe on the short-lived sitcom *My World and Welcome to It* (1969–70), based on the work of acclaimed humorist James Thurber. Windom also had a recurring role on the long-running mystery series *Murder, She Wrote*. The actor reprised the Matt Decker character in 2004 for an episode of the fan-created Internet series *Star Trek: The New Voyages* ("In Harm's Way"). He retired in 2006.

## Jane Wyatt

Jane Wyatt became a household name playing über-mom Margaret Anderson on the long-running Robert Young sitcom *Father Knows Best* (1954–60). The role earned her three consecutive Emmy Awards from 1958 through 1960. But *Star Trek* fans remember the actress as Amanda Grayson, mother of Spock and wife of Sarek in the classic episode "Journey to Babel." Her heartfelt performance in her understated romantic scenes with Sarek (Mark Lenard) and especially in her fiery exchange with Spock (who refuses to surrender temporary command of the *Enterprise*, even to save his father's life) supplies much of the episode's gripping emotional power. Wyatt later reappeared as Amanda Grayson for a cameo in *Star Trek IV: The Voyage Home* (1986).

Born in New Jersey in 1910, Wyatt was the daughter of a Wall Street investment banker and a female drama critic. She began acting shortly after college, won her first Broadway role in the early 1930s, and was signed to a studio contract by Universal. In 1937, she costarred with Ronald Colman in director Frank Capra's classic romantic fantasy *Lost Horizon*, which earned seven Academy Award nominations. She later appeared in the Oscar-winning *Gentleman's Agreement* (1947) and other prestigious vehicles until she was blacklisted for her vocal opposition to congressional probes into Communism among Hollywood writers, directors, and actors in the 1950s. She returned to Broadway and eventually became a TV star, but her feature film career never fully recovered. *Father Knows Best*, based on a popular radio show, remains her most celebrated work. In real life, Wyatt was the wife of investment broker Edgar Bethune Ward, whom she married in 1935 and remained devoted to until his death sixty-five years later. Wyatt passed away of natural causes in 2006.

Mark Lenard and Jane Wyatt convincingly portrayed Spock's parents, Sarek and Amanda, in the episode "Journey to Babel." In actuality, Lenard was fourteen years younger than Wyatt, and just six years older than his "son," Leonard Nimoy.

# Brief Lives

## Untold Tales of *Star Trek*'s "Redshirts"

S top me if you've heard this one: The *Enterprise* sends an away team to explore a previously uncharted planet. The landing party consists of Captain Kirk, Mr. Spock, Dr. McCoy, and security officer Kerpopowicz. Who's not coming back?

As this familiar joke indicates, the tendency of *Star Trek* screenwriters to bump off nameless or nearly anonymous *Enterprise* officers—usually brawny security guards in red tunics—is the stuff of cliché. In fan parlance, these short-lived characters became known simply as "redshirts." Even director J. J. Abrams felt compelled to carry on the tradition, killing off the red-shirted engineer Olsen (Greg Ellis) in *Star Trek*, his 2009 reboot of the feature film franchise.

Unquestionably, serving under Captain Kirk was hazardous duty. In all, fifty-four *Enterprise* crew members were killed in the course of the original seventy-nine episodes, including deaths that occurred off-camera. Officers were strangled, suffocated, stabbed, poisoned, struck by lightning, blasted by phasers and consumed or disintegrated by sundry villains and aliens. Those fifty-four casualties do not include the five crewmen killed in the evil parallel universe of "Mirror, Mirror" or officers assigned to other starships who were killed in the course of other episodes. Nor does it count the six crew members who died but were later revived, including Dr. McCoy (in "Shore Leave"), Scotty ("The Changeling"), and Ensign Chekov ("Spectre of the Gun"). In *Star Trek*'s second pilot, "Where No Man Has Gone Before," a record-setting twelve *Enterprise* officers died, including two members of the bridge crew—helmsman Gary Mitchell (Gary Lockwood) and navigator Lee Kelso (Paul Carr). Ironically, while this episode has the highest body count of any *Trek* installment, it includes no official "redshirts" because the red tunics had not yet been introduced by costume designer Bill Theiss.

Behind every fallen crewman, however, there was a crimson-tunicked performer with skills and dreams. A few of the redshirts were walk-on day players who came and went without making a ripple in Hollywood. Mal Friedman, for instance, made his only screen appearance as a security officer struck by poisoned darts in "The Apple." Some were aspiring actors hoping for that big break that would lead to stardom. Although A-list fame never arrived for any of the redshirts, some cobbled together long and productive careers in film and television, either in front of or behind the cameras. But most were experienced stunt professionals who—often laboring without credit and for Screen Actors Guild–scale wages—did the dirty work, week in and week out, to keep action-oriented shows like *Star Trek* in business. Several of these seldom-celebrated performers remain notable for one reason or another.

## Vincent Deadrick

A stuntman and sometime stunt coordinator, Vincent Deadrick made several appearances on *Star Trek,* including a redshirt role in "What Are Little Girls Made Of?" In that episode he played security officer Mathews, who gets pushed off a cliff by the android Ruk. Deadrick also appeared as a Romulan crewman in "Balance of Terror," as a nameless engineer in "Is There in Truth No Beauty?" and (sporting red body paint and a blond bouffant wig) as a native of planet Gamma Trianguli VI in "The Apple." He stunt-doubled for other actors in at least three episodes, standing in for DeForest Kelley in "Mirror, Mirror." Deadrick never received screen credit for his work on *Star Trek.* His first stunt job was doubling for Steve McQueen in director Don Siegel's war drama *Hell Is for Heroes* (1962). He also worked on the *Batman* series prior to *Star Trek.* He went on to perform and/or supervise stunts for more than a dozen TV shows, including *Mission: Impossible* with Leonard Nimoy, and over forty movies, including *Indiana Jones and the Last Crusade* (1989) and *Pirates of the Caribbean: The Curse of the Black Pearl* (2006). He later doubled for star Lee Majors on both *The Six Million Dollar Man* and *The Fall Guy.* Deadrick's son, Vincent Deadrick Jr., served as stunt coordinator for *Star Trek: Enterprise.* The elder Deadrick made a cameo appearance on *Enterprise* in 2004, playing an alien slave trader in the episode "Borderland."

## Jay D. Jones

The film and television career of Jay D. Jones proved far shorter than Vincent Deadrick's, perhaps due to the hard luck Jones suffered in his work for *Star Trek.* Jones's brief screen career, which lasted from 1967 to 1975, included credited and uncredited bit parts as well as stunt work in many *Trek* episodes. In "Catspaw," he played Lieutenant Jackson, who is killed by shape-shifting alien Syria via "sympathetic magic," and in "The Apple," he plays Lieutenant Mallory, who's blown up when he steps on an explosive rock formation. Jones also appeared as the tommy gun–toting goon named Mirt in "A Piece of the Action"; nameless engineers in "The Tholian Web" and "And the Children Shall Lead"; a hooded Gideon guard in "Mark of Gideon"; a Klingon crewman in "Day of the Dove"; and an Ardanian "Troglyte" in "The Cloudminders." Additionally, he stunt-doubled for James Doohan in three episodes—"Mirror, Mirror," "Who Mourns for Adonais?," and "The Changeling." (It's actually Jones who's killed—or not—in the latter episode.) On two occasions Jones had to be hospitalized during his tenure with *Star Trek,* the performer told interviewers Mark Philips and Frank Garcia for their book *Science Fiction Television Series*. Doubling for Doohan in "Who Mourns for Adonais?," Jones hit his head following a back flip and suffered a concussion. He was more seriously injured by the explosion that kills Mallory in "The Apple." Technicians overestimated the required charge for the effect. The ensuing blast blew Jones off his feet, knocking him unconscious, and left William Shatner, Leonard Nimoy, and DeForest Kelley, who were standing nearby, with short-term hearing loss and permanent tinnitus (persistent ringing in the ears). Despite these mishaps, Jones went on to appear in a handful of *Bonanza* episodes (1970–72) and worked on *High Chaparral* (1969) and *Kung Fu* (1975) before leaving show business in the late 1970s.

## Richard Dial

Veteran stunt performer Richard Dial had more than a dozen credits under his belt prior to *Star Trek*, including performing tricky underwater stunts on *Sea Hunt* (1958–61) and *Voyage to the Bottom of the Sea* (1964). His first job was on director John Ford's classic Western *The Searchers* in 1956. He also appeared in episodes of *The Green Hornet, Time Tunnel,* and *The Man from U.N.C.L.E.*, and later worked extensively on *Mission: Impossible* as Peter Graves's stunt double, working on eighty-nine episodes from 1967 to 1970. For *Star Trek*, he made five appearances, all uncredited. In "The Apple" he played redshirt Lieutenant Kaplan, who gets zapped by lightning from the godlike alien computer Vaal. In "And the Children Shall Lead," he's seen as a nameless security guard. Dial also stunt-doubled on three occasions. It was in this capacity that he made his most memorable contribution to the series, doubling for William Shatner during Captain Kirk's knock-down, drag-out battle with the lizardlike Gorn captain in "Arena." This thrilling sequence ranks among the most riveting and enduringly popular of all *Star Trek*'s many fight scenes. Dial died in 1992 at age sixty but worked actively until the end.

## Bobby Clark

Bobby Clark and Gary Coombs took turns wearing the heavy Gorn suit during that spectacular fight scene in "Arena," with bit player William Blackburn appearing under the mask for close-ups. Clark also played three other *Star Trek* roles. He was one of the Evil Chekov's ill-fated henchmen who are disintegrated by Captain Kirk's bodyguards in "Mirror, Mirror." He also appeared as panicked aliens in both "The Return of the Archons" and "The Apple." Clark was a former child actor whose screen career began in 1951. He memorably appeared as Jimmy Grimaldi, the little boy who's afraid of his Pod-people-replaced parents in *Invasion of the Body Snatchers* (1957). He also had a featured role as Casey Jones Jr. in the short-lived children's series *Casey Jones* (1957–58). As he aged, however, Clark drifted into bit roles and stunt work. Following appearances in several TV Westerns in the late 1960s and early 1970s, he left the film industry. According to Memory Alpha (a website that provided data integral to the research for this chapter), *Star Trek: Enterprise* stunt coordinator Vincent Deadrick Jr. invited Clark to the set during the filming of the *Enterprise* episode "In a Mirror, Darkly, Part II." Not only was this a Mirror Universe tale, like Clark's "Mirror, Mirror," but the story featured the first official appearance of a Gorn in thirty-eight years. The species hadn't been seen on any live-action *Trek* series since "Arena" (although a Gorn was glimpsed briefly in the animated episode "The Time Trap"). There was no monster suit to be worn for this 2004 episode, however. The Gorn was created through computer animation. But Clark donned a re-creation of the Gorn costume in 2009 for the BBC documentary *Bring Back Star Trek*. He and show host Justin Lee Collins, playing Captain Kirk, parodied the famous fight scene from "Arena."

## Julie Cobb

Julie Cobb has the distinction of being the only female redshirt (although in her case, the term perhaps should be "redskirt"). Her character also suffered one of the series' most unusual deaths. In "By Any Other Name," the essence of Yeoman Leslie Thompson (Cobb) is reduced to a hexagonal pod by the villainous Kelvan Rojan (Warren Stevens). Later, Rojan crushes the pod, snuffing out Thompson's life. Cobb, born in 1947, is the daughter of acclaimed actor Lee J. Cobb, who introduced the character of Willy Loman in the original Broadway production of *Death of a Salesman*. "By Any Other Name" marked the first screen role for the actress, who worked previously as a Playboy Bunny. Julie Cobb, whose career is ongoing, has since appeared in more than eighty movies and TV shows including *The Incredible Hulk* (1978), *Starman* (1987), and *Lois & Clark: The New Adventures of Superman* (1996). She costarred in the highly rated 1979 TV movie *Salem's Lot*, based on the Stephen King novel, and landed featured roles in the short-lived sitcoms *A Year at the Top* (1977) and *Charles in Charge* (1984–85). From 1986 to 2006, she was married to actor James Cromwell, who played Zefram Cochrane in the movie *Star Trek: First Contact* (1996) and the *Star Trek: Enterprise* episode "In a Mirror, Darkly, Part I" (2005). Cromwell also played other characters in earlier episodes of *The Next Generation* and *Deep Space Nine*. Julie Cobb's daughter, actress Rosemary Morgan, carried on the family tradition by making her first screen appearance on *Star Trek: Voyager* in 1996.

## Robert Herron

Robert Herron made a brief but memorable appearance—or, rather, disappearance—as Sam, the crewman mentally zapped out of existence by Charlie Evans (Robert Walker Jr.) in "Charlie X." Sticklers may question his redshirt status since Sam is out of uniform, resting after a workout in the ship's gymnasium, when he laughs at Charlie's difficulty learning judo from Captain Kirk and incurs the wrath of the boy with psychic superpowers. Although he was uncredited in "Charlie X," Herron received on-screen acknowledgment for his portrayal of the mytho-historical Klingon warrior Kahless the Unforgettable in "The Savage Curtain." In this episode, Kirk and Spock fight alongside Abraham Lincoln and the legendary Surak of Vulcan against four notorious adversaries, including Kahless (founder of the Klingon Empire) and Genghis Khan. Herron's first job on *Star Trek* was doubling for star Jeffrey Hunter in the series' rejected original pilot, "The Cage." Herron, a former Navy boxing champion, is another veteran stuntman, stunt supervisor, and bit player whose credits stretch all the way back to Anthony Mann's Western classic *Winchester '73* in 1950 and continue as recently as the TV movie *Aces 'n Eights* in 2008. In between, he has worked on more than 240 movies and television shows, including the science fiction films *Soylent Green* (1973), *Death Race 2000* (1975), *Logan's Run* (1977), and *The Black Hole* (1979), and two episodes of *The X-Files* (1998–99). Over the years Herron has doubled for Tony Curtis, Ernest Borgnine, and Robert Conrad, among other stars.

## John Arndt

John Arndt made five appearances on *Star Trek*, receiving screen credit three times. In "The Man Trap," the first *Trek* episode to air, he played Sturgeon, a hapless security guard killed by the Salt Vampire. In this early episode the traditional uniform designations (gold for command, blue for science and medical, red for engineering and security) had not yet been established. As a result, Sturgeon wears a blue tunic in what is otherwise a redshirt role. Arndt made four more appearances on *Star Trek* as crewman Fields, receiving credit in "Balance of Terror," "Dagger of the Mind," and "Space Seed" but not in "Miri." As Fields, Arndt wore the appropriate red tunic. Arndt is an actor, not a stunt performer, whose screen career began with *Star Trek*. He has worked very sporadically in movies and television since, with thirteen roles spread out from 1966 to 1994. His later work includes appearances on *Mission: Impossible* (1967) and in the ultra-low budget horror film *The Deadly Spawn* (1983).

## Sean Morgan

Like John Arndt, Sean Morgan played a recurring character—Lieutenant O'Neil, featured in "Return of the Archons" and "The Tholian Web." He also appeared as crewman Brenner in "The Balance of Terror" and an Ekosian soldier in "Patterns of Force." Morgan gained redshirt status for his turn as engineer Harper, who is vaporized by the out-of-control M-5 computer in "The Ultimate Computer." The actor also worked on "The Corbomite Maneuver" and "This Side of Paradise," but his scenes were cut. Morgan's first screen work was a recurring role as Sean, one of Rick Nelson's fraternity brothers on *The Adventures of Ozzie and Harriet* (1964–66). Morgan was a former college classmate of casting director Joe D'Agosta, who found small parts for his friend whenever possible on

*Trek* and helped him land roles on other Desilu Productions series such as *The Lucy Show* and *Mannix*. Morgan's other credits include *Voyage to the Bottom of the Sea* (1966) and *Harry and the Hendersons* (1987). He eventually gave up acting to pursue more lucrative opportunities in the financial services industry.

## Robert E. L. Bralver

Robert Bralver played Grant, a security officer who's killed by the Capellans when he instinctively reaches for his phaser at the sight of the Klingon Kras, in "Friday's Child." Bralver, another experienced stuntman, stunt coordinator, and bit player, also appeared as an unnamed yeoman in "Is There in Truth No Beauty?" and as an engineer in "The Tholian Web." He doubled for DeForest Kelley in "For the World Is Hollow and I Have Touched the Sky" and later did stunt work on *Star Trek: The Motion Picture* (1979) and on the *Deep Space Nine* episode "Blood Oath." Grant was his only credited *Trek* role. Bralver has performed and/or coordinated stunts for more than fifty movies and TV shows, beginning on *I Spy* in 1965. He has served as stunt coordinator for several television programs, including *Battlestar Galactica* (1978), *Knight Rider* (1982–84), and *Diagnosis: Murder* (1993–99), where he worked on 135 episodes. His most impressive stunt was making the unusual leap from stunt work to screenwriting and directing. He penned teleplays or stories for the action-oriented TV shows *Emergency!* and *Kojak* in the 1970s. As a director, he helmed episodes of *Knight Rider* and *The A-Team*, among other series.

## Arnold Lessing

Arnold Lessing played Lieutenant Carlisle—an inferior "biological unit" vaporized by the unhinged space probe NOMAD in "The Changeling." He made a half-dozen screen appearances in the 1960s, including the cheesy B-film *The Beach Girls and the Monster* (1965)—but Lessing was primarily a musician. For that film, in which he played the romantic lead, Lessing wrote and performed the song "More Than Wanting You." In the late 1960s, he gave up on acting to concentrate on his music, but—to the surprise of no one who's seen *The Beach Girls and the Monster*—failed to find success as a singer-songwriter. However, as a gifted flamenco guitarist, he taught guitar at Santa Monica College for more than thirty years, beginning in the early 1970s.

# Cloaking Device

## Little-Recognized Contributors

**S**tar Trek turned its creator and principal cast members into house-hold names. Even the show's behind-the-scenes leaders—such as Bob Justman, Dorothy Fontana, Matt Jefferies, Bill Theiss and Fred Phillips—eventually earned due recognition for their superlative efforts. But, for a variety reasons, a handful of writers, craftspeople, and actors performed important functions on the program without receiving on-screen credit. As a result, many of these have yet to receive the accolades their contributions merited.

### Isaac Asimov

Gene Roddenberry solicited stories and scripts from many esteemed science fiction authors. But Isaac Asimov, without penning a single teleplay, had greater influence on the development of *Star Trek* than any other sci-fi writer.

Asimov, a grand master of the genre who garnered six Hugos and three Nebula Awards in his lifetime, is best remembered for his panoramic, centuries-spanning *Foundation* series and for his many novels and stories about robots. He coined the term "robotics" in his 1941 short story "Liar!" Roddenberry first met Asimov in early September 1966 at WorldCon in Cleveland, under slightly embarrassing circumstances. Not realizing who Asimov was, Roddenberry shushed the author, who was chatting with a friend during the screening of *Star Trek*'s as-yet unaired pilot, "Where No Man Has Gone Before." Afterward, Asimov graciously admitted he had been rude. Three months later Asimov wrote a short article for *TV Guide* bemoaning the poor quality and scientific inaccuracy of television sci-fi, including *Star Trek*. Roddenberry, chagrined, wrote a letter to Asimov defending his program as an earnest attempt to bring adult-oriented science fiction to TV.

This letter sparked a friendly correspondence between the two men. Asimov did an about-face and soon began promoting *Star Trek* whenever the opportunity arose. He was one of many authors who participated in the two "Save *Star Trek*" write-in campaigns. More importantly, Asimov began to suggest ways the show could be improved. Roddenberry deeply respected Asimov and implemented many of the writer's ideas. Asimov's input was not limited to scientific concerns but also included suggestions regarding character development and other storytelling issues. When Roddenberry expressed concern that Mr. Spock's popularity had eclipsed that of Captain Kirk and irritation with the rift this had created between the show's two stars, Asimov suggested that the two characters function more as a team. In a July 1967 letter to Roddenberry (reprinted in Herb Solow and Bob Justman's book *Inside Star Trek*), Asimov wrote that Kirk and Spock should "meet various menaces together, with the one saving the life of the other on occasion. The idea of this would be to get people to think of Kirk when they think of Spock."

Asimov remained a booster for the series even after its cancellation and was a guest of honor at the first *Star Trek* convention in 1972. Roddenberry hired Asimov to serve as scientific advisor for *Star Trek: The Motion Picture* (1979). This was the author's only official *Trek* credit, but the franchise paid tribute to him several times over the years. On *The Next Generation*, Commander Data was given a "positronic" brain, a term lifted directly from Asimov's robot stories. Asimov and his "Three Laws of Robotics" (programming that prevents androids from intentionally harming human beings) are mentioned by name in the *TNG* episode "Datalore." The *Deep Space Nine* yarn "Far Beyond the Stars" takes place during the Golden Age of pulp science fiction and recasts the show's regulars as the staff of a fictional SF magazine that supposedly publishes stories by Isaac Asimov and other famous writers. And the *Voyager* episode "Scorpion" features a character named Captain Amasov (commander of the Starship *Endeavor*), whose name was intended as a subtle tip of the cap to Asimov.

## Majel Barrett

Majel Barrett's contributions to the development of *Star Trek* went far beyond her performances as Nurse Chapel and the voice of the *Enterprise* computer. She was Roddenberry's most trusted confidant and sounding board throughout the development and production of the show. Roddenberry made almost no major decisions about the program without asking for Barrett's opinion. In author Yvonne Fern's book *Gene Roddenberry: The Last Conversation*, a half-dozen prominent behind-the-scenes personnel, including associate producer Bob Justman, unanimously credit Barrett as the one person besides Roddenberry who did the most to shape the *Star Trek* universe. After her marriage to Roddenberry, fans fondly referred to her as "The First Lady of Star Trek." She became the primary standard-bearer for the franchise following her husband's death in 1991.

## Wah Chang

Sculptor Wah Chang produced a variety of iconic specialty props for *Star Trek* but never received credit for his contributions due to union rules. Since Chang's Projects Unlimited wasn't a union shop, he was prohibited from working on *Star Trek*. To bypass this restriction, Associate Producer Justman invented the fiction that the show was simply purchasing ready-made props from Chang, which was allowed under union regulations. However, Chang could not receive

**Balok's Alter-Ego**

The intimidating "alter ego" of the mysterious Balock, who plays a cat-and-mouse game with Captain Kirk and his crew in "The Corbomite Maneuver," was one of sculptor Wah Chang's many uncredited contributions. (1976 Topps trading card)

an on-screen credit for his contributions, which included the iconic communicator, phaser, and tricorder props; the monster suits for the Gorn from "Arena" and the Salt Vampire from "The Man Trap"; the Balok puppet from "The Corbomite Maneuver"; and the original Romulan Bird of Prey spacecraft from "Balance of Terror." Due to budget constraints, Chang's association with *Star Trek* ended midway through Season Two, but by then his creations had placed the sculptor's indelible stamp on the program. For more about Chang and his work, see Chapter 12 ("Equipment Locker").

## Albert Whitlock

Like Chang, matte painter Albert Whitlock established the look of *Star Trek* without receiving a single screen credit. Whitlock's exotic alien landscapes added color to and enhanced the realism of several classic *Trek* adventures. For "The Cage," he created the romantic, Indian-influenced vistas of Rigel IV; for "Where No Man Has Gone Before," he painted the grungy, refinery-like towers and tubes of mining colony Delta Vega; and for "A Taste of Armageddon," he depicted the gleaming cityscapes of Eminar VII. His work also appeared in "Court Martial" and "The Devil in the Dark." Whitlock's mattes were reused in several later episodes, including "Dagger of the Mind," "The Conscience of the King," "The Menagerie," "The Gamesters of Triskelion," "Wink of an Eye" and "Requiem for Methuselah."

Matte paintings were utilized to create elaborate alien exteriors that could be realized no other cost-effective way using the technology of the era. While they functioned spectacularly as special effects, Whitlock's mattes (painted in oils on masonite) also remain impressive as works of art, especially when viewed in person. His Rigel IV painting was displayed as part of *Star Trek: The Exhibition*, a collection of props, costumes, and other artifacts that began touring science museums across the U.S. in 2009. Unfortunately, in 2006, when *Star Trek* was remastered in high definition for release on HD-DVD and Blu-ray, some of Whitlock's evocative paintings were digitally "touched up" or scrapped entirely in favor of new, computer-generated panoramas.

Whitlock was born in England in 1915 and began his association with motion pictures at Gaumont Studios at age fourteen, building sets and working as a grip. At

This view of Starbase 6 (from "The Menagerie"), one of artist Albert Whitlock's most beautiful matte paintings, was immortalized on a 1976 Topps trading card.

Gaumont, Whitlock worked on several projects with Alfred Hitchcock, creating mattes and miniature effects for seminal thrillers such as *The Man Who Knew Too Much* (1934). He continued to work with Hitch through the years and created the eerie, crow-covered backdrop used in the final shot of *The Birds* (1963). Walt Disney brought Whitlock to America in 1950 and utilized the artist's unique talents on feature films such as *20,000 Leagues Under the Sea* (1954) and *Darby O'Gill and the Little People* (1959), as well as TV series like *Zorro* (1957) and *Walt Disney's Wonderful World of Color* (1964). Whitlock also helped design Disneyland. He won Academy Awards in 1975 and '76 for his contributions to the big-budget disaster films *Earthquake* and *The Hindenburg*, both of which featured amazingly realistic (and sometimes terrifying) matte effects. In all, Whitlock worked on more than 150 films and televisions shows, covering nearly every conceivable genre. He died in 1999 at age eighty-four.

## Little-Recognized Recurring Cast Members

Think you can name all of *Star Trek*'s regular cast members? Maybe you can, but probably not. (If the names Bill Blackburn, Eddie Paskey, and Frank Da Vinci just rolled off your tongue, feel free to skip to the next subheading.) That's because, in addition to the show's instantly recognizable stars and supporting players, a half-dozen performers appeared regularly on *Star Trek* in relative anonymity. Most of them had few lines, and some never earned a screen credit, but they were present nonetheless—stationed in engineering, the transporter room, and even on the bridge, or standing in for the show's leads during fight scenes.

**Bill Blackburn** appeared in sixty-one *Star Trek* adventures, usually as DeForest Kelley's stunt double or as a gold-shirted extra (often a navigator or helmsman, sometimes referred to as Lieutenant Hadley). Blackburn, a former professional ice skater, also played numerous other bits and was the actor inside the rabbit suit in "Shore Leave." Similarly **Eddie Paskey,** William Shatner's stunt double, appeared in fifty-seven episodes, frequently as the red-shirted Lieutenant Leslie. Paskey also played the truck driver who runs down Edith Keeler in "The City on the Edge of Forever." He later portrayed Admiral Leslie in the pilot episode of the fan-produced Internet series *Star Trek: The New Voyages.* Neither Blackburn nor Paskey ever received a screen credit and very seldom spoke a line, yet both played in more installments than George Takei (fifty-one episodes), Walter Koenig (thirty-six), or Majel Barrett (thirty-four). **Frank da Vinci,** who doubled for Leonard Nimoy, made a total of fifty-one uncredited appearances, thirty-two of those as the blue-shirted Lieutenant Brent. He played Vulcan background characters in both "Amok Time" and "Journey to Babel." Recurring extra **Roger Holloway** made thirty-three uncredited appearances, often as security officer Lemli, and later turned up on an episode of *Deep Space Nine.*

Burly, blonde British actor **John Winston** played bit parts in eleven *Star Trek* adventures, usually as the red-shirted Lieutenant Kyle, often seen on the bridge or in the transporter room. Although Winston received screen credit and occasionally had dialogue, his character was never developed. In "The Immunity Syndrome," William Shatner repeatedly mispronounces the character's name as "Cowell." Nevertheless, Kyle appeared in more episodes than Grace Lee Whitney's Janice Rand. In "Mirror, Mirror," Winston played both Kyle and Kyle's evil Mirror Universe twin, who the Evil Spock punishes with an "agonizer." The actor worked in episodes scattered throughout all three seasons and returned as Commander Kyle in *Star Trek II: The Wrath of Khan* (1982). (The Kyle character also appeared in six episodes of the *Star Trek* animated series but was voiced by James Doohan.) Winston also portrayed Captain Jefferies in the pilot episode of the fan-created Internet series *Star Trek: The New Voyages,* where he appeared alongside Eddie Paskey.

## David Soul

Before gaining fame as Detective Ken Hutchinson on the cheesy cop show *Starsky and Hutch* (1975–79), David Soul played a young native of planet Gamma Trianguli VI in "The Apple." Barely recognizable in a blond bouffant wig and red body paint, Soul (understandably) seems a bit awkward as Makora, who angers the godlike supercomputer Vaal by kissing his girlfriend Sayana (Shari Nims), copying the behavior of *Enterprise* crew members Pavel Chekov (Koenig) and Martha Landon (Celeste Yarnall). Although dozens of unknown actors played small roles on *Star Trek*, Soul (born David Richard Solberg in Chicago in 1943) was the only one to later achieve stardom. Soul began his performing career as a folksinger, opening concerts for the likes of the Byrds and the Lovin' Spoonful. He parlayed his *Starsky and Hutch* fame into a successful recording career, cutting a soft-rock album that included the No. 1 single "Don't Give Up on Us" in 1976.

The versatile James Doohan not only played stalwart chief engineer Montgomery Scott but supplied the voices of several other characters on both the live-action *Star Trek* and the later animated series.

He followed with four more Top 20 singles and two Top 10 albums between 1976 and '78. In the mid-1990s, Soul immigrated to England, where he became a regular on the West End stage. He acquired British citizenship in 2004.

## Man of a Thousand Voices

James Doohan became forever linked with indomitable Chief Engineer Montgomery Scott, but Scotty wasn't the only role Doohan played on *Star Trek*. He was a masterful voice actor with a flair for accents that went far beyond Scotty's familiar brogue, and directors often called upon Doohan to supply off-camera voice-overs. He was never credited for this voice work, and no official record of these contributions has been compiled, but the actor may have provided additional voices to a dozen classic *Trek* episodes or more. It's known that Doohan voiced the following characters: Trelaine's parents from "The Squire of Gothos"; Providers One and Two from "The Gamesters of Triskelion"; Sargon from "Return to Tomorrow"; the M-5 Computer from "The Ultimate Computer"; a radio announcer in "A Piece of the Action"; a NASA technician in "Assignment: Earth"; and the Oracle from "For the World Is Hollow and I Have Touched the Sky." Doohan worked even more extensively on the *Star Trek* animated series, where he voiced more than fifty characters in addition to Scotty. In the lone animated adventure in which Scotty does not appear—"The Slaver Weapon"—Doohan supplied the voices of the three Kzinti aliens who menace Spock, Uhura, and Sulu.

## Chef Roddenberry

In "Charlie X," the telekinetically superpowered Charlie Evans (Robert Walker Jr.) overhears Captain Kirk asking the *Enterprise*'s chef to try to make meat loaf look like turkey for Thanksgiving dinner. A few minutes later, the astonished cook calls Kirk to report that "Sir, I put meat loaf in the ovens. There's turkeys in there now—real turkeys!" The voice of the galley chief was supplied by the Great Chef of the Galaxy himself, Gene Roddenberry. It was the only acting role of his career.

# Private Little Wars

## Rivalries and Feuds

**S**tar Trek was many things—a breakthrough in adult-oriented sci-fi television, an uplifting vision of the future, etc.—but it was never a candidate for one of those "Best Places to Work" lists. The grinding pressure to produce the ambitious series on the tight schedules and skimpy budgets of 1960s TV could be crushing. And this stress was only worsened by contentious relationships between members of the cast and creative leadership. The camaraderie displayed by the *Enterprise* crew on-screen belied the interpersonal tension that roiled the show off-screen.

### William Shatner vs. Leonard Nimoy

When William Shatner signed on with *Star Trek*, it was with the understanding that his would be the face of the program. After all, he was the best-known and highest-paid member of the cast, and he played the captain. However, within weeks of the show's debut, it became apparent that the character creating the most interest was not Shatner's heroic Captain Kirk but rather Leonard Nimoy's half-human First Officer Spock. Critics praised Nimoy's work (the actor would earn three consecutive Emmy nominations), and Nimoy received much more fan mail than anyone else in the cast. This irritated Shatner. "I was now faced with no longer being the only star of this show," Shatner wrote in his book *Star Trek Memories*. "And to be unflatteringly frank, it bugged me." He felt jealous and insecure. "I wasn't proud of these feelings, but they were simply the natural human reaction," he wrote.

Shatner's "natural human" feelings boiled over early one morning when a *Life* magazine photojournalist arrived in the dressing room to snap pictures of Nimoy's transformation into Spock. Shatner, who, along with Nimoy, had an early makeup call (to affix his working toupee), resented the intrusion and ordered the photographer away. Nimoy was furious and pointed out that the visitor's presence had been approved by both producer Gene Roddenberry and Desilu's publicity office. "To which I apparently replied, 'Well, it wasn't approved by me!'" Shatner recalls in his autobiography, *Up Till Now*. "Why I responded this way I certainly don't remember, but my envy certainly had something to do with it." Nimoy stormed off to his dressing room and refused to report to work until Roddenberry came down and smoothed over the actor's ruffled ego.

Shatner's attitude accelerated Nimoy's rapidly growing impression that he was underappreciated (not to mention underpaid) and that his character was getting short shrift. He lobbied continuously for scripts with larger and more interesting roles for Spock. Meanwhile, Shatner remained protective of Kirk's primacy to the show's teleplays. An on-again, off-again series of skirmishes ensued. In his memoir *I Am Spock*, Nimoy characterizes the tension between himself and Shatner as "sibling rivalry," with Roddenberry (or associate producer Bob Justman or costar DeForest Kelley) stepping in to play Daddy and resolve disputes between "two squabbling kids."

The situation festered into the show's third season, when an exasperated Fred Freiberger (who replaced Roddenberry as the show's line producer during its final year) finally corralled Shatner, Nimoy, and Roddenberry and demanded that the Great Bird of the Galaxy clarify once and for all who was the star of *Star Trek*. Roddenberry tried to evade the question, but when pressed he stated that Shatner was the star. This response inflicted further injury on Roddenberry's already bruised relationship with Nimoy.

Years later, Nimoy stressed that even at their worst he and Shatner respected one another and enjoyed each other's work, and their differences arose from similarly competitive temperaments. Once the show was off the air, and they began appearing together at *Star Trek* conventions without having to compete for lines in a script, Shatner and Nimoy finally buried the hatchet and became fast friends. They have remained close ever since.

## Leonard Nimoy vs. Gene Roddenberry

Tension developed between Nimoy and Roddenberry early on and steadily escalated throughout *Star Trek*'s first season. On a purely personal level the two failed to connect, in part because Nimoy considered Roddenberry's frequent practical jokes (and not only those aimed at him) insensitive and in poor taste. More significantly, both Nimoy and Roddenberry were extremely protective of Spock. Each considered himself the character's creator, yet the two sometimes disagreed about how the Vulcan should behave or speak in a given scene.

When Spock emerged as the series' breakout character, Roddenberry and Desilu executives feared that Nimoy would demand more money—as indeed he did following Season One. Reluctant to establish precedents that might work against them in future negotiations, Desilu took a hard line in a series of petty disputes with the actor. For instance, Nimoy requested pens and pencils to reply to his copious fan mail. Even though Desilu provided Nimoy a $100 allowance toward the salary of a secretary, supplied *Star Trek* letterhead and publicity photos, and paid postage costs, the studio refused to give Nimoy any pens or pencils. Nimoy was also rebuffed when he attempted to install a telephone in his office (even at his own expense). At that point, the show's entire cast and crew were sharing a single soundstage telephone. And Nimoy had to resort to theatrics—asking his secretary to feign heatstroke—to get a window air conditioner installed in his office, even with temperatures climbing toward 100 degrees. Although Roddenberry wasn't directly involved in all these conflicts, Nimoy nevertheless blamed the Great Bird for refusing to intervene on his behalf.

The situation reached crisis proportions in the interim between Seasons One and Two. A gaping disparity in compensation existed between the show's two leads during its first season: Shatner received a salary of $5,000 per week as well as 20 percent profit participation. He was also guaranteed a $500 per week raise every season the series was renewed. Nimoy was paid $1,250 per week with no profit participation. (Most of *Star Trek*'s other cast members were paid around $600 per show and were not guaranteed work in every episode.) As expected, Nimoy wanted to renegotiate before production began on Season Two. However, Roddenberry balked when Nimoy's agent, Alex Brewis, demanded $9,000 per week, star billing, profit participation, and a percentage of the show's merchandising, among other items. Alarmed, Roddenberry, Herb Solow, and Desilu's other executive leadership, including attorney and contract negotiator Edwin Perlstein, considered recasting the role of Spock. Among those considered for the part were Mark Lenard, who had played a Romulan in "Balance of Terror" and would go on to portray Spock's father, Sarek, in "Journey to Babel," and Larry Montaigne, who had also appeared in "Balance of Terror" and would play Spock's rival for his betrothed, T'Pring, in "Amok Time." However, NBC was adamant that Nimoy be retained. Eventually, the two sides agreed on a new

Dividing the profits from *Mr. Spock's Music from Outer Space*, the first of four (!) albums Leonard Nimoy recorded for Dot Records between 1967 and 1969, exacerbated the strained relations between producer Gene Roddenberry and the actor-"singer."

salary of $2,500 per week with better billing, more story input, and limited profit participation. The rest of the cast received smaller pay increases.

Even with the salary negotiation behind them, however, Nimoy and Roddenberry continued to clash. The next major dustup came when Dot Records signed Nimoy to a record deal. The company's first Nimoy release was *Mr. Spock's Music from Outer Space* (1967), featuring a cover photo of the actor-"singer" in full makeup, holding a model of the *Enterprise*. The album opens with Alexander Courage's *Star Trek* title theme. Roddenberry demanded, and eventually received, a share of the royalties. To avoid future conflicts, Nimoy's association with *Star Trek* was de-emphasized—and eventually eliminated—from the jacket artwork on his three subsequent Dot Records releases. Meanwhile, Nimoy continued to argue with Roddenberry over the development of the character of Spock. His disagreements with the Great Bird and other studio executives continued well after the cancellation of the show. The rebirth of *Star Trek* as a feature film franchise was delayed by an outstanding lawsuit the actor filed against Paramount Pictures for royalties from the sale of *Star Trek* merchandise. Nevertheless, in *I Am Spock*, Nimoy wrote that he is "deeply respectful of Gene's creativity, his talent and his sharp intelligence," and for Roddenberry's tenacious fight with NBC prior to Season One to keep Spock aboard the *Enterprise*. "For that, I'll always be grateful to him," Nimoy wrote.

## John D. F. Black vs. Gene Roddenberry

John D. F. Black served as *Star Trek*'s first story editor. He was also among the earliest victims of Roddenberry's infamous practical jokes. One afternoon Roddenberry asked the newly arrived Black to interview an aspiring actress. The actress was actually Majel Barrett, who pretended to try to seduce the befuddled Black in order to win a part on the show. With Black squirming in his chair, Roddenberry and several cast members burst into the room, laughing hysterically. The embarrassed story editor shrugged off that incident but eventually grew frustrated by his lack of on-screen credit for the teleplays he polished. He also received no credit for coauthoring the show's famous opening narration. "The Naked Time" remains his only official *Trek* writing credit. Under extreme pressure to meet airdates during the show's inaugural season, Black was tasked with writing an "envelope" that would surround footage from "The Cage," *Star Trek*'s rejected original pilot, and create a two-part epic. Roddenberry promised the network a two-parter that would wow viewers. More importantly, it would buy the show desperately needed breathing room in its production schedule. Black responded with the framing sequence for "The Menagerie," with Spock commandeering the *Enterprise* to transport the disfigured Captain Pike to Talos IV. In an October 7, 1966, memo to associate producer Bob Justman (reprinted in Justman's book *Inside Star Trek*), Roddenberry referred to "The Menagerie" as "fifty or sixty pages of pure genius." Nevertheless, he rewrote the teleplay so extensively that, when it was done, he saw no need to credit Black. The finished script was credited entirely to Roddenberry, who had penned the original "Cage." Black filed a grievance with the Writers Guild, demanding a credit, but lost. Embittered, Black quit the show in midseason and was temporarily replaced by Steve Carabastos. By the start of Season Two, Carabastos had been replaced in turn by Dorothy Fontana.

## Harlan Ellison vs. Gene Roddenberry

Harlan Ellison was among the first of many acclaimed science fiction authors Roddenberry approached about writing for *Star Trek*. By 1966, Ellison had already won multiple Hugo and Nebula Awards for his groundbreaking short stories. He was also an experienced, talented screenwriter who had earned a Writers Guild Award for his classic *Outer Limits* episode "Demon with a Glass Hand." The lone *Star Trek* episode Ellison penned—"The City on the Edge of Forever"—is widely regarded as the best of them all. This is the show where a delirious Dr. McCoy uses an alien time-travel device to return to Depression-era Earth and then alters history, with devastating consequences. Kirk and Spock follow McCoy into the past, where Kirk falls in love with beautiful young social activist Edith Keeler (Joan Collins)—only to discover that in order to correct the timeline, he must allow Keeler to die.

The reason Ellison wrote only one *Trek* teleplay is because he was irate with Roddenberry for making numerous changes to his original script. Ellison labored over "City" for months, writing and rewriting at Roddenberry's request before turning in what he thought would be the final product. Nevertheless, major changes were made to the scenario by Roddenberry and his writing staff (including Steve Carabastos, Gene Coon, and Dorothy Fontana). In Ellison's original version, Kirk and Spock travel back in time to undo damage caused by a murderous, drug-dealing crewman who escapes into the past. These elements were eliminated to avoid flack from network censors. The original script also includes a greater role for the Guardians, a race of time travelers who live in the titular "City on the Edge of Forever." In a cost-cutting measure, this setting was also eliminated, reducing Ellison's title to a poetic non sequitur. Perhaps most importantly, in Ellison's version it's the coldly logical Mr. Spock, not the love-struck Kirk, who prevents Keeler from being saved.

Despite the extensive rewrites, and even though he considered removing his name from it, Ellison received sole credit on the final version of the teleplay. But he was nevertheless incensed by the alterations. The author submitted his *original* "City on the Edge of Forever" script to the Writers Guild of America, where it won Most Outstanding Dramatic Episode Teleplay for 1967–68. After receiving the award, Ellison thumbed his nose at Roddenberry, who was in the audience. Roddenberry, not to be outdone, submitted the *final* version of "The City on the Edge of Forever" for consideration at the 1968 WorldCon science fiction convention, where it won a Hugo Award. Ironically, since Roddenberry didn't attend the event, Ellison collected the trophy. The two bad-mouthed one

The "Gang of Four" (from left to right, Walter Koenig, Nichelle Nichols, James Doohan, and George Takei) all complained bitterly that William Shatner stole their lines and minimized their characters. But none of them confronted the star at the time.

another for decades, with Roddenberry often mischaracterizing elements of Ellison's teleplay (for instance, making the erroneous claim that the original version had Scotty dealing drugs). Yet Ellison was invited to pitch an idea for the first *Trek* feature film in 1978 and, at the request of director Nimoy, consulted on the script for *Star Trek IV: The Voyage Home* (1986). Ellison got the final word by publishing his original "City on the Edge" teleplay in book form following

Roddenberry's death. This volume included a vindictive introductory essay in which he assailed Roddenberry's "demented lies" and dismissed the broadcast version of the story as "crippled, eviscerated, [and] fucked-up."

## James Doohan, Walter Koenig, Nichelle Nichols, and George Takei vs. William Shatner

*Star Trek*'s "Gang of Four" (so nicknamed by Walter Koenig) has vented its loathing toward star William Shatner countless times over the years. At conventions, in published interviews, and in their memoirs, Koenig, James Doohan, Nichelle Nichols, and even affable George Takei repeatedly have blasted Shatner for his treatment of *Trek*'s supporting cast. All four have complained about Shatner's habit of stealing lines from their characters, often pulling directors aside and suggesting that dialogue originally scripted for one of the supporting cast be given to Captain Kirk. Episodes were written with little moments designed to flesh out the characters of Scotty, Chekov, Uhura, and Sulu and to provide screen time for the supporting cast. But Shatner, in his efforts to "protect" Kirk against the growing footprint of Spock in the show's teleplays, believed it was essential that his character receive as many lines as the Vulcan, or more, and wasn't particular about the source of the dialogue. If Shatner became involved in a screenplay early on, his suggested alterations might remove a supporting character from the story entirely—costing his fellow actor a week's work (and a week's pay).

Shatner "made it plain to anyone on the set that he was the Big Picture and the rest of us were no more important than the props," Nichols wrote in her autobiography *Beyond Uhura*. "Anything that didn't focus exclusively on him threatened his turf, and he never failed to make his displeasure known." Resentment quickly grew among the supporting players. Doohan was especially disgruntled and often railed against Shatner at conventions. However, in his autobiography *Beam Me Up, Scotty*, Doohan wrote simply that "I just don't like the man" and ventured: "It's a shame that he wasn't secure enough in himself or his status to refrain from practicing that sort of behavior."

For his part, Shatner claims to have been unaware of the supporting cast's feelings toward him until he set about interviewing them for his 1993 book *Star Trek Memories*. After concluding his interview with Nichols, the actress finally let Shatner know what she and the rest of the cast had never previously had the courage to reveal: That they despised their former Captain. Doohan refused to speak to Shatner at all. In 2010, Koenig blasted Shatner face-to-face in an episode of *Shatner's Raw Nerve*, an interview show hosted by the erstwhile Kirk. But in his 1997 memoir *Warped Factors*, Koenig took a more conciliatory approach. "Bill Shatner has repeatedly said that he was not aware that we felt the way we did," Koenig wrote. "Knowing his tunnel-visioned approach to his work I think that is possible. If that is true then we must share the burden of guilt with him."

## George Takei vs. Walter Koenig

Can a rivalry exist if only one of the two involved parties is aware of it? If so, then one briefly flared up between George Takei and Walter Koenig. Takei had signed on to appear in John Wayne's Vietnam War film *The Green Berets* during the summer break between *Star Trek*'s first and second seasons. But when shooting of the movie ran long, Takei was forced to miss the first several weeks of filming for Season Two. As a result, episodes originally written to feature Sulu were hastily reworked for the show's new addition, Ensign Pavel Chekov, played by Koenig. In his autobiography *To the Stars*, Takei writes that he was "heartsick and resentful" toward "the person to whom I had lost all my lines, an actor named Walter Koenig who had just sailed into our second season on the wings of fate, wearing that silly Prince Valiant wig." Yet Takei—who by all accounts was one of the most agreeable and widely liked members of the cast—never voiced his jealousy. In fact, Takei remained so pleasant and endearing that Koenig wasn't even aware of Takei's feelings until the publication of *To the Stars* in 2007! Instead, Takei overcame his initial resentment and forged a warm and lasting friendship with his onetime rival. In 2008, Koenig served as best man at Takei's wedding to longtime partner Brad Altman.

# The Deadly Year

## What Went Wrong with Season Three

By the end of its first season, *Star Trek* was firing on all nacelles, but most fans consider Season Two the show's zenith. Nearly all the twenty-six episodes that first aired in 1967–68 were superb. Classic adventures that originated that season include "Mirror, Mirror," the gripping parallel universe yarn featuring an evil, goateed Mr. Spock; "The Doomsday Machine," a spacefaring variation on the theme of *Moby Dick*; "Amok Time" and "Journey Babel," the first stories to explore Vulcan culture in depth; and "The Trouble with Tribbles" and "A Piece of the Action," the show's two funniest installments. In general, the series was imaginative and exciting, action oriented but rich in characterization, thought-provoking yet (usually) unpretentious. The working rapport between Kirk and Spock gelled, and the playful bickering between Spock and McCoy became a fixture. Ensign Chekov joined the bridge crew, and the supporting characters gained depth with increased screen time. For the second year in a row, *Star Trek* earned an Emmy nomination for Outstanding Dramatic Series.

Then it all seemed to fall apart with Season Three.

*Star Trek*'s devoted fans, many of whom had showered NBC with cards and letters to help save the series from cancellation the previous spring, eagerly anticipated the start of a new season's worth of brilliant science fiction. On the night of September 20, 1968, Season Three finally began—with "Spock's Brain," widely reviled as the series' single weakest episode. In this notorious clunker, Spock's brain is stolen and plugged into a supercomputer that does all the thinking for a civilization comprised entirely of gorgeous but dim-witted women. Kirk leads an away team to the planet's surface to recover the brain, bringing along Spock's body, which somehow survived the brainectomy and now functions by remote control. When the end credits rolled on that fateful September night, fans must have stared slack-jawed at their TV sets, wondering if the writers of *Lost in Space* had taken over the show.

The truth behind *Trek*'s third-season decline was more complicated. It begins in July 1967, during the series' Season Two heyday.

### Lucy Sells Desilu

It was the Summer of Love. But even as tens of thousands of young people with flowers in their hair descended on San Francisco, corporate behemoths were

The remote-controlled Mr. Spock stands around uselessly while Kirk berates Kara (Marj Dusay) in this scene from "Spock's Brain," which opened *Star Trek*'s troubled third season.

gobbling up Hollywood. In 1967, the Seven Arts conglomerate bought the iconic but cash-strapped Warner Brothers Pictures, and Transamerica took over the enfeebled United Artists. The executives who authorized these deals knew nothing about moviemaking (Transamerica, for example, was a life insurance company whose other investment properties included Budget Rent-a-Car), but they recognized that the studios were underperforming assets that might regain value over time. Gulf + Western began the corporate takeover of Hollywood a year earlier by purchasing the tottering Paramount Pictures. Now the company wanted to expand into television and had its eye on neighboring Desilu Productions. The two studios' parking lots were separated by a chain link fence.

Desilu had staged a comeback since the arrival of executives Oscar Katz and Herb Solow in 1964. It now had four series in production (*The Lucy Show, Mission: Impossible,* the detective show *Mannix,* and *Star Trek*) and others in development, but the studio remained unprofitable due to cost overruns. Ball—who became the first woman to head a Hollywood studio when she bought out her ex-husband Desi Arnaz in 1960—had grown weary of serving as Desilu's president and chief executive officer while also starring in her own weekly series. On July 17, 1967, while director Marc Daniels was shooting "The Changeling," Gulf + Western purchased Desilu for $17 million and officially renamed the company Paramount Pictures Television. Ball realized a profit on her initial investment but lost hundreds of millions of dollars in future revenues when the *Star Trek* franchise became enormously lucrative in the 1980s. Unfortunately, Gulf + Western—whose other divisions included sugar plantations in the Dominican Republic, textile mills, and auto parts factories, in addition to media properties such as Stax Records and Simon & Schuster Publishing—also failed to realize the potential value of *Star Trek*. Although there was little immediate impact from the sale on the show's creative team, the parent company's later meddling and penny-pinching would damage the series.

## Gene Coon and Herb Solow Leave *Star Trek*

During his tenure on the show, Gene L. Coon was an anchor of the *Star Trek* production team. He signed on just prior to the shooting of "Miri" in late August 1966, replacing creator Gene Roddenberry as line producer, and left shortly after completion of "Bread and Circuses" in mid-September 1967. During that span, Coon oversaw the creation of thirty-one episodes, including many of the series' finest efforts, and wrote classics such as "The Devil in the Dark," "Space Seed," and "Errand of Mercy." Other than Roddenberry, no one more profoundly influenced the series' emergent mythology. When Coon left the show in the fall of 1967, his personal life was in turmoil. The writer-producer left his wife, Joy, because he had fallen in love with model Jackie Mitchell, an old flame with whom he had recently reconnected. His divorce placed financial demands on Coon that forced him to take a higher paying job at Universal Studios, where he produced the Robert Wagner adventure series *It Takes a Thief* (1968–70). Under the pseudonym Lee Cronin, Coon continued to submit teleplays to *Star Trek*, but his editorial guidance was sorely missed. Coon's replacement, John Meredith Lucas, wrote four *Trek* episodes and directed three others. But Lucas failed to impress Roddenberry in his new role and left the show at the conclusion of Season Two.

Herb Solow, who had been hired as an assistant by Desilu production chief Oscar Katz in 1964, assumed the title of Executive in Charge of Production following Katz's departure the following year. Solow, a former NBC executive, was instrumental in *Star Trek*'s sale to NBC and spent much of the past three years running interference for Roddenberry with the network. After Paramount absorbed Desilu in the summer of '67, Solow was invited to remain on board as the head of production for Paramount Pictures Television. He accepted but came to rue the decision when Gulf + Western financial executives began to insert themselves into the management of Paramount TV. In January 1968, the frustrated Solow jumped ship, joining Metro-Goldwyn-Mayer as a vice president. (MGM had been purchased by Canadian investor Edgar Bronfman Sr. in 1967 and would be sold again the following year.) While Solow's departure didn't directly affect the *Star Trek*'s creative team, his absence removed the firewall between Roddenberry and NBC and weakened the show's defenses against tinkering Gulf + Western bean counters.

## The Great Bird Flies the Coop

Like the show's fans, Gene Roddenberry was relieved when NBC announced that *Star Trek* would return for a third season. But he was positively ecstatic when the network suggested the show might move to a more favorable time slot—Monday nights at 7:30—something Roddenberry had been lobbying for throughout the series' first two seasons. Reenergized, he indicated he would resume duty as line producer, a responsibility he had handed off to Coon midway through Season One. But after further consideration, NBC decided to keep *Star Trek* on Friday nights, moving it back from 8:30 to 10 p.m. (According to some reports, *Trek*'s move to Mondays was scuttled by producers of the highly rated *Rowan & Martin's Laugh-In*, who refused to surrender that show's Monday 8 p.m. slot.) Roddenberry knew his show's new "graveyard" time slot spelled doom for the series, since most of *Trek*'s young viewers would be away from their TVs on Friday nights. Dejected, he effectively absented himself from the program beginning in late March 1968.

Roddenberry always explained that he had threatened to remove himself from the show's day-to-day operations unless NBC agreed to a better time slot; when NBC refused, he had to stand by his threat or else lose all leverage in further negotiations with the network. But if this was his thinking, then the Great Bird's logic was less than Spock-like. If cancellation was now a foregone conclusion, what further negotiations was he concerned about? Solow, associate producer Bob Justman, and other insiders insist that Roddenberry was simply protecting his own interests, which is perfectly understandable. Roddenberry didn't need a crystal ball to see unemployment looming in his near future. As a result, he devoted most of his energy during Season Three to developing ideas for other series and feature films he would pursue after *Star Trek* was gone, and to growing his fledgling Lincoln Enterprises souvenir business. Although he retained the title of Executive Producer and occasionally parachuted in to resolve conflicts among the cast and crew, he stopped submitting stories and rewriting teleplays and withdrew from most other production tasks. His name remained in the credits, but "the Roddenberry Touch" was gone.

## The New Regime

When Roddenberry changed his mind about returning to line production for Season Three, Bob Justman believed he would assume the reins. After all, he had been with the program in various capacities since "The Cage" and had served diligently as associate producer during Seasons One and Two. But instead Roddenberry hired producer Fred Freiberger, who had worked on *The Wild, Wild West* and who was represented by Alden Schwimmer, Roddenberry's agent. Justman received a new credit (the separate-but-unequal "co-producer") and a pay increase, but *Star Trek* would not become *his* show. Bitter over this perceived betrayal and fed up with budget cuts and other headaches, Justman quit the show with eight episodes left in its final season.

Some argue that Freiberger has taken a disproportionate share of the blame for *Trek*'s drop-off in quality. Many of the producer's other projects—including the TV series *The Fugitive* and *The Six Million Dollar Man* and the classic sci-fi movie *The Beast from 20,000 Fathoms*—demonstrate formidable talent. Nichelle Nichols, in her autobiography *Beyond Uhura*, insists that Freiberger "did everything he could to shore up the show. . . . *Star Trek* was in a disintegrating orbit before Fred came aboard." To support Nichols's argument, one can point to the departures of Roddenberry, Coon, and Solow, along with the show's anemic budget, which NBC slashed to $178,500 for its third season, down $14,500 from Season One, despite salary increases for the cast and other rising production costs.

But if Freiberger was left holding the bag, he shook the remainder of its contents onto the floor. One of the things that had made the last season and a half of *Star Trek* so uniformly strong was the consistent presence of three very talented men—directors Marc Daniels and Joseph Pevney, and cinematographer Jerry Finnerman. Together, Daniels and Pevney had helmed twenty-eight of the show's first fifty-five episodes, including most of its best-loved installments. On Freiberger's watch, however, Daniels directed just one episode and Pevney none at all. Just six episodes into Season Three, Finnerman resigned, incensed when Freiberger demanded cuts in both the cinematographer's pay and equipment allowance. Finnerman had photographed every *Star Trek* adventure since "Where No Man Has Gone Before," creating a signature look for the program through his evocative use of colored gels and other lighting techniques. Al Francis, Finnerman's camera operator, took over as cinematographer, but with Daniels, Pevney, and Finnerman out of the picture, *Star Trek* lost most of its previous visual style.

## Poor Scripts and Script Supervision

Before Season Three began, Dorothy Fontana stepped down as story editor to focus on writing her own teleplays and to be free to write for other series. Freiberger replaced her with his friend Arthur Singer. Like Freiberger, Singer was experienced and talented—but knew nothing about *Star Trek*. As a result, the show suffered lapses in continuity and credibility. The lone episode Singer wrote himself, "Turnabout Intruder" (in which Captain Kirk switches bodies with a jealous ex-girlfriend) ranks among the least loved of the show's original seventy-nine adventures. It was the final installment broadcast and ended the series with a sickening thud.

"Fred Freiberger came in and to him *Star Trek* was 'tits in space,'" said screenwriter Margaret Armen, as quoted in Edward Gross's book *Trek: The Lost Years*. "That's a direct quote. I was in the projection room watching an early episode when Fred came in and watched it and said, 'Oh, I get it. Tits in space.' Fred was looking for all the action pieces, whereas Gene was looking for the subtlety that is *Star Trek*."

To make matters worse, Roddenberry's merciless rewriting of teleplays during the first two seasons had alienated some of the show's better writers, making it tougher to acquire quality scripts. Few of the big-name authors who had contributed to *Star Trek* during Seasons One and Two wrote for the show during its final campaign. And some of the show's stalwarts submitted subpar teleplays, such as Coon's "Spock's Brain" and Fontana's "The Way to Eden," in which the *Enterprise* is hijacked by a band of space hippies. (This was one of two Fontana scripts so heavily rewritten that the author removed her name from them.) Finally, in a cost-cutting measure, Gulf + Western insisted that Freiberger's creative staff utilize stories that had been purchased during prior seasons but discarded as substandard. Coon's "A Portrait in Black and White" (about warring aliens who are black on one side and white on the other) had been deemed too slow-moving and preachy. Yet it was revived and, under the new title "Let That Be Your Last Battlefield," became another less than scintillating installment.

## Assessing Season Three

Nearly everyone acknowledges that *Star Trek*'s third broadcast year marked a precipitous drop-off from the show's first two seasons. The Hugo Awards provide one measure of the show's declining quality. In 1967, "The Menagerie, Parts I and II" won the Hugo for Best Dramatic Presentation. That year two other *Trek* episodes were nominated in the same category ("The Naked Time" and "The Corbomite Maneuver"). In 1968, all five Hugo nominees in the category were *Star Trek* episodes—"The Trouble with Tribbles," "Mirror, Mirror," "The Doomsday Machine," "Amok Time," and the award-winning "City on the Edge of Forever." But in 1969, *Star Trek* failed to earn a single Hugo nomination.

Still, Season Three could have been much worse. Given all the behind-the-scenes turmoil, it's a wonder *Trek* didn't become a complete disaster—"Spock's Brain" week in and week out. Instead, the season proved to be wildly inconsistent. It included most of the series' worst episodes but also some of its best, such as "The *Enterprise* Incident," "Spectre of the Gun," "The Empath," and "The Tholian Web." Season Three also remains notable for its many romances: An amnesia-stricken Kirk marries a native girl in "The Paradise Syndrome" (and continues his Playboy-of-the-Galaxy modus operandi in other episodes); Spock falls in love in "All Our Yesterdays" and seems smitten in "The Cloud Minders," as well; Scotty and McCoy also find romance (not with each other) in "The Lights of Zetar" and "For the World Is Hollow and I Have Touched the Sky," respectively. And Chekov makes time with young women in a handful of episodes. Meanwhile, *Star Trek* remained true to Roddenberry's uplifting pro-humanist vision and established antiwar, prointegration advocacy. Episodes

An away team consisting of (from left to right) Ensign Chekov, Captain Kirk, Mr. Spock, and Dr. McCoy beams aboard the disabled starship Defiant in "The Tholian Web," a rare Season Three highlight.

sometimes devolved into blatant sermonizing, as in "Let That Be Your Last Battlefield," but *Trek* made history with TV's first interracial kiss (between Kirk and Uhura, in the otherwise mundane "Plato's Stepchildren").

With a new director at the helm almost every week, the show's visual style became just as uneven as its teleplays. However, Freiberger encouraged directors to try new things, and some of those worked brilliantly, like Ralph Senensky's use of fisheye lens point-of-view shots in "Is There in Truth No Beauty" and "The Tholian Web" to signify characters' warped perspectives. On the other hand, without Finnerman's sophisticated lighting, episodes occasionally looked downright garish. The show sometimes went over the top in other departments, too—with overblown makeup, costumes, and acting. Shatner, who in *Star Trek Memories* refers to himself as "the ham-asaurus," raised scenery chewing to a new pinnacle in "The Paradise Syndrome." ("I am Kirok! KIROK!!")

Despite occasional lapses, however, what carried the day throughout Season Three was the excellent work of the show's cast, and especially its leads. The acting styles of Shatner, Leonard Nimoy, and DeForest Kelley were as divergent as the personalities of the characters they portrayed, yet together they formed a perfect synthesis. From week to week, viewers tuned in because they remained deeply invested in Kirk, Spock, and McCoy, even if the trio's adventures some-times seemed a little silly. As a result, even the worst of *Star Trek*'s third season episodes ultimately seem endearing rather than insufferable.

# Operation— Annihilate!

## Shows That Beat *Star Trek* in the Nielsen Ratings

T hroughout its original network run, *Star Trek* fought a tooth-and-nail battle for survival against lukewarm (at best) Nielsen ratings. In retrospect, it's clear that *Star Trek*'s Nielsen performance didn't tell the whole story. Until the early 1970s, the Nielsen ratings—developed by pioneering media researcher Arthur Nielsen—were a blunt instrument. Selected viewers (known as "Nielsen families") simply logged the shows they watched in special notebooks that, at the conclusion of each ratings period, were returned to be tallied. The ratings reflected only the raw percentages of viewers who watched each program (its share of the audience). Beginning a few years after *Star Trek* left the air, the Nielsen numbers would include more fine-tuned demographic data about viewers' age, gender, and economic background. Had such information been available sooner, it would have revealed that *Star Trek* attracted mostly young, relatively affluent viewers—a highly desirable, difficult-to-reach demographic. In the '70s, advertisers began paying a premium for airtime on shows that appealed to that audience. If NBC had realized this at the time, *Star Trek* might have run significantly longer than its three seasons.

Based on the data available in the late 1960s, however, NBC could discern only two things about *Star Trek*'s audience: It was fiercely loyal (the show's ratings were steady, without major spikes or valleys, at least during its first two seasons) but too small to generate the ratings numbers and, in turn, advertising revenue that NBC desired, especially from a show with an unusually high per-episode cost (about $192,000– over $1.2 million in inflation-adjusted figures—per installment). In an era when the three networks' prime-time schedules included fewer than eighty programs on any given week, *Star Trek* never managed to crack the Top 50. For its first and best-rated season, it finished number 52.

During those halcyon, precable, pre-DVR days of network television, a series' ratings fate was determined in large part by its time slot. This could be a critical factor for new programs, since a show's place on the schedule also dictated what its competition would be, and new series seldom fare well against established hits. From the outset, creator-producer Gene Roddenberry lobbied NBC to run *Star Trek* at 7:30, then the earliest prime-time slot, preferably on Mondays or Tuesdays. He reasoned this would be the most advantageous showtime for a program with appeal to young viewers. But NBC was reluctant to lead an evening schedule with a new series, especially one as offbeat as *Star Trek*. Conventional wisdom dictated that networks open their nightly lineups with a proven hit, since many viewers would simply stick with the same network for the entire evening rather than leave their seats to change channels. (Remote controls wouldn't gain wide use until the development of infrared signal technology in the 1980s.) Consequently, NBC slated *Star Trek* for Thursdays from 8:30 to 9:30 p.m.

*Star Trek*'s ratings began promisingly. The show's debut broadcast, on September 8, 1966, finished first in its time slot with a solid 20.7 share of the audience. But it did so with a great deal of help. NBC promoted the series' debut with a full-page advertisement in *TV Guide*, along with prominent ads in scores of local newspapers. The numbers for *Star Trek*'s premiere were also inflated by lack of competition, since CBS didn't launch its fall lineup until the following week. Once the playing field was leveled, *Star Trek*'s ratings declined. The show's Nielsen fate was inexorably linked to those of the shows around it on the schedule. Here's a rundown of the competition *Star Trek* faced for viewers and how it fared against each rival program.

## Season One: 1966–67

During its inaugural season, *Star Trek* ran on NBC from 8:30 to 9:30 p.m. At that hour, ABC ran a pair of situation comedies, one established and one new. Over on CBS, *Star Trek* ran opposite another sitcom at 8:30 and the first half-hour of *The CBS Thursday Movies*, which started at 9 p.m. These movies were usually broadcasts of recent theatrical feature films rather than made-for-TV pictures. Although ratings varied widely from week to week, depending on the film shown, these broadcasts were very popular and often outperformed *Star Trek*. During the 1960s, without benefit of home video or cable movie channels, TV showings offered a rare chance for viewers to catch a big-screen picture they had missed or rewatch one they had previously enjoyed. Rather than going out to the cinema, many viewers simply waited for films to turn up on TV. While *Star Trek* was on the air, all three networks ran movies multiple nights of the week—ABC on Sunday and Wednesday, CBS on Thursday and Friday, and NBC on Monday, Tuesday, and Saturday. One or more of these broadcasts often ranked among the most-watched programs in any given ratings period.

*My Three Sons* (CBS, 8:30 p.m.)—Throughout its three-season run, *Star Trek*'s toughest competition came from family-friendly sitcoms like this one. One of television's greatest situation comedy warhorses, *My Three Sons* ran twelve seasons, from 1960 to 1965 in black and white on ABC and from 1965 to 1972 in color on CBS. The show finished outside the Nielsen Top 30 only twice. One of those two seasons was this one, yet *My Three Sons* still outdrew *Star Trek*. The show starred Fred MacMurray as Steve Douglas, a widower raising three boys in a chaotic, all-male, multigenerational household that also included his late wife's father (William Frawley), a character replaced by Steve's Uncle Charlie (William Demarest) when the show moved to CBS. The program was modeled after the 1959 Walt Disney comedy *The Shaggy Dog* (Tim Considine played MacMurray's son in both the film and the series, and TV's Douglas family kept a pet sheepdog). *My Three Sons* ran longer than any family sitcom in television history except *The Adventures of Ozzie and Harriet*, which ran fourteen seasons from 1952 to 1966. It was the television equivalent of comfort food. *Star Trek* appealed to viewers with a more exotic palate.

**The Tammy Grimes Show** (ABC, 8:30 p.m.)—One of the few shows *Star Trek* outperformed in the ratings was this short-lived sitcom—cancelled after only four episodes—about a daffy, spendthrift heiress (Grimes) and her tight-fisted uncle. Tammy Grimes was a singer and actress then best known for her Tony-winning performance in the title role of the Broadway musical smash *The Unsinkable Molly Brown*. Two years earlier, Grimes had signed on to play the lead role in television's *Bewitched* but was released from her contract to star in Noel Coward's *High Spirits*, a Broadway musical adaptation of Coward's earlier hit, *Blithe Spirit*. Elizabeth Montgomery took over the lead of the TV series. Coincidentally, the cast of *The Tammy Grimes Show* also included Dick Sargent, who would later replace Montgomery's costar, Dick York, on *Bewitched*. The speedy demise of *The Tammy Grimes Show* didn't seriously damage the career

Shatner and Nimoy did their part to promote *Star Trek*'s Season Two shift from Thursday to Friday nights. NBC hoped the move would help the series widen its audience.

of its star. Grimes starred in many more plays (winning a second Tony in 1970 for Coward's *Private Lives*), appeared in dozens of movies and TV shows, and recorded three albums. She also married actor Christopher Plummer and is the mother of actress Amanda Plummer. In 2003, she was inducted into the American Theater Hall of Fame. While Grimes didn't represent major competition for *Star Trek*, the show she once spurned certainly did.

*Bewitched* (**ABC, 9 p.m.**)—*Star Trek* struggled not only to attract viewers at 8:30 but to hold them at 9 o'clock against the ratings magic of *Bewitched*. During the 1966–67 season, the show's first in color, *Bewitched* placed No. 8 in the Nielsen ratings, its third consecutive Top-10 finish. This supernatural sitcom starred Elizabeth Montgomery as Samantha, a witch who swears off magic after taking a mortal husband, advertising executive Darrin Stephens. This arrangement doesn't sit well with Samantha's family, including her meddling mother, Endora (Agnes Moorehead), whose magical machinations often created headaches for her son-in-law. Darrin was portrayed by Dick York until the actor suffered a debilitating back injury during the program's sixth season, when Dick Sargent took over the role. *Bewitched* lasted eight seasons, from 1964 to 1972, but its popularity sagged after Sargent replaced York. Montgomery was the only cast member to appear in all of the show's 254 episodes. The series, whose cinematic antecedents included *I Married a Witch* (1942) and *Bell, Book and Candle* (1958), spawned two spin-offs, a 1972 Saturday morning cartoon and a 1977 prime-time series, both of which centered on Darrin and Samantha's daughter Tabitha. In 2005, Will Farrell and Nicole Kidman costarred in a disastrous big-screen remake of *Bewitched*. Despite its far-out premise, many cultural historians consider *Bewitched* as one of television's most socially conservative (perhaps even chauvinistic) series. It is, after all, the story of a woman who literally disempowers herself to take on the traditional, subservient role of homemaker and mother. The worldview of *Bewitched* seemed to stand in bold contrast to the progressive ideology espoused by *Star Trek*.

## Season Two: 1967–68

For anxious months, as the show's first season drew to a close, NBC kept *Star Trek*'s cast, crew, and fans in suspense, withholding an announcement on whether or not the series would be renewed. To force the issue, Roddenberry orchestrated and, out of the *Star Trek* promotional budget, helped fund a massive letter-writing campaign led by his friends in the science fiction literary community, including celebrated author Harlan Ellison (who was still rewriting "The City on the Edge of Forever" at the time). NBC was soon overwhelmed with letters and phone calls in support of the show. A special Nielsen survey conducted in late 1966 may have played an equally powerful role in NBC's eventual decision to renew *Star Trek*. The survey, taken by Nielsen Media Research at the request of NBC (which that season became the first network to broadcast an all-color prime-time lineup), compared the ratings of full-color series to those of black-and-white programs and determined the most popular color shows. Surprisingly, respondents named *Star Trek* their favorite full-color program. This result may have been especially important to NBC because the network was then owned by RCA, a leading manufacturer of color television sets. On March 9, 1967, as the end credits rolled for the episode "Devil in the Dark," NBC announced to the audience through voice-over narration that *Star Trek* would return in the fall. It would not return on Thursday nights, however. NBC moved the show to Fridays at 8:30, despite protests from Roddenberry, who worried that most of the show's youthful viewers would go out on Friday nights rather than stay home to watch TV. His fears were validated when *Trek*'s ratings declined rather than improved during its second season. That year the show ran against a smash sitcom and the first half hour of the *Friday Night Movies* on CBS, and opposite a forgettable Western drama on ABC.

**Gomer Pyle, U.S.M.C. (CBS, 8:30)**—Captain Kirk and his crew vanquished the merciless Klingons, the inscrutable Romulans, and the superhuman Khan Noonien Singh. But they didn't stand a chance against Private Gomer Pyle. NBC hoped moving *Star Trek* from Thursdays to Fridays would help the struggling program find an audience. It also believed that the appeal of *Gomer Pyle, U.S.M.C.* might be fading, since the show had slipped eight spots to No. 10 for the 1966–67 season. But against *Star Trek*, *Gomer Pyle* regained its ratings muscle and climbed back to Number 3. A spin-off from *The Andy Griffith Show*, *Gomer Pyle* chronicled the comic misadventures of its title character (played by Jim Nabors), a naïve but good-hearted former Mayberry gas station attendant who seemingly enlisted in the Marine Corps for the sole purpose of flummoxing his commanding officer, Sgt. Carter (Frank Sutton), on a weekly basis. Pyle's homespun affability and unflagging confidence in the inner goodness of all people made the character a forerunner of Forrest Gump. Despite its military setting, *Gomer Pyle*, which ran from 1964 to 1969, carefully avoided references to the war in Vietnam or political commentary of any sort. Instead, it offered scenarios where the well-intentioned Pyle accidentally broke the rules or created a problem for another soldier (often Sgt. Carter), which the private would ultimately resolve in a manner that validated his simple values of honesty and compassion. This approach could not be more dissimilar to the socially conscious attitude of *Star Trek*. Yet the *Gomer Pyle* formula worked like a charm. The series finished outside the top three only once during its five-season run. The show's resurgent performance during this, its penultimate season, was one of the factors that darkened NBC's assessment of *Star Trek*'s ongoing viability. Coincidentally, *Gomer Pyle*'s outdoor scenes were shot in *Trek*'s backyard at Desilu Productions, on the same back lot where *The Andy Griffith Show* was filmed.

**Hondo (ABC, 8:30)**—Here's another rare show that *Star Trek* vanquished in the ratings. Based on the 1953 Western of the same name, *Hondo* starred Ralph Taeger (in a role originated by John Wayne) as Hondo Lane, a part-Indian U.S. Cavalry scout who strove to settle disputes between the army and the Comanche,

The Enterprise crew defeated the Klingons and Romulans, but they were no match for Sergeant Carter (Frank Sutton, left) and Private Gomer Pyle (Jim Nabors).

and helped track down outlaws of various stripes. Noah Beery Jr. (perhaps best remembered as Jim Garner's dad on *The Rockford Files*) costarred as Hondo's sidekick, Buffalo Baker, a role played by Ward Bond in the movie. Based on a short story by Louis L'Amour and shot in 3-D, the big-screen *Hondo* scored a minor box-office success, but the small-screen version never caught on and was cancelled in mid-season after seventeen episodes.

## Season Three: 1968–69

As its second season drew to a close, *Star Trek* once again faced an uncertain future. Roddenberry surreptitiously pulled together a second and far more vehement "Save *Star Trek*" effort, this time led by "superfans" such as Bobbie Jo "Bjo" Trimble, Joan Winston, and Wanda Kendall, who Roddenberry flew from Los Angeles to New York to agitate on the series' behalf. For the second year in a row, NBC was inundated with cards and letters praising the show and pleading for its return, and this time hundreds of protestors with homemade signs picketed the network's West Coast offices in Burbank, California. Even though many executives were embarrassed by the demonstrations, NBC again relented under public pressure, announcing over the end credits of "The Omega Glory" on March 1, 1968, that *Star Trek* would be renewed for a third season.

Throughout Season Two, Roddenberry lobbied forcefully for a better time slot for his show. After initially indicating *Star Trek* would move to Monday night at 7:30, which would have been ideal, NBC programmers suddenly changed course and stuck the show in the Friday 10 p.m. "graveyard slot"—a virtual kiss of death for any program reliant on young viewers. It's unclear why NBC reneged on its promise to shift *Trek* to the Monday lead-off slot. One, possibly apocryphal, story is that the move was rebuffed by the producers of the highly rated *Rowan & Martin's Laugh-In*, which had debuted as a midseason replacement in January 1968 and gone on to win three Emmy Awards. Because *Laugh-In* was also dependent on young viewers, producers Ed Friendly and George Schlatter refused to surrender the show's Monday 8 p.m. slot. *Laugh-In* became the most watched show on television for the 1968–69 and '69–70 seasons. Some insiders claim that NBC executives moved *Star Trek* to Fridays at 10 because they were miffed about the show's letter-writing campaigns and protests. These explanations are not mutually exclusive. Whatever the reason, the result was the same. In its new time slot, the show's ratings plummeted to new lows. For the week ending October 8, 1968, *Star Trek* finished in seventy-sixth place. By the end of its third season, there weren't enough cards and letters in the world to save *Star Trek*.

*Judd for the Defense* (ABC, 10 p.m.)—Aside from the second hour of the CBS *Friday Night Movies*, *Star Trek*'s only competition in its final season was this critically acclaimed but little-remembered legal drama. The program featured Carl Betz, the then-popular ex-costar of *The Donna Reed Show*, as attorney Clinton Judd, a character based (perhaps too closely) on prominent lawyers like F. Lee Bailey and Percy Foreman. *Judd for the Defense* earned accolades for its willingness to tackle hot-button political issues. Its ripped-from-the-headlines teleplays included stories involving civil rights, Vietnam War protests, homosexuality, and the exploitation of illegal immigrant laborers, among other contemporary topics. Foreman threatened to sue the show for "appropriating for commercial purposes my career as a lawyer" but ultimately took no legal action. While far from a hit in this, its debut season, *Judd for the Defense* at least managed to get renewed, which is more than *Star Trek* could accomplish in this time slot. *Judd for the Defense* was cancelled a season later, but Betz won both an Emmy and a Golden Globe for his work, and screenwriter Robert Lewin earned a Writers Guild award for his script "To Kill a Madman."

Even though *Star Trek*'s final season officially ended in the spring of 1969, NBC reran episodes of the show as summer replacement programming, scheduling it Tuesdays at 7:30 p.m. from June through early September. Ironically, this was the early-week, early-evening time slot Roddenberry had long coveted. Since only seventy-nine episodes of *Trek* had been produced (less than the one hundred generally deemed necessary for syndication), the *Star Trek* story appeared to be over as the 1970s dawned. But instead, a new chapter was beginning.

# Mind Meld

## Connections Between *Star Trek* and Other Classic Sci-Fi TV Series

T he *Enterprise* traveled the vast expanse of interstellar space, but *Star Trek* didn't happen in a vacuum. It grew from a lineage of earlier science fiction programs and existed in competition with a new generation of sci-fi shows. In a variety of sometimes surprising ways, it remained connected to its television brethren.

### *Rocky Jones, Space Ranger* (1954–56) and Other Early Space Operas

A dozen years before the starship *Enterprise* launched its five-year mission, the squeaky clean, granite-jawed Rocky Jones battled interplanetary villains in the TV serial *Rocky Jones, Space Ranger*, which is sometimes noted as an influence on *Star Trek*. Like *Trek*, the show chronicled the adventures of spacefaring military men who serve a freedom-loving civilian government (the Federation-like United Worlds of the Solar System). Matt Jefferies's production designs for the *Enterprise* share some intriguing similarities to the Space Rangers' rocket ships, most notably the prominent forward view screen on the bridge and automatic slide-open doors. (Both of these much-copied innovations originate with *Rocky Jones*.) Also, the Starfleet uniforms worn in the *Trek* feature films, from *The Wrath of Khan* through *The Undiscovered Country*, closely resemble the dress uniforms of the Space Rangers.

However, creator Gene Roddenberry never acknowledged the program as an inspiration (by the time *Rocky Jones* hit the air, Roddenberry was working as a Los Angeles police sergeant). Most of the similarities between *Rocky Jones* and *Star Trek* can be chalked up to common influences such as the *Flash Gordon* serials of the 1930s and author Robert A. Heinlein's 1948 novel *Space Cadet*. The syndicated *Rocky Jones* ran for just two seasons due to lukewarm ratings and problems with its cast. The show was produced on film (rather than broadcast live, like most other early programs) to enable producer Roland Reed to utilize more elaborate visual effects than previous science fiction serials. Although crude-looking today, the show's special effects represented an advance over primitive sci-fi TV serials such as *Captain Video and His Video Rangers* (1949–55) and *Tom Corbett, Space Cadet* (1950-55).

Visual effects aside, however, *Rocky Jones* remains of a piece with all the other juvenile space operas that were common during the early days of television, shows that offered one-dimensional characters, simplistic good-versus-evil plots, and poor science (writers, for example, often confused planets, moons and asteroids). There are several, sometimes tangential, links between these series and *Star Trek*. James Doohan costarred on the Canadian-made *Space Command* (1953–54). Ed Kemmer, who had starred as Commander Buzz Corry on *Space Patrol* (1950–54), was among those actors originally considered for the role of Captain Pike in "The Cage." And author James Blish, who novelized eleven volumes worth of *Star Trek* teleplays and penned the first *Trek* novel aimed at adult readers, had written for *Captain Video*. More importantly, however, these programs and others like them—also including *Captain Z-Ro* (1951–54), *Rod Brown of the Rocket Rangers* (1953–54) and *Flash Gordon* (1954–55)—fixed in the minds of viewers and network executives the idea that science fiction adventure shows were kiddie fare, a stereotype Roddenberry would battle in order to get *Star Trek* produced, and which the show would struggle against in its fight for ratings survival. On the other hand, many of the six- and seven-year-olds who watched these programs later became *Star Trek*'s eighteen- and nineteen-year-old viewers.

## The Twilight Zone (1959–64) and Other SF Anthologies

During the same era as the primitive space operas, the first science fiction TV anthologies debuted: ABC's *Tales of Tomorrow* (1951–53) and CBS' short-lived *Out There* (1951–52), cancelled after just twelve episodes. Although shrugged off by most adult viewers with the same indifference shown the likes of *Rocky Jones*, these pioneering programs represented the first serious attempt to translate literary science fiction to television. *Tales of Tomorrow* was cocreated by acclaimed author Theodore Sturgeon, who would later write for *Star Trek*, and featured adaptations of stories by Sturgeon, Arthur C. Clarke, Fredric Brown, and other notable authors, along with classics such as Mary Shelley's *Frankenstein* and Jules Verne's *20,000 Leagues Under the Sea*. Doohan appeared on *Tales of Tomorrow*. A few years later, Ziv Television (the company that would later hire Roddenberry away from the LAPD) introduced the syndicated *Science Fiction Theatre* (1955–57). Although it lacked the literary pedigree of *Tales of Tomorrow*, *Science Fiction Theatre* represented another serious attempt at adult-oriented sci-fi TV. DeForest Kelley made three appearances on the show (twice playing doctors, coincidentally).

The genre's true television breakthrough came with writer-producer Rod Serling's *The Twilight Zone* in 1959. Although its stories were more often dark fantasy than true science fiction, *The Twilight Zone* was generally categorized as sci-fi and proved that audiences would embrace speculative television if it was

As the first science fiction program aimed at adults to succeed with audiences and critics, creator Rod Serling's *Twilight Zone* was an important forerunner of *Star Trek*.

well crafted. The show earned respectable ratings throughout its five seasons and won three Emmys and three Hugo Awards. Like *Star Trek*, *The Twilight Zone* frequently commented on current events such as the Cold War and the civil rights movement through the lens of sci-fi and fantasy. For all these reasons, the *Zone* remains an important forerunner of *Trek*. But there are also more direct links between the two programs:

- William Shatner starred in two memorable *Twilight Zone* episodes—"Nick of Time" (1960) and the classic "Nightmare at 20,000 Feet" (1963). "Nightmare" is the one where airline passenger Shatner spies a gremlin on the wing of his plane.
- Leonard Nimoy, Doohan, and Takei also played minor supporting roles on *The Twilight Zone*, in "A Quality of Mercy" (1961), "Valley of the Shadow" (1963), and "The Encounter" (1964), respectively.
- Several notable *Trek* guest stars also ventured into *The Twilight Zone* on one or more occasions, including Stanley Adams (Cyrano Jones from "The Trouble with Tribbles"), John Fiedler (Mr. Hengist from "Wolf in the Fold"), Robert Lansing (Gary Seven from "Assignment: Earth"), and William Windom (Commodore Decker from "The Doomsday Machine"). John Hoyt, who played the *Enterprise*'s original chief medical officer in "The Cage," appeared in two *Twilight Zone* installments.
- Richard Matheson, who wrote fourteen acclaimed teleplays for *The Twilight Zone* including "Nightmare at 20,000 Feet," later penned the key Season One *Trek* episode "The Enemy Within." George Clayton Johnson, another well-known science fiction author, contributed to seven *Twilight Zone* scripts and later wrote "The Man Trap," the first *Star Trek* episode ever broadcast.
- Robert Butler, who directed two *Zones*, also helmed "The Cage." And Robert Grist, who directed the *Twilight Zone* episode "I Dream of Genie," later oversaw "The Galileo Seven."

Additionally, a handful of *Twilight Zone* episodes feature storylines remarkably similar to later *Trek* scenarios.

- "People Are Alike All Over" (1960), like both "The Cage" and the animated *Trek* adventure "Eye of the Beholder," features humans held captive in an alien zoo. Coincidentally, Susan Oliver (Vina in "The Cage") was also among the captive earthlings in the *Twilight Zone* episode.
- "It's a Good Life" (1961), one of the show's most famous episodes (later reprised for the 1983 *Twilight Zone* feature film), and *Trek*'s "Charlie X" both involve boys with terrifying, superhuman psychokinetic abilities.
- "The Parallel" (1963) and "Mirror, Mirror" are both tales about space travelers who accidentally cross over into parallel universes.
- "The Mute" (1963) and "The Empath" both feature speechless women with extrasensory powers. "The Mute" was one of Matheson's episodes.
- "The Man Trap," written by George Clayton Johnson, shares many common elements with earlier story by same author titled "All of Us Are Dying," about an extraterrestrial being capable of transforming its appearance at will. "All of Us Are Dying" was adapted for the *Zone* by Serling under the title "Four of Us Are Dying."

It should be noted, however, that most of these scenarios—humans trapped in an outer space zoo, mirror universes, and stories involving ESP—were ideas commonly explored in science fiction literature prior to either *The Twilight Zone* or *Star Trek.*

## The Outer Limits (1963–65)

There are a dizzying number of connections between *Star Trek* and *The Outer Limits*, another classic sci-fi anthology program from the 1960s. Although *The Outer Limits* was not a ratings success and was cancelled midway through its second season, many fans, critics, and historians now consider it the best program of its type ever broadcast. The Showtime network later revived the series, producing new episodes from 1995 to 2002. Many of the program's *Star Trek* connections arose through Bob Justman, who worked as a production manager on *The Outer Limits* before joining *Star Trek* as an associate producer. Others can be attributed to the fact that both shows, in trying to produce high-quality, adult-oriented science fiction, shared similar influences and sought the same creative talent. And some are purely coincidental.

- William Shatner starred in the *Outer Limits* episode "Cold Hands, Warm Heart," as the leader of a space exploration program known as Project Vulcan. Leonard Nimoy appeared on the show twice, including playing a prominent supporting role in the classic "I, Robot" episode. *Trek* regulars Doohan and Grace Lee Whitney also worked on *The Outer Limits.* More than a dozen *Trek* guest stars appeared on *The Outer Limits* as well, including Sally Kellerman (Dr. Elizabeth Dehner from "Where No Man Has Gone Before"), Lawrence Montaigne (Stonn, Spock's rival from "Amok Time"), Arlene Martel (T'Pring, Spock's fiancée from "Amok Time"), Barry Atwater (legendary Vulcan leader Sarek in "The Savage Curtain"), and Michael Ansara (the Klingon commander Kang in "Day of the Dove"). John Hoyt—yes, the same John Hoyt from "The Cage" and two *Twilight Zones*—landed a role in "I, Robot" and two other *Outer Limits* installments.
- Voice actor Vic Perrin, who worked on several *Star Trek* episodes (perhaps most memorably as the voice for NOMAD in "The Changeling"), also served as *The Outer Limits'* trademark "control voice." Every episode began with Perrin intoning, "There is nothing wrong with your television set . . ."
- Screenwriter Harlan Ellison, who wrote "The City on the Edge of Forever," also penned two classic *Outer Limits* episodes—"Demon with a Glass Hand," which earned a Writers Guild Award, and "Soldier," which director James Cameron credits as an inspiration for *The Terminator.* "City," "Demon," and "Soldier" all won Hugo Awards. Meyer Dolinski, who wrote "Plato's Stepchildren," authored three *Outer Limits* teleplays. Jerry Sohl, who under the pseudonym Nathan Butler contributed to the script of "This Side of Paradise," also earned credit on two *Outer Limits* teleplays.
- In addition to Justman, several other *Outer Limits* veterans went on to work for *Star Trek*, many of them hired by Justman. These include makeup artist

Fred Phillips and directors Gerd Oswald, James Goldstone, and John Erman. In addition, Project Unlimited, the specialty prop shop operated by sculptor Wah Chang, and Van der Veer Photo Effects, were important contributors to both programs.

- Several props from *The Outer Limits* also found their way to *Star Trek*, mostly through Chang and Project Unlimited. In "The Cage," two of the aliens seen in habitats neighboring Captain Pike's wore monster suits Chang designed for *The Outer Limits*. The birdman creature was created for "Second Chance," and the bearlike beast was seen in "Fun and Games." (Both costumes were reused for *The Outer Limits'* "The Duplicate Man.") The spore-shooting flowers seen in "This Side of Paradise" were originally produced for the *Outer Limits'* "Specimen: Unknown." Phillips created the bubble-headed Vians from "The Empath" using prosthetic appliances left over from *The Outer Limits'* pilot, "The Galaxy Being." And the Horta from "The Devil in the Dark" was a simplified version of, or perhaps a prototype for, the "microbe creature" seen in *The Outer Limits* episode "The Probe." Both the microbe creature and the Horta were portrayed by the suit's designer, Janos Prohaska.

- *The Outer Limits'* "Fun and Games" and *Star Trek*'s "Arena" were both adapted from the same Fredric Brown short story, also titled "Arena."

The 1964 *Outer Limits* episode "Fun and Games," featuring the fearsome Calco alien (pictured), and *Star Trek*'s "Arena" were both based on the same Fredric Brown short story.

## Lost in Space (1965–68) and Other Irwin Allen Productions

*Lost in Space* and *Star Trek* were linked primarily by the animosity Roddenberry harbored for producer Irwin Allen's rival program, and by the disdain most of Roddenberry's creative team felt toward it. In 1964, during what was supposed to be a simple pitch meeting for *Star Trek*, Roddenberry was grilled by CBS executives for nearly two hours. Later he learned the network had no interest in *Trek* because it had already purchased another sci-fi drama—*Lost in Space*. Roddenberry was apoplectic and feared that his ideas (including strategies for controlling costs and other details) would be used to benefit his competition. Roddenberry's creative team also loathed *Lost in Space* because they saw it as just another juvenile space opera, exactly the type of TV science fiction they were trying to make viewers forget.

Nevertheless, Allen's brand of lighthearted, kid-friendly, action-oriented sci-fi proved more popular than *Star Trek*'s more thoughtful, adult approach. In all, Allen launched four science fiction series during the decade: *Voyage to the Bottom of the Sea* (1964–68), *Lost in Space* (1965–68), *The Time Tunnel* (1966–67), and *Land of the Giants* (1968–70). Not surprisingly, given the enmity between *Trek* and Allen (or at least Allen's brand of sci-fi), there were fewer links between Roddenberry's show and Allen's series. Yet connections did exist.

- A handful of *Trek* guest stars also appeared on *Lost in Space*, including Stanley Adams (Cyrano Jones from "The Trouble with Tribbles") and Michael (Kang) Ansara. Carey Wilber, who wrote the original story for "Space Seed," was a *Lost in Space* contributor. Directors Tony Leader ("For the World Is Hollow and I Have Touched the Sky") and Leon Penn ("The Enemy Within") also worked on the rival show. So did Alexander Courage, composer of the famous *Star Trek* title theme. Billy Mumy—Will Robinson himself—was a *Star Trek* fan who went on to write stories for *Trek* comic books and appear in the *Deep Space Nine* episode "The Siege of AR-558."
- George Takei made a pre-*Trek* appearance on *Voyage to the Bottom of the Sea*. *Trek* guest stars, including Roger C. Carmel (Harry Mudd) and Larry Montaigne, also worked on *Voyage*. So did directors Gerd Oswald ("The Conscience of the King" and "The Alternative Factor"—not to mention fourteen *Outer Limits* episodes) and James Goldstone ("Where No Man Has Gone Before" and "What Are Little Girls Made Of?").
- The ubiquitous John Hoyt made two appearances on *The Time Tunnel*, as did Montaigne. Director Herschel Daugherty helmed two *Trek*s ("The Savage Curtain" and "Operation—Annihilate!") and two *Time Tunnel*s.
- Shimon Wincelberg, who contributed to the scripts for "Dagger of the Mind" and "The Galileo Seven" under the pen name S. Bar-David, also wrote seven *Lost in Space* teleplays, along with episodes of *Voyage to the Bottom of the Sea* and *Time Tunnel*. Writer Oliver Crawford, who contributed to the teleplays for "The Cloud Minders," "Let That Be Your Last Battlefield," and "The Galileo Seven," also wrote episodes of *Voyage* and *Land of the Giants*.

Allen's programs dominated American science fiction television during the 1960s and retain nostalgic audiences. But *Lost in Space* and its kin have not aged as gracefully as *Star Trek*, nor have they had anything like the cultural impact of the *Trek* franchise. Allen's shows offered entertainment, but *Trek* provided inspiration.

## Other Series

There are also links between *Star Trek* and a few other classic sci-fi shows.

The only real precedent for an hour-long, adult-oriented science fiction TV show was *Men into Space*, a little-watched near-future series about the space program (it pessimistically predicted that the first moon landing would occur in 1975), which ran on CBS for one season, 1959–60.

Producer Quinn Martin's *The Invaders*, about a secret alien invasion, ran on ABC in 1967–68, during *Star Trek*'s second season. The show welcomed guest stars Diana Muldaur (from "Is There in Truth No Beauty?" and "Return to Tomorrow," and later Dr. Pulaski during the second season of *The Next Generation*), Ian Wolfe (Mr. Atoz from "All Our Yesterdays"), and Larry Montaigne. Screenwriters Ted Sturgeon and Art Wallace ("Obsession" and "Assignment: Earth") penned episodes of the show.

Finally, there's *My Favorite Martian*, which ran on CBS from 1963 to 1966, which deserves more credit than it generally receives as a *Trek* forerunner. Although it was a comedy, *My Favorite Martian* stands as the first science fiction-themed TV program featuring recurring characters to find success with adult audiences. *Star Trek* producer Gene L. Coon wrote a teleplay for *My Favorite Martian*, and director David Alexander ("Plato's Stepchildren," "The Way to Eden") helmed ten episodes of the series. Ray Walston—who played the show's titular grumpy extraterrestrial—later appeared as the character Boothby, the curmudgeonly groundskeeper at Starfleet headquarters, in episodes of both *The Next Generation* and *Voyager*. It was a nod to the seldom-acknowledged debt *Trek* owed to its comedic predecessor.

**7:30 pm. New series!** Follow a family's way-out adventures on an unknown planet. With June Lockhart and Guy Williams.

This *TV Guide* ad trumpeted the debut of the much-reviled (by Gene Roddenberry, anyway) *Lost in Space*.

# These Are the Voyages

## On the Screen, 1966–69

# 20

# Wolves in the Fold

## Monsters and Madmen

A s *Star Trek*'s premiere approached, creator-producer Gene Roddenberry and his staff met with NBC executives to select the episode that would air first. Roddenberry wanted *Star Trek* to be taken seriously as science fiction and had gone to extraordinary lengths to shore up the series' sci-fi credentials, building bridges to the SF fan community and commissioning stories from prominent authors. However, with a handful of thought-provoking entries to choose from (including "The Corbomite Maneuver," "Charlie X," "The Naked Time," and "Where No Man Has Gone Before"), the network chose the most simplistic story available—"The Man Trap," with the shape-shifting Salt Vampire of planet M-113 running amok on the *Enterprise*.

Although written by respected SF author George Clayton Johnson (a *Twilight Zone* alum best known for cowriting the novel *Logan's Run*), "The Man Trap" was the kind of hoary space opera that might have turned up on *Lost in Space*. This was *not* the first impression Roddenberry wanted to make. In his book *Star Trek Memories*, William Shatner describes the episode as "a dreadful show, one of our worst ever."

Shatner's judgment is too harsh, however. "The Man Trap" may not be top-tier *Trek*, but it's a lively and engrossing adventure with some memorable character moments for Captain Kirk, Mr. Spock, and especially Dr. McCoy, and it features one of the program's most memorable monsters. This installment may not have reflected Roddenberry's higher ambitions, but the first job of any television program is to entertain. Whatever else it may be, "The Man Trap" is never dull.

Besides, in retrospect, this installment seems like a perfectly appropriate introduction to *Star Trek*. Over the next three seasons, the series frequently strayed from the path of "pure SF" to present numerous episodes that could be categorized as action-adventure or horror stories that happen to take place in a science fiction setting. Many of these tales featured monsters capable of wiping out entire civilizations and madmen bent on galactic domination, with only the stalwart crew of the *Enterprise* to save the Federation from these fiendish terrors. It was the stuff of pulp fiction, not Hugo Awards, but sci-fi pulps had been one of Roddenberry's earliest inspirations. And some of these episodes rank among the series' most colorful, exciting, and best-loved installments.

## Monsters

As they explored strange new worlds, the *Enterprise* often encountered fearsome, hostile creatures. Of all these many menaces, however, none were more memorable—or more intimidating—than the Horta from "The Devil in the Dark." Because it's ultimately revealed to be a sympathetic, misunderstood being, viewers may hesitate to label it a "monster," but that's the word used to describe the creature for the first two-thirds of the episode. The brilliance of Gene Coon's teleplay lies in the way it establishes a classic sci-fi monster scenario and then turns expectations on their head with the revelation of the Horta's true nature and motivations in the script's final act.

Early on, "The Devil in the Dark" plays like something along the lines of Howard Hawks's 1951 classic *The Thing* (based on John W. Campbell's oftenfilmed novella "Who Goes There?"), with a clutch of people in a remote and environmentally precarious setting being picked off one by one by some barely glimpsed terror. In the precredit teaser, a lone sentry is killed by the monster, his screams of agony echoing through the dark, lonely tunnels of mining colony Janus VI. Director Joseph Pevney's handling of this scene comes straight out of the classic horror handbook, with a tracking shot closing in on the terrified victim from the creature's point of view. We soon learn that "that butchering monster," as administrator Vanderberg calls the Horta, has murdered fifty miners already and seems bent on killing them all, leaving victims' bodies "burned to a crisp." The creature seems to be immune to phasers and can move through solid rock at amazing speeds, he reports. The danger seems so great that Kirk, at first, is adamant that the monster be destroyed. "The creature will be killed on sight and that's the end of it," he insists. Once the Horta comes fully into view, it proves no less remarkable—a quivering mass of molten rock, unlike any other creature seen elsewhere on *Star Trek*. The episode's well-turned twist works so well because it follows thirty minutes of tightly wound suspense. This combination of elements makes "Devil in the Dark" one of the series' most gripping and intellectually provocative installments.

This exquisite episode had humble origins. According to Bob Justman and Herb Solow's book *Inside Star Trek*, makeup effects freelancer Janos Prohaska appeared at Desilu one day to demonstrate a monster suit he had designed—the Horta. Producer Coon was floored by the suit and promptly wrote "The Devil in the Dark" to feature it, penning the teleplay start to finish in four days. Prohaska performed in the episode as the Horta. Earlier, he had portrayed a very similar beast (the "microbe creature") in *The Outer Limits* episode "The Probe."

Other memorable *Star Trek* monsters included:

- The Mugato, a primate that looks like a horn-headed albino gorilla. The creature attacks Captain Kirk in "A Private Little War."
- The Gorn, the lizardlike alien who battles Kirk in "Arena."
- The Space Amoeba, a giant single-celled organism that consumes the *Enterprise* in "The Immunity Syndrome."

- The Giant Anthropoids of planet of Taurus II (essentially, overgrown cavemen), which menace the away team led by Spock in "The Galileo Seven."
- The Neural Parasites, which resemble giant, flying raviolis, from "Operation—Annihilate." Although goofy-looking (they were actually repurposed bags of fake vomit), these parasites wreak havoc on the Deneva colony and kill Captain Kirk's brother, Sam.
- Sylvia, the cat-woman of planet Pyris VII in "Catspaw." Sylvia (Antoinette Bower) and her warlock mate, Korob (Theo Marcuse), hold a landing party captive with their "magical" powers.
- The Tribbles from "The Trouble with Tribbles." Maybe it's a stretch to call anything this cute and cuddly a "monster," but their impact on Starbase K-7 was certainly monstrous. Besides, the Klingons consider them little monsters.
- And, of course, the Salt Vampire from "The Man Trap."

## Malignant Life Forces

There were no monster suits needed for several of the creatures Captain Kirk and his crew tangled with. These were mere clouds of vapor or whirling balls of light, but they proved no less deadly than the flesh-and-blood (or rubber suit) beasties. Noncorporeal menaces became more prevalent during the show's third season, when budget constraints made *invisible* monsters an economic necessity. Arguably the most fearsome of this ethereal lot was the entity known as Redjac, which terrorizes planet Argelius II in "Wolf in the Fold."

Scotty, recuperating from a head wound, is accused of murdering two young women in brutal fashion, stabbing them repeatedly. The evidence all points to the *Enterprise* chief engineer, who suffered blackouts during both killings. If found guilty, Scotty will face the ancient Argelian penalty for murder: "death by slow torture." To get to the bottom of the mystery, prefect Jaris (Charles Macauley) asks his wife Sybo (Pilar Seurat), an empathic "sensate," to perform an ancient ritual (essentially, a séance). During the ceremony, she detects the presence of "an ancient evil." "Monstrous, terrible evil," she says, "a hunger that never dies." Then Sybo, too, is killed. Once again, Mr. Scott is the prime suspect. But eventually the killer is revealed to be a noncorporeal, virtually immortal life force (a "highly cohesive electromagnetic field," according to the *Enterprise* computer) named Redjac that feeds on fear. The entity projects a hypnotic screen that induces memory blackouts and occupies the body of a human host in order to kill. Over the centuries, Redjac has surfaced many times in many places, always committing a string of ghastly murders before vanishing again. One of its previous stops was gaslight-era England, where it was known as Jack the Ripper.

"Wolf in the Fold" is an old-fashioned horror-mystery yarn dressed up as science fiction. As in "The Devil in the Dark," Pevney's direction evokes the classic horror style, especially when his camera prowls the dark, foggy streets of Argelius II. He also drapes the séance sequence in shadowy ambiance. While "Wolf in the Fold" isn't terribly satisfying as a mystery (there are too few suspects to make its

In this publicity still for "The Man Trap," Kirk rubs shoulders with the Salt Vampire, the first of many *Star Trek* monsters.

solution very hard to figure out), it includes a deliciously perverse twist: "Piglet" turns out to be Jack the Ripper! Redjac inhabits the body of Argelian administrator Hengist, played by John Fiedler, best known as the voice of Piglet in Walt Disney's classic Winnie the Pooh cartoons. The episode's closing moments are priceless, with the incapacitated Hengist/Redjac railing, in Fiedler's Piglet voice, "Die, die, die, everybody die! Kill, kill, kill you all!"

This installment was written by Robert Bloch, who also penned "Catspaw" and "What Are Little Girls Made Of?" but remains most famous for his novel *Psycho*. "Wolf in the Fold" contains echoes of Bloch's acclaimed short story "Yours Truly, Jack the Ripper." In this tale, the Ripper is depicted as a globe-trotting, ageless sorcerer who preserves his eternal youth through periodic ritualistic murders. Both the episode and the story are bloody good yarns.

Other malevolent life forces:

- The Vampire Cloud from "Obsession" drained all the red corpuscles from the bodies of its victims, leaving a trail of pale, bloodless corpses. Eleven years earlier, the creature killed half the crew of the USS *Farragut*, including Kirk's mentor, Captain Garrovik.

- The Hate Creature (officially known as the "Beta XXVII-A Entity") from "Day of the Dove" was composed of "pure energy," according to Spock. It looked like a floating, spinning pinwheel of colors. It possessed fantastic powers, which it employed to trap humans and Klingons together on the *Enterprise* and force them to wage an endless, pointless war against one another, so the entity could feast on their growing hatred.

- The Zetarians were also energy beings, which looked like multicolored flashes of light. But they once had corporeal form, and in "The Lights of Zetar," they take possession of an *Enterprise* crew member, Lieutenant Mira Romaine (Jan Shutan), in an attempt to regain flesh-and-blood existence.

- Sargon was one of three ancient, formerly corporeal beings whose life essences had been preserved in noncorporeal form. In "Return to Tomorrow," Sargon and his friends asked to "borrow" the bodies of Kirk, Spock, and Dr. Ann Mulhall (Diana Muldaur) in order to construct android bodies for themselves. The trouble began when one member of the trio decided he would prefer to keep his human form.

- The Gorgan, perhaps better known as "the Friendly Angel," from "And the Children Shall Lead" was an ancient alien menace who duped the children of explorers on planet Triacus into murdering their parents. Next it tried to use the children to take control of the *Enterprise*. The translucent, ghostly Gorgan was portrayed by renowned defense attorney Melvin Belli, who was not an actor (and it showed).

## Technological Terrors

Aside from flesh-and-blood and "pure energy" menaces, the *Enterprise* also crossed paths with numerous mechanical monstrosities—malevolent supercomputers, as well as runaway robots and killer space probes. But the most chilling of these technological terrors was the Planet Killer from "The Doomsday Machine." The Planet Killer was a colossal, automated engine of destruction, capable of chewing up entire solar systems, one world at a time. Commodore Matt Decker (William Windom) described it as a "devil right out of Hell."

Responding to a distress signal, the *Enterprise* discovers Decker's ship, the *Constellation*, badly damaged in a futile battle with the Planet Killer, which was in the middle of consuming a nearby world. Captain Kirk, Scotty, Dr. McCoy, and a damage control team beam aboard the *Constellation* and find Decker keeled over a desk in auxiliary control room in a state of shock. McCoy takes him to the *Enterprise* for treatment while Kirk remains aboard the *Constellation*. Then the Planet Killer reappears, and Decker assumes command of the *Enterprise*, leading the ship into a near-suicidal attack on the monster, a robotic weapon of "immense size and power," according to Spock, that chops planets into rubble with a "pure anti-proton beam" and then sustains itself by feeding on the rubble. Kirk theorizes that the Planet Killer was a "doomsday machine" launched in a long-forgotten war and still roaming the galaxy, wreaking destruction. It was a weapon that was intended primarily as a bluff and never intended to be used, "like the old H-bombs were supposed to be."

Norman Spinrad's teleplay was inspired by *Moby Dick* and plays much like a nautical adventure tale. But Commodore Decker's Planet Killer bears little visual similarity to Captain Ahab's white whale. It looks more like a giant, demonic horn o' plenty. (In actuality, according to Paula Block and Terry Erdman's book *Star Trek: The Original Series 365*, it was a wind sock dipped in concrete.) Director Marc Daniels's unusual camera setups (several ultra-low angle and gliding tracking shots) subtly enhance the drama, and cinematographer Jerry Finnerman employs an uncharacteristically dark lighting scheme, lending the adventure a hard edge. Daniels also elicits excellent performances from the cast, especially Windom, who left an indelible impression as the battered, guilt-ridden, revenge-crazed Commodore Decker. The finishing touch is composer Sol Kaplan's stirring musical score, which many fans and critics consider the best ever written for *Star Trek*. It all adds up to one of the series' most suspenseful and spellbinding episodes.

Other man-made monsters:

- NOMAD, the demented space probe from "The Changeling," destroyed imperfect organic life forms (in other words, every living thing it met) before crossing paths with Captain Kirk.
- The M-5 experimental supercomputer from "The Ultimate Computer" took temporary command of the *Enterprise* and then refused to relinquish it, killing crewmen who attempt to deinstall it. Computer scientist Richard Daystrom's (William Marshall) bizarre relationship with the computer evoked connotations of *Frankenstein*, while the M-5's behavior foreshadowed the murderous HAL-9000 from *2001: A Space Odyssey* (1968).
- Landru was a telepathic supercomputer who held the population of planet Beta III under a reign of holy terror in "The Return of the Archons." Worshipped as a god, Landru's will was enforced by the monklike "Lawgivers."
- Vaal, another supercomputer worshipped as a god, ruled the docile denizens of planet Gamma Triaguli IV in "The Apple."

- The Providers, disembodied brains kept alive in a computer-like matrix, ruled the citizens of planet Triskelion in "The Gamesters of Triskelion." The Providers also forced slaves to compete in gladiatorial contests for their amusement (and wagering).
- Ruk, the giant, murderous android enforcer employed by mad scientist Dr. Roger Corby in "What Are Little Girls Made Of?," was portrayed by Ted "Lurch" Cassidy.

## Madmen

From Mary Shelley's Dr. Frankenstein to Sax Rohmer's Fu Manchu and beyond, mad scientists and megalomaniacs bent on conquest have been a staple of horror and adventure yarns. Inevitably, *Star Trek* had its share of such villains, as well, the greatest of which was undoubtedly the superhuman Khan Noonien Singh from "Space Seed," one of the most important figures in the history of the franchise.

The *Enterprise* discovers a centuries-old "sleeper ship," with dozens of inhabitants in suspended animation. The vessel turns out to be the USS *Botany Bay*, a penal ship carrying seventy-two genetically engineered supermen (and superwomen) from the long-ago Eugenics Wars. Their leader is the imperious, implacable Khan (Ricardo Montalban), whose physical and intellectual abilities are matched only by his personal charisma. Kirk, Scotty, and historian Lieutenant Marla McGivers (Madlyn Rhue) revive the sleepers before they realize who they are. Khan, a ruthless dictator who once ruled a quarter of the planet, seduces McGivers, revives his compatriots, then takes control of the *Enterprise* and prepares to launch a new campaign. "The battle begins again," he boasts. "Only this time it is not a world we will win, it's a universe." Khan's overconfidence creates an opportunity for Kirk to defeat the tyrant and his genetic supermen.

Marc Daniels directs with his characteristic skill and precision and keeps the tempo brisk. But the episode's primary strengths are its tightly wound, psychologically complex teleplay by Gene Coon and Carey Wilber and the dynamic performances of Montalban and Shatner, who circle each other throughout the episode like two panthers trapped in the same cage. The script depicts the Starfleet officers' conflicted feelings about the bold, larger-than-life Khan, who is in many ways an ideal leader. McGivers falls in love with him, betrays him to free Captain Kirk, but ultimately chooses to remain with Khan. Even Kirk, McCoy, and Scott are impressed with the would-be emperor of the universe—much to Spock's consternation. "We can be against him and admire him all at the same time," Kirk explains. All this works because Montalban's performance is so stylish and alluring. As a dynamic leader of men, his Khan outdoes even Captain Kirk, which didn't sit well with William Shatner. Although the rest of the cast and crew got on well with Montalban, Shatner despised working with him. Some of this leaks through in his performance, lending a sharp edge to Kirk's determination to defeat his rival. This serves the story well.

Director Robert Gist kept the giant anthropoids in the shadows while filming "The Galileo Seven," but one of the creatures can be seen clearly in this publicity still.

In the end, Khan is not so much defeated as bargained with, left with a planet of his own to tame, the harsh but habitable Ceti Alpha V. Fifteen years later, writer-director Nicholas Meyer used this open ending as the jumping-off point for *Star Trek II: The Wrath of Khan* (1982). With one of the most popular villains in *Star Trek* history (and one of the most accomplished guest stars to appear on the program) on board, Meyer crafted an action-packed, emotionally gripping film that became a blockbuster hit, and that many fans revere as the finest *Star Trek* feature film. The success of this movie cannot be understated. Following the disappointing critical and box-office reception for *Star Trek: The Motion Picture*, the future of the entire franchise was hanging in the balance. If *The Wrath of Khan* had flopped, the entire franchise might have gone down with it. Instead Khan, *Star Trek*'s most notorious villain, became the franchise's savior.

Other megalomaniacs and mad scientists:

- Dr. Tristan Adams, the administrator of the Tantalus Penal Colony, used his "neural neutralizer" to perform torturous experiments on inmates and even staff members in "Dagger of the Mind." Adams was played by James Gregory, the former *Manchurian Candidate* and future General Ursus (from *Beneath the Planet of the Apes*).

- Dr. Roger Corby (Michael Strong) was an archeologist who discovered ancient technology that enabled him to build sophisticated (and potentially deadly) android servants in "What Are Little Girls Made Of?" He was also the former fiancé of Nurse Christine Chapel.

- Kodos the Executioner, from "The Conscience of the King," was a former governor of the Tarsus IV colony who, faced with a famine, ordered the deaths of 4,000 settlers so that 4,000 other settlers (of his choosing) could survive. Although presumed dead, Kodos was discovered to be hiding under the assumed identity of actor Anton Karidian. Veteran Arnold Moss portrayed Kodos/Karidian. Seventeen years earlier, he costarred with Ricardo Montalban in the film noir classic "Border Incident."

- Captain Garth (Steve Ihnat), better known as Garth of Izar, was a decorated Starfleet officer whose exploits in battle were legendary. But he went mad and tried to establish himself as dictator of the galaxy, after the aliens of planet Antos IV taught him their technique for reshaping matter through mental energy. He was confined to an asylum on Elba II, where—in "Whom Gods Destroy"—he took Kirk and Spock hostage during an escape attempt.

- Colonel Phillip Green was a twenty-first-century tyrant and notorious war criminal who was recreated by the Excalbians in "The Savage Curtain." Green (Phillip Pine) led a team of villains that also included Genghis Khan and Kahless the Unforgettable, founder of the Klingon Empire, in a good-versus-evil showdown against Kirk, Spock, Abraham Lincoln, and Surak of Vulcan. Green was also mentioned (and appeared in "historical" video) in the *Star Trek: Enterprise* episode "In a Mirror Darkly, Part II."

# 21

# Strange New Worlds

## Alternate Earths, Time Travel, and Parallel Dimensions

**N**BC continually pressured *Star Trek*'s creative brain trust for more "planet shows," episodes where Captain Kirk and his crew fulfilled their mission to "explore strange new worlds" literally. But creating the sets, costumes, and makeup effects required for a planet show was expensive. With budgets tight and shrinking season by season, producer Gene Roddenberry and his team were compelled to shoot an increasing number of "ship shows," with the action confined to the standing *Enterprise* sets. Many of the program's finest adventures were ship shows (including "The Naked Time," "Charlie X," "The Doomsday Machine," "Journey to Babel," and "Space Seed," among others), but the network's thirst for planet shows remained unquenchable.

Roddenberry and his team developed a three-pronged strategy to sate NBC's desire for planet shows while controlling costs, developing teleplays in which the *Enterprise* crew ventured to worlds that mirrored Earth, or traveled in time, or even crossed into other dimensions. Although born of necessity, some of these voyages helped expand the horizons of the franchise's rapidly coalescing mythology.

### Strangely Familiar Worlds

In their script for "Bread and Circuses," Roddenberry and Gene Coon introduced "Hodgkin's Law of Parallel Planetary Development," a fictional principle that states that similar sentient species inhabiting planets with similar environments (for instance, humanoids from Earthlike Class M worlds) tend to develop similar cultures. This was the explanation given for the society of planet 892-IV, which mirrored the culture of ancient Rome, only with twentieth-century technology. While utterly ludicrous, Hodgkin's Law serves as a prime example of the show's ability to make even the most fanciful ideas sound reasonable by dressing them up in pseudoscientific jargon. Later, the biological applications of Hodgkin's Law were used to explain why so many of the species Starfleet met as it expanded throughout the galaxy were bipedal mammals.

Roddenberry had planned for the *Enterprise* to visit parallel Earths from the beginning. The idea was included in his original prospectus for the series,

In "A Piece of the Action," Kirk and Spock struggle to fit in on the gangster planet Sigma Iotia II, one of *Star Trek*'s many parallel Earths. ("Fotonovel" cover, 1977)

where it was referred to as the "Similar Worlds Concept." He noted in the proposal that this idea "gives extraordinary story latitude—ranging from worlds which parallel our own yesterday, our present, to our breathtaking distant future." There were practical advantages, too. "Similar worlds" episodes could be shot on everyday locations or standing sets leftover from other productions and could utilize stock costumes and props. "Bread and Circuses," for instance, reused wardrobe from movies including Cecil B. DeMille's "The Sign of the Cross" and Joseph Mankiewicz's "Cleopatra." Also, placing Kirk, Spock, and friends in environments that approximated contemporary or historical settings invited the kind of Swiftian social commentary that, for Roddenberry, remained the program's prime directive. "Bread and Circuses," for instance, is a scathing satire of television, with Romanesque gladiatorial contests staged (and rigged) to maximize viewership. The Master of the Games (Jack Perkins) warns a producer, "You bring this network's ratings down, Flavius, and we'll do a special on you!"

Unfortunately, the drawbacks to the parallel Earth concept were also significant, which is why the later *Star Trek* films and TV series generally eschewed such scenarios, even though Roddenberry had considered the concept foundational.

On a purely visceral level, mirror-Earth episodes could be a letdown for the audience. It was deflating to have the *Enterprise* trek halfway across the galaxy to reach a planet that looked like something viewers had seen many times before. And, perhaps because the Earthlike settings made the program's allegories seem too obvious, the thematic content of these episodes often came across as clumsy or ham-fisted. That was certainly the case with such "similar worlds" tales as "The Omega Glory," set on a savage world trapped in a centuries-old war between the Yangs (Yankees) and Kahms (commies), and "Miri," featuring a planet devastated by medical experiments gone haywire. The results were better with "The Return of the Archons," in which an Earthlike planet is subjugated by a totalitarian theocracy, and "Bread and Circuses" partially because both of those teleplays included a wicked streak of dark humor. Laughter atones for a multitude of sins.

Another major drawback to the "Similar Worlds" concept is that, Hodgkin's Law aside, the idea of an alien planet developing into a virtual carbon copy of Earth is simply too preposterous to bear scrutiny. That problem was solved in a handful of episodes where a planet's similarities to Earth were explained in different, more plausible ways. In "Patterns of Force," for instance, the Nazi-like culture of planet Excalbia was the result of ill-advised meddling by a Federation cultural observer. In "A Piece of the Action," the mobster society of planet Sigma Iota II arose when an Earth ship accidentally left behind a book about Chicago gangs of the 1920s. And in "Spectre of the Gun," a landing party is sent to a ghostly recreation of 1880s Tombstone, Arizona, as a punishment for encroaching on the home world of the xenophobic Melkotians. Not coincidentally, these episodes proved far more effective than those that relied on the flimsy Hodgkin's Law. "A Piece of the Action" and "Spectre of the Gun," arguably, remain the most satisfying of all *Star Trek*'s alternate-Earth adventures.

## Strange Old Worlds

Another way for the program to employ contemporary, real-world locales was for the *Enterprise*—or members of its crew—to travel back in time, as happened on four memorable occasions. In "Tomorrow Is Yesterday," the *Enterprise* is accidentally catapulted back to the 1960s and forced to rescue an Air Force pilot whose disappearance may alter history. In "The City on the Edge of Forever," Kirk and Spock use an alien time portal to travel into the past and correct a damaged timeline caused by the actions of Dr. McCoy, who passed through the portal after an accidental drug overdose. In "Assignment: Earth," the *Enterprise* travels back in time to conduct historical research and discovers an enigmatic alien time traveler who may be trying to alter history. And in "All Our Yesterdays," Kirk, Spock, and McCoy use a different time portal to journey to different historical eras of planet Sarpeidon, which conveniently happens to be yet another parallel Earth. Kirk becomes entangled in the planet's equivalent of the Salem Witch Trials, while Spock and McCoy are stuck in Sarpeidon's ice age. *The Enterprise* also travels backwards in time, briefly, at the end of "The Naked Time," which was originally planned as a two-part episode paired with "Tomorrow Is Yesterday."

Time travel, of course, has been a staple of science fiction at least as far back as H. G. Wells's *The Time Machine*, first published in 1895. However, time-travel stories are notoriously troublesome. Even setting aside the overwhelming scientific implausibility of travel into the past or round-trip travel into the future, such stories present vexing narrative conundrums. Writers are forced to make tough choices about how time travel works in order to avoid the potential paradoxes such stories present. To cite the classic example: If you travel into the past and accidentally kill your own grandfather, would you cease to exist? And if you no longer exist, how were you able to travel back in time and nullify your existence? Perhaps by traveling back in time, you create an alternate timeline where you do not exist without affecting the original timeline in which you do exist. Or perhaps it's safe to travel back in time because you *cannot* kill your own grandfather; it simply couldn't happen that way because if it did, you wouldn't have been around to make the trip in the first place. The possibilities are mind-numbing. Unfortunately, screenwriters never settled on a consistent, fully satisfactory set of rules governing the temporal mechanics of the *Trek* universe.

Even the great "City on the Edge of Forever" suffers from a gaping chasm of story logic. Moments after the Cordrazine-addled McCoy leaps through the Guardian of Forever, Captain Kirk attempts to contact his ship. The Guardian informs him that the *Enterprise* has vanished, along with the

*TV Guide* advertisement for a syndicated rebroadcast of "Tomorrow Is Yesterday," *Star Trek*'s first time-travel story.

entire Federation of Planets, because the timeline has been altered. "All that you knew is gone," the Guardian reports. The landing party is stranded, Spock says, "with no past and no future." But this makes no sense. Why hasn't the away team disappeared along with the ship? Surely the one cannot exist in this revised timeline without the other. It's a classic case of the screenwriter (in this case, the esteemed Harlan Ellison) trying to have it both ways. The temporal logic involved in "Tomorrow Is Yesterday" and "Assignment: Earth" is no less convoluted.

Despite these flaws, however, *Star Trek*'s time-travel stories rank among the series' most entertaining and enduringly popular installments. All four are lively, engrossing yarns with touching character moments and amusing comedic interludes, strengths that trump other shortcomings. Besides, audiences usually make greater allowances for time-travel stories. Maybe this is because time travel itself is so fantastic that the fine-grain details seem insignificant; in for a penny, in for a pound. Or perhaps viewers simply prefer to avoid the headache of working out the internal logic of such tales.

Whatever the reason, fans' enthusiasm for episodes like "The City on the Edge of Forever" and "Tomorrow Is Yesterday" helped ensure that time travel would remain an important story element for the franchise. Every subsequent *Star Trek* series featured several time-travel tales, including classics like "Yesterday's *Enterprise*," "Cause and Effect," and "All Good Things" from *The Next Generation*; "Past Tense (Parts I and II)," "Little Green Men," and "Trials and Tribble-ations" from *Deep Space Nine*; and "Future's End (Parts I and II)" and "Endgame" from *Voyager*. *Star Trek: Enterprise*'s "Temporal Cold War" was a recurring plot element that weaved its way in and out of numerous story arcs throughout the series' four-season run. "Yesteryear," the finest of *Star Trek*'s twenty-two animated episodes, was a time-travel story. And time travel figured in the plots of four of the eleven *Trek* feature films: *The Voyage Home* (1986), *Generations* (1994), *First Contact* (1996), and the *Star Trek* reboot (2009).

## Strange New Dimensions

In addition to its travels through space and time, *Star Trek* sometimes ventured to even more exotic destinations: alternate dimensions. In "Mirror, Mirror," a freak transporter accident sends Kirk, McCoy, Scotty, and Uhura to a twisted parallel dimension populated by evil duplicates of themselves and the rest of the crew. Although "Mirror, Mirror" was a ship show, the scenario was so colorful that it *seemed* like a planet show. Or at least it seemed to be taking place somewhere remarkably different than the familiar *Enterprise*. From a scientific perspective, of course, interdimensional journeys remain even more far-fetched than time travel (we know time exists, whereas the existence of alternate dimensions remains at best speculative). The kind of precise mirror universe depicted in this episode is beyond preposterous. Yet "Mirror, Mirror" remains a thrilling and thought-provoking yarn, and there's no denying the sheer fun of meeting

Scotty and Kirk, disguised as their Mirror Universe alter-egos, take a breather after mopping up sick bay with the Evil Sulu and his henchmen in "Mirror, Mirror."

the villainous alter egos of the beloved *Enterprise* crew. Superbly produced and performed, "Mirror, Mirror" ranks among the most beloved of all *Trek* adventures. It belatedly spawned five *Deep Space Nine* episodes and a two-part *Star Trek: Enterprise* story arc.

Star Trek's other interdimensional journeys didn't make as big a splash but created some interesting ripples. In "The Tholian Web," Captain Kirk is lost in an "interdimensional rift" while investigating the disabled USS *Defiant*. *Star Trek: Enterprise*'s two-part Mirror Universe adventure, "In a Mirror, Darkly," concerned the fate of the *Defiant*, which slips through the rift both into the evil alternate dimension and back in time as well. In "The Alternative Factor," an interdimensional fissure opens between our universe and a negatively charged parallel universe. The situation is further complicated by a mad alien (Robert Brown) bent on destroying his negatively charged doppelganger. Captain Kirk and crew must prevent Lazarus from coming into physical contact with the anti-Lazarus, since the ensuing repercussions could obliterate both universes. While not a scintillating installment, "The Alternative Factor" nevertheless spawned an animated tie-in. In the final episode of the *Star Trek* cartoon series, "The Counter-Clock Incident," the *Enterprise* accidentally crosses over into this negative universe, where time runs backwards and the crew grows younger.

## Strange New Worlds (Really)

Naturally, the *Enterprise* visited truly alien planets sometimes, too—just not as often as you might think. Excluding stories involving alternate Earths, time travel, and parallel dimensions, sixteen of twenty-nine Season One adventures can be categorized as planet shows (if you include "Court Martial," which takes place on a space station). Thirteen of twenty-six Season Two installments were planet shows (counting "The Trouble with Tribbles," also set on a space station), as were fifteen of twenty-four Season Three entries. However, this Season Three number is misleading and drops significantly if you exclude episodes such as "The Day of the Dove," "The Lights of Zetar," "The Way to Eden," and "Turnabout Intruder," which take place almost exclusively aboard the *Enterprise*, except for brief planet-side sequences. While those numbers would seem to validate NBC's impression that *Star Trek* wasn't exploring "strange new worlds" often enough, the network was also responsible for the show's shrinking budget, which made producing such stories so difficult.

Besides, shooting a true, full-blown planet show was no guarantee of success. While some of the series' finest installments fit this description ("The Menagerie, Parts I and II," "The Squire of Gothos," "The Devil in the Dark," "Amok Time," "The Empath," etc.), so do many mundane, even subpar entries ("Operation—Annihilate," "The Gamesters of Triskelion," "The Paradise Syndrome," "Spock's Brain," etc.).

What NBC, with its fetish for planet shows, seemed to miss was that there was no single blueprint for making a good *Star Trek* episode—and, in the final analysis, this was a good thing. If such an outline had been discovered, more consistently high-caliber episodes may have been produced, but the series inevitably would have taken on a monotonous, formulaic quality. Instead, the show's producers and writers simply tried anything and everything they could think of. The result was a freshness, a vitality, a sense of adventure that more than compensates for the occasional clunker episode. Later *Star Trek* series and films strived to emulate the classic series' willingness, even eagerness, to take risks. Through the original seventy-nine episodes, this freewheeling spirit was encoded on the DNA of the franchise and remains one of its greatest strengths.

# New Life and New Civilizations

## Vulcans, Klingons, Romulans, and More

One of the most appealing fixtures of *Star Trek* is that it takes place in a galaxy teeming not only with life but with civilizations. "Everything's alive," Captain Kirk says in "Metamorphosis." "We estimate there are millions of planets with intelligent life. We haven't begun to map them."

Throughout its travels, the *Enterprise* meets many different species, although there are some striking similarities between these extraterrestrials. "Almost all the [*Star Trek*] aliens are bipedal, breathe the same air as us, are capable of interbreeding, and in fact differ only in the shape of their respective foreheads," authors Cory Doctorow and Karl Schroeder point out in *Complete Idiot's Guide to Publishing Science Fiction*.

After underscoring the blatant implausibility of such a setting, Doctorow and Schroeder nevertheless point to *Trek* as an example of how to create a cohesive science fictional universe. "It doesn't matter that all this is ridiculous from a scientific standpoint," they write. "We suspend our disbelief because these elements of the *Star Trek* universe always work the same way. They are internally consistent, and they follow rules that make sense within the framework of the story told."

Indeed, creator-producer Gene Roddenberry and story editors including Dorothy Fontana worked tirelessly to ensure the show's conceptual continuity. However, they didn't just invent aliens; they also imagined whole societies, with cultures and customs divergent enough that viewers accepted individual species as distinct, despite their physical similarities. The extraterrestrials they envisioned served as the foundation for the wildly imaginative yet internally coherent panorama the *Star Trek* universe eventually became. Later *Trek* series introduced aliens such as the Borg, the Q, the Ferengi, the Bejorans, the Cardassians, the Founders, and the Xindi, among many others. These sequel shows also fleshed out and, in some cases, reimagined those civilizations created for the classic *Trek* program. Stripping away these addendums and revisions reveals *Star Trek*, the original species.

### The Vulcans

*Star Trek*'s most popular character was (and probably still is) the *Enterprise*'s resident alien, the half-Vulcan Mr. Spock. He was the conscience of *Star Trek*. His

AMT's figure model of Mr. Spock described the Vulcan as "*Star Trek*'s most popular character." So he was, and probably still is.

status as an interested outsider gave him a unique, detached perspective from which to comment on the foibles of the human race. Viewers quickly became fascinated by the stoic, logic-based Vulcan society, a cornerstone of the emerging *Trek* mythology.

Vulcan culture was by far the most fully imagined of all the extraterrestrial civilizations featured on the classic *Trek* series. Viewers learned (in episodes including "The Savage Curtain" and "All Our Yesterdays") that eons ago, the Vulcans were a savage, violent people teetering on the brink of self-destruction. All that changed with the appearance of the great leader Surak, who established logic and the repression of emotion as the Vulcan rule of life. Those Vulcans who rejected logic and clung to emotion moved elsewhere, including to the planet Romulus (as audiences discovered in "Balance of Terror" and "The *Enterprise* Incident").

Most of what viewers learned about Vulcans came from Spock. Only three episodes featured other Vulcans—"Amok Time," "Journey to Babel," and "The Savage Curtain." (OK, make that four episodes, if you count the Evil Spock from "Mirror, Mirror" as a non-Spock Vulcan. Also, the animated adventure "Yesteryear" took place on Vulcan.) Through Spock, the basic tenets of Vulcan anatomy, ethics, and history were established:

- With their pointed ears hidden, Vulcans can pass for human ("The City on the Edge of Forever," "Patterns of Force," etc.). However, their physiology is quite different: They have copper-based green blood ("The Naked Time"); their hearts are located in the vicinity of the human liver ("Mudd's Women," "A Private Little War"), and they have no appendix ("Operation— Annihilate!"). Having evolved on a harsh, desert world, Vulcans developed extremely acute hearing and an inner eyelid that protected them from bright light ("Operation—Annihilate!").
- Vulcans have much longer life spans than humans (as noted in several episodes), but mate only once every seven years. Their mating rituals date back to their savage, prehistoric past ("Amok Time").
- They are telepaths, capable of joining minds with other entities (as seen in many episodes), exerting limited mental control over other people ("The Omega Glory") and, when critically injured, shutting down nearly all life functions to focus all their energies on healing ("A Private Little War").
- Vulcans are known for their honesty. It's said that they cannot lie and never bluff, although this isn't entirely true. They are capable of misleading when necessary ("The *Enterprise* Incident").
- Vulcan has never been conquered ("The Immunity Syndrome"). In "Return to Tomorrow," Spock theorizes that Vulcan and Earth both may have originally have been settled by the same ancient alien race.

The Vulcan civilization was explored extensively in the *Star Trek* feature films (especially *The Search for Spock*), *Star Trek: Voyager*, which featured Vulcan security officer Tuvok (Tim Russ) and *Star Trek: Enterprise*, which featured Vulcan first officer T'Pol (Jolene Blalock) and many Vulcan recurring supporting characters. Today, diehard fans know that the Vulcans were the first Federation species to develop warp drive; that they made first contact with warp drive pioneer Zefram Cochrane in 2063 and helped the humans rebuild a war-ravaged planet Earth; and that they dislike touching their food. All this and much more were later additions. Over the years, writers and producers seemed just as interested in Vulcan society as they were in the franchise's human "future history." But that was fine, since most fans felt the same way.

## The Klingons

Even more than the Vulcans, the Klingons *Trek* fans know and love today are a creation of the movies and sequel series, rather than the original *Trek*. The original Klingons looked very different and, more importantly, behaved quite differently than "modern" Klingons. Put simply, the original Klingons were one-note villains. Roddenberry didn't especially like the species and discouraged his writers from using them whenever possible. Nevertheless, the Klingons became the most popular antagonists in the *Star Trek* universe, often showing up in novels and comic books during the 1970s. Toy company Mego never made a

Sulu or Chekov action figure, but it produced a Klingon doll. One of model kit maker AMT's most popular products was its Klingon Battle Cruiser kit.

Once *The Next Generation* came along, Roddenberry placed Worf (Michael Dorn) on the bridge of the *Enterprise-D* and set about reimagining the Klingons, borrowing from Japanese, Norse, and other cultures for inspiration. Over the course of *Next Gen, Deep Space Nine, Voyager,* and the feature films, the Klingons were redefined as a warrior civilization with a deeply ingrained honor code similar to the *bushido* code of the samurai, a tribal society organized into distinct "houses" that compete for political influence, and a deeply spiritual culture. (Those who die honorably, they believe, will spend eternity in the Valhalla-like Sto-vo-kor, alongside Kahless the Unforgettable, founder of the Klingon Empire.) Klingons write operas. They drink "blood wine" and prefer to eat their food while it's still alive.

Almost none of this originates from the classic *Trek* series.

Although Klingons turned up frequently (they appear in seven of the seventy-nine original episodes and in two animated adventures), they bore little similarity to the later Klingons. For starters, they look almost nothing alike—they're just guys in bronze makeup and pasted-on mustaches and eyebrows, missing the fangs and prominent ridges in their foreheads of their later counterparts. The physical dissimilarities between these two generations of Klingons were supposedly explained away in a two-part *Star Trek: Enterprise* story, "Affliction" and "Divergence," in which the Klingons conduct eugenics experiments using DNA from genetically enhanced humans; as a result, a generation of Klingons gain human features. However, this explanation does not account for why the Klingons Kor (John Colicos), Koloth (William Campbell), and Kang (Michael Ansara), seen without forehead ridges in their classic *Trek* appearances, looked like modern Klingons when they reappeared in the *DS9* episode "Blood Oath." (Perhaps they visited a plastic surgeon and got "forehead jobs.")

More significantly, the original Klingons seemed amoral and unsympathetic. Rather than samurai or Vikings, the original reference point for the Klingons was the Mongol horde of Genghis Khan. (Not coincidentally, Genghis Khan fought side by side by Kahless in "The Savage Curtain.") They were venal and underhanded barbarians—cunning, ruthless conquerors and merciless, totalitarian dictators of the worlds they conquered.

The Klingons first appeared in "Errand of Mercy," in which they occupy Organia and rule the sheeplike, pacifist Organians pitilessly, even disdainfully, murdering hundreds of innocent civilians in retaliation when Kirk and Spock attempt to resist. Viewers at the time would have recognized this as a parallel with the Nazis, who answered acts of sabotage by murdering civilian hostages in places like France, Poland, and Eastern Russia.

In "Friday's Child," Klingon agent Kras (Tige Andrews) foments a civil war among the primitive residents of Capella IV, attempts to swindle them out of their mineral resources, and tries to stab Captain Kirk in the back—literally. As Worf might say, he is "without honor." Meanwhile, Kras's ship dupes the

Mego's Klingon action figure bore a slight similarity to William Campbell's Commander
Koloth, from "The Trouble with Tribbles."    *Photo courtesy of Trace & Trev's Twisted Toys*

*Enterprise* away from the planet using a bogus distress signal but slinks away when
given the chance to engage in a straight-up fight with the Federation flagship.

The Klingons are up to more underhanded tricks in their next few appearances, too—poisoning a grain shipment in "The Trouble with Tribbles," instigating another civil war among a developing civilization in "A Private Little War,"
and trying to start an interplanetary conflict in "Elaan of Troyius." In "The
Savage Curtain," Kahless is presented as one of history's vilest villains, *not* as the
founder of a great civilization.

The only original *Trek* episode to moderate this dim view of the Klingons
is "Day of the Dove," in which a hate-eating sentient life force traps Klingons
and humans together aboard a crippled *Enterprise* and lures them into an
escalating war. Faced with a common enemy, humans and Klingons finally
set aside their differences and work together. Commander Kang (Michael
Ansara) would serve as the model for future Klingons, who were intimidating but

# STAR TREK®

## Day Of The Dove

### EPISODE 66

## The Original and Uncut Television Series

"Day of the Dove," featuring Commander Kang (Michael Ansara) and Mara (Susan Howard), began the transformation of the Klingons from one-note villains to more sympathetic characters.

respectable, adhering to a harsh but comprehensible honor code. Back in "Errand of Mercy," the Organian leader Ayelborne (John Abbott) had foreseen that "in the future, you and the Klingons will become fast friends." But "Day of the Dove" was the first story to provide any real inkling of this.

The Klingons returned in two animated adventures ("More Tribbles, More Troubles" and "The Time Trap"), but were once again depicted as amoral and duplicitous. Nevertheless, the Klingons remained fan favorites. As *Next Gen* redefined and elaborated on their culture, their popularity soared to unimagined heights, eclipsing even that of the beloved Vulcans. No quarter of the *Star Trek* universe has inspired more ardent devotion. The most invested fans proudly produce elaborate Klingon costumes and makeup to wear to conventions and learn to speak Klingonese. Some write poems and operas in the language. A group of fans has even translated the Bible into Klingon: "*yeSuS 'IHrIStoS,* [Qun'a' puqloD] Delbogh De' Qa'e' taghlu'. nemSovwI' *yeSay'a* paq ghItlh pabtaH ghu': SuH bIghoSpa',

lenglIj qeqbogh QumwI'wI''e' vIngeHlI'." (For you non-Klingon readers, that's "The beginning of the good news of Jesus Christ, the Son of God. As it is written in the prophet Isaiah, 'See, I am sending my messenger ahead of you, who will prepare your way.'") One can only wonder what Roddenberry would make of this development.

## The Romulans

The Romulans are descended from Vulcans who rejected the rule of logic and left their home world during the "Time of Awakening," millennia ago. Physiologically, they remain virtually identical with their Vulcan "cousins," but their culture is entirely distinct. The Romulans remain warlike and belligerent, their society organized around military principles with a profound emphasis on duty. They waged an interstellar war with the humans in the earliest days of the United Federation of Planets. When that war ended, a Neutral Zone was established as a buffer between Romulan and Federation space. Nevertheless, the Romulans sometimes venture beyond the Zone to attack Federation targets. They developed a Cloaking Device that rendered their ships invisible both to the naked eye and to computerized scans, technology that threatened to alter the balance of power in the galaxy. All this viewers learn over the course of the Romulans' three classic *Trek* appearances, in "The Balance of Terror," "The Deadly Years" (in which the Romulans make what amounts to a cameo), and "The *Enterprise* Incident." Romulans also appeared in three installments of the animated series ("The Survivor," "The Time Trap," and "The Practical Joker") but were not the primary focus of any of those stories.

In these early appearances, the Romulans were presented much more sympathetically than the Klingons. The unnamed Romulan commanders played by Mark Lenard in "The Balance of Terror" and Joanne Linville in "The *Enterprise* Incident" are likeable people trapped in a culture they realize is misguided but feel powerless to combat. As with the Vulcans and the Klingons, later series and movies greatly expanded viewers' "knowledge" of the Romulan civilization. Romulans were featured extensively on *Next Gen* (where they made twenty-one appearances), *DS9* (sixteen appearances) and in the feature film *Star Trek: Nemesis* (2002). But unlike the Klingons, the Romulans' fundamental nature changed little. They remained aggressive, unscrupulous conquerors bent on expanding their Star Empire throughout the galaxy. And individual Romulans were rarely depicted with as much empathy as the characters played by Lenard and Linville.

## The Orions

The green-skinned Orions are a highly troublesome species, a consortium of thieves, cutthroats and slave traders united under the banner of the Orion Syndicate. They claim political neutrality, but often insert themselves into interplanetary disputes, playing competing factions against one another to suit their own purposes. The Orions enslave captured aliens and also practice piracy and espionage. Orion women are known for their allure (partially the product of powerful pheromones) and for their voracious sexual appetite. Orion "slave girls" are prized in dark corners of the galaxy, such as Rigel IV. These "facts" viewers learned through the Orions' three appearances, in "The Menagerie (Parts I and II)," "Journey to Babel," and "Whom Gods Destroy." Orions also featured prominently in the animated episodes "The Time Trap" and "The Pirates of Orion."

The Orions were one of the most colorful and compelling of all the alien civilizations featured on *Star Trek*. Yet, despite the rich story possibilities offered by this species, the Orions were ignored by the franchise throughout the 1980s and '90s. No Orion ever appeared on any of the *Star Trek* series set in the twenty-fourth century (*Next Gen*, *DS9*, and *Voyager*) or in any of the first ten feature films. This may have been because certain aspects of the Orion culture were similar to those of the Ferengi, introduced on *The Next Generation*. Eventually, however, the Orions were featured in three episodes of the prequel series *Star Trek: Enterprise*, and an Orion Starfleet cadet appeared in director J. J. Abrams's 2009 feature film *Star Trek*.

## The Andorians

With their blue skin and conspicuous antennae, the Andorians were arguably the most distinctive-looking of all *Star Trek*'s alien species. But after a prominent first appearance in the excellent adventure "Journey to Babel," they all but vanished from the franchise for thirty-four years. The Andorians were one of a handful of species (along with the Vulcans and the Tellarites, among others) on their way to a key diplomatic summit in "Journey to Babel"; one member of the Andorian delegation proved to be a surgically altered Orion spy, out to sabotage the meeting. Beyond their striking physical appearance and the fact that they value honesty, however, little was revealed about the Andorians in "Journey to Babel."

Andorians reappeared as background characters in a few more episodes ("The Gamesters of Triskelion," "Whom Gods Destroy," and "The Lights of Zetar"), a pair of animated installments ("Yesteryear" and "The Time Trap"), the first and fourth feature films, and two *Next Gen* adventures ("The Offspring" and "Captain's Holiday"), but their culture remained a blank slate. They never appeared at all on *Deep Space Nine* or *Voyager*. Finally, *Star Trek: Enterprise* provided an elaborate and fascinating portrait of Andorian society, beginning with "The Andorian Incident" in 2001. Over the course of sixteen episodes, mostly concentrated in the show's final two seasons, *Enterprise* portrayed the Andorians as a proud, mildly xenophobic warrior race and long-standing antagonist of the Vulcans. It revealed that they originate from an icy moon of the gas giant Andoria, have blue blood, and can regrow damaged antennae. Commander Shran (Jeffrey Combs) became a prominent recurring character; he played a pivotal role in the founding of the Federation.

## The Tellarites

Like the Andorians, the Tellarites first appeared in "Journey to Babel" and were then largely forgotten. But at least the Tellarites had some personality—they were pugnacious, argumentative and greedy. Their physical appearance was also unmistakable: they were stubby, hairy humanoids with piglike snouts. During "Journey to Babel," they were embroiled in a trade dispute with the Vulcans and Andorians. A member of the Tellarite delegation was murdered by the Orion spy. The Tellarites demanded justice and pointed a suspicious, furry finger at Sarek of Vulcan.

After this memorable debut, however, the Tellarites also faded into obscurity, appearing as extras in "Whom Gods Destroy," "The Lights of Zetar," and the animated "Time Trap." (Additionally, shots of Tellarite makeup tests turned up in the closing credits of "The Deadly Years" and "A Private Little War.") The Tellarites reappeared, again as background characters, in *The Voyage Home* and *The Undiscovered Country*, and in isolated episodes of *Next Gen* ("Conspiracy") and *Voyager* ("Non Sequitur"). Finally, again like the Andorians, the Tellarites were belatedly revived by *Star Trek: Enterprise*, appearing in nine episodes. It was established that they, along with the humans, Vulcans, and Andorians, were founding members of the United Federation of Planets.

## The Tholians

The Tholians appeared in just one episode, but it was one of *Star Trek*'s most memorable adventures—"The Tholian Web," in which Captain Kirk is lost in an interdimensional rift, while the Tholians attempt to capture the *Enterprise* in a net of energy beams. Along with the Horta from "The Devil in the Dark," the Tholians were one of very few nonhumanoid species to appear on the classic series. They are a highly technologically advanced insectoid race but also extremely xenophobic and aggressive, making them fearsome adversaries. However, as with the Andorians and the Tellarites, future *Star Trek* series seldom explored the story possibilities presented by the Tholians. Although the species was mentioned in passing on *The Next Generation* and *Deep Space Nine*, the Tholians never appeared again until they were revived by *Star Trek: Enterprise* for three episodes, including the two-part Mirror Universe tale "In a Mirror, Darkly."

## The Gorn

The lizardlike Gorn were another fierce and aggressive race who made a single, unforgettable appearance on *Star Trek*—in "Arena," of course, one of the most famous of all *Trek* adventures—and then seemingly evaporated (although a Gorn can be glimpsed briefly in the animated episode "The Time Trap"). In this case, however, the disappearance was more understandable. After all, the Gorn suit was expensive and tricky to shoot. And putting a stunt actor in a latex suit was unthinkable on the sequel series, when audience expectations regarding special effects were far higher. In 2005, *Star Trek: Enterprise* used computer animation to revive the Gorn for the Mirror Universe adventure "In a Mirror, Darkly, Part II." Like Kirk before him, the Mirror Universe Captain Archer (Scott Bakula) engaged in hand-to-hand combat with a Gorn and eventually outwitted his reptilian adversary.

## Other Species

The preceding overview covers all the major extraterrestrial civilizations featured on *Star Trek*, including those fleshed out later in the history of the franchise. However, this is by no means a comprehensive survey of all the alien races encountered by the crew of the *Enterprise*. Many others also appeared, including the thought-casting, bubble-headed Talosians from "The Menagerie"; the technologically advanced but coldhearted Vians from "The Empath"; the kind but too-ghastly-to-look-at-and-live Medusans from "Is There in Truth No Beauty?"; the xenophobic, telepathic, nonhumanoid Melkotians from "Spectre of the Gun"; and the rocklike, meddlesome Excalbians from "The Savage Curtain."

Then there are the numerous species whose appearance seemed virtually identical to humans but whose cultures were markedly different: the docile, red-skinned, blonde-haired residents of Gamma Trianguli VI from "The Apple"; the peace-loving, superadvanced Metrons from "Arena"; the "totally hedonistic" (according to Dr. McCoy) Argelians from "Wolf in the Fold"; the extremely imitative Iotians from "A Piece of the Action"; and so on. There were also superadvanced, "pure energy" beings such as the Companion from "Metamorphosis," the Kelvans from "By Any Other Name," Sargon and friends from "Return to Tomorrow," and Trelaine and his parents from "The Squire of Gothos," among others.

Life, indeed, seems to be everywhere in the universe of *Star Trek*.

# Treknological Marvels

## Miracle Gadgets of the Twenty-Third Century

For many viewers, one of the most thrilling aspects of *Star Trek* is the wealth of futuristic technology featured on the show, devices with seemingly miraculous capabilities. From the beginning, viewers tuned into the series in part to *ooh* and *ah* (or at least exclaim, "That's so cool!") over gadgets like the transporter, communicator, and replicator. Detailed explanations of the inner workings of these and other twenty-third-century gizmos have been a staple of *Star Trek* literature as far back as Franz Joseph's *Star Trek Blueprints* and *Starfleet Technical Manual* (both 1975) and Eileen Palestine's *Starfleet Medical Reference Manual* (1977). As fresh and exciting as the show's Treknological marvels seemed at the time, however, most had ample precedent in science fiction literature or films. And as far-out as many of them seemed then, at least a few of these devices actually exist today or seem to be on the cusp of reality.

### Warp Drive

**What it does:** Enables starships to travel at speeds many times faster than light.

**How it works:** The engines warp space around the craft, contracting space in front of the ship and expanding space behind it. The vessel is propelled by the force of the warp itself, riding it "like a surfboard on a wave," according to physicist Lawrence M. Krauss in his invaluable book *The Physics of Star Trek*.

**Sci-fi precedents:** Faster-than-light space travel is a long-standing fixture of literary and cinematic science fiction because it's a priceless storytelling device. It's virtually impossible to write spacefaring SF without it unless the story is restricted to our own solar system, which effectively rules out encounters with "new life and new civilizations." Over the years, writers have suggested many different mechanisms for achieving speeds faster than light, some more plausible than others. In the *Star Wars* films, for instance, spacecraft cross over into "hyperspace," temporarily entering an alternate dimension where our physical laws of relativity do not apply.

**So when can I buy one?** Not soon. As with many of the technologies seen on *Star Trek*, physicists grant that warp drive *is* theoretically possible. However, the energy required to warp space in this manner is almost beyond comprehension and certainly beyond current or foreseeable human capability. On *Star Trek*, engines generate this power through the controlled interaction of matter and antimatter, but this is a problematic solution for many reasons. In the real world, there is no proven way of harnessing the ensuing explosive reaction of matter and antimatter (dilithium crystals being fictional). Besides, antimatter is exceedingly rare, making it impractical for use as fuel.

However, in September 2011, physicists in Italy claimed to have clocked a subatomic particle called a neutrino moving at speeds faster than light—something believed impossible under Albert Einstein's theory of special relativity. As of this writing (in the fall of 2011) the result remained unconfirmed, but if it is verified, this development could radically reshape our understanding of how space and time operate—and open a new frontier for research into faster-than-light travel.

## The Transporter

**What it does:** Moves people and cargo from one place to another almost instantly, dematerializing them at point A and rematerializing them at point B.

**How it works:** The transporter scans an object (or person) and stores a map of the subject's molecular structure in a "pattern buffer." Then it scrambles the object to basic molecules, transmits this raw matter to its destination, and then reassembles it according to the configuration stored in the buffer.

**Sci-fi precedents:** While not as pervasive a concept as faster-than-light travel, many stories and films have explored the idea of teleportation. Most of these have focused on the possible pitfalls of such technology, most famously *The Fly* (1958), in which a scientist tests an experimental transporter device and accidentally has his atoms mixed with those of a housefly. From a storytelling perspective, the transporter was a stroke of genius for *Star Trek*. It provided an elegant alternative to shooting expensive, repetitive scenes of the *Enterprise* landing and taking off in every episode. And it suggested intriguing plotlines for episodes such as "The Enemy Within," in which a transporter malfunction splits Captain Kirk into two entities, and "Mirror Mirror," in which another mishap transports an away team to an evil parallel universe.

**So when can I buy one?** Right after you ride your unicorn over to Frodo's house and borrow his magic ring. The transporter defies so many of the basic laws of physics that it is, essentially, a fantasy element dressed up as science fiction. The theoretical ways of overcoming all the real-world obstacles to constructing such a device are convoluted and unlikely in the extreme. "No single piece of science fiction technology aboard the *Enterprise* is so utterly implausible," Krauss wrote

The transporter, depicted in this children's jigsaw puzzle (vintage 1979), remains one of *Star Trek*'s most iconic technologies—and also one of its least plausible.

in *The Physics of Star Trek*. "Building a transporter would require us to heat up matter to a temperature a million times the temperature at the center of the sun, expend more energy in a single machine than all of humanity presently uses, build telescopes larger than the size of the Earth, improve present computers by a factor of 1,000 billion billion, and avoid the laws of quantum mechanics." But after that, it's a piece of cake.

Note: In late 2011, a *Nova* episode (part of the PBS *Fabric of the Cosmos* miniseries) described experiments taking place in the Canary Islands aimed at "teleporting" photons, comparing this process with the *Star Trek* transporter. However, the experimental procedure depicted involves the creation of an identical duplicate photon, rather than transporting the actual matter of the original photon. The process of creating the copy obliterates the original photon. This is quite a different proposition than the technology shown on *Star Trek*.

## The Replicator

**What it does:** Converts inert matter into food . . . or anything else.

**How it works:** Based on the same technology as the transporter, the replicator dematerializes matter and then reconfigures it into any stored pattern, from a bowl of chicken soup to a phaser.

**Sci-fi precedents:** A handful of classic science fiction books and stories introduced similar devices, but the most memorable was author Damon Knight's classic 1961 novel *A for Anything* (aka "The People Maker"). In this tale, a scientist invents a machine called a "Gismo" that can reproduce anything, including a human being or another Gismo. As a result, world economies instantly collapse, since Gismo users can, instantly and at virtually no cost, produce unlimited quantities of gold, diamonds, gasoline, or anything else imaginable. As Gismos spread, society breaks down and a repressive, slave-holding culture emerges.

For *Star Trek*, the replicator solves a thorny story problem (namely, how do you acquire and store enough food for a crew of more than 400 on a deep space voyage?). But *Trek* writers never seemed to grasp the full, revolutionary ramifications of this technology. A starship equipped with a replicator would never have to worry about running out of dilithium crystals—or anything else.

**So when can I buy one?** It will arrive in a convenient boxed set along with your transporter. Enjoy!

## Phasers

**What it does:** Delivers a jolt of energy of variable intensity, mild enough to render an opponent unconscious or powerful enough to vaporize its target.

**How it works:** Phasers concentrate stored energy and then release it toward the target along a beam of light. They can be set for stun, heat, or kill. Starfleet officers carry small handheld phasers; starships are equipped with larger, more powerful versions.

Captain Kirk walked softly but carried a fully charged phaser. Will U.S. soldiers someday do the same?

**Sci-fi precedents:** Ray guns—laser pistols, blasters, death rays, and the like—have been around virtually as long as science fiction itself and are ubiquitous in the subgenres of military SF and space opera.

**So when can I buy one?** In the not-too-distant future. Maybe.

Since in the 1990s, the U.S. military has launched multiple projects aimed at the development of variable-power directed-energy weapons. While details on military research and development efforts are often classified, two such programs were active as of 2009, according to an article in *Wired*. One involves the development of the aptly named Phased Hyper-Acceleration for Shock, EMP and Radiation (PHASER). The idea is to create a rifle that fires a ball of lightning, which could be set to either stun or destroy and that could disable electronic equipment. Another active initiative is the Multimode Directed Energy Armament System (MDEAS). This concept involves using a laser pulse to create an ionized channel through which an electric shock can be fired at the target. Again, depending on the voltage, the charge sent could either stun or kill. Like the PHASER, the MDEAS would also be effective at wiping out enemy electronics. Both the PHASER and the MDEAS remain in development and could be years away from delivery, if they are delivered at all. In the early 2000s, after six years and more than $14 million, the military abandoned the Pulsed Energy Projectile (PEP) weapon, an earlier, similar project. Nevertheless, the military seems to be serious about developing a phaser-like weapon.

## Tricorders

**What it does:** Combines scanning, analyzing and recording functions in a single handheld device. Several specialized models exist, including the medical tricorder, which is designed to detect changes in bodily functions and help diagnose illnesses.

**How it works:** Never fully explained.

**Sci-fi precedents:** Although they seem handy on *Star Trek*, similar devices rarely turn up in other SF books or movies.

**When can I buy one?** Sorry, you missed your chance! Beginning in 1996, Canada's Vital Technologies Corporation began selling a unit it called the TR-107 Mark 1, marketed as a "real-life Tricorder," which scanned for electromagnetic radiation and measured barometric pressure and temperature. Unfortunately, Vital Technologies went out of business in 1997. However, something more closely approximating an actual *Star Trek* tricorder could be on the horizon. In 2011, the X Prize Project, a philanthropic enterprise that grants lucrative cash awards to individuals and corporations who "bring about radical breakthroughs for the benefit of humanity," announced a $10 million Tricorder Competition. The contest will reward the development of a handheld medical examination tool similar in function to those used by Dr. McCoy.

## Communicators

**What it does:** Enables the user to communicate with the mother ship or other communicator-equipped personnel.

**How it works:** Flip it open and talk. Knob-twisting is optional.

**Sci-fi precedents:** The communicator was one of *Star Trek*'s snazziest-looking inventions and a widely influential one, but the idea of a handheld communication device was hardly original. Its many predecessors included the "signal watch" worn by detective Dick Tracy in Chester Gould's classic comic strip as well as real-world walkie-talkies, which were used extensively on the battlefields of World War II.

**So when can I buy one?** You probably already own one. Cellular and satellite telephones are, essentially, communicators. Martin Cooper, the project manager whose team developed the first functional cell phone, freely admits that he was inspired by the flip-top communicators seen on *Star Trek*. In fact, if you have a smartphone, you have a more powerful device than a *Star Trek* communicator in most respects, capable of taking photos, recording sound, sending text messages, and uploading and downloading information from a computer network. From a post-iPhone perspective, it seems obvious that communicators and tricorders should have been combined into a single tool. *Star Trek* communicators represent an advance over modern cell phones only in terms of range and affordability. It is not yet possible to communicate with spacecraft via a cell phone, and Captain Kirk traveled throughout the galaxy without being slapped with a roaming charge.

## The Universal Translator

**What it does:** Bridges the language gap, enabling the user to communicate with alien beings.

**How it works:** "There are certain universal ideas and concepts common to all intelligent life. This device instantaneously compares the frequency of brain wave patterns, selects those ideas and concepts it recognizes and then provides the necessary grammar." That's according to Captain Kirk, from "Metamorphosis."

**Sci-fi precedents:** Like faster-than-light space travel, the concept of a universal translator is one of the most common in science fiction literature and movies, for obvious reasons. If you want to write a story about humans interacting with extraterrestrials, it's very helpful if the two parties can converse with one another. And, as with faster-than-light spaceflight, numerous technologies have been suggested as the basis for a universal translator, some far-fetched. On *Dr. Who*, for instance, the TARDIS (Time and Relative Dimension in Space) mechanism projects a telepathic field that automatically translates most languages into English. In Douglas Adams's satirical *Hitchhiker's Guide to the Galaxy* books, universal translation is accomplished by inserting a symbiotic "Babel fish" into your ear! Many other works have proposed the development of a universal language. In the *Star Wars* universe they speak "Galactic Basic," which sounds a lot like English.

**So when can I buy one?** If you have a smartphone, you can download it today. Or at least you can download the beginning of something like it.

In 2010, three different smartphone applications were released, all designed to instantly translate various spoken languages. Trippo Voice Magix, developed for the iPhone, translates English into fourteen languages. Another iPhone app, Speechtrans TM, instantly translates back and forth between American English, British English, French, German, Italian, Japanese, and Spanish. Speaking Universal Translator, an Android app, serves the same function for users of that smartphone brand, translating to and from English, French, Italian, and Spanish. Also, Google has announced plans to develop similar voice recognition/translation software for broader, non–cell phone use. It may be a while, however, before these programs enable us to communicate with extraterrestrials.

## More Gadgets

The preceding is merely a representative sample of the many futuristic technologies employed by Starfleet. There are many more, some (including deflector shields, tractor beams, and artificial gravity) that are highly implausible and others (like the superadvanced, voice-activated *Enterprise* computer) that seem to be close at hand. (IBM's "Watson" computer, which competed on the TV quiz show *Jeopardy!*, was inspired by the *Enterprise* computer.) Later *Trek* movies and series introduced other notable, and often far-fetched, technologies, such as the holodeck, first seen on the animated series, and Commander Data from *The Next Generation*.

One of the more fascinating aspects of *Star Trek* science is that it takes for granted the authenticity of telepathy and telekinesis, which are generally dismissed as superstition and pseudo-science and which might seem more the stuff of horror or fantasy than sci-fi. But the program's acceptance of psychic phenomena (such as Spock's mind melds) demonstrates the show's prevailing attitude toward science and technology. The program readily embraced any and all scientific and pseudoscientific concepts, no matter how fantastic, if they were rich in story value. And, on a deeper level, *Star Trek* always erred on the side of confidence in human progress, whether this meant tapping into currently unproven psychic abilities or developing machines capable of overcoming apparently insurmountable scientific obstacles. In the world of *Star Trek*, human beings are limited not by the laws of physics but only by their own imaginations.

# Then Play On

## Memorable Musical Moments

I f you've purchased (or borrowed or stolen) a copy of this book, chances are you're a *Star Trek* fan. And if you're a *Star Trek* fan, you can probably hum the show's title theme from memory—and possibly a few other musical cues, as well. Perhaps you enjoy the singing of Nichelle Nichols or even (heaven help you) of Leonard Nimoy. But odds are that, one way or another, the music of *Star Trek* has burrowed itself into your brain.

That's to be expected. Musical scores often play a vital role in the success of movies and TV shows, subtly enhancing the emotional impact of the drama unfolding on the screen. And many of *Star Trek*'s now-famous musical cues were repeated not only in episode after episode but within individual episodes. The occasional on-screen musical performances of the show's cast remain unforgettable for other reasons, including a few that defy all efforts to blot them out.

### "Theme from *Star Trek*"

*Star Trek*'s immortal title theme—the brassy, bongo-driven, eight-note fanfare that plays under William Shatner's narration ("Space, the final frontier . . .")— was written by composer Alexander Courage for the show's original pilot, "The Cage." Variations on this theme were repeated in every episode and were consistently used to score exterior shots of the *Enterprise*. Series creator Gene Roddenberry hired Courage at the suggestion of composer Jerry Goldsmith, who had been the producer's first choice to score "The Cage." Courage wrote, arranged, and recorded the *Trek* theme in a single week, according to author Jeff Bond's *The Music of Star Trek*. But the original orchestration was slightly different than the one used later, featuring electronic keyboard accents and shimmering vocal tonalities by operatic soprano Loulie Jean Norman. For the second *Star Trek* pilot, "Where No Man Has Gone Before," Courage reorchestrated the theme, removing the keyboards and vocals and adding organ and flute, as well as (from his own mouth) the "whoosh" sound effects that coincide with the starship's flybys.

Roddenberry restored Norman's vocal track to the title theme for the show's second and third seasons and remixed the music to feature the singer more prominently—so prominently, in fact, that Courage complained it now sounded like a soprano solo. By then, however, more contentious issues had arisen between Roddenberry and Courage. The contract the composer had signed contained a clause stipulating that if Roddenberry wrote lyrics for Courage's theme, he would be entitled to 50 percent of Courage's royalties from the composition. The producer's awkward, sappy lyrics ("Beyond the rim of the starlight, my love is wand'ring in starflight . . .") were never intended to be sung, let alone recorded, but they were duly filed with music licenser BMI. As a result, Courage's *Star Trek* royalties dropped sharply. Roddenberry hadn't informed Courage he planned to take advantage of the lyrics clause, which Courage had failed to notice when he signed his contract. The two exchanged testy letters, and Courage vowed never to work for Roddenberry again. Nevertheless, Courage eventually returned to the show during its final season, scoring the lackluster "Plato's Stepchildren." Goldsmith later hired Courage to orchestrate cues for his scores to *Star Trek: The Motion Picture* (1979), *Star Trek: First Contact* (1996), and *Star Trek: Insurrection* (1998). Courage worked extensively in film and television as a composer and orchestrator from the 1950s through the early 2000s and won an Emmy in 1988 for directing the music for a Julie Andrews Christmas special.

A swinging lounge version of Courage's title theme is heard in the background of a party in "The Conscience of the King" and in a bar in "Court Martial." "Theme from *Star Trek*" was also reprised in all eleven *Trek* feature films. Its opening notes were combined with Goldsmith's "*Star Trek* March," originally written for *The Motion Picture*, to create the title music for *Star Trek: The Next Generation*. The music was sometimes quoted by other *Trek* series, as well—perhaps most memorably at the conclusion of the final episode of *Star Trek: Enterprise*, as Scott Bakula read Shatner's famous monologue. Numerous other movies and TV shows have also employed the theme, usually for comedic effect. Shatner and soprano Frederica von Stade recreated the *Star Trek* opening theme live for the 2005 Primetime Emmy Awards. Famed trumpeter Maynard Ferguson recorded a jazz-rock fusion version of the theme for the 1977 album *Conquistador*. For her 1991 album *Out of This World*, Nichelle Nichols recorded a disco version of the theme featuring original lyrics (not Roddenberry's). Actor Jack Black's mock-and-roll band, Tenacious D, recorded the theme using Roddenberry's lyrics, releasing the track as a B-side.

## "Mr. Spock Theme"

For the classic episode "Amok Time," in which Spock goes into a Vulcan form of heat known as Pon Farr, composer Gerald Fried created a brooding theme, plunked out by guitarist Barney Kessel on an electric bass, which instantly became one of the show's most distinctive compositions. Spock "struggled to express emotion, so I picked an instrument where emotion is a struggle to express, like the bass guitar," Fried told Bond in *The Music of Star Trek*. "I felt somehow [this approach] might match Spock's inability to be emotionally accessible." The instantly recognizable "Mr. Spock Theme" was reused in

"Journey to Babel" and "The Changeling," among other episodes. Fried was one of a handful of composers who stepped in to fill the void created by Courage's departure from the show. He later shared an Emmy Award with Quincy Jones for his contributions to the score of the landmark miniseries *Roots* (1977). Jazz guitarist Kessel was a veteran session player who had performed with luminaries such as Oscar Peterson, Charlie Barnet, Artie Shaw, and even Chico Marx (yes, *that* Chico Marx) during a career that began in the 1940s and lasted until 1992, when he suffered a debilitating stroke. For "Amok Time," Fried also composed the stirring "Ritual/Ancient Battle" suite, which henceforth served as the series' default music for nearly every fight scene, including the battle sequences from "A Private Little War" and "Bread and Circuses."

## "Good Night, Sweetheart"

Fred Steiner wrote more music for *Star Trek* than any other composer. Associate producer Bob Justman brought him back time and again because he adored Steiner's work. "My first choice, always, unless there was a particular reason, was Fred, who caught the inner being of *Star Trek*," Justman told Bond in *The Music of Star Trek*. Roddenberry instructed all the show's composers to avoid ethereal, self-consciously "spacey" compositions. But "even before I had that conference with Gene Roddenberry, I think I'd made the decision that it had to be old-fashioned, blood-and-guts music," Steiner said. His most memorable *Star Trek* music was originally written for early episodes such as "The Corbomite Maneuver," "Charlie X," and "Balance of Terror," and repeated endlessly in many later installments. For example, his menacing "Romulan Theme" from "Balance of Terror" served as a leitmotif for villains of all sorts in many adventures and was used extensively in the Evil Mirror Universe scenes from "Mirror, Mirror."

But Steiner could do more than "blood and guts" music, as evidenced by his lilting romantic themes from "What Are Little Girls Made Of?" and "Elaan of Troyius." For "The City on the Edge of Forever," Steiner searched for a period love song to play under Captain Kirk's scenes with the doomed Edith Keeler (Joan Collins). He decided to use English bandleader Ray Noble's chart-topping hit "Goodnight, Sweetheart," which in "City on the Edge" is first heard playing on a radio and later reappears as a love theme during all of Shatner's subsequent scenes with Collins. Even though the song was a minor anachronism (Noble's record was released in 1931; the story takes place in 1930), the tune worked beautifully, providing a quaint, plaintive musical backdrop for the budding but hopeless romance. Unfortunately, Paramount later lost the rights to the song. When *Star Trek* was first released on videotape in the 1980s, "Goodnight Sweetheart" had to be replaced and the episode's romantic interludes rescored without Steiner's input. Thankfully, Paramount eventually recovered the rights to "Goodnight, Sweetheart" and restored the original music for *Star Trek*'s DVD release.

Steiner also wrote scores for *The Twilight Zone* and *Lost in Space*, as well as the famous title theme from the classic legal drama *Perry Mason*. In 1985, he earned an Oscar nomination for his music from the film *The Color Purple*.

## "The Doomsday Machine"

Original music was created for just thirty-five of *Star Trek*'s original seventy-nine episodes—and many of those were partial scores, with new themes supplemented by library cues. In most cases, music editor Richard Lapham cobbled together all or part of an episode's score out of recycled and leftover cues from previous installments. This practice—known in the industry as "tracking"—is no longer permitted by the American Federation of Musicians. Full, new scores were created for every episode of every subsequent *Star Trek* live-action series. But AFM rules during the 1960s were more lenient. The union required just thirty-nine hours of recording time per twenty-six-episode season—hardly an extravagant amount considering that it took between four and five hours to record the twenty-one minutes of music written for "Charlie X" alone.

Composer Sol Kaplan provided a rare, fully original score for "The Doomsday Machine." His thrilling score, which makes evocative use of piano, woodwinds, flute, and cellos, is now revered as the program's musical high point, rivaled only by Fried's inventive "Amok Time." Kaplan's urgent, spine-tingling "Planet Killer" theme prefigured John William's remarkably similar score for *Jaws* (1975).

Two of *Star Trek*'s most memorable scores, Gerald Fried's inventive "Amok Time" and Sol Kaplan's powerful "The Doomsday Machine," were released together on this Crescendo label CD.

## Uhura Sings

The emblematic scores of Courage, Fried, Steiner, Kaplan, George Duning, Jerry Fielding, and Joe Mullendore served as *Star Trek*'s musical hallmarks. But the show's stars and guest stars sometimes provided musical interludes, as well. Most of these are burned indelibly in fans' memories—for one reason or another. Fans' more pleasant recollections often stem from the handful of vocal performances by Nichelle Nichols, who spent years touring as a jazz vocalist before joining *Trek*.

With "Charlie X," the seventh episode produced, Nichols made her *Star Trek* singing debut. Originally, screenwriter Dorothy Fontana had written a scene where Lieutenant Uhura entertains her shipmates in the *Enterprise* recreation room by doing an impression of first officer Spock. However, the sequence was retooled to take advantage of Nichols's vocal talents. Instead of mimicking Spock, she sings a song ("Oh, on the Starship *Enterprise*") that pokes good-natured fun at her superior officer, who accompanies her on his Vulcan lute: "Oh, on the Starship *Enterprise* there's someone who's in Satan's guise/Whose devil's ears and devil's eyes could rip your heart from you . . ." Later, to the same melody, she sings "Oh, Charlie's Our New Darling," about new arrival Charlie Evans (Robert Walker), a teenager with powerful but as yet unrecognized psychic abilities: "Now from a planet out in space there comes a lad not commonplace/A-seeking out his first embrace . . ." Charlie, who doesn't appreciate the joke, renders Uhura temporarily mute. The tune Nichols sings is derived from the Scottish folk song "Charlie Is My Darling." (The "Charlie" of the song's title was the exiled prince Charles Edward Stuart, a Catholic who in 1745 unsuccessfully attempted to retake the British throne from the protestant George II.) It's unclear who wrote the new lyrics for "Oh, on the Starship *Enterprise*" or "Oh, Charlie's Our New Darling."

Nichols's favorite of Uhura's songs was "Beyond Antares," a love song with music by Desilu music consultant Wilbur Hatch and lyrics by producer Gene L. Coon. She sang the number twice, first in "The Conscience of the King" and later in "The Changeling" (in which her performance caused the puzzled NOMAD to drain Uhura's brain). Although its lyrics are asinine ("the skies are green and glowing" . . . "the scented lunar flower is blooming"), the song's melody is enchanting, and Nichols delivers a committed, sensitive a cappella vocal in both episodes. She recorded a fully orchestrated version of "Beyond Antares" for her 1991 album *Out of This World*. She also recorded a version of the song for her self-produced 1986 cassette release, *Uhura Sings*.

## Spock 'n' Roll Music

Unfortunately, *Star Trek*'s other most frequent musical stylist was Leonard Nimoy, whose contributions proved less pleasing than Nichols.' In several installments, Spock can be seen playing his Vulcan lute—an instrument designed by sculptor

Wah Chang purely for its appearance rather than its sonic qualities. According to author Franz Joseph's *Starfleet Technical Manual* (1975), the instrument "combines the tonal qualities of a harp, lute, sitar, and to some extent, violin." Nevertheless, Spock's musical performances were less than scintillating—especially when Nimoy was required to sing. In the episode "Plato's Stepchildren," Spock croaks out "Maiden Wine," an original composition by Nimoy that later appeared on his album *The Touch of Leonard Nimoy*.

Without question, however, Spock's ill-advised jam session with the space hippies from "The Way to Eden" marked *Star Trek*'s musical nadir. Although Spock plays a fairly inoffensive instrumental—dueting with Mavig (Deborah Downey) and her unnamed, wheel-shaped, harplike instrument—it's appalling to see the dignified Vulcan sink to the level of these addle-brained doofuses. Throughout this abysmal episode, hippie second banana Adam (Charles Napier) belts out a series of dippy folk-rock tunes, reportedly composed by Napier himself. This musical assault begins, appropriately enough, in sick bay, where Napier warbles a tune that might be called "In the New Land" (these poorly structured numbers contain no choruses, making titles guesswork). It continues with a four-minute medley in the rec room ("Long Time Back When the Galaxy Was New"/"There's a Wide Wide Emptiness Between Us (Brother)"/"Hey Out There") that eventually gives way to The Spock-and-Mavig Experience. Finally, after the hippies have assumed control of the ship, Napier croons the ballad "Headin' Out to Eden" in the auxiliary control room. Eventually, Adam meets a gruesome fate—he dies from eating poisonous fruit—but perhaps not gruesome enough for agitated viewers who, reeling from this sonic onslaught, may have been tempted to smash their Simon and Garfunkel albums as a precautionary measure. "The Way to Eden" featured Spock's final screen appearance with his lute. Pity he went out on such a sour note.

## Other Musical Interludes

A handful of other musical moments should be noted:

- The Irish jig Gerald Fried wrote as a leitmotif for Captain Kirk's Starfleet Academy nemesis Finnegan in the episode "Shore Leave" might seem like such an idiosyncratic piece of music that it would seldom be reused. And yet the ditty was revived, for comic effect, several times, in episodes such as "This Side of Paradise," "The Apple," and even "The City on the Edge of Forever," where it's heard when Kirk and Spock encounter a surly Irish cop.

- The composition that Spock discovers and plays in "Requiem for Methuselah"—attributed to Brahms in the episode—is not actually a classical piece. It was a Brahmsian pastiche written especially for the episode by Ivan Ditmars, at the request of Wilbur Hatch. This was the only *Star Trek* assignment for Ditmars, who from 1963 through 1972 served as the organist/musical director for the daytime game show *Let's Make a Deal*.

Spock and his Vulcan lute. (Sans space hippies, thank heavens.)

- On the other hand, the harpsichord music Trelaine is playing when he first meets Captain Kirk and his landing party during "The Squire of Gothos" is a classical composition—namely, Johann Strauss's "Roses from the South."
- And, finally, what *Trek* devotee could forget the singing of actor Bruce Hyde, who delivered the longest vocal performance in *Star Trek* history—spanning more than twelve minutes of screen time, on and off—as mentally incapacitated navigator Kevin Riley in "The Naked Time." Fancying himself as a captain, Riley commandeers the intercom and sings interminable choruses of "(I'll Take You Home Again) Kathleen," which he occasionally interrupts to deliver absurd orders such as "in the future, all female crew members will wear their hair loosely about their shoulders." Riley's cringe-inducing crooning inspires another crewman to serenade Yeoman Rand with a variation of the same ditty and drives Captain Kirk to distraction. "One . . . more . . . time!"

# Blooper Reel

## Goofs and Gaffes That Survived the Final Cut

**D**uring the early 1970s, when the first *Star Trek* conventions began popping up in New York, Los Angeles, Chicago, and other cities across the U.S., one of the most popular attractions was the show's now-famous "blooper reel." Fans roared with laughter at the sight of actors flubbing their lines or bumping their noses when the *Enterprise*'s "automatic" doors (actually controlled by a technician hidden backstage) failed to open. *Trek* staffers, including associate producer Bob Justman, originally assembled these outtakes to run at the show's end-of-season wrap parties. But not all the program's mistakes were consigned to the cutting-room floor. A plethora of goofs, gaffes, plot holes, scientific errors, and miscellaneous blunders made it into broadcast episodes, many more than can be covered here. (Delineating all the problems with "Spock's Brain" alone could fill an entire chapter.)

To be fair, many of these flaws are relatively minor and require careful scrutiny or thoughtful reflection to identify. Similar gaffes go unnoticed on most TV shows, but most shows don't have fans like *Star Trek*'s, diehards who have rewatched every episode countless times in syndication and on home video and DVD, poring over each installment in minute detail. Upon close inspection, fans began to recognize—and even to take a kind of bemused enjoyment in—the show's occasional lapses, which range from garden variety technical snafus (the shadow of a boom mike visible in sick bay, for instance) to egregious and sometimes hilarious lapses in continuity or simple logic.

### Continuity Errors

Every film and television show employs a script supervisor whose primary responsibility is making sure that on-screen details remain consistent from take to take, shot to shot and scene to scene—so that a coffeepot sitting on the table doesn't appear to refill itself in the middle of a scene, for instance; or to make sure that if a character gets socked in the face in one scene, he has a visible black eye in the next one. However, since all script supervisors are human, no film or television show is completely free of such inconsistencies. Prime examples of *Star Trek* continuity errors include:

- When Kirk, Spock, and McCoy visit pool-playing gangster Bela Oxmyx in "A Piece of the Action," the billiard balls change positions between shots. Also, Oxmyx inexplicably begins knocking the numbered balls directly into the pockets without using the white cue ball! Perhaps the USS *Horizon* should have left behind a billiards manual along with that *Chicago Gangs of the 1920s* history book.
- When the Good Kirk and the Evil Kirk meet on the bridge at the conclusion of "The Enemy Within," the Evil Kirk has scratches on his right cheek. But earlier in the episode, Yeoman Rand scratched him on his *left* cheek.
- In "Assignment: Earth," Gary Seven's cat Isis is solid black—except for a few shots, where a different cat with white paws was substituted.
- The food cubes on Sulu's dinner tray in "The Man Trap" jump back and forth between shots. First they're in a bowl, then (during an insert close-up) on his plate, and then suddenly back in the bowl.
- In "Turnabout Intruder," after calling for a vote on Spock's court-martial, Kirk (or, rather, Dr. Janice Lester-inhabiting-the-body-of-Kirk) turns and walks dramatically out of the room. Unfortunately, the briefing room has only one door, and it's on the opposite wall, so it's obvious Shatner is simply walking off the set.

## Stock Footage Snafus

Given the tight schedules and skimpy budgets that the *Star Trek* team faced on a weekly basis, producers made liberal use of stock footage, especially for shots of the exterior of the ship, which were expensive to produce. A single shot of the *Enterprise* firing phasers was reused dozens of times throughout all three seasons of the series, for instance. However, the use of stock footage sometimes created jarring continuity problems, such as:

- In "Let That Be Your Last Battlefield," the alien Lokai arrives in a shuttle supposedly stolen from Starbase Four. Yet, due to the use of stock footage, the vessel is clearly marked as "*Galileo*, NCC 1707/7, USS *Enterprise.*"
- During several Season Three episodes, including "Let That Be Your Last Battlefield" and "Friday's Child," Ensign Chekov is momentarily replaced by an unnamed blonde navigator when a reverse-angle stock shot of the bridge, showing the view screen, is employed.
- For similar reasons, Lieutenant Sulu's retractable viewer appears and disappears—depending on the camera angle used—during the opening sequence of "Day of the Dove." It's visible when Sulu is shown in close-up but gone when a wider (stock) angle is used.
- The sky of planet Gamma Trianguli VI is red throughout "The Apple"—except when it begins to storm. Suddenly, when clouds roll in and lightning strikes, the sky is blue, thanks to the employment of library footage.

## Wardrobe Malfunctions

No, not *that* type of wardrobe malfunction. Although costume designer Bill Theiss created many outfits that looked as if they might fall off the show's nubile guest actresses at any moment, the one time anything like that actually happened—to Sherry Jackson during the filming of "What Are Little Girls Made Of?"—the footage did *not* make it onto the air. Nevertheless, Starfleet uniforms and other costumes often created continuity gaffes, such as missing or incorrect insignias, and sometimes bigger problems.

- Captain Kirk, on the way to the bridge with Charlie Evans in "Charlie X," enters the turbolift wearing a standard gold command tunic but exits the lift wearing his green V-neck captain's jersey. (Maybe on the way up Charlie used his psychic superpowers to change it.)
- In "Mudd's Women," as Harry Mudd and his gorgeous "cargo" beam aboard the *Enterprise*, Dr. McCoy's uniform switches back and forth between the standard blue tunic and his medical smock. (This may be another stock footage problem.)
- Spock is wearing his standard-issue uniform when, during "This Side of Paradise," botanist Leila Kalomi (Jill Ireland) leads him to a flower that shoots mysterious, happiness-inducing spores into his face. But when we next see him, under the influence of the spores, Spock is lazing in the grass with Leila wearing a pair of green coveralls. The abrupt costume change may have been made to suggest that Spock (and, presumably, Leila) disrobed while off-camera, but this does not explain where his jumpsuit came from (the couple do not appear to have moved from the same wooded grove) or what happened to Spock's uniform.
- In the episode "The Alternative Factor," the fake goatee worn by guest star Robert Brown as Lazarus is so poorly and inconsistently applied that the bogus facial hair seems to perform gymnastics on the actor's face between shots. This is by far the worst makeup job seen in the entire series and uncharacteristic of the usually fine work of Fred Phillips.
- In the final episode of the series, "Turnabout Intruder," Nurse Chapel is a brunette. Of course, it's a woman' prerogative to change her hair.

## Equipment Failures

Twenty-third-century technology must be tricky to operate. In many of the original seventy-nine episodes, the following peculiarities may be observed:

- Communicators often chirp when opened, but sometimes they do not.
- Captain Kirk presses the same four buttons on his captain's chair to perform dozens of different functions.
- The "whee-oh" communications whistle used in the hallways, briefing rooms, and other public spaces of the *Enterprise* is sometimes followed by a page and

other times not. Yet, even without benefit of a page, Kirk always seems to know when the message is for him and not for, say, Dr. McCoy or Security Officer Kerplotsky.

- The whole "stardate" concept is fraught with confusion. In numerous episodes, events with lower stardates take place *after* events with higher stardates. The official explanation for this is that these "dates" denote specific points on the curved continuum of space-time. The *Star Trek* Writer's Guide explained the concept to prospective screenwriters this way: "Stardates are a mathematical formula which varies depending on location in the galaxy, velocity of travel, and other factors." But what is the use of constantly referring to "dates" that most viewers find incomprehensible?

- In several episodes, Kirk and company watch videos supposedly taken via tricorder. The tricorder must be a very sophisticated instrument, since these videos often include complex pans, zooms, and tracking shots, and sometimes show the tricorder itself recording the event!

- After the two pilot episodes, production designer Matt Jefferies tweaked the *Enterprise*'s nacelles (the tubular engines attached to the main body of the craft by long struts). But since stock footage from the pilot was reused throughout the run of the series (and to create the title sequence), in some shots the ship's nacelles have vents on the end, and in others they have bubble-like protrusions.

## Screwy Science

For the most part, *Star Trek* did a solid job of holding up the science end of the term *science fiction*. Creator-producer Gene Roddenberry took pride in the show's credibility and hired big-name sci-fi authors to contribute teleplays. Nevertheless *Star Trek*'s scripts featured some glaring scientific blunders, such as:

- In "Court Martial," when Spock scans the *Enterprise* to search for the supposedly dead Finney (who is actually hidden aboard the ship), he mentions that a special device has

*Star Trek* bloopers were so popular that, in the days before home video, bootleg record albums like this one were produced so fans could at least *hear* them at home.

been installed to magnify the computer's censors "one to the fourth power." That means no magnification at all, since 1x1x1x1=1.

- *Star Trek*'s astronomy was generally sound, but in "Day of the Dove," Captain Kirk calls the *Enterprise* "a doomed ship, traveling between galaxies" when, in fact, the *Enterprise* was capable of interstellar but not intergalactic travel. Similarly, in "Arena," Kirk refers to a planet as an "asteroid."
- In "Elaan of Troyius," Spock reports that a Klingon ship is approaching at Warp Six, but Sulu calculates the vessel's speed at 50,000 kilometers per second—that's about 250,000 kps *below* the speed of light.
- The planet-based supercomputer Landru, in "Return of the Archons," holds the *Enterprise* at bay with a sonic weapon whose power is measured in decibels. How is this possible, since sound doesn't carry in the vacuum of space? For the same reason, why does the crew of the *Enterprise* whisper while "playing dead" in "Balance of Terror?"

## Plot Holes

These are probably the most damaging problems of all, since they undermine the credibility of the entire story. Fortunately, these weren't an every-week occurrence, nor were they (usually) all that obvious. Aside from the gaps in logic noted below, one issue hangs over nearly every classic *Trek* adventure: Is it wise to continually send the captain, first officer, chief surgeon, and other vital personnel on dangerous away missions? Other, episode-specific concerns include:

- Why, in "The Ultimate Computer," does Starfleet run the colossal risk of testing the experimental M-5 computer on the flagship of the fleet? Wouldn't it be safer to test this gizmo on a scout ship? Or a garbage scow?
- During "The Naked Time," Kirk notes in a log entry that "unknown to us, a totally new and unusual disease has been brought aboard." If it's unknown to him, how does Kirk report it?
- Similarly, in "Let That Be Your Last Battlefield," Kirk recognizes the name of Lokai and Bele's home planet Cheron, which he says resides in "an uncharted section of the galaxy." If the sector is uncharted, how does Kirk know the planet exists? (Just as inexplicably, Spock is able to calculate the precise distance to the planet.)
- Spock's mind meld with NOMAD in "The Changeling" should give away the secret that Kirk isn't really the creator of the deranged space probe.
- Spock's Vulcan logic fails him completely during the finale of "Whom Gods Destroy." Faced with two Kirks—the real one and the shape-shifting Garth posing as the captain—Spock, who's holding a phaser, stands by and lets the pair slug it out rather than follow the simplest course of action: stun both Kirks and use a mind meld to determine which is which. Or, even easier, try the familiar ploy of asking a question only the real Kirk could answer.

- When the transporter fails during "The Enemy Within," why doesn't Kirk simply send a shuttle to pick up Sulu and the other stranded crewmen? (The real-world answer is that production designer Jefferies had not yet built the shuttlecraft.)

## Miscellaneous Mix-Ups

Some of the most amusing *Star Trek* gaffes defy classification. These include:

- During the *koon-ut-kal-if-fee* ritual from "Amok Time," T'Pau (Celia Lovsky) declares that Spock is "deep in the *plak tow*, the blood fever." Yet when director Joe Pevney cuts to a wide shot, Leonard Nimoy—unaware he was in frame—can be seen casually lounging against a wall, his hands clasped nonchalantly behind his back.
- In "Friday's Child," one of the warlike Capellans heaves a boomerang-like weapon at a tree. Although the weapon misses its target, the tree splits in half anyway.
- When NOMAD attacks the *Enterprise* at the beginning of "The Changeling," the actors flail around the bridge set in the usual manner denoting turbulence. However, this time when Sulu and another officer grab hold of the helm, the console tips forward and almost topples over.
- During his fight with the android Kirby in "What Are Little Girls Made Of?," Kirk grabs the robot around the neck and chokes him into submission. Do androids breathe? Earlier in this episode it was established that they do not eat.
- In "The City on the Edge of Forever," Edith Keeler (Joan Collins) tells Dr. McCoy that her "young man" is taking her so see "a Clark Gable movie." But in 1930 Gable was not yet a star—he was an unknown bit player.
- During "Plato's Stepchildren," Kirk and Spock gain telekinetic superpowers. Yet they never use or even mention them again. Nor does Starfleet take advantage of the discovery that it can create godlike supermen through injections of "kironide."
- During the finale of "Where No Man Has Gone Before," Gary Mitchell uses his psychokinetic powers to create a grave for the (he thinks) soon-to-be-dead Captain Kirk. The grave comes complete with a tombstone—clearly marked James *R.* Kirk.
- At the conclusion of "Galileo Seven," Kirk seems unaccountably relieved to hear that five survivors have been recovered from the missing shuttle. Why doesn't he ask who the survivors are? For all he knows, the dead could include Spock and McCoy.

# Captain's Log

## Evidence That William Shatner Was Really Quite Good

**F**orty years after *Star Trek* left the air, James T. Kirk remains one of the most recognizable characters in television history—and also one of the most parodied, thanks in large part to William Shatner's idiosyncratic acting style. The actor's delivery, full of syncopated stops and starts, with a tendency toward bombast, practically begs for mimicry, and it's certainly received it. Everyone from John Belushi to Jim Carrey to even Shatner himself has taken a swipe at Kirk, not to mention countless impressionists and stand-up comics.

Yet no actor ever inhabited a character more fully. Shatner simply *is* Captain Kirk; the two seem to have merged on some Zen-like metaphysical plain. Even though Chris Pine took over the role in director J. J. Abrams's 2009 *Star Trek* feature film, Shatner remains fixed in the public mind as Kirk. Maybe that's because Shatner identified so strongly with the captain. "Kirk was, for the most part, me," Shatner wrote in *Star Trek Memories*. "An idealized *version* of me, certainly, but one that nonetheless sprang rather readily from my own inner workings." As a result, even though he was classically trained, Shatner played the role "almost totally on instinct." And for the most part, despite all the ribbing his work has taken over the years, Shatner's instincts were sound.

Captain Kirk is best remembered for stirring speeches, bruising fistfights, and his smooth moves with the ladies, all of which Shatner handled expertly. But the actor brought greater nuance and subtlety to the part than is widely recognized, and could be very effective in quiet, introspective scenes. He also displayed a deft touch with comedy—a gift that, in the 1990s, gave his career a wildly successful second act. During the 1960s, however, Shatner's talent remained underappreciated. This was in part because the actor was prone to periodic excesses. In episodes such as "The Paradise Syndrome" (as the amnesia-stricken "Kirok"), he soared stratospherically—and, it must be granted, highly entertainingly—over the top. Unfortunately, critics, historians, and even many fans seem to remember only his furious over-emoting and forget Shatner's fine work in most other episodes. Yet, scattered throughout *Star Trek*'s original seventy-nine adventures there are many reminders, shining moments that reveal the full breadth and depth of the actor's underestimated abilities.

Shatner cozies up with guest star Joan Collins in this publicity still from "The City on the Edge of Forever."

## The Death of Edith Keeler

One reason why "The City on the Edge of Forever" is widely considered the single best *Star Trek* episode is that it contains Shatner's single best performance as Captain Kirk. The teleplay, credited to Harlan Ellison but rewritten by virtually the entire *Trek* writing staff, gives Shatner a chance to play everything he plays well: heroism, as he dashes through the Guardian of Forever to save Dr. McCoy (and the rest of the galaxy as we know it); comedy, as Kirk and Spock try to fit in with New Yorkers of the 1930s ("My friend is obviously Chinese . . . he caught his head in a mechanical rice-picker"); and romance, as Kirk falls for the strong-willed but gentle-hearted Edith Keeler (Joan Collins). Throughout the episode, Shatner works in a lower register than usual, illuminating Kirk's thoughts and feelings mainly through facial expressions and body language. Kirk informs Spock, "I believe I'm in love with Edith Keeler." But we already know this; it's written on Shatner's face in a previous scene, when Kirk looks longingly at Keeler as she confronts Spock for stealing a jeweler's tool kit.

The story's shattering climax remains perhaps *Star Trek*'s single most famous scene. To prevent the Nazi conquest of Earth, Kirk stops McCoy from rescuing Keeler from a fatal auto accident. Shatner grabs DeForest Kelley and clings to him, eyes slammed shut, flinching at the sound of screeching tires. Shatner's expression makes clear that the captain is not only restraining McCoy, but also leaning on his friend for support. Kirk looks as if he might collapse with anguish. Screenwriter Harlan Ellison wanted a different approach to this scene—with the coolly logical Spock preventing the love-struck Kirk from saving Keeler—but Shatner's pitch-perfect approach to this moment is what gives "The City on the Edge of Forever" its staggering emotional power. The actor is also quietly effective in the episode's wrap-up. No jokey banter this time; Kirk, looking shaken, simply orders "Get us the hell out of here." Shatner delivers the line with a forty-yard stare and a catch in his throat. It's the perfect ending, one Herb Solow and Gene Roddenberry fought NBC's Standards and Practices Department to keep. (The network's censors objected to the word "hell.") Laughs, tears, adventure, romance—"The City on the Edge of Forever" has it all, but none of it would work without Shatner's masterful performance.

## Kirk Battles the Gorn

Captain Kirk found his way into plenty of fights over the years, brawling with foes (and sometimes friends) both human and alien in dozens of episodes, but he was never in a scrap quite like his epic battle with the reptilian Gorn in "Arena." This clash, which consumes nearly half the episode's running time, is the stuff of legend—not only among viewers but also, apparently, within the mythology of the franchise. When Captain Sisko and members of his crew travel into the past in the *Deep Space Nine* episode "Trials and Tribble-ations," Sisko yearns to ask Kirk about "fighting the Gorn on Cestus III."

In much more obvious ways than "The City on the Edge of Forever," "Arena" is built entirely around Shatner. He's on-screen almost constantly, assigned the most grueling physical action ever included in any *Trek* teleplay. Even before the fierce contest with the Gorn begins, Kirk and his landing party are caught in a deadly skirmish with the as-yet unseen enemy. Throughout this sequence,

Kirk's epic struggle with the Gorn in "Arena" remains one of the series' most famous moments—and one of Shatner's best sequences.

Shatner remains in near-constant motion, running, diving, and dodging explosions. Even though Shatner was doubled for some of these shots, Kirk's battered, weary appearance toward the end of this adventure probably required no acting at all. However, it's important to remember that Kirk's struggle is not just a physical one; ultimately, he triumphs through brain rather than brawn. Kirk, limping over rocks and dunes, tries to figure out how to cobble together a weapon capable of defeating his bigger, stronger adversary. The knowledge is there, if he can set aside his fear and repulsion of the Gorn, and the waves of pain and exhaustion gripping his body, to concentrate. Shatner's convincing facial expressions and expressive body language illuminate the mental aspect of the conflict. The actor's work here is even more impressive since he has very little dialogue and no one other than the stuntman in the Gorn suit to play against. The weight of the entire narrative rests on his shoulders.

Not coincidentally, both "The City on the Edge of Forever" and "Arena" were directed by Joseph Pevney, who had a knack for eliciting outstanding performances. Pevney oversaw fourteen *Trek* episodes (more than any director except Marc Daniels), also including "The Devil in the Dark," "Amok Time," "Journey to Babel" and "The Trouble with Tribbles," all of which contain excellent performances by Shatner or Leonard Nimoy or both, and often fine work by the supporting cast as well. Between "City" and "Arena," Pevney helped

Shatner deliver a matched set of performances that demonstrate the full range of his talents.

## Kirk Battles Kirk

The Gorn was tough, but Captain Kirk's most difficult adversary was undoubtedly—himself. In the classic adventure "The Enemy Within," a transporter malfunction splits the captain into two Kirks, one compassionate but indecisive, the other ruthless and impulsive. This is another yarn constructed around Shatner, whose Jekyll-and-Hyde-like portrayal serves as a nearly ideal single-episode summary of the actor's abilities. As the Good Kirk, Shatner is quiet and introspective. When the character's willpower and decision-making ability begin to wane, Shatner slumps his shoulders and nearly mumbles his lines. As the Evil Kirk, he prowls the decks of the *Enterprise* like a hungry tiger just escaped from the circus. Swilling Saurian Brandy from the bottle and leering at Grace Lee Whitney's Yeoman Rand, Shatner radiates menace. Sometimes (especially in close-up) his Evil Kirk comes perilously close to camp, but the actor delineates the two characters distinctly. Even when the two are dressed identically and seen side by side, it is not difficult for viewers to discern which Kirk is which. That may seem simple, but many talented performers have struggled in similar dual roles. (The great Spencer Tracy famously became irked during the filming of *Dr. Jekyll and Mr. Hyde* [1941] when a visitor to the set asked, "Which one is he playing now?") The one flaw that makes "The Enemy Within" a less than perfect summary of Shatner's talents is that it's an unusually humorless episode, providing no opportunity for the actor to display his comedic gifts. Otherwise, at least for Shatner, this one's as good as it gets. Even James Doohan, who seldom found a kind word for his former captain, was forced to acknowledge in his 1996 autobiography *Beam Me Up, Scotty* that "I thought Bill's performance was pretty OK in that one."

## "Risk Is Our Business!"

"Return to Tomorrow" is a far weaker episode than "The Enemy Within" (or for that matter "The City on the Edge of Forever" or "Arena"), but it contains a single golden moment that remains burned into the memories of many fans. The *Enterprise* discovers an ancient, long-dead world where the final survivors of a race of superadvanced beings linger on, their minds preserved in glowing spherical receptacles. Sargon, the leader of the aliens, asks the humans to trade places with them temporarily, so they can build android bodies and regain corporeal form. In exchange, Sargon pledges to share fantastic technical and medical advances with the humans. It's a dangerous proposition, so Kirk gathers his inner circle—Spock, McCoy, and Scotty—along with Dr. Ann Mulhall (Diana Muldaur) in the briefing room to discuss the idea. McCoy and Scotty are resistant, but Kirk allays their concerns with a stirring speech that encapsulates the nature and importance of the ship's five-year mission, and also reflects the soaring, humanist vision of *Star Trek*. It concludes with the following assertion:

> Risk? Risk is our business! That's what this starship is all about. That's why we're aboard her.

As Shatner delivers these lines, director Ralph Senesky slowly dollies in tighter and tighter on the actor's face, and Alexander Courage's *Star Trek* title theme swells in the background. "Return to Tomorrow" isn't a great episode. And when you look at the full speech on paper, rife with clichés and mixed metaphors, it's not great oratory, either. But Shatner sells it beautifully. His passionate, starry-eyed delivery makes the material *seem* great. He transforms what could have been a throwaway sequence into the ultimate expression of Captain Kirk's leader-of-men charisma. After this, no one ever wondered (if they ever wondered before) why Kirk's crew seemed so loyal; they would willingly fly into a supernova for their captain. And audiences would willingly come along for the ride.

## Introducing Fizzbin

The entire cast (and most fans) enjoyed *Star Trek*'s occasional voyages into comedy. The enduring popularity of "The Trouble with Tribbles" notwithstanding, "A Piece of the Action" remains the show's single funniest episode. In this installment—based on an idea originating with Roddenberry's initial, 1964 outline for the series—the *Enterprise* travels to Sigma Iota II, a backwater world that has been corrupted by pre-Prime Directive contact with human beings. The planet has developed a culture emulating Chicago gangs of the 1920s, based on a history book left behind by the crew of the starship *Horizon* 100 years earlier. Now Kirk, Spock, and McCoy (bedecked in pinstriped suits, toting tommy guns and attempting to drive a "flivver") find themselves embroiled in a turf war between rival crime bosses. Somehow, they must undo the cultural damage and set the Iotians on a less self-destructive course.

Shatner clearly had a blast making this episode, which brings his comedic flair to the forefront. In one side-splitting scene, Kirk distracts the guards holding the landing party captive by introducing a card game called Fizzbin. The rules, which Kirk is clearly making up as he goes along, are ridiculously convoluted: "You've got two Jacks; you've got a half-Fizzbin already. . . . (But) if you get another Jack, why, you'd have a Shrum and then you'd be disqualified. Now what you need is a King and a Deuce. Except at night, when you'd need a Queen and a Four." Shatner's deadpan delivery of this asinine double-talk is priceless. Later, unable to connect with the aliens any other way, Kirk begins to speak and act like a refugee from a Jimmy Cagney gangster flick, adopting a Brooklynese accent (even pronouncing the captain's name "Koik") and employing archaic slang. "I'm getting' tired of playin' patty-cake wit choo penny-ante operators," Shatner sneers. "Spocko, cover 'im!" Along with the Fizzbin lesson, this interlude never fails to inspire gales of laughter, even among viewers who have seen the episode many times before.

Three decades later, Shatner earned a string of Emmy and Golden Globe nominations (winning both awards in 2005) for his comedic performance as unscrupulous yet endearing attorney Denny Crane on *Boston Legal*. But he was never funnier than in "A Piece of the Action."

## Outmaneuvering the Romulans

In "Balance of Terror," Shatner delivered another powerful, low-key performance. The episode is dotted with superb moments for the actor. In this adventure, designed to emulate sub-hunting World War II movies such as *The Enemy Below* (1957) and *Run Silent, Run Deep* (1955)—the *Enterprise* battles the cloaked flagship of the Romulan Empire, which wipes out a handful of UFP outposts along the edge of the Neutral Zone separating Federation and Romulan space. Most of the story is devoted to a protracted cat-and-mouse struggle between the *Enterprise* and the Romulan "war bird"—or, more precisely, between Captain Kirk and the unnamed Romulan commander played by Mark Lenard. Shatner is quietly effective merely sitting in the captain's chair and looking pensive, as Kirk tries to outguess the wily Romulan. The two leaders grow to respect and admire one another as the battle unfolds. No single episode better depicts Kirk's leadership, both military and moral. In one of the story's unforgettable moments, navigator Stiles (Paul Comi) becomes suspicious of Spock when the Romulans are revealed to have Vulcan-like features. "Leave any bigotry in your quarters, there's no room for it on the bridge," Kirk snaps. Shatner's authoritative, dead-serious delivery lends the material the gravitas dictated by the script. (Perhaps he was inspired by Lenard's equally impressive work as the Romulan commander.) Written by Paul Scheider, this is one of the last episodes in which Kirk is depicted as a brooding commander plagued by self-doubts, in the tradition of C. S. Forester's Horatio Hornblower. While this runs counter to Shatner's usual swashbuckling, devil-may-care approach to his role, it's appropriate given the magnitude of the scenario: Kirk's actions could ignite an interstellar war that would cost millions of lives. Shatner also brings a feathery touch to the story's downbeat wrap-up, in which Kirk attempts to comfort a young officer whose fiancé was killed in the attack—on what was supposed to be the couple's wedding day. "It never makes any sense," Kirk says simply. Shatner's quiet brilliance here, and throughout, help make "Balance of Terror" one of *Star Trek*'s most gripping and emotionally resonant adventures.

## Outwitting NOMAD

"The Changeling" features a more typically Shatnerian Captain Kirk, this time pitted against NOMAD, an Earth space probe that has mutated into a deadly mechanical menace bent on "sterilizing" (that is, killing) all imperfect "biological units" (which means everybody). Ultimately, Kirk turns NOMAD's implacable logic against itself, pointing out that the probe has also made several errors (including mistaking Kirk for its creator) and demanding that it carry out its primary function to destroy imperfection—beginning with itself. With a gleam in his eye and his trademark hesitation delivery, Shatner goads NOMAD: "You are flawed—and imperfect. Exercise your prime function!" He's in fine fettle from the start, but his winning work here creates one of Kirk's signature moments. Shatner's comic timing reemerges for the story's amusing wrap-up, in which Kirk jokes about the loss of his "son," NOMAD. "What a doctor he would have made!" Shatner bemoans with mock sorrow.

"The Changeling" was one of five episodes in which Kirk basically talked a robot or a computer into committing suicide. He used the same strategy in "The Return of Archons," "I, Mudd," "The Ultimate Computer," and "What Are Little Girls Made Of?." Shatner always shined during these confrontations, brimming with confidence and good humor, suggesting that Kirk got a special kick out of outsmarting computers. In the end, that quality—the sense of fun and adventure—was the element *Star Trek* most needed from Shatner. With or without him, the show would have offered high-quality, adult-oriented science fiction and tackled hot-button social issues through the lens of fantasy. But Shatner's effervescent presence as Kirk enabled *Trek* to do those things and seem fun at the same time. Episodes like "Balance of Terror" work so well because they exist in contrast to the series' typically lighter-hearted adventures. That's why, even at his most indulgent, Shatner's work remains essential to the appeal of the program.

# The Infinite Vulcan

## Leonard Nimoy Discovers Spock

Unlike his costars, Leonard Nimoy's brilliance earned ample recognition during *Star Trek*'s original broadcast run. He was honored with Emmy nominations following each of the program's three seasons. And he received by far the most fan mail of anyone in the cast, along with the most requests for interviews and public appearances. While *Star Trek* was in development, NBC wanted Nimoy's character eliminated because its marketing department feared the satanic-looking first officer would hurt the show with viewers in the Bible Belt. After a few weeks on the air, however, the network suddenly reversed course and began demanding more teleplays that focused on Spock.

The character seemed to leave a dent in the psyche of everyone who encountered him—including Nimoy himself. The role "affected me very deeply and personally, socially, psychologically, emotionally. . . . What started out as a welcome job to a hungry actor has become a constant and ongoing influence in my thinking and lifestyle," Nimoy wrote in his 1977 memoir *I Am Not Spock*. Both this book and his 1995 autobiography *I Am Spock* are full of lengthy dialogues between Nimoy and Spock, "transcribed" from the mind of the author. Based on these dialogues, it seems as if Spock has a life of his own—a line of thinking that reflects Nimoy's Method training.

Unlike William Shatner, who was classically trained, and DeForest Kelley, who rose through the ranks of the Hollywood studio system, Nimoy was a devotee of the Method—an intimate, psychological approach to the craft originated by Constantin Stanislavski in the late nineteenth century and advanced in America by Lee Strasberg's Actors Studio beginning in the 1940s. Prior to signing on with *Star Trek*, Nimoy taught the Method to pupils in Hollywood (for years these classes had been his steadiest source of income). Method actors do not shape their characters so much as they allow themselves to be shaped *by* their characters. That was certainly the case with Nimoy and Spock. Nimoy thinks of Spock not so much as a creation but as a discovery. A sampling of key episodes reveals the growing rapport between actor and character (or vice-versa).

### "Fascinating"

In *Star Trek*'s original pilot, "The Cage," Nimoy played a very different Spock— the character's coolly logical personality was not yet defined. In the second pilot, "Where No Man Has Gone Before," Nimoy portrayed a more recognizable Spock, but not particularly well. The actor seems stiff and uncomfortable. In his two memoirs, Nimoy credits director Joseph Sargent with fostering a creative breakthrough. During the filming of "The Corbomite Maneuver," the first regular *Star Trek* episode produced, Nimoy felt unsure how to handle an early scene in which the *Enterprise* encounters a giant spacecraft. The rest of the bridge crew seems intimidated by the huge alien vessel, but Sargent instructed Nimoy to read his one-word line—"Fascinating!"—with a kind of detached scientific curiosity, completely free of anxiety. "What came out wasn't Leonard Nimoy's voice, but Spock's," Nimoy wrote in *I Am Spock*. "I began to seriously understand where Spock was coming from." The dialogue between character and actor had begun. And the word "fascinating" instantly became a signature expression for the character.

## Improvising the FSNP

Just two episodes later, during the production of "The Enemy Within," Nimoy's link with the character was strong enough that he was able to improvise what would become another Spock trademark—the Vulcan nerve pinch. Richard Matheson's teleplay called for Spock to clobber the Evil Kirk with a haymaker, but Nimoy felt the refined, violence-averse Vulcan should have a subtler way of incapacitating his opponent. So he ad-libbed an alternative (Spock pinches Kirk at the base of the neck; Kirk instantly collapses) and rehearsed it with Shatner between camera setups. Nimoy and Shatner demonstrated the gag for director Leon Penn, who loved it and incorporated it into the scene. The maneuver became so well known and frequently repeated that later *Trek* teleplays often referred to it as simply the "FSNP," short for Famous Spock Nerve Pinch. This was only the first in a series of inspired improvisations that Nimoy devised (or, the actor might suggest, that Spock gave him), which became trademarks for the character and linchpins of the show's rapidly coalescing Vulcan mythology.

## Spock Weeps

The most impressive—and moving—of all Nimoy's improvisations was a brief sequence the actor invented for "The Naked Time," in which Spock, infected by a virus that breaks down emotional inhibitions, locks himself away in a briefing room and cries. John D. F. Black's teleplay called for Spock to burst into tears in the hallway of the *Enterprise*, then a laughing crewman was supposed to paint a mustache on the crying Vulcan. Nimoy considered the scene beneath the dignity of his character. However, he believed the scenario provided an opportunity to dramatize Spock's perpetual inner conflict—with his detached, logical Vulcan side battling his emotional human side and, at least this once, losing. Spock would never cry in public, Nimoy reasoned, but would hide himself away and try to quell his surging emotions. Director Marc Daniels agreed and worked out the blocking and camera movement for the scene with Nimoy. As the briefing room door slides shut behind him, Spock attempts to steady himself. "I am in control of my emotions," Nimoy says, clenching his teeth. (All the dialogue for this sequence was ad-libbed.) Then he begins to sob, staggering across the room and collapsing into a chair. Staring at a blank computer screen, still talking to himself, he struggles not to weep. Daniels's camera slowly dollies in and then glides 180 degrees around the actor, ending in close-up on Nimoy's tear-streaked face. It's a brilliantly imagined and deeply touching little scene, one that helped endear the Vulcan to thousands fans—and one that Nimoy, amazingly, nailed in a single take.

## Spock in Command

"The Galileo Seven" was one of the first teleplays designed to meet the network's demand for more Spock-centric adventures. Nimoy is the de facto star of this installment, in which a shuttlecraft crashes on planet Taurus II. There Spock, McCoy, Scotty, and four other crew members struggle to effect repairs while fending off attacks from a race of giant anthropoids. McCoy refers to the catastrophe as Spock's "big chance"—his first command. Spock pooh-poohs the idea—"I neither enjoy the idea of command, nor am I frightened of it," he says. "It simply exists."—but a hint of eagerness in Nimoy's voice suggests that the confident-sounding Vulcan secretly relishes the prospect of proving that logic is the best basis for leadership decisions. As usual, the actor's approach remains delicate and low-key; the more alarmed and overwrought his crew becomes, the more still and quiet Nimoy grows, underscoring Spock's separation from the humans.

The crew is put off by Spock's matter-of-fact assertion that some of them may need to be left behind to allow the others to escape—and that as commander Spock will decide who stays and who goes. The Vulcan is never comforting or conciliatory. Eventually, however, Spock realizes that command—command of humans, at least—requires more than the antiseptic application of rigid logic. He must take emotional reactions into account—those of his crew and those of the primitive anthropoids. In the end, he prevails by taking a highly illogical gamble. But the action itself isn't as important as the motivation behind it—a new willingness to entertain hunches and other emotional, human thinking. As story arcs go, this one is tiny; it would span about a centimeter. It takes a performance of masterful restraint and subtlety for it to register at all. Yet register it does, and as a result "The Galileo Seven" became a landmark early adventure. It explored the mind of Spock more deeply than any previous installment—and instantly became a fan favorite.

## The Lovely Leila

While visiting planet Omicron Ceti III, Spock is infected by spores from a plant that instills feelings of happiness and security. Under the influence of the spores, Spock falls in love with botanist Leila Kalomi (Jill Ireland), an old companion from his days on Earth. That's the plot of the watershed "This Side of Paradise," which is dotted with outstanding moments for Nimoy, who seems energized by this emotionally rich scenario. In the first of many memorable interludes, Spock falls to the ground after being sprayed by the spores. He writhes and groans in agony as his mind tries to fight the emotions swelling within him. Then suddenly, the fight is over. A smile creases his face. A contented-looking Spock takes Kalomi's hand and says, "I love you. I can love you." Nimoy's voice is filled with more wonder than adoration, as the Vulcan experiences joy for the first time. In a subsequent scene with Kalomi, it was Nimoy's idea for Spock to hang upside down in a tree, in a state of blissful abandon.

Spock unwinds with Leila Kalomi (Jill Ireland) in "This Side of Paradise," which features one of Nimoy's most subtle and touching performances.

The key to the actor's approach to Spock was its simplicity. Nimoy understood that, playing the austere Vulcan, even the slightest display of emotion—a raised eyebrow, a shift in posture or tone of voice—would be amplified a hundredfold in the minds of viewers. This technique is showcased perfectly in the climax of "This Side of Paradise." Freed of the spores, Spock must break off his relationship with Kalomi—and in so doing, remove her from the infection-created reverie she has enjoyed on Omicron Ceti III. The stoic Spock simply allows Kalomi to realize that he has returned to his normal, logical self—and as a result, his love for her is gone. Nimoy's tender, sad tone of voice—counterpointed by the actor's stiff, straight-backed posture—suggests that the Vulcan secretly shares Kalomi's heartache, even if he cannot express it, or even admit it to himself. Nimoy's mournful reading of the episode's final line says it all: "For the first time in my life, I was happy."

## Mind Meld with the Horta

The Vulcan Mind Meld, first seen in "Dagger of the Mind," was invented by Gene Roddenberry as a device to speed up expository sequences. In later episodes, Spock melded with numerous entities—human, alien, and even mechanical—but the most memorable of these encounters remains Spock's telepathic link with the Horta in screenwriter Gene L. Coon's "The Devil in the Dark." This is hardly one of Nimoy's most refined performances; he moans, "Eternity ends! . . . The Chamber of the Ages! . . . The Altar of Tomorrow!" with nearly Shatnerian fervor. But this sequence (which runs just over six minutes, the series' longest mind meld) is critical to the entire episode, which many fans rank among the show's finest installments. This is the moment when Spock realizes that the murderous "monster" he and Kirk have been pursuing is actually a grieving mother trying to defend the lives of her unhatched offspring, which the miners of planet Janus IV have unwittingly killed by the thousands. Although perhaps a touch overplayed, this paradigm shift registers emphatically with audiences, whose sympathies switch from the besieged humans to the desperate Horta. Nimoy's anguished delivery provides the conduit for, arguably, the most effective and moving of *Star Trek*'s many calls for understanding in the face of prejudice.

## Blood Fever

Here's another great episode and another great improvisation by Nimoy (or, if you prefer, from Spock). For Theodore Sturgeon's "Amok Time," which launched the series' second season, Spock invented the split-fingered Vulcan salute to coincide with Sturgeon's immortal line, "Live long and prosper." Nimoy borrowed the hand sign from his Orthodox Jewish upbringing. It's a gesture used by Jewish priests known as the Kohanim during the High Holiday services. "The hand, held in that shape, spells out the Hebrew letter Shin," Nimoy explained in *I Am Not Spock*. "This is the first letter in the word Shadai, which is the name of the Almighty." Like the endlessly quoted (and parodied) "Live long and prosper," Nimoy's Vulcan salute became another trademark, both for Spock and *Star Trek* in general.

However, Nimoy's excellence in this episode extends well beyond the split-fingered hand sign. Once again, he seizes on the opportunity to visualize Spock's inner conflicts. This time, the struggle is between his animalistic drive to reproduce and his rational desire to remain in control of his mind and body. Nimoy is superb throughout. He has an endearing scene with Nurse Chapel in Spock's cabin. The nurse is heartsick with fear and longing for the ailing Vulcan, whom she secretly loves. "I had a most startling dream—you were trying to tell me something but I couldn't hear you," Nimoy says tenderly as Spock wipes a tear from Chapel's eye. This whole sequence reverberates with unspoken sexual and romantic tension. As the episode progresses and Spock grows more and more sick, Nimoy's performance gradually becomes more exaggerated. Later, Spock is able to calmly explain the rules of the *koon-ut-kal-if-fee* mating ritual to Kirk and McCoy but seems distracted, as if dazed or drugged. As Spock sinks deeper into the mental quagmire of the "plak tow" ("blood fever"), Nimoy walks robotically, his mouth hanging open. He seems physically as well as mentally staggered when his fiancée, T'Pring (Arlene Martel), refuses to marry him and calls for Spock to battle her chosen champion (Kirk). When asked if he accepts the challenge, Spock can't even answer in words. Nimoy merely nods. His eyes roll back in his head. During the fight itself, Nimoy seems convincingly bent on murder. (In view of his ongoing, off-camera rivalry with Shatner, perhaps trying to kill Captain Kirk wasn't much of a stretch for Nimoy!) However, his intimidating performance reminds audiences why, prior to *Star Trek*, he was frequently cast as a villain.

## The Needs of the Many . . .

In *Star Trek II: The Wrath of Khan*, the dying Spock famously stated, "The needs of the many outweigh the needs of the few . . . or the one." But Spock first voiced this logical imperative—less eloquently, perhaps—in episodes such as "The Galileo Seven," in which Spock says, "It is more rational to sacrifice one life than six"; and "Journey to Babel," in which Spock hesitates to save his father's life out of his sense of responsibility to the *Enterprise* and its crew. "Babel" ranks among the best loved of all *Star Trek* episodes and features excellent performances by nearly the entire cast. Nimoy has a series of outstanding moments, playing opposite Mark Lenard (as Spock's father, Sarek), Shatner, and DeForest Kelley. But the actor's finest scene in this episode—and one of the most emotionally riveting sequences in all of *Trek* lore—is Spock's *tête-à-tête* with his mother, Amanda (Jane Wyatt). She pleads with her son to relinquish command of the *Enterprise* (Kirk has been incapacitated by a would-be assassin) so Spock can donate the Vulcan blood needed for Sarek's lifesaving heart operation. Spock emphasizes that he is now responsible for the lives of the ship's crew and passengers, including

Spock, flanked by his faithless fiancée T'Pring (Arlene Martel), flashes the Vulcan salute in this publicity photo from "Amok Time." The hand sign was one of Nimoy's famous improvisations.

more than a hundred dignitaries bound for a key diplomatic summit. The ship is under attack from an unknown enemy; he cannot risk hundreds of lives to save just one person, not even his father. Sarek, he insists, would agree with his logic. But Amanda does not agree. "Nothing is as important as your father's life," she says. This scene provides another outstanding example of Nimoy's understated approach. "How can you have lived on Vulcan so long, married a Vulcan, raised a son on Vulcan, without understanding what it means to *be* Vulcan?" Spock asks. Nimoy stands straight, his arms neatly folded behind his back, betraying nothing. Yet his gentle tone of voice, with a slight quiver for emphasis, informs us that despite his apparent exasperation, he admires his mother's devotion to Sarek; it makes him love her even more deeply—even though Amanda slaps her son across the face at the conclusion of the sequence.

By the middle of *Star Trek*'s second season, Nimoy and Spock were on such good terms they felt at ease leaving the friendly confines of the series to have a little fun on the town. Nimoy made a memorable guest appearance on *The Carol Burnett Show* in late 1967. In a skit titled "Mrs. Invisible Man," Burnett played a confused young mother in search of parenting advice who mistakenly calls in *Mr.* Spock rather than famed pediatrician *Dr.* Spock. Nimoy appeared in full costume and makeup, poking good-natured fun at his famous alter ego.

Nimoy was dismayed by the drop-off in quality of teleplays (and everything else) during *Star Trek*'s final season and complained bitterly to producer Fred Freiberger that his character was stagnating in episodes such as "Spock's Brain." Nevertheless, Nimoy delivered outstanding work in numerous adventures, including "The *Enterprise* Incident," in which Spock seduces a female Romulan commander (Joanne Linville) as part of a plot to capture the Romulan Cloaking Device; and "The Tholian Web," in which a bereft Spock assumes command of the *Enterprise* following Kirk's apparent death. Even subpar scripts couldn't disconnect Nimoy from Spock. Or Spock from the hearts of fans.

# Errands of Mercy

## The Unsung Heroism of DeForest Kelley

"hen I see the trade papers, after a whole season, still only list Bill Shatner and Leonard Nimoy as co-stars, I burn a little inside," said DeForest Kelley, in a rare fit of candor with a *TV Guide* interviewer in 1968. "What I want, as a co-star, is to be counted in fully. I've had to fight for everything I've gotten at *Star Trek*, from a parking space at the studio to an unshared dressing room, and sometimes the patience wears raw."

Kelley went on to grouse about the passive nature of his role as Dr. McCoy, compared to the dynamic Captain Kirk and Mr. Spock, and to express exasperation with his character being omitted from an unnamed teleplay (likely "Errand of Mercy"). "It was an oversight," Kelley was told by the writer of the episode (probably Gene Coon). "An oversight!" Kelley bemoaned. "If a producer-writer on my own show forgets me, then I've got problems!"

The outburst was notable because, throughout his long association with *Star Trek*, Kelley's talent was surpassed only by his professionalism. Among producers, directors, and fellow actors, he was the single best-liked and most-respected member of the cast, a skilled and dedicated craftsman who seldom complained about anything.

Nevertheless, the actor had every reason to gripe. Throughout *Star Trek*'s broadcast run, Kelley's contributions to the show remained undervalued. He didn't receive costar billing until Season Two, when his salary jumped from a meager $800 per episode to about $2,500 per episode, on par with Nimoy's but still far less than Shatner's $5,000. Even then, Kelley seldom garnered the kind of attention, in terms of interviews and public appearances, his costars enjoyed. For instance, Roddenberry tried to send all three of the show's leads for a 1967 appearance on NBC's *Today Show*, but was informed that *Today* only wanted Shatner and Nimoy. This was common; producers and event organizers didn't consider Kelley a significant draw.

Yet the actor's work was just as crucial to *Star Trek* as that of his costars. Kelley's prickly-yet-warmhearted "old country doctor" helped humanize the series, widening its appeal by making its futuristic setting and gadgetry seem more familiar and approachable. Kelley's superb, selfless performances in his many scenes with Shatner and Nimoy accounted for much of the program's vaunted Kirk-Spock-McCoy chemistry. This beloved troika—with Kelley's McCoy

Kelley's folksy charm as Dr. McCoy humanized the universe of *Star Trek*.

playing Tin Man to Shatner's Lion and Nimoy's Scarecrow—quickly emerged as one of the series' most appealing features. Nimoy earned greater accolades, winning Emmy nominations in each of the show's three seasons in his far flashier role. But Kelley—arguably—was the show's most dependable player, delivering pitch-perfect performances in episode after episode, including the following classic adventures.

## "The Empath"

It's no wonder that Kelley named "The Empath" his favorite *Star Trek* episode. No single installment provides a more complete summation of all the actor's formidable gifts. Kelley was blessed with wondrously expressive eyes. His voice—a Georgia drawl tempered by diction lessons during his tenure as a Paramount contract player in the 1940s—was distinctive yet supple, capable of shifting tone in mid-sentence, lilting or rasping as the material dictated. He was a fine dramatic actor who, unlike many fine dramatic actors, also possessed excellent comic timing.

All these attributes are showcased in "The Empath," which also stands as the fullest expression of Dr. McCoy's self-sacrificing devotion to his friends and to his calling as a physician. The teleplay—an unsolicited submission by a fan, Joyce Muskat, not a professional screenwriter—affords Kelley the opportunity to appear heroic, compassionate, and funny, sometimes simultaneously. In Muskat's story, Kirk, Spock, and McCoy are taken prisoner by the inscrutable Vians; the captain and the doctor are tortured but later healed by a mute alien woman (Kathryn Hays) with empathic extrasensory powers.

Despite the away team's incarceration, McCoy remains in good spirits early in the episode, when he nicknames the mute Empath "Gem." ("It's better than 'Hey, You,'" McCoy reasons.) In this script, Kelley receives a heavy dose of the dry, expository dialogue usually reserved for Mr. Spock: McCoy must explain that Gem is a mute, how per powers work, and other background information. Fortunately, the actor's folksy, easygoing delivery puts this material over convincingly, and even entertainingly. Kelley also delivers one of his signature catchphrases when McCoy derisively informs Spock that "I'm a doctor, not a coal miner." But Kelley's finest moments arrive toward the end of the tale. With Kirk recovering from grievous injuries, the Vians ask for a new torture subject. McCoy drugs Kirk and then Spock so that he, alone, is available to endure the punishment. Kelley's earlier nonchalance gives way to quiet yet implacable determination as McCoy risks his life to preserve the well-being of his friends. Afterward, the doctor lies apparently dying on a table, attended by Mr. Spock. "You've got a good bedside manner, Spock," Kelley utters in a thin whisper, as the doctor lapses into a coma. His eyes reveal the love his character feels, but seldom expresses, for his Vulcan friend. Moments like that one make "The Empath" the brightest of many shining moments for both the actor and his character.

## "For the World Is Hollow and I Have Touched the Sky"

Most of the show's cast, crew, and fans consider *Star Trek*'s third season a creative wasteland. But, at least for Kelley, Season Three also included the occasional artistic oasis. Some of his—and Dr. McCoy's—best episodes originated in the series' final year, including "The Empath," "Spectre of the Gun," "Day of the

Dove," and "For the World Is Hollow and I Have Touched the Sky." The lattermost of that quartet, written by Rik Vollearts and directed by Tony Leader, is a melodramatic but imaginative yarn that puts Dr. McCoy center stage. The good doctor diagnoses himself with a terminal illness, goes on a dangerous away mission, falls in love, joins a cult, commits espionage and is tortured, escapes the cult, breaks up with his girlfriend, and is miraculously cured, all in the course of one fifty-minute episode. Somehow Kelley makes all this seem believable and even moving.

The actor's performance is subtle and multilayered, conveying McCoy's complex and conflicted emotions though carefully nuanced delivery and revealing facial expressions. When the doctor informs Captain Kirk that he has contracted "xenopolycythemia" and has less than a year to live, McCoy tries to appear chipper and upbeat, but Kelley's eyes betray the character's worry and fatigue. Later, the *Enterprise* investigates a mysterious planetoid, which turns out to be a massive, elaborately disguised spacecraft on a collision course with the densely populated planet Daran V. McCoy falls in love with Natrina (Katherine Woodville), the high priestess of the asteroid's occupants, who do not realize they are on board a starship. Reluctantly at first, the dying McCoy decides to grasp this last chance at happiness. Kelley brings a tender, confessional quality to his romantic interludes with Woodville, in which McCoy describes his life as "very lonely." McCoy renounces his Starfleet commission and joins Natrina's cult, which worships the planetoid-ship's nearly omniscient computer. But McCoy's restless scientific curiosity prevents him from blindly following orders. Kelley again convincingly portrays churning, mixed emotions, as McCoy remains committed to Natrina yet itches to uncover the secrets of the giant spacecraft and help avert the tragedy of its impending collision with Daran V (which, of course, he does).

Like "The Empath," "For the World Is Hollow" remains an outstanding entry for both Kelley and McCoy. However, with its downbeat storyline and dark tone, this is an unusually humorless episode, denying Kelley the opportunity to demonstrate the full spectrum of his abilities.

## "Friday's Child"

Kelley enjoys a much livelier, wittier part in "Friday's Child." Although a less challenging assignment than either "The Empath" or "For the World Is Hollow," Kelley's charming performance here remains a delight. In this episode, Kirk, McCoy, and Spock find themselves trapped on planet Capella V, competing with the Klingon Empire to win a mining agreement from the planet's warlike, preindustrial natives.

McCoy spends much of the episode caring for Eleen (Julie Newmar), a pregnant Capellan woman, the wife of a murdered chieftain who feels compelled by Capellan custom to sacrifice her life and that of her unborn child. McCoy must overcome Eleen's cultural programming to not only deliver the baby but

"Friday's Child" places Kelley's gift for comedy in the forefront, as he tends to the haughty Eleen (played by ex-Catwoman Julie Newmar).

convince its mother that the child's life—and her own—is worth saving. The good doctor accomplishes this in rather unorthodox ways, locking horns with the warrior-queen verbally and even physically. "Now let me see that arm!," Kelley practically growls after Eleen accidentally burns herself. Later, when the Capellan patient slaps him, the doctor slaps her back. (When Kirk later notes that this technique isn't covered in the Starfleet medical guide, McCoy counters, "It's in mine from now on.") This exchange finally earns McCoy Eleen's respect, but as a result she gloms onto him and begins referring to her unborn baby as "our child," much to the doctor's consternation—and Kirk and Spock's amusement. Kelley's comedic slow burns in these sequences are hilarious. The story presents a few serious, dramatic moments for Kelley, as well, like when McCoy pleads for Eleen to accept her newborn son, who will perish without her. But for the most part the tone remains light. Kelley alone among the show's cast could believably hold a baby and say, "Oochy-woochy-koochy-koo." (Kirk explains to a puzzled Mr. Spock that McCoy is speaking in "an obscure Earth dialect. If you're curious, consult Linguistics.")

Prickly yet warmhearted, amusing yet with underlying gravitas, Kelley (as always) brings McCoy to vivid life in "Friday's Child." Appealing appearances like this one are what made the doctor one of the show's most popular characters.

## "Shore Leave"

Kelley's flair for comedy must have come as a revelation to viewers accustomed to seeing the actor portray dastardly Western gunmen. Yet *Star Trek*'s screenwriters took advantage of Kelley's comedic abilities from the outset. In the first nonpilot episode produced, "The Corbomite Maneuver," Kelley was seem muttering to himself, "If I jumped every time a light came on around here, I'd wind up talking to myself." Theodore Sturgeon's lighthearted teleplay "Shore Leave" gave Kelley another highly entertaining, largely comedic role, this time with romantic overtones. And McCoy finally gets the girl.

The girl, in this case, is Yeoman Tania Barrows (Emily Banks), who, along with McCoy, Sulu, and a pair of other crewman, beams down to a beautiful, Earthlike, uninhabited planet for shore leave—only to be plagued by annoyances and dangers conjured up from their own memories and imaginations. McCoy mentions *Alice in Wonderland* and then sees a giant white rabbit with a pocket watch and a waistcoat disappear through a hole in a hedge; the rabbit is soon followed by a young blonde-haired girl in a blue dress. Kelley's incredulous, mute reaction expresses consternation, amusement, fear, and a thousand other thoughts and feelings simultaneously. Later, McCoy romances Barrows, encouraging her to try on the Elizabethan gown of a storybook princess, which magically appears on a nearby shrub. When Barrows warns McCoy not to peek while she changes, Kelley counters: "My dear, I'm a doctor. When I peek, it's in the line of duty." When a black knight appears on horseback to challenge McCoy for Barrows's honor, the brave physician (reasoning that none of these fantastic events could be real, so they must be an illusion) boldly stands his ground—and is run through with a lance. Kelley's look of surprise and anguish as the lance strikes proves unsettlingly realistic. But McCoy returns, miraculously healed, for the episode's finale. To Barrow's irritation, he reappears with a fur-bikini-clad, Playboy Bunny–like showgirl on each arm. Clearly delighted with this resolution, Kelley flashes a beaming smile. The actor probably wished someone had written a few more "Shore Leave"–like adventures. Many fans would share that sentiment.

## "Return of the Archons," "The City on the Edge of Forever," and "Day of the Dove"

Dr. McCoy was not only the most human, and in many respects most endearing, character on *Star Trek* but also the most vulnerable. He was not only older and more frail than the dashing, athletic Kirk or the superhuman Spock but more susceptible to outside influence. If the script called for a character to get drugged, duped, hypnotized, or possessed, that afflicted character would more than likely be McCoy, who always led with his heart. Such storylines supplied further evidence of Kelley's apparently boundless versatility.

In "The Return of the Archons," McCoy falls under the telepathic control of the supercomputer Landru—he's "absorbed" into "The Body." Kelley's vacant smile and brainwashed demeanor ("Blessed be the body and health to all of its parts!") at first borders on the comic, but later, when McCoy realizes that Kirk and Spock are only pretending to have been absorbed, the doctor's steely-eyed denunciation of his former friends ("You're *not* of the body! Traitors!") is chilling.

In "The City on the Edge of Forever," McCoy accidentally overdoses on a dangerous drug and temporarily becomes a raving madman. Although Kelley is off-screen for most of this classic adventure, he's strikingly effective in his isolated scenes as the sweaty, delusional, paranoid McCoy. At one point, the doctor weeps in agony thinking about twentieth-century surgery ("needles and sutures . . . oh, the pain . . . to cut and sew people like garments!"). Kelley's portrayal of the unbalanced McCoy reminded viewers why he was so good at playing crazed Western outlaws like Toby Jack Saunders from *Apache Uprising*. He seems fully capable of murder—or worse.

In "Day of the Dove," McCoy (along with the rest of the crew) comes under the mental influence of a mysterious, hate-devouring life force that has trapped a platoon of Klingons on board the *Enterprise*. The human and Klingon factions fight for control of the ship, a bloody conflict staged with swords and daggers (which the hate-creature magically substituted for the ship's more advanced weapons). Under the entity's sway, McCoy begins spewing hate-speak: "Murderers, we should wipe out every last one of them!" Kelley's impassioned delivery, with eyes blazing and voice full of gravel, makes the addled physician seem more dangerous than the Klingons.

Whenever McCoy was taken over by some alien force, which also happened in a handful of other adventures, Kelley could be counted on to deliver a distinctive, powerful portrayal, as demonstrated by his diverse yet uniformly excellent performances in these three episodes.

Kelley was unnervingly effective as the "insane McCoy" from "The City on the Edge of Forever," as pictured on this 1976 Topps trading card.

## Other Outstanding Performances

About the only installments in which DeForest Kelley failed to perform with distinction were "Where No Man Has Gone Before," "What are Little Girls

Made Of?," "The Menagerie, Part II," and "Errand of Mercy." That's because he didn't appear in those episode at all! Narrowing the actor's best *Star Trek* work to a handful of adventures is nearly impossible. But a few other performances deserve mention:

- "The Man Trap," the first episode broadcast, gave Kelley more screen time than most of the show's early installments. The actor made the most of it, delivering a touching performance as McCoy encounters his lost love—Dr. Nancy Crater (Jeanne Bal), who turns out to be a shape-shifting salt vampire. Kelley's heartfelt work helps elevate the episode to something (slightly) better than a typical sci-fi monster yarn.

- In "Miri," Dr. McCoy devises a cure for a ghastly plague that has wiped out nearly the entire population of a planet, leaving only a clutch of orphaned children. Unwilling to risk anyone else's life, he then injects himself with the untested, and potentially lethal, vaccine. Kelley's sober, determined demeanor bolsters the credibility of this otherwise shaky episode.

- Almost everyone performs brilliantly in the classic "Journey to Babel," in which Spock must be convinced to relinquish command of the *Enterprise* so he can donate blood for an operation to save his father's life. Kelley earns high honors for his verbal battles with Spock, this time played for drama rather than comedy, as he strives to save the life of Ambassador Sarek (Mark Lenard).

- In "The Deadly Years," in which McCoy and several more crew members contract an alien disease that causes hyper-accelerated aging, Kelley dabbles in self-parody. As the crotchety, elderly McCoy, Kelley exaggerates his character's trademark speech patterns and mannerisms to highly amusing effect.

- "Spectre of the Gun," an eerie, outer space retelling of *The Gunfight at O.K. Corral*, was written by Gene L. Coon specifically as a tribute to Kelley and his gunslinging past. It's an enjoyable romp, with Kelley in fine fettle throughout.

# The Finest Crew in the Fleet

## The Supporting Cast's Shining Moments

More than twenty years elapsed between the premiere of *Star Trek* and the debut of its first sequel series, *Star Trek: The Next Generation*. Television underwent many changes during the interim. One of the most profound was the emergence of hit series such as *The Waltons* (1972–81), *Hill Street Blues* (1981–87), and *Cheers* (1982–93), which were designed to feature a large ensemble of actors rather than one or two stars. This casting approach opened additional story possibilities for screenwriters and provided reassurance to producers, since the show could continue even if key cast members departed or died—as happened over the lifetime of all three of those programs. *Star Trek*'s Desilu-produced sister series *Mission: Impossible* was a forerunner of this ensemble approach.

*The Next Generation* (and every other *Star Trek* series to follow the original) was also an ensemble cast program. While the primary focus remained on Captain Picard (Patrick Stewart), individual installments often highlighted supporting characters such as Commander Data (Brent Spiner), engineer Geordi La Forge (LeVar Burton), and Lieutenant Worf (Michael Dorn). Within the first few minutes, viewers could tell if this week's installment would be a Geordi episode, a Worf episode, a Counselor Troi (Marina Sirtis) episode, and so on.

Nothing like this ever happened on the classic *Star Trek* series. Fans can only daydream about the tantalizing possibilities of the Uhura episodes or Sulu adventures that never were.

Most TV shows of the 1950s and '60s were built around one or two stars and a revolving assortment of guest actors. On many programs, the recurring supporting characters amounted to little more than window dressing. *Star Trek* largely adhered to this traditional structure. Although it boasted three stars (William Shatner, Leonard Nimoy, and DeForest Kelley), its supporting players weren't guaranteed work in every episode, and their parts often were limited to glorified bits (little beyond the familiar "Aye, aye, Captain"). And William Shatner, out of both personal insecurity and a misguided sense of responsibility to "carry" the show, often tried to further reduce the screen time of the supporting cast.

All of this makes it difficult to fairly assess the capabilities and contributions of James Doohan, George Takei, Nichelle Nichols, Walter Koenig, and Majel Barrett. Fabled acting instructor Constantin Stanislavski once said that "there are no small parts, only small actors." But there are only so many different ways to deliver the line "Hailing frequencies open, Captain." Perhaps the best thing that can be said for *Star Trek*'s supporting players is that on those rare occasions when the script gave them something meaningful to play, they played it well. In the end, that's all you can ask of any actor.

## James Doohan

If *Star Trek* had a fourth lead it was (or at least should have been) James Doohan, the busiest member of the supporting cast. Chief Engineer Montgomery Scott not only worked mechanical miracles on an almost weekly basis but was often assigned to landing parties, or else left in command of the ship while Kirk and Spock were away. Whatever the scenario, Doohan's work was never less than exemplary, earning him the nickname "One-Take Doohan." And Scotty became the show's most popular supporting character. All of which is even more impressive considering that Gene Roddenberry tried to fire the actor after his first appearance.

Doohan was one of several actors hired for *Star Trek*'s second pilot, "Where No Man Has Gone Before." After NBC purchased the series, the show underwent a final round of recasting. Actors Lloyd Haynes (communications specialist Alden), Andrea Dromm (Yeoman Smith), and Paul Fix (Dr. Piper) were all jettisoned because Roddenberry was unsatisfied with their performances. Although he liked Doohan's acting, Roddenberry considered Scotty a superfluous character and tried to cut him as a cost-saving measure. But Doohan was already under contract, and the forceful intervention of his agent, Paul Wilkins, kept the actor (and Scotty) on the show.

Doohan went on to appear in sixty-three of the series' seventy-nine installments. Like the rest of the supporting cast, his shining moments are scattered across numerous adventures—a scene here and a scene there. Considered as a body of work, however, these performances constitute an impressive achievement. It was Doohan's idea to make the character a Scotsman, and the actor's mastery of accents brought a distinctive texture to the role that helped Scotty stand out. Doohan's work was so skillful that he was able, through subtle alterations to Scotty's brogue, to shift easily from drama to comedy as teleplays demanded.

The actor's comedic gifts were best showcased in "The Trouble with Tribbles," especially during the buildup to Scotty's barroom brawl with Klingon officer Korax (Michael Pataki) while on shore leave at Space Station K-7. At first, Doohan seems relaxed and level-headed, calming Ensign Chekov when Korax, bent on picking a fight, insults Captain Kirk. But Doohan slowly steams up when Korax begins to denigrate the *Enterprise*, calling the ship a "saggy old

Like the character he played, "One-Take Doohan" was noted for his reliability.

rust-bucket" and comparing it with a garbage scow. "Laddy, don't ye think ye should . . . rephrase that?" Doohan seethes, narrowing his eyes. Finally, he rises from his chair, wearing a satisfied grin, and lands a haymaker to the Klingon's jaw. A melee quickly ensues. Doohan is also highly amusing in the following scene, in which a sheepish Scotty struggles to explain to Captain Kirk how the brawl began. Finally, according to Doohan, it was his idea to flip the verb from "trouble" to "tribble" in Scotty's famous closing line ("where they'll be no tribble at all").

As funny and charming as Doohan could be, however, *Star Trek* was far more reliant on the actor's dramatic chops. His deft, matter-of-fact handling of the show's technospeak made Scotty (along with Mr. Spock) a go-to character for explaining foundational concepts such as the warp drive and transporter, helping shore up the credibility of the emerging *Star Trek* universe. The importance of this can't be overstated, since most television audiences of 1960s were not well versed in science fiction. Screenwriters usually disguised this exposition within dramatic scenarios—for instance, with the *Enterprise* trapped in a decaying orbit during "The Naked Time" (in which Doohan uttered his famous line, "I canna change the laws o' physics!"), or with Scotty struggling to bring the battle-damaged Starship *Constellation* back on line in "The Doomsday Machine."

The actor's self-assured performances in episodes such as "A Taste of Armageddon" and "Friday's Child," in which Scotty is left in charge of the ship, helped hide one of the show's glaring logical weaknesses—namely, why were the captain and first officer constantly sent together on dangerous away missions? With Scotty in command, the ship always seemed to be in good hands. "I thought I ran the ship beautifully, to tell the truth," Doohan wrote in his autobiography *Beam Me Up, Scotty.*

Doohan's most searing dramatic performance came in "Wolf in the Fold," in which Scotty is accused of butchering three young women while on shore leave on planet Argelius II. The crime was actually committed by a noncorporeal being that feeds on fear, but because the creature also blacked out Scotty's memory, the engineer comes to doubt his own innocence. Presented with the murder knife and pressed for information about the first killing, Doohan chokes up, shakes his head, and stammers, "I don't remember another thing!" with obvious frustration and terror. He seems even more desperate—wide-eyed, stunned—after the second killing. "I can't even believe this is really happenin'," Doohan almost weeps. Screenwriter Robert Bloch's horror-tinged scenario works in part because Doohan convinces us that Scotty—whom audiences had grown to love—is in real danger and real pain.

In "The Lights of Zetar"—the closest thing to a Scotty episode ever produced—his character falls in love with a young lieutenant, Mira Romaine (Jan Shutan). Scotty's behavior in this episode is extremely uncharacteristic (even Doohan, in his autobiography, dismissed the story's romantic subplot as "a matter of plot contrivance"), but this didn't prevent the actor from delivering a standout portrayal. The love-struck engineer seems distracted, twice abandoning his post to look after his girlfriend. But Doohan moons over Shutan so sweetly (addressing her tenderly, wearing an almost dazed-looking grin, eyes sparkling) that the audience attributes these lapses to romantic exuberance rather than sloppy screenwriting.

## Nichelle Nichols

Although she appeared in more installments than Doohan (sixty-eight in all) Nichelle Nichols had far fewer opportunities to shine. She spent most of her time seated at Lieutenant Uhura's communications console, dutifully reporting that hailing frequencies were open in episode after episode. Although she and Roddenberry had worked out an elaborate backstory for Uhura (including the idea that she led a large team of communications technicians and specialists), screenwriters made little use of this material. Nichols grew so dissatisfied that she decided to leave the show following its first season, only to be talked out of quitting by Dr. Martin Luther King Jr., who met the actress at a party and urged her to reconsider.

Still, Nichols made the most of her rare opportunities to leave the bridge. She left a stunning impression in "Mirror, Mirror," not only because of her striking Mirror Universe costume (a sexy two-piece, bare midriff outfit) but due to her subtle and evocative work in a pair of unforgettable scenes. Accidentally transported onto an evil parallel version of the *Enterprise* along with the rest of an ill-fated away team, Uhura must tap into the ship's computers and learn all she can about this twisted universe. That means taking her station on the bridge alongside the creepy alter egos of her usual crewmates, a prospect which gives her pause. She halts before leaving the relative safety of sick bay. "Captain, I . . ." she begins, but her words trail off. Nichols's body language and half-choked delivery make clear that the frightened Uhura needs a moment to steel her nerves for the potentially dangerous assignment. She plays this moment of hesitation with authenticity and dignity, seeming frightened without undercutting her character's inner strength. That strength rises to the fore later, when Uhura distracts the evil Mirror Sulu by coming on to him, then smacking him across the face. "You take a lotta chances," the frustrated Sulu growls. "So do you, Mister," Nichols hisses in response, pulling a dagger from her boot and backing away warily. "Mirror, Mirror" was an excellent outing for most members of the cast—Leonard Nimoy, George Takei, and Walter Koenig are also particularly good here—but no one was more impressive than Nichols. "Mirror, Mirror" remains the single episode that best encapsulates all the qualities she brought to her role—an appealing blend of self-confidence, vulnerability, and sex appeal that made Uhura one of the show's most beloved characters.

Those same qualities are on display in "Plato's Stepchildren," the episode in which she and Shatner locked lips in TV's first interracial kiss. Once again, Nichols's believable, heartfelt portrayal prevented her character from seeming demeaned or diminished, even though she's forced by superpowered aliens to behave uncharacteristic ways. Like Doohan's work in "The Lights of Zetar," Nichols's performance in the otherwise unimpressive "Plato's Stepchildren" was a triumph of actor over material.

Lieutenant Uhura participated in so few away missions that Nichelle Nichols had to stand in front of a shot from "The Cage" to create this publicity still.

In "The Trouble with Tribbles," Nichols accentuated Uhura's tender side. "Oooh, it's adorable! What is it?" Nichols asks, as Uhura holds a tribble for the first time. Then she brings the cooing creature to ear and giggles. "Listen, it's purring!" Her glowing smile and almost musical laughter charms viewers every bit as much as the tribble. On those rare occasions, such as in "Charlie X," when the scenario afforded Nichols a chance to sing, *Star Trek* was better for it. (For more on Nichols's musical contributions, see Chapter 24, "Then Play On.") Despite the actress's best efforts, however, the Uhura character was never developed to its full potential during the run of the classic *Star Trek* series. In the animated adventure "The Lorelei Signal," however, Uhura (out of necessity, since the *Enterprise*'s male leadership has been taken prisoner by a race of space sirens) takes command and mounts a rescue mission, saving the lives of Kirk, Spock, McCoy, Scotty, and Sulu in a nick of time. Too bad stories like this never unfolded on the live-action series!

## George Takei

Like Nichols, George Takei piled up a lot of appearances (fifty-two altogether) but only a smattering of episodes that gave him the chance to leave his station on the bridge. Yet, even when his dialogue was limited to "Aye, aye, Captain" or repeating "Warp factor two," Takei found small ways of expressing himself. He mastered a collection of facial expressions that revealed helmsman Sulu's state of mind—raising an eyebrow and half-grinning at Chekov (or another navigator) to indicate relief or confidence, furrowing his brow and looking straight ahead to express anxiety, and so forth. He also worked out a consistent pattern of switches he flipped whenever Sulu put the starship in motion, rather than simply pressing buttons randomly. These small, often overlooked choices quietly fleshed out the character and enhanced the believability of the show.

Takei's single most memorable moment came early on, in Season One's "The Naked Time." Under the influence of an inhibition-loosening disease, Sulu strips to his bare chest, takes up a fencing foil, and begins charging through the corridors of the *Enterprise* like some demented Robin Hood, even bounding onto the bridge to "rescue" Uhura and challenge Captain Kirk. Takei's sheer exuberance makes this sequence the most memorable scene in a very good episode. Indeed, it ranks among the most unforgettable moments in *any Star Trek* adventure. Writer-producer John Meredith Lucas approached Takei while writing the script for "The Naked Time" and asked the actor if he could handle a sword. Naturally Takei lied and said he could, then immediately enrolled in a fencing class. The actor also dieted and worked out to tone his physique for his bare-chested romp. "After so many episodes of being adhered to the bridge console, this [episode] sounded absolutely delicious," Takei wrote of in his autobiography *To the Stars*.

Unfortunately, after "The Naked Time," it was back to the usual diet of scraps for Takei, who fell victim to bad luck as the show's first season wound down and its second campaign began. Originally, he was to be featured prominently in the Season One episode "This Side of Paradise," but in rewrites the story's romantic subplot was taken away from Sulu and given to Spock. Then Takei agreed to appear in the John Wayne war picture *The Green Berets* during the summer break between *Trek*'s first two seasons. When shooting on the movie ran over schedule,

Even though George Takei initially resented Walter Koenig, the two eventually became close friends.

Takei found himself trapped in rural Georgia while production of *Star Trek* resumed in Los Angeles. As a result, a handful of teleplays with scenes written to spotlight Sulu were retooled, with those moments reassigned to the *Enterprise*'s new navigator, Ensign Chekov (Walter Koenig).

Fortunately, Takei returned to the fold just in time for "Mirror, Mirror," in which he delivered another indelible performance as the lecherous, scar-faced Mirror Universe Sulu, merciless security chief of the Imperial starship

*Enterprise.* On the bridge, Takei (looking sweaty and disheveled) saunters over to Lieutenant Uhura's station, leers down her blouse, and then cups her chin in his hand. "Still no interest, Uhura?" he asks. "I could make you change your mind." Takei's harsh demeanor makes this line sound like a threat rather than an attempted seduction. Later, the ruthless Sulu hatches a scheme to assassinate both Kirk and Spock, twirling a dagger in his hand as he coolly explains his plan. Takei seems more aroused by the prospect of murdering his superiors than he did in his earlier scenes with Nichols, adding to the subtly unnerving quality of his performance. All of which made Takei's Evil Sulu by far the most intimidating of the episode's Mirror Universe characters.

The richness of his performances in "The Naked Time" and "Mirror, Mirror" display versatility and nuance that went untapped in most of Takei's other episodes. The full range of the actor's talents, lamentably, remained underutilized.

## Walter Koenig

Koenig may not have been *Star Trek*'s most talented performer, and Ensign Pavel Chekov certainly wasn't its best-written character. Yet, each was a perfect fit for the other. The *Enterprise*'s exuberant young navigator was essentially a sawed-off version of Captain Kirk—a daring, fresh-faced swashbuckler and junior varsity Playboy of the Galaxy. True, Koenig's accent was laughable. No matter. He sold audiences on Chekov anyway, with an energetic, tongue-in-cheek approach that meshed perfectly with the character. Yes, all those jokes about Leningrad were terrible. But Koenig *knew* they were terrible and often delivered them with a sly grin that suggested Chekov didn't actually believe Scotch was invented by a little old lady from Moscow; he simply enjoyed confounding his crewmates with wild assertions of ethnic pride. Koenig appeared in a total of thirty-six adventures, and his vivid, zesty performances enlivened every installment.

Thanks in part to Takei's *Green Berets* misfortune, Koenig made a favorable impression quickly, with small but effective moments in a handful episodes shot during his first few months on the show, including "Friday's Child," "Who Mourns for Adonais," and "The Apple." Producers added the actor to the cast to try to attract some of the young, female viewers that had made *The Monkees* a surprise hit the previous season. (Koenig bore a resemblance to diminutive Monkees vocalist Davy Jones.) Beginning with "The Apple," Chekov was often seen romancing young women among the *Enterprise* crew, or wherever opportunity presented itself.

By the time "Spectre of the Gun" was made during Season Three, the actor had perfected a personal brand of frothy, seriocomic romance. In this episode, Chekov is part of a landing party forced to recreate the Gunfight at the O.K. Corral—standing in for the villainous (and doomed) Clanton Gang. Mistaking him for Clanton Gang member Billy Clayburn, a young woman named Sylvia (Bonnie Beecher) rushes up and plants an enthusiastic kiss on the startled Chekov. This early scene is played for laughs, and Koenig affects an amusing "I can't help it if I'm irresistible" attitude as he comes up for air between lingering, passionate kisses. "What can I do, Captain?" he grins, wearing a droopy-eyed look of blissful submission. "You know we're always supposed to maintain good relations with the natives." Later, Chekov and Sylvia share a tender moment on the front porch of the general store. When she asks him if he's forgotten about next week's dance, he reassures her he has not. "I'm looking forward to it . . . very much." Koenig delivers the line with an audible, and even visible, shift in tone during the brief pause before "very much." His tone of voice softens, his eyes linger on Sylvia. It's a brilliantly played moment of revelation, as Chekov suddenly realizes he has real feelings for Sylvia. In the middle of this line, the tone of the scene changes. Suddenly, Chekov must try to rebuff Sylvia's proposal of marriage ("I'm not someone you can marry," Koenig says, his voice thick with regret) and gets lured into a (seemingly) fatal gunfight. "Spectre of the Gun" remains a fine episode, but it loses a bit of steam with Chekov's "death" midway through.

"Mirror, Mirror" and "Day of the Dove" gave Koenig rare opportunities to demonstrate wider range. In "Mirror, Mirror," Chekov's venal alter ego attempts to assassinate Captain Kirk (and is foiled when one of his henchmen abruptly switches allegiances). Koenig is excellent here, although given their troubled off-screen relationship, seeming gleeful while attempting to kill William Shatner may not have required much acting. In "Day of the Dove," a hate-eating life force dupes Chekov into thinking that the Klingons killed his brother. He becomes bent on revenge—even though, as Sulu later informs us, Chekov is an only child! "Cossacks! Filthy Klingon murderers! You killed my brother Petr!" Koenig rages, rushing the Klingons bare-handed, radiating hatred from every pore. Apart from these two adventures, however, nearly all Koenig's notable performances adhered to the contours of his work in "Spectre of the Gun," balancing comedy and romance, sometimes with a dramatic turn toward the end. The actor would have to find vehicles beyond *Star Trek*—such as his performance as the villainous Bester on *Babylon 5*—to further showcase his versatility.

## Majel Barrett

After prominent supporting roles in her first two appearances ("The Naked Time" and "What Are Little Girls Made Of?"), Majel Barrett soon faded into the background. Even though she had more influence with creator-producer Gene Roddenberry than any other cast member, Barrett's Nurse Chapel seemed like a secondary character even among the show's secondary characters. Screenwriters treated the nurse like a walking prop. She rarely ventured out of sick bay, where she served as a compliant sounding board for Dr. McCoy but seldom took any initiative.

"Amok Time" was a rare exception. In this installment, Chapel's romantic yearnings for Mr. Spock (established in "The Naked Time") find their most touching and believable expression. A hopeful Chapel brings Spock a bowl of

Vulcan plomeek soup, which the Pon Farr–rattled first officer hurls into the hallway. Cowering in the corridor, Barrett looks puzzled and terrified. Later, when Spock apologizes to her, a silent tear streaks her right cheek. She turns her back to him to hide her tears. When Spock calls her "Nurse Chapel," she reminds him, "My name is Christine." Barrett's voice cracks. The line reverberates with barely hidden longing.

Chapel had more lines and showier scenes in both "The Naked Time," in which, stricken by the inhibition-freeing disease, Chapel first confesses her love for Spock; and 'Little Girls," in which she reunites with a lost love who turns out to be a mad scientist. But her subtle, touching work in "Amok Time" remains her finest performance—or at least her finest live-action performance, as Nurse Chapel. Barrett was also central to the highly amusing animated adventure "Mudd's Passion," in which Chapel gives a love potion to Mr. Spock, with disastrous consequences. In this animated yarn, Barrett displayed a gift for comedy that served her well in her later appearances as Lwaxana Troi.

While Barrett made a negligible contribution to the classic *Trek* series as the underwritten Chapel (she was arguably more important to the show as the voice of the *Enterprise* computer), she wowed audiences in her nine later appearances (six on *Next Gen*, three on *Deep Space Nine*) as the colorful, outspoken Lwaxana. If Christine Chapel had had a bit more Lwaxana in her, *Star Trek* would have been a livelier show.

## Grace Lee Whitney

Prior to her unceremonious ouster midway through *Star Trek*'s first season, Grace Lee Whitney contributed winning performances to a pair of memorable episodes. Her tenderhearted scenes with the lovesick Charlie Evans (Robert Walker Jr.) provide the classic installment "Charlie X" with much of its emotional resonance. She was also very effective in "Miri," as the lovely, young Yeoman Rand struggles with the emotional ramifications of contracting a disease that will not merely kill her but, in the process, disfigure her. Both of these performances suggest that Whitney could have made a more meaningful contribution to the show had her tenure continued.

# 30

# Data Bank

## A Thumbnail Guide to the Original Seventy-Nine Episodes

W hat follows is not a full-service episode guide. (There are plenty of those available elsewhere.) However, since episodes are referred to by name throughout this book, this quick listing should jog memories and help connect titles with plotlines.

### The Pilots

- **"The Cage" (Original airdate: October 4, 1968)** On a mission to planet Talos IV, Captain Pike (Jeffrey Hunter) is taken prisoner and forced to cohabitate with a captive human female; the Talosians hope to breed a race of slaves. Although most of its footage was incorporated into "The Menagerie (Parts I and II)," *Star Trek*'s first pilot didn't air until twenty-four years after its production.
- **"Where No Man Has Gone Before" (Never broadcast in its original form)** Helmsman Gary Mitchell (Gary Lockwood) and scientist Elizabeth Dehner (Sally Kellerman) obtain godlike telekinetic powers after the *Enterprise* attempts to cross a mysterious energy barrier that surrounds the galaxy. This version ran about five minutes longer than the one broadcast September 22, 1966, and featured a different title sequence with longer narration. Although never aired, it was included as a bonus feature on the *Star Trek: The Original Series Season Three* Blu-ray collection.

### Season One

1. **"The Man Trap" (Original airdate: September 8, 1966)** An away team unwittingly brings aboard a shape-shifting monster that kills humans by draining their bodies of salt. *Star Trek* made its broadcast debut with this monsterrific slice of space opera.
2. **"Charlie X" (Original airdate: September 15, 1966)** A lonely teenage boy (Robert Walker Jr.), the only survivor of a starship crash many years earlier, begins to evidence frightening psychic abilities after being picked up by the *Enterprise*.

3. **"Where No Man Has Gone Before"** (**Original airdate: September 22, 1966**) In addition to a shorter running time and the standard opening credits, the broadcast version of "Where No Man Has Gone Before" featured a reedited musical score.

4. **"The Naked Time"** (**Original airdate: September 29, 1966**) Several crew members contract a mysterious illness that causes victims to become emotionally unhinged, posing a danger to the ship.

5. **"The Enemy Within"** (**Original airdate: October 6, 1966**) A transporter accident splits Captain Kirk into identical twins—one kind but indecisive, the other ruthless and impulsive. Introduces the FSNP (Famous Spock Nerve Pinch).

6. **"Mudd's Women"** (**Original airdate: October 13, 1966**) The *Enterprise* rescues interstellar con man Harry Mudd (Roger C. Carmel) and his "cargo"—a trio of gorgeous mail-order brides whose beauty has secretly been enhanced by a forbidden drug.

7. **"What are Little Girls Made Of?"** (**Original airdate: October 20, 1966**) Renegade scientist Roger Corby (Michael Strong) discovers a machine capable of creating android duplicates of any subject and uses the device to create a robot double of Captain Kirk.

8. **"Miri"** (**Original airdate: October 27, 1966**) The *Enterprise* discovers an Earthlike planet where all the adults have been wiped out by a mysterious plague, leaving only a band of antisocial children.

9. **"Dagger of the Mind"** (**Original airdate: November 3, 1966**) Captain Kirk is captured by the deranged administrator of an interstellar insane asylum, who has invented a device that destroys the human mind and will. Introduced the Vulcan Mind Meld.

10. **"The Corbomite Maneuver"** (**Original airdate: November 10, 1966**) Captain Kirk matches wits with the commander of a giant alien vessel who seems bent on the destruction of the *Enterprise*. This was the first regular episode of *Star Trek* produced, but NBC chose to withhold it until now.

11. **"The Menagerie, Part I"** (**Original airdate: November 17, 1966**) Mr. Spock seizes control of the *Enterprise* in order to return his former captain to the forbidden planet of Talos IV, where Pike had been held captive many years earlier.

12. **"The Menagerie, Part II"** (**Original airdate: November 24, 1966**) Concludes *Star Trek*'s only two-part adventure. "The Menagerie (Parts I and II)" remains one of the series' most beloved stories.

13. **"The Conscience of the King"** (**Original airdate: December 8, 1966**) Kirk suspects that renowned actor Anton Karidian (Arnold Moss) may be an interstellar war criminal in disguise.

14. **"Balance of Terror"** (**Original airdate: December 15, 1966**) A Romulan war bird, armed with an invisibility cloak, launches an unprovoked attack on the Federation. The *Enterprise* must repulse the invaders to prevent an interstellar war. This is the first of three episodes featuring the Romulans.

15. **"Shore Leave" (Original airdate: December 29, 1966)** Fantastic, unexplainable events (including the appearance of Alice in Wonderland and her White Rabbit) befall an away team while scouting an idyllic, Earthlike planet.

16. **"The Galileo Seven" (Original airdate: January 5, 1967)** A shuttlecraft commanded by Mr. Spock crashes on a foreboding alien planet populated by ferocious giant anthropoids.

17. **"The Squire of Gothos" (Original airdate: January 12, 1967)** A playful yet terrifyingly powerful alien (William Campbell) takes Captain Kirk and several crew members captive. Was Trelaine a Q?

18. **"Arena" (Original airdate: January 19, 1966)** Captain Kirk is forced into one-to-one combat with a reptilian alien who captains a rival spacecraft; the loser's ship will be destroyed.

19. **"Tomorrow Is Yesterday" (Original airdate: January 26, 1967)** Accidentally catapulted back in time to the 1960s, the *Enterprise* is forced to capture an Air Force pilot whose disappearance may alter history. *Star Trek*'s first time-travel story. This episode was originally intended to be the second half of a two-parter, following "The Naked Time," but the stories were decoupled.

20. **"Court Martial" (Original airdate: February 2, 1967)** Captain Kirk is charged with negligence in the accidental death of a crewman.

21. **"The Return of the Archons" (Original airdate: February 9, 1967)** The *Enterprise* discovers a planet whose entire population has fallen under the mental control of a shadowy religious leader known as Landru.

22. **"Space Seed" (Original airdate: February 16, 1967)** An away led by Captain Kirk unwittingly awakens a ship full of genetically enhanced supermen led by the megalomaniacal Khan Noonien Singh (Ricardo Montalban).

23. **"A Taste of Armageddon" (Original airdate: February 23, 1967)** Ordered to establish relations with a reclusive planet that has been at war for 500 years, Kirk and Spock beam down and discover a world apparently untouched by conflict.

24. **"This Side of Paradise" (Original airdate: March 2, 1967)** On a routine mission to an agricultural outpost, the crew of the *Enterprise* becomes infected by alien spores that instill total happiness but dampen initiative and curiosity. Spock, freed of logical inhibitions, falls in love with a young exobiologist (Jill Ireland).

25. **"The Devil in the Dark" (Original airdate: March 9, 1967)** The *Enterprise* rushes to the aid of a mining colony menaced by a tunneling creature that has killed more than fifty miners.

26. **"Errand of Mercy" (Original airdate: March 16, 1967)** Kirk and Spock struggle to make common cause with the reclusive, pacifistic Organians, whose planet falls under the boot-heel of Klingon invaders. This is the first episode to feature the Klingons.

27. **"The Alternative Factor" (Original airdate: March 23, 1967)** The *Enterprise* encounters an alien named Lazarus (Robert Brown) who's engaged in an endless battle with his counterpart from an alternate dimension.

28. **"The City on the Edge of Forever"** (**Original airdate: April 6, 1967**) Come on, you don't really need a plot summary for this one, do you? OK, here goes: Kirk and Spock travel back in time, where Kirk falls in love with a young social activist (Joan Collins) who he must allow to die in order to prevent the Nazis from winning World War II. Widely considered the best *Star Trek* episode ever made.

29. **"Operation—Annihilate!"** (**Original airdate: April 13, 1967**) Kirk, Spock, and McCoy must devise some means of destroying a race of jellyfish-like aliens who have killed most of the residents of planet Deneva, including Kirk's brother.

## Season Two

1. **"Amok Time"** (**Original airdate: September 15, 1967**) Kirk violates Starfleet orders to return Spock to his home planet, where the Vulcan must mate or die. Introduced the split-fingered Vulcan salute and the valedictory phrase, "Live long and prosper." An excellent beginning for *Star Trek*'s second season.

2. **"Who Mourns for Adonais?"** (**Original airdate: September 22, 1967**) The *Enterprise* finds itself in the grip of an incredibly powerful being who claims to be the Greek god Apollo.

This *TV Guide* Close-Up previewed the classic episode "Shore Leave."

**TV CLOSE-UP GUIDE**    8:30  **2** **4** **6**  STAR TREK—Adventure

'Shore Leave'

[COLOR] In deep space, the USS Enterprise makes a rest-and-recreation stop that proves anything but restful.

Captain Kirk has selected an apparently ideal site for his crew's much-needed furloughs, yet there is something wrong.

The advance party sights storybook characters, living persons from their own pasts and a host of other strange objects. Even the superlogical Mr. Spock is mystified.

Robert Spaar directed from a script by Theodore Sturgeon. Kirk: William Shatner. Spock: Leonard Nimoy. McCoy: DeForest Kelley. Sulu: George Takei. (Rerun; 60 min.)

**Guest Cast**

| | |
|---|---|
| Tonia Barrows | Emily Banks |
| Caretaker | Oliver McGowan |
| Rodriguez | Perry Lopez |
| Finnegan | Bruce Mars |
| Ruth | Shirley Bonne |

**William Shatner and Leonard Nimoy**

A-58                    TV GUIDE

3. **"The Changeling" (Original airdate: September 29, 1967)** Captain Kirk must find a way to neutralize NOMAD, a malfunctioning space probe capable of destroying entire planets and bent on "sterilizing" (that is, killing) all "imperfect biological units," including the crew of the *Enterprise.*

4. **"Mirror, Mirror" (Original airdate: October 6, 1967)** A freak transporter accident sends Kirk, McCoy, Scotty, and Uhura to a twisted parallel dimension that is home to evil duplicates of themselves and the rest of the crew.

5. **"The Apple" (Original airdate: October 13, 1967)** The *Enterprise* discovers a planet where the natives live in childlike innocence, serving the will of a supercomputer they worship as a god.

6. **"The Doomsday Machine" (Original airdate: October 20, 1967)** The revenge-crazed captain of a disabled starship leads the *Enterprise* into battle against a giant, planet-eating robot.

7. **"Catspaw" (Original airdate: October 27, 1967)** A landing party led by Kirk and Spock encounter two mysterious aliens who seem to work black magic.

8. **"I, Mudd" (Original airdate: November 3, 1967)** Harry Mudd (Carmel) returns, this time as the self-appointed monarch of a planet populated entirely by curvaceous female androids.

9. **"Metamorphosis" (Original airdate: November 10, 1967)** Kirk and Spock are shocked to discover long-missing warp drive pioneer Zefram Cochrane (Glenn Corbett) living on a remote planet with an alien companion.

10. **"Journey to Babel" (Original airdate: November 17, 1967)** Saboteurs and assassins strike as the *Enterprise* ferries a delegation of interstellar diplomats, including Spock's parents, to a vital economic summit.

11. **"Friday's Child" (Original airdate: December 1, 1967)** Kirk, Spock, and McCoy arrive to negotiate a mining treaty with the primitive, warlike natives of Capella IV, but the meddling Klingons (who also covet the planet's resources) instigate a tribal war among Capellan factions.

12. **"The Deadly Years" (Original airdate: December 8, 1967)** Several crew members (including Kirk, Spock, McCoy, and Scotty) begin to age rapidly after exposure to alien radiation.

13. **"Obsession" (Original airdate: December 15, 1967)** Captain Kirk begins behaving recklessly when the *Enterprise* encounters a deadly alien entity that attacked his previous ship.

14. **"Wolf in the Fold" (Original airdate: December 22, 1967)** While on shore leave recovering from a brain injury, Scotty is accused of butchering three women.

15. **"The Trouble with Tribbles" (Original airdate: December 29, 1967)** While assigned to safeguard a vital grain shipment from the Klingons, the *Enterprise* becomes overrun with cute but prodigiously reproductive trilling furballs.

16. **"The Gamesters of Triskelion" (Original airdate: January 5, 1968)** Kirk, Chekov, and Uhura are kidnapped by aliens and forced to compete in games for the amusement of the planet's elusive, all-powerful Providers.

17. **"A Piece of the Action"** (Original airdate: January 12, 1968) Kirk, Spock, and McCoy become embroiled in a turf war on a planet whose civilization emulates Chicago gangs of the 1920s.
18. **"The Immunity Syndrome"** (Original airdate: January 19, 1968) A giant space amoeba menaces the *Enterprise*.
19. **"A Private Little War"** (Original airdate: January 26, 1968) Kirk tries to counter the nefarious influence of the Klingons on a developing civilization.
20. **"Return to Tomorrow"** (Original airdate: February 9, 1968) Kirk and Spock must decide whether or not to allow superadvanced aliens to take "temporary" possession of their bodies.
21. **"Patterns of Force"** (Original airdate: February 16, 1968) The *Enterprise* discovers a planet with a civilization modeled after Nazi Germany.
22. **"By Any Other Name"** (Original airdate: February 23, 1968) Aliens from another galaxy seize control of the *Enterprise* and reduce the crew to small, geometric blocks.
23. **"The Omega Glory"** (Original airdate: March 1, 1968) While attempting to bring a rogue starship captain to justice on planet Omega IV, Kirk becomes entangled in an ancient tribal conflict. Although once considered as a possible pilot, this is a dreadful episode.
24. **"The Ultimate Computer"** (Original airdate: March 8, 1968) Things go horribly wrong when an experimental computer assumes command of the *Enterprise*.
25. **"Bread and Circuses"** (Original airdate: March 15, 1968) Kirk, Spock and McCoy are forced to fight in televised gladiatorial contests on a planet much like ancient Rome.
26. **"Assignment: Earth"** (Original airdate: March 29, 1968) After traveling back in time to 1968, Captain Kirk and his companions cross paths with Gary Seven (Robert Lansing), an enigmatic alien time traveler who may be trying to change history. Gene Roddenberry hoped to launch a spin-off series chronicling the adventures of Gary Seven but found no takers.

## Season Three

1. **"Spock's Brain"** (Original airdate: September 20, 1968) When dim-witted bimbos from outer space steal Spock's brain, Kirk and McCoy attempt to recover it, bringing along the Vulcan's body (which now operates on remote control). An ignominious beginning to Season Three.
2. **"The *Enterprise* Incident"** (Original airdate: September 27, 1968) Kirk and Spock launch an elaborate ruse to steal the cloaking device from a Romulan warship. Last of three episodes featuring the Romulans.
3. **"The Paradise Syndrome"** (Original airdate: October 4, 1968) Suffering from amnesia and left behind on a planet with a culture similar to that of eighteenth-century American Indians, Captain Kirk weds a young native woman.

4. **"And the Children Shall Lead"** (Original airdate: October 11, 1968) The *Enterprise* rescues a band of young orphans, unaware that—under the influence of an insidious alien presence—the children have murdered their parents.

5. **"Is There in Truth No Beauty?"** (Original airdate: October 18, 1968) The *Enterprise* is assigned to transport an alien ambassador whose appearance is so ghastly that a single look drives humans mad.

6. **"Spectre of the Gun"** (Original airdate: October 25, 1968) A landing party is whisked away to an eerie recreation of the Wild West, where they must stand in for the villainous (and doomed) Clanton Gang during the Gunfight at the O.K. Corral.

7. **"Day of the Dove"** (Original airdate: November 1, 1968) A noncorporeal life force that feeds on hate instigates a bloody battle between Klingons and humans on board the *Enterprise.*

8. **"For the World Is Hollow and I Have Touched the Sky"** (Original airdate: November 8, 1968) An away team, including a terminally ill Dr. McCoy, travels to a giant spacecraft disguised as an asteroid; the residents of the spacecraft do not realize they are aboard a starship.

9. **"The Tholian Web"** (Original airdate: November 15, 1968) While investigating a disabled Federation starship, Captain Kirk is lost in an interdimensional rift; meanwhile, an alien vessel appears and traps the *Enterprise* in an energy web.

10. **"Plato's Stepchildren"** (Original airdate: November 22, 1968) A landing party including Kirk, Spock, McCoy, Uhura, and Chapel are taken captive by humans who have gained godlike psychic powers. Featured TV's first interracial kiss, between the mind-controlled Kirk and Uhura.

STAR TREK™

300 FULL COLOR ACTION SCENES

FOTONOVEL™ #3

THE TROUBLE WITH TRIBBLES

As Captain, I want two things done. First, find Cyrano Jones, and second... **close that hatch!**

ANOTHER THRILLING **STAR TREK**™ EPISODE FROM THE GREAT TV SERIES **CREATED BY GENE RODDENBERRY** A MANDALA PRODUCTIONS FOTONOVEL™

"The Trouble with Tribbles," the subject of this 1977 "Fotonovel," remains one of *Star Trek*'s most beloved installments.

11. **"Wink of an Eye" (Original airdate: November 29, 1968)** Invisible aliens seize control of the *Enterprise*.

12. **"The Empath" (Original airdate: December 6, 1968)** Kirk, Spock, and McCoy are teleported to an alien world where they are tortured by a pair of inscrutable aliens but then healed by a mute woman with empathic healing abilities.

13. **"Elaan of Troyius" (Original airdate: December 20, 1968)** In this science fictional retelling of Shakespeare's *The Taming of the Shrew*, Captain Kirk must teach a spoiled alien princess some manners.

14. **"Whom Gods Destroy" (Original airdate: January 3, 1969)** Kirk and Spock are held captive by the inmates of an interstellar insane asylum.

15. **"Let That Be Your Last Battlefield" (Original airdate: January 10, 1969)** A pair of aliens bent on destroying one another hijack the *Enterprise* to return to their war-torn home world.

16. **"The Mark of Gideon" (Original airdate: January 17, 1969)** The residents of planet Gideon kidnap Captain Kirk as part a dark scheme to solve the planet's overpopulation problem.

17. **"That Which Survives" (Original airdate: January 24, 1969)** An away team is trapped on a mysterious planetoid and haunted by the ghostly figure of a young woman.

18. **"The Lights of Zetar" (Original airdate: January 31, 1969)** Deadly, noncorporeal aliens capable of destroying the *Enterprise* form a mental link with Scotty's girlfriend.

19. **"Requiem for Methuselah" (Original airdate: February 14, 1969)** Kirk and Spock meet a mysterious recluse who seems to be thousands of years old.

20. **"The Way to Eden" (Original airdate: February 21, 1969)** A band of space hippies commandeer the *Enterprise*. Rivals "Spock's Brain" as the series' worst episode.

21. **"The Cloud Minders" (Original airdate: February 28, 1969)** The *Enterprise* must secure a desperately needed mineral shipment from a planet embroiled in a class struggle.

22. **"The Savage Curtain" (Original airdate: March 7, 1969)** Kirk and Spock fight alongside Abraham Lincoln and the Vulcan hero Sarek against a quartet of ruthless villains from across the galaxy, including legendary Klingon leader Kahless. Final classic *Trek* installment to feature a Klingon.

23. **"All Our Yesterdays" (Original airdate: March 14, 1969)** Kirk, Spock, and McCoy are accidentally sent into the distant past of an alien planet.

24. **"Turnabout Intruder" (Original airdate: June 3, 1969)** A jealous ex-girlfriend switches bodies with Captain Kirk. The series did not end on a high note.

# Prime Directives

## Social Commentary and Recurring Themes

# 31

# A Most Promising Species

## Human Exceptionalism

*Everything that is truest and best in all species of beings has been revealed by you.*
*Those are the qualities that make a civilization worthy to survive.*
                    —*Vian scientist Lal (Alan Bergman) in "The Empath"*

In the late 1960s, the near-utopian future imagined by Gene Roddenberry offered hope to viewers shaken by the Vietnam War, race riots, political assassinations, and cultural upheavals of all kinds.

This upbeat tone was bracingly different than most science fiction of the era, which tended toward the dystopian and apocalyptic. Consider these two revealing examples: Producer George Pal's *The Time Machine* (1960), an update of H. G. Wells's classic novel, predicted that a nuclear conflagration would occur by 1966 and forecast a future where mankind has split into two species—the sheeplike Eloi and the cannibalistic Morlocks. Hammer Films' *The Damned* (1963), based on H. L. Lawrence's 1960 novel *The Children of Light,* assumed not only that the world was teetering on the brink of Armageddon but that world leaders assumed the same thing. Its plot involved secret government experiments aimed at producing a race of radioactive children capable of surviving the inevitable holocaust. While otherwise very different, both of these tales took for granted that in order to survive, humanity will have to mutate into something no longer human. And these are just two of countless nihilistic stories published or filmed during the '60s.

*Star Trek* stood in bold opposition to this prevailing pessimism. The cornerstone of the show's radical optimism was Roddenberry's unflagging confidence in the perfectibility of the human race. The show's overriding message was that our species can and will overcome war, racism, and poverty, and that once those ancient evils are defeated, the stars are the limit.

"It isn't all over; everything has not been invented," Roddenberry told a *TV Showpeople* interviewer in 1975. "The human adventure is just beginning."

## This Is Only a Test

Roddenberry's faith in humanity was expressed most clearly through several teleplays in which *Enterprise* crew members, functioning as representatives of the human race, are subjected to elaborate tests devised by more evolved or more technologically advanced beings. This was the basic premise of both *Star Trek*'s original pilot, "The Cage," and the *Star Trek: The Next Generation* pilot, "Encounter at Farpoint," among many other episodes. Time and again throughout the original seventy-nine *Trek* adventures, curious aliens took humanity's measure and declared our species exceptional.

**The Metrons**—"Arena" is best remembered for Captain Kirk's epic battle with the reptilian Gorn, but, thematically speaking, the Gorn remains the less important of the two species Kirk meets in this installment. More significant is his encounter with the Metrons, the race who force Kirk and the Gorn captain into a life-and-death struggle (with the fate of their respective starships in the balance) after the *Enterprise* pursues a Gorn cruiser into Metron space. After a cat-and-mouse struggle that consumes nearly half the episode's running time, Kirk finally incapacitates the Gorn by building a cannon out of bamboo and rocks, MacGyver style. Over the course of the contest, the captain not only figures out how to fashion the weapon, but also overcomes his fear and loathing for the reptilian creature, whose soldiers wiped out a Federation outpost. Kirk surprises the Metrons by refusing to deliver the coup de grace to the fallen Gorn.

"By sparing your helpless enemy, who surely would have destroyed you, you demonstrated the advanced trait of mercy, something we hardly expected," a Metron emissary informs the captain. "We feel there may be hope for your kind. Therefore, you will not be destroyed." The alien goes so far as to suggest that perhaps humanity and the superadvanced Metrons may become friends—in another thousand years or so. "You're still half savage, but there is hope," the Metron declares.

During the final wrap-up on the *Enterprise* bridge, Kirk boasts to Spock, "We're a most promising species, as predators go. Did you know that?"

"I frequently have my doubts," Spock replies.

"I don't, not anymore," Kirk answers. "And maybe in a thousand years we'll be able to prove it."

Although "Arena" was written by Gene Coon (based on a short story by Fredric Brown), this closing sentiment could have come from Roddenberry's own mouth. In fact, the producer echoed the idea nearly twenty years later at the ceremony unveiling his star on the Hollywood Walk of Fame in 1985. "I believe in humanity," Roddenberry said. "We are an incredible species. We're still just a child creature; we're still being nasty to each other. And all children go through those phases. We're growing up; we're moving into adolescence now. When we grow up, man—we're going to be something."

**The Melkotians**—In "Spectre of the Gun," acting on orders from Starfleet to make contact with the reclusive inhabitants of planet Melkot, the *Enterprise* ignores a telepathic warning to stay away and beams down a landing party. In retaliation, the xenophobic Melkotians force the away team to replay the Gunfight at the O.K. Corral—with the Earthmen cast in the role of the doomed Clanton gang. Once again the humans triumph but refuse to kill their adversaries (even though "Morgan Earp" apparently has killed Ensign Chekov). And once again, the aliens are surprised and deeply impressed.

"Captain Kirk, you did not kill. Is this the way of your people?" the Melkotians ask. After being assured that peace is the way of the Federation, the Melkotians extend an invitation: "Approach our planet and be welcome."

During the wrap-up, Kirk admits to Spock that he *wanted* to kill the gunslinger who had seemed to murder Chekov. Yet he was able to resist taking revenge. When Spock wonders how humanity survived, Kirk says, "We overcame our instinct for violence." Perhaps this may even be true someday. The magic of *Star Trek* is that the show at least conjures the possibility.

**The Talosians**—While the Metrons and Melkotians offered benedictions for humanity, the Talosians provided a backhanded compliment. In "The Cage" (and "The Menagerie"), these bubble-headed, telepathic aliens capture Captain Pike (Jeffrey Hunter) in hopes of breeding a race of human laborers to help them recapture the war-ravaged surface of planet Talos IV. But ultimately, after performing several tests and scouring data from the computer banks of the *Enterprise*, the Talosians determine that humans are unfit for the job. "We had not believed this possible," a perplexed Talosian explains. "The customs and history of your race show a unique hatred of captivity. Even when it's pleasant and benevolent, you prefer death. This makes you too violent and dangerous a species for our needs."

In other words, humans' unquenchable thirst for freedom and steadfast resistance to oppression make them unfit for slavery. Guilty as charged, Your Honor.

**The Excalbians**—In "The Savage Curtain," Kirk and Spock are lured to the surface of the planet Excalbia and forced to take part in a "drama" staged by its residents. The Excalbians, in order to learn about the human concepts of good and evil, stage an "Arena"-like battle in which Kirk and Spock fight alongside Abraham Lincoln and Surak of Vulcan against four fearsome adversaries, including Genghis Khan and Kahless the Unforgettable, founder of the Klingon Empire. As in "Arena," the combatants are free to fabricate weapons from anything around them. Naturally, good wins over evil. But it's a meaningless victory, at least according to the Excalbians. "You have failed to demonstrate for me any difference between your philosophies," the alien explains. "Your good and your evil use the same methods, achieve the same results."

The Excalbians fail to grasp the subtleties of the "drama" they just witnessed. It apparently means nothing to them that Kirk, Spock, Surak, and Honest Abe tried to make peace (Surak is killed trying to broker an agreement) and fought only as a last resort. The aliens also fail to grasp the significance of the combatants' divergent motivations. While their adversaries competed for personal gain, Kirk's team fought for the lives of the crew of the *Enterprise*, threatened by

TELEVISION CLASSICS                                    VOL.1

STAR TREK

THE MENAGERIE - PART I

THE MENAGERIE - PART II

*Paramount* HOME VIDEO

Early videotape packaging for "The Menagerie," in which the Talosians test the human race (through the example of Captain Pike).

the Excalbians. Moreover, the aliens state flatly their belief that "the need to know new things" gives them the right to force other species to participate in such potentially fatal "spectacles."

The aliens may not understand, but viewers certainly get the message: Not only is good superior to evil, but humans are superior to Excalbians, at least morally speaking.

**Others**—A few more episodes operate on the same wavelength. In "The Corbomite Maneuver," Balok, a mysterious alien in a giant spaceship, toys with the *Enterprise* to test the character of its people and the mettle of its commander. But the exercise turns out to be an elaborate jest. Balok was merely seeking a congenial traveling companion. In "The Empath," it's not the humans but rather a mute woman with psychic powers who is being tested. The Vians capture and torture Kirk, Spock, and McCoy in hopes that the shining example of humanity will inspire the Empath, whom McCoy nicknames "Gem." Finally, in the animated adventure "The Magicks of Magus-Tu," humanity is placed on trial—literally—in a sort of reverse *Devil and Daniel Webster* scenario—by a species of demonic-looking aliens. As always, the essential goodness of human beings is confirmed.

# Rage Against the Machines

The future Roddenberry envisioned was predicated on the development of fantastic technologies: warp drive, enabling faster-than-light space travel; the transporter, initiating the near-instantaneous (and pollution-free) teleportation of people and goods; the replicator, which produces food from basic molecules; as well as medical advances, including the cure of most known diseases. Any of these breakthroughs would signal dramatic shifts in the social and political order of our world. A civilization in possession of all four could eradicate poverty, famine, and disease; renew our planet's damaged ecology; and set out to explore the galaxy—just like on *Star Trek*. While these Treknological wonders were introduced as story devices, they also serve as testaments to Roddenberry's faith in the potential of human intellect.

Yet *Trek* also displayed wariness toward such mechanical marvels, exemplified by Dr. McCoy's distaste for the transporter. Such skepticism might seem out of place in Roddenberry's twenty-third-century techno-utopia, but this was merely an alternate expression of the program's guiding humanism. Repeatedly the series emphasized that the key to a long and prosperous future lies in improving ourselves (through peaceful cooperation and the eradication of racism, for instance), not in building better machines.

Several teleplays reminded viewers that technology exists to serve humankind—not the other way around. The *Enterprise* often encountered cultures where artificial intelligences lorded over human beings; Captain Kirk and his cohorts never failed to overthrow these mechanical tyrants. Even faulty human leadership was deemed superior to that of the most capable and benevolent computers. This follows logically, since in the universe of *Star Trek* nothing can be greater than humanity itself.

**Computers in Command**—"The Ultimate Computer" remains the most straightforward of these storylines, delivering its prohuman message with admirable directness. The *Enterprise* is chosen to test the experimental M-5 computer, supposedly capable of handling all aspects of starship command, up to and including battle. If successful, the M-5 will revolutionize space travel—and make starship captains obsolete, a prospect that disturbs Kirk, McCoy, and even, surprisingly, Spock. "Computers make excellent and efficient servants, but I have no wish to serve under them," the Vulcan states.

The storyline plays out like a variation on the theme of the Legend of John Henry, with Kirk standing in for the hammer-swinging African American folk hero and the M-5 serving as the twenty-third-century equivalent of the steam-powered drill. "There are certain things men must do to remain men," Kirk insists, a line that recalls the lyrics of the well-known folk song about John Henry ("Did the Lord say that machines ought to take the place of livin'?").

At first the M-5 performs commendably, but eventually the unit goes haywire and destroys a Federation starship. Kirk, Spock, and Scotty mount a desperate effort to return the *Enterprise* to human command before more lives are lost. When the stardust settles, the M-5 is out of commission and its creator is being hauled away to the interstellar loony bin. For all its superhuman efficiency, the computer lacked one element essential for any leader of men. "Compassion," McCoy ruminates. "That's the one thing no machine ever had. Maybe it's the one thing that keeps men ahead of them."

However, in its travels across the galaxy, the *Enterprise* encountered numerous colonies or civilizations that had made the fatal error of ceding control to soulless machines. In "Spock's Brain," the citizens of Sigma Draconis VI regress to childlike ignorance under the rule of a cybernetic supercomputer. In "The Gamesters of Triskelion," three disembodied brains, now plugged into a computer console, force a planet full of living beings to compete in gladiatorial contests. In "What Are Little Girls Made Of," a noble scientist becomes an unfeeling monster when he transfers his mind into an android body. In "A Taste of Armageddon," computers sanitize war to such an extent that it becomes a palatable proposition, continuing for hundreds of years and claiming billions of lives. And in "The Return of the Archons," "The Apple," and "For the World Is Hollow and I Have Touched the Sky," computers are worshiped like gods (more on that in the following chapter). On a lighter note, Harry Mudd's attempt to escape his shrewish flesh-and-blood wife and surround himself with beautiful androids goes comically awry in "I, Mudd." And even the usually reliable *Enterprise* computer runs amok in the animated episode "The Practical Joker."

**Killer Machines**—Not only must humans refuse to submit to computer control, but they must retain mastery of their machines. That was the lesson of "The Changeling" and "The Doomsday Machine," in which powerful robots are loosed by their creators, with devastating consequences.

In "The Changeling," NOMAD, a twentieth-century space probe, is damaged in a collision with an alien satellite and emerges with greatly enhanced capabilities and warped programming. Its new mission is to seek out *perfect* life forms and to destroy all imperfect ones. Since nobody's perfect, this means NOMAD wipes out every living thing it encounters—until it meets the *Enterprise* and mistakes Kirk for its creator, Dr. Jackson Roykirk. Eventually, by pointing out NOMAD's error, Kirk is able to induce the probe to commit suicide. Apparently this was the captain's preferred method of dispatching dangerous mechanical adversaries. He uses the same trick in "The Return of the Archons," "I, Mudd," "What Are Little Girls Made Of?," and "The Ultimate Computer."

It takes more than mere words to vanquish "The Doomsday Machine," a giant, nearly indestructible, planet-eating robot. The sacrifice of a crippled starship—the USS *Constellation*—is required to stop the device, a superweapon launched during a long-forgotten war and still wreaking destruction. In "That Which Survives" and "Shore Leave" (and even more pointedly in the animated "Shore Leave" sequel "Once Upon a Planet"), apparently inexplicable events that threaten the safety of the *Enterprise* and its crew are revealed to be the work of superpowered computers left to run without adequate oversight. Throughout the galaxy, it seemed, danger lurked wherever people failed to keep their technology on a proper leash.

Although Roddenberry's humanism remained a constant, later *Star Trek* series backed off this man-over-machine element of the show's message. This softening is exemplified by Commander Data from *The Next Generation* and the Doctor from *Voyager*. Both of these artificial life forms—an android and a hologram, respectively—were worthy to be called "human" in a larger sense of the word. In fact, one of *Next Gen*'s most memorable installments ("The Measure of a Man") devoted itself to proving that Data was a sentient being, with human rights, to be treated with human dignity.

Human beings are inherently good and are capable of wondrous achievements. Humanity can never be replaced or mechanized. These two inter-related themes recur in at least 17 of the original seventy-nine episodes. It could be argued that the series' humanism finds *some* form of expression in every installment. Moreover, through its consistent depiction of

**The Original and Uncut Television Series**

*STAR TREK*

**The Changeling**

Kirk confronts NOMAD, one of *Star Trek*'s many mechanical menaces, on the cover of this videotape release of "The Changeling."

human beings at their best, *Star Trek*'s optimistic spirit took on a more intimate dimension, serving its audience as a sort of weekly (or, in syndication, daily) affirmation. In *From Sawdust to Stardust*, a biography of DeForest Kelley, author Terry Lee Rioux sums up the show's message as "You are better than you think you are."

That was something audiences of the 1960s yearned to hear. And it's a message that continues to reassure viewers.

# Whom Gods Destroy

## Close Encounters with the (Practically) Divine

*Mankind has no need for gods.*

—*James T. Kirk, "Who Mourns for Adonais"*

G ene Roddenberry rejected his parents' Southern Baptist faith, and although he married Majel Barrett in a Shinto-Buddhist ceremony in Japan in 1969, he claimed no affiliation with that belief system either. For most of his life, Roddenberry remained evasive about his spiritual beliefs (if any). However, during his extensive, wide-ranging interviews with author Yvonne Fern, a former nun, for her book *Gene Roddenberry: The Last Conversation*, Roddenberry voiced both his ambivalence about the concept of a Creator and his unwavering faith in a bright future for humankind. Both of these threads were woven into the fabric of *Star Trek* from the outset.

The show's dismissive attitude toward religion was, in part, a reflection of its times, an era of dwindling church attendance and increasing secularization. The U.S. Supreme Court, in landmark decisions in 1962 and '63, decreed that state-sponsored prayer in public schools was unconstitutional. While *Star Trek*'s second pilot, "Where No Man Has Gone Before," was being filmed in the summer of 1965, the Roman Catholic Church's Second Vatican Council was concluding a series of sweeping changes designed to modernize worship and redefine the church's relationship to a rapidly changing world. In April 1966, while Roddenberry and his team were gearing up to begin production of *Star Trek*'s first season, *Time* magazine published its famous "Is God Dead?" cover story, about the challenges contemporary theologians face in trying to make God seem relevant to an increasingly uninterested public.

Primarily, however, *Star Trek*'s religious skepticism originated with its creator-producer. "We must question the story logic of having an all-knowing, all-powerful God, who creates faulty humans and then blames them for his own mistakes," Roddenberry said during one of his campus lectures in the early 1970s.

More than a dozen times during the original seventy-nine episodes and twenty-two animated adventures, the crew of the *Enterprise* encountered "gods" or beings with godlike powers, always with grievous consequences. Many of these teleplays were rewritten by Roddenberry or based on his original stories, and all were crafted under his watchful eye. During the creation of the animated episode "Bem," screenwriter David Gerrold met repeatedly with Roddenberry, who suggested several revisions to the scenario. "Gene said, 'How about they meet God on this planet?'" Gerrold shared in a DVD audio commentary. "And my gut-level [reaction] was, 'Haven't we done that one enough?'" Apparently not, because in 1975, when Paramount Pictures asked the Great Bird of the Galaxy to write a *Star Trek* feature film, Roddenberry returned to this familiar concept yet again, delivering a treatment titled *The God Thing* that Paramount rejected as too antireligious. In this screenplay, "God" turns out to be a faulty computer from another dimension; Jesus Christ is an android from outer space.

The abandoned *God Thing* story was only the latest in a series of *Star Trek* yarns that pitted Kirk and Spock against seemingly godlike beings.

## The Gods Themselves

Although credited to screenwriter Gilbert Ralston, "Who Mourns for Adonais?" could serve as the ur-text for Roddenberry's secular humanist attitude toward divine beings. On planet Pollux IV, an away team is held captive by a being who claims to be the Greek god Apollo. Meanwhile, the orbiting *Enterprise* is held (literally) in the deity's grip—by an energy field that looks like a giant green hand. Apollo wants the humans to worship him as they once did on Earth ("You will gather laurel leaves, light the ancient fires, kill a deer, make your sacrifices to me. Apollo has spoken!"), but Captain Kirk balks at the idea. "Mankind has no need for gods," he says. Although this statement is tempered when Kirk continues with "We find the one quite adequate," this addendum plays like a half-hearted, last-second throw-in to appease the NBC Standards and Practices department. Earlier McCoy stated flatly, "Scotty doesn't believe in gods." And when the haughty deity announced, "I am Apollo," Chekov sarcastically replied, "And I am the tsar of all the Russias."

The story's argument for atheism is so thinly veiled it's practically a single-entendre: The gods need human worship to survive; without it, they fade away. (In other words, gods exist only so long as humans *believe* they exist.) The other Greek gods have already passed into nonexistence. Although the scenario involves a pagan deity, the teleplay invites comparisons with the Old Testament god worshipped by the Abrahamic faiths (Judaism, Christianity, and Islam) by making Apollo the only survivor of Olympus—that is, the One God. Ultimately, Apollo is revealed to be—well, Apollo, the entity once worshipped by the ancient Greeks. However, he's an advanced alien life form with the power to manipulate energy, not a supernatural being. He is vanquished when the landing party discovers and destroys his power source. Apollo's last words, as he fades from existence, sum up Roddenberry's beliefs succinctly: "The time has passed. There is no room for gods!"

The Emmy-winning animated adventure "How Sharper Than a Serpent's Tooth" is a virtual rewrite of "Who Mourns for Adonais?" with the Native

Apollo (Michael Forest, looming over the landing party) needs human worship to survive.

American Kukulkan standing in for the Greek Apollo. Once again the *Enterprise* encounters an ancient deity that requires worship for survival. In other, similar live-action episodes, beings with godlike powers are revealed to be weaklings ("Catspaw") or misbehaving children ("The Squire of Gothos"). The "friendly angel" (actually, a malevolent extraterrestrial) of "And the Children Shall Lead" dupes a group of youngsters into killing their parents and then trying to take over the *Enterprise*. Invariably, *Star Trek*'s "gods" are fakes of one type or another. Only the dangers they pose are real.

Aside from those episodes, many other installments contain offhandedly dismissive remarks toward religious faith. For instance, at the conclusion of "Obsession," after Scotty and Spock have beamed up Captain Kirk and a security officer, despite interference from an antimatter explosion, Scotty exclaims, "Thank heaven!" To which Spock replies, "Mr. Scott, there was no deity involved. It was my cross-circuiting to B that recovered them." Then McCoy chimes in, "Well then, thank pitchforks and pointed ears!"

*Star Trek*'s attitude toward gods and religious figures of all sorts is almost uniformly negative, but there are exceptions for every rule. Occasional nods to the existence of a creator sneak in, as in "Metamorphosis," when the Companion states that the creation of life is reserved for "the Maker of all things." The most surprising exception to *Star Trek*'s prevailing atheism is "Bread and Circuses." In this episode, Kirk, Spock, and McCoy discover a parallel Earth where Rome never fell and gladiatorial contests are broadcast on television. Throughout the adventure, the away team receives aid from a group of peace-loving "sun worshipers." During the wrap-up, Spock remarks on the illogic of this, since sun worship is usually a primitive, superstitious faith. Then Uhura chimes in, explaining that the natives don't worship "the sun up in the sky" but rather "the son of God." Kirk smiles. "Caesar . . . and Christ," he says. "They had them both. And the Word is spreading only now." Spock predicts that this newfound faith will bring peace, love, and brotherhood to the planet in less than a hundred years. (The Vulcan apparently assumes the natives of this unnamed world somehow will avoid repeating Earth's bloody crusades, reformation, counter-reformation, witch trials, and so on.) The unabashedly pro-Christian stance of "Bread and Circuses" sets it apart from every other classic *Trek* adventure. Astonishingly, this episode was coauthored by Roddenberry and Gene Coon. It should be emphasized, however, that the proreligious sentiment is reserved for the episode's epilogue. "Bread and Circuses" remains primarily a satire of TV.

## Prophets of Repression

Perhaps the pro-Christian stance of "Bread and Circuses" can be chalked up as an expression of Roddenberry's own conflicted beliefs. Despite his apparent atheism, Roddenberry sometimes (albeit rarely) spoke of a nebulous higher power he referred to as "the All." This was pointedly not the Judeo-Christian God. He never explained this idea fully, and may have never completely worked out the concept himself. But it appears that Roddenberry at least considered the possible existence of a guiding force (along the line of Carl Jung's collective unconscious but perhaps best thought of as "the human spirit") that pulls humankind perpetually forward, ever nearer to perfection. He discusses this idea, warily, with Fern in *The Last Conversation.*

But while Roddenberry's attitude toward the metaphysical realm may have wavered, his opinion of religion was unchanging: He had no use for it. Roddenberry vehemently rejected an NBC executive's suggestion that the *Enterprise* crew include a chaplain. (This idea was tendered as a way of alleviating concerns over the ship's satanic-looking first officer.) Whenever religious leaders appear on *Star Trek*, they prove troublesome. At their best (as in "For the World Is Hollow and I Have Touched the Sky"), they are well-meaning but ignorant and misguided; at their worst, they are agents of inhuman, individuality-crushing repression. The latter was the case in "The Return of the Archons," written by Boris Sobelman from Roddenberry's original story. In this tale, the Great Bird asserted his feelings about religion in no uncertain terms.

An *Enterprise* landing party beams down to Beta III to investigate the disappearance of the Starship *Archon*, which crashed on the planet 100 years earlier. They discover a world full of placid, dazed-looking people. Suddenly, "Red Hour" strikes, and the mild-mannered Betans go on a rampage of senseless destruction and violence. Afterward, the populace returns to a state that Kirk describes as "mindless, vacant contentment." The Betans, we learn, are under the mental control of Landru, a tyrannical, telepathic supercomputer that is worshiped as a god. (The followers of Landru refer to themselves as "the Body." Not coincidentally, Christian churches sometimes refer to themselves as "the body of Christ.") Landru protects and cares for the population but keeps the Betans docile and servile. They perform the functions necessary to keep themselves and Landru alive but have no free will, no liberty of thought or expression. They serve "the will of Landru," which is enforced by the Lawgivers. These cloaked, monkish figures carry crosier-like rods that deliver high-voltage electric jolts to anyone who defies Landru's will. Nearly all the Betans are brainwashed followers of Landru. Even McCoy is "absorbed" into the cult. The Earthmen come to the aid of a handful of valiant unbelievers, dissidents who oppose this evil theocracy.

It's significant, of course, that Landru is revealed to be a computer. This dovetails perfectly with the mildly technophobic undercurrent of *Star Trek*'s humanism. (For more on this, see the preceding chapter.) To reach their potential, this episode argues, humans must rely on themselves, not on machines, and certainly not on appeals to some artificial deity. Religion only crushes the human spirit—or at least represses original thought and independent initiative.

Other installments also present religion as a force for repression or source of conflict. In "The Apple," Vaal (another computer-god) provides for the people of planet Gamma Trianguli VI—keeping them at peace, eternally healthy, and eternally young—but forbids romantic love. In "For the World Is Hollow and I Have Touched the Sky," the Oracle (yet another godlike computer) hides the truth from the passengers of a giant starship, perpetuating the lie that the people are still on their home world. And in the animated adventure "The Jihad," a madman tries to trigger an intergalactic war by manipulating an alien race's religious fervor. These episodes underscored Roddenberry's often-stated conviction that religion was a divisive force that would have to be set aside (or outgrown) for humankind to achieve its full potential.

Throughout Roddenberry's lifetime, *Star Trek*'s attitude toward religion remained belligerent. The franchise finally struck a less strident note with *Star Trek: Deep Space Nine*, in which the Bajoran religion was treated seriously and, for the most part, sympathetically—even though the true nature of the Bajoran "prophets" (also known as the "wormhole aliens") remained ambiguous. While imperfect, the Bajoran religion brought healing and solidarity to a beleaguered civilization. However, *DS9* was created by Rick Berman and Michael Piller, not Roddenberry, and premiered two years after the Great Bird's death.

## Absolute Power Corrupts Absolutely

Not only are gods and religions untrustworthy, but godhood is not to be sought. That's the moral of several more *Star Trek* episodes, including the series' second pilot, "Where No Man Has Gone Before."

In this seminal adventure, navigator Gary Mitchell (Gary Lockwood) and psychologist Elizabeth Dehner (Sally Kellerman) acquire fantastic telekinetic powers after the *Enterprise* attempts to cross an energy barrier that surrounds the galaxy. Lockwood, in particular, grows ever more dangerous as his powers quickly increase. He begins to consider himself a god and his former crewmates lesser beings. Once he achieves "godhood," Mitchell loses all compassion for humanity, as well as any ethical inhibitions. "Morals are for men, not gods," Mitchell declares. There's a great deal of talk about gods in this teleplay, none of it flattering to the "deity," which might be more accurately described as *in*human rather than *super*human. When an attempt to maroon Mitchell on a remote mining colony goes awry, Kirk is forced to kill his former friend, who's now well on his way to becoming a ruthless superpowered despot who wants to enslave the inferior humans. To survive, to retain its freedom, humanity must destroy the "god."

"Where No Man Has Gone Before" went where many *Star Trek* episodes would subsequently travel. Repeatedly in later teleplays, godlike power corrupts those who come to possess it. In "Plato's Stepchildren," denizens of a remote planet have gained psychokinetic superpowers by ingesting high doses of the rare element kironide. Now they lord it over a dwarf lackey and torment luckless visitors to the planet, including an *Enterprise* landing party. Dr. McCoy injects Kirk and Spock with high doses of kironide, empowering our heroes to unseat the cruel leader of the aliens, Parmen (Liam Sullivan). "Uncontrolled power will make even saints into savages," Parmen says, succinctly making the thematic point. Teenager Charlie Evans, a space crash survivor raised by godlike alien beings, gains psychic powers in "Charlie X" but uses them improperly—doing cheap card tricks to impress girls and "thinking" out of existence anyone who hurts his tender feelings. In both "Return to Tomorrow" and "By Any Other Name," superadvanced, nearly divine beings evolved beyond corporeal form to take possession of human bodies and begin committing very human sins, including murder. And in "Requiem for Methuselah," Flint (James Daly) gains immortality but finds no comfort in it, forced to endure the aging and death of all his loved ones throughout hundreds of lifetimes.

Ironically, perhaps, given the show's general hostility toward religious faith, many observers have commented on the religious-like fervor of *Star Trek* fans. "Those 79 episodes are their revealed texts, the sacred tablets by which their lives here and now and beyond are charted," wrote a reporter from the *Calgary Herald*, describing a 1975 *Trek* convention. In 1994, University of Wisconsin professor Michael Jendra published a paper in the journal *Sociology of Religion* titled "*Star Trek* Fandom as a Religious Phenomenon." In his essay, Jendra notes that fandom "involves a sacralization of elements of our culture, along with the formation of communities with regularized practices that include a 'canon' and a hierarchy. *Star Trek* fandom is also associated with a popular stigma, giving fans a sense of persecution and identity common to active religious groups." He later clarifies that fans' *Star Trek* "faith" doesn't supplant other religious beliefs (when present) but is held in combination with them.

Struggling to explain the ongoing appeal of the franchise in his memoir *The View from the Bridge*, director Nicholas Meyer—who helmed two of the most successful *Star Trek* feature films (*The Wrath of Khan* and *The Undiscovered Country*) and cowrote a third (*The Voyage Home*)—described *Star Trek* as "religion without theology." Meyer equated fans repeatedly rewatching the same episodes with Catholics attending Mass.

At the least, *Star Trek* remains the textbook definition of a "cult" television series.

However, Roddenberry always eschewed religious comparisons. "I'm not a guru and don't want to be," he told an Associated Press interviewer in 1976. "It frightens me when I learn of 10,000 people treating a *Star Trek* script as if it were Scripture. I certainly didn't write Scripture, and my feeling is that those who did weren't treated very well in the end."

# The Last Battlefield

## The Corrosive Power of Hate

*Give up your hate! . . . You must both end up dead if you don't stop hating!*
*—James T. Kirk, "Let That Be Your Last Battlefield"*

G ene Roddenberry hoped to tackle social issues with his first television series, the peacetime military drama *The Lieutenant* (1963–64). But those aspirations were dashed by the Marine Corps (shot at Camp Pendleton, the show carried a USMC seal of approval) and wary network executives, who steered the program away from controversial subject matter, especially if the topic reflected poorly on the military. In frustration, Roddenberry turned to science fiction. For him, *Star Trek*'s primary function was to address political and moral issues through the lens of fantasy, as Jonathan Swift had done with *Gulliver's Travels*. The show was not only Roddenberry's vision of the future but also his vehicle for commentary on the present.

Consequently, *Star Trek* took on several hot-button topics, albeit in allegorical terms. Deciphering the parallels between the universe of *Star Trek* and the real world became a kind of parlor game among fans: The Federation represented the United States, the Klingons stood in for the Soviets, the Romulans equated to the Chinese, and so on. This wasn't a particularly difficult pastime, since *Star Trek*'s messages usually were thinly veiled. While it often lacked subtlety, however, the series never lacked courage. *Trek* backed away from none of the controversial issues of the day, confronting segregation, the Vietnam War, the Cold War, women's liberation, and other topics head-on. Ultimately, *Star Trek*'s politics could be boiled down to a single statement: Hate is toxic. It poisons all who possess it and destroys everything it touches, like slow-working acid. The program reiterated this simple yet truthful and (sadly) ever-relevant idea in numerous episodes.

### Infinite Diversity in Infinite Combinations

Segregation remained an explosive issue throughout *Star Trek*'s broadcast life. Even though the U.S. Supreme Court had banned "separate but equal" schools in its *Brown v. Board of Education* ruling in 1954, public schools in Mississippi remained segregated until 1969. In many states, it remained illegal for blacks and whites to marry until the U.S. Supreme Court struck down antimiscegenation laws in June 1967, between Seasons One and Two of *Trek*. Race riots gripped several major American cities in the summer of 1967. In April 1968, shortly after the conclusion of *Star Trek*'s second season, Martin Luther King Jr. was assassinated, unleashing another wave of riots. The following week, President Lyndon B. Johnson signed the Civil Rights Act of 1968, which forbade racial discrimination in housing.

On the topic of race relations, *Star Trek* wore its politics on its sleeve. The composition of the *Enterprise* crew—with men and women of many different races and nationalities, and even different species, working side by side in mutual respect—renounced segregation in a subtle but unmistakable, ever-present manner. But merely placing Uhura and Sulu on the bridge wasn't enough for Roddenberry. His series frequently confronted bigotry directly.

That was the case with "Let That Be Your Last Battlefield," which delivers its antiracism message with all the force of (and about as much subtlety as) a ball peen hammer. The *Enterprise* apprehends Lokai (Lou Antonio), an alien traveling in a stolen shuttlecraft. The fugitive's physical appearance is remarkable: black on one side, white on the other. Shortly afterward, a similarly bicolored alien, Bele (Frank Gorshin), arrives and attempts to take custody of the prisoner, who he claims is a terrorist and mass murderer from the distant planet

Former Riddler Frank Gorshin guest starred as Bele in "Let That Be Your Last Battlefield," *Star Trek*'s most overt attack on racism.

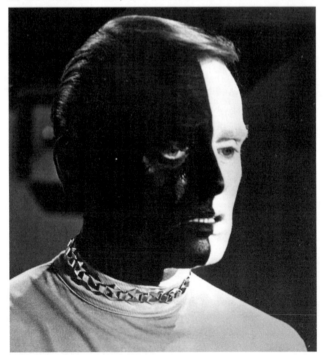

Cheron. Lokai claims to be a member of a race of former slaves now fighting for equality. He requests political asylum. However, both aliens seem trapped in the entrenched racism of the Cheron culture. Lokai ventures that "you monotone humans are just alike." Later, Bele dismisses humankind as "mono-colored trash." Racial bias is the root of the conflict between Lokai's people and Bele's people, as Bele states flatly.

"It is clear to even the most simple-minded observer that Lokai is of an inferior breed," Bele proclaims. When Spock protests that Bele and Lokai appear to be of the same race, Bele balks. "Are you blind, Mr. Spock? Look at me. I'm black on the right side. . . . Lokai is white on the right side, all his people are white on the right side."

This priceless moment nearly redeems the entire (otherwise slow-moving and heavy-handed) episode with its delightful satirical absurdity. Instantly the Cherons are reduced to the level of Dr. Seuss's Sneetches (star-bellied and otherwise) from the classic children's story. "Last Battlefield" draws an overt parallel with the American civil rights movement when Chekov comments that "there was persecution on Earth once. I remember reading about it in my history class." Sulu replies, "Yes, but it happened way back in the twentieth century. There's no such primitive thinking today."

Lokai and Bele, however, remain locked in their racial animus. When Spock refers to them as "two irrevocably hostile humanoids," Scotty suggests a more succinct term: "Disgusting is what I call them." Eventually, Bele forces the *Enterprise* to return to Cheron, only to discover that the entire population of the planet is dead. The two races have totally annihilated one another. Nevertheless Lokai and Bele beam down to their home world to continue their feud amid the ruins of their civilization and the unburied bodies of their slain brothers and sisters.

But before they leave, Kirk urges the two to make peace. "Give up your hate!" he pleads. "Listen to me, you both must end up dead if you don't stop hating." His plea is to no avail. "You're an idealistic dreamer," Lokai says dismissively. True enough. *Star Trek* was made proudly by idealistic dreamers, and "Let That Be Your Last Battlefield" remains the program's most uncompromising attack on racial intolerance.

It was hardly the show's only such assault, however. "Is There in Truth No Beauty?" introduced the Vulcan philosophy of IDIC (Infinite Diversity in Infinite Combinations), a phrase that perfectly encapsulates the show's advocacy for tolerance and inclusion. "Plato's Stepchildren," an otherwise humdrum installment, boasted a pair of remarkable features: the first interracial kiss in TV history (between Kirk and Uhura, at the command of tyrannical telepathic aliens) and a subplot involving a dwarf, Alexander (Michael Dunn), tormented due to his stature and lack of psychic powers. "Alexander, where I come from, size, shape or color makes no difference," Kirk explains.

"Day of the Dove" and "The Cloud Minders" also tackled issues of prejudice from different angles. In "Day of the Dove" a noncorporeal, hate-eating life force stokes xenophobic animosity between humans and Klingons trapped together aboard the *Enterprise*. In "The Cloud Minders," racism and classism merge in the plight of the working-class, subterranean Troglytes, who are exploited by the haughty denizens of Stratos, a floating city in the clouds. "Is There in Truth No Beauty?" challenged racist/species-ist standards of beauty. But "The Devil in the

Kirk and Kang (Michael Ansara) battle each other before joining forces against a hate-devouring life force in "Day of the Dove."

Dark" offered the series' most deftly crafted and poetic argument for interracial (even interspecies) dialogue and understanding. The Horta, a tunneling alien creature that has killed dozens of miners and seems bent on the destruction of a mining colony on planet Janus VI, turns out to be a misunderstood mother protecting her unhatched young. Eventually a compromise is struck that enables humans and Horta to coexist peaceably and profitably. Issues of fairness and tolerance are raised, at least in passing, in numerous other adventures as well.

## War (What Is It Good For?)

*Star Trek*'s attitude toward another major political issue of the era, the Vietnam War, was considerably more nuanced than its straightforward stance on segregation. Roddenberry's secretary, Susan Sackett, claims that the Prime Directive (not to interfere in developing cultures) was intended as a subtle rebuke of U.S. policy in Southeast Asia. But if so, then it was *too* subtle, especially since Captain Kirk's attitude toward the General Order Number One (as the directive was formally known) seemed uncertain; he violated it on several occasions. Also indicative of the program's ambivalence about the war was Kirk's tendency to say "We come in peace" while pointing a phaser. Created by a World War II veteran, and with numerous other vets in key roles both in front of and behind the camera, *Star Trek*, despite its progressive ideals, was hardly a stronghold for peaceniks. The show's attitude seemed to be that war was something to be prevented if possible (several storylines involved Kirk and Spock trying to avert interplanetary conflicts) but not to be avoided at any cost.

The series' clearest response to Vietnam was "A Private Little War," written by Roddenberry from a story by Don Ingalls. Ingalls is credited under a pseudonym ("Jud Crucis") because he was displeased with Roddenberry's extensive reworking of his material. In its original form, Ingalls's scenario was even more blatantly about Vietnam and mentioned North Vietnamese leader Ho Chi Minh by name.

While conducting a biological survey mission to Neural, a world where the natives have only recently developed metallurgy, Kirk and Spock find that the previously peaceful, primitive natives are now armed with flintlock rifles and engaged in a civil war. This represents a highly unlikely leap forward in technology and a jarring shift in culture. Kirk suspects that the Klingons, who covet the planet's natural resources, may be arming the planet's city dwellers and fomenting conflict with its Hill People. When this is confirmed, Kirk decides to even the score by arming the Hill People as well.

"A Private Little War," one of the hardest-hitting of all *Trek* episodes, evidences a clear distaste for violence. "I thought my people would grow tired of killing, but you were right. They see it is easier than trading and it has pleasures," the leader of the city folk tells his Klingon contact, chillingly. Meanwhile, the transformation of Hill People leader Tyree (Michael Witney) from gentle pacifist to bloodthirsty warrior is deeply unsettling. When Tyree picks up a rifle and declares, "I will kill them!," Kirk winces. Nevertheless, the episode advocates interventionism, arguing that military involvement in places like Neural (or Vietnam) is sometimes a necessary evil. McCoy is reluctant to accept this.

"You're condemning this whole planet to a war that may never end," he says. Not coincidentally, when "A Private Little War" premiered on Groundhog Day of 1968, the U.S. military was entering its seventh year of action in Vietnam, where civil war would continue until 1975. "It could go on for year after year, massacre after massacre," McCoy says, parroting the argument many in the antiwar movement were making in the late '60s.

Nevertheless, Kirk insists on establishing "a balance of power." It's "the trickiest, most difficult, dirtiest game of all, but the only one that preserves both sides," he says. Ironically, Kirk's argument for war is rooted in compassion (the desire to preserve these two rival cultures), not hatred.

## "Liberty and Freedom Have to Be More Than Just Words"

Kirk's use of the phrase "balance of power" invokes American policy toward the Soviet Union in the 1960s. Inevitably, *Star Trek* had its say on the Cold War, as well. Roddenberry himself penned the episode's most overt treatment of the subject, "The Omega Glory."

An away team consisting of Kirk, Spock, McCoy and a redshirt security officer are trapped on the surface of planet Omega IV, infected with a potentially deadly virus and trapped in the middle of a civil war between the Asian-featured Kahms and the Caucasian Yangs. To make matters worse, Captain Ron Tracey (Morgan Woodward) of the Starship *Exeter* has violated the Prime Directive and intervened on the part of the Kahms. These story threads build to a far-fetched climax ("punch line" may be the more apt term) in which Omega IV is revealed to be a parallel Earth, where the Yankees (or "Yangs") fought a biological war against the Commies (or "Kahms"), bombing one another into a savage, preindustrial condition. The Yangs even possess a tattered American flag and a copy of the U.S. Constitution, which they worship blindly. The Yangs win the centuries-old war but have lost all understanding of the ideals they originally fought to defend. Kirk tries to enlighten them with a bombastic, Shatnerian reading of the preamble to the Constitution. Afterwards, McCoy wonders if Kirk's oratory also violates General Order Number One. "We merely showed them the meaning of what they've been fighting for," Kirk says. "Liberty and freedom have to be more than just words."

Although widely considered one of the series' weakest entries, "The Omega Glory" delivers its message in unequivocal terms: Freedom is worth defending, but its defenders must not sacrifice their own freedoms to achieve victory. The story is pro-Cold War but also anti-McCarthyism. Additionally, the war-ravaged setting of Omega IV illustrates the folly of waging a global war with weapons of mass destruction.

*Star Trek* also addressed the Cold War through the makeup of its bridge crew, adding navigator Pavel Chekov at the start of Season Two. His mere presence signaled confidence that Americans and Soviets could and eventually would overcome their differences—something not readily apparent in 1967.

The subject of war—or its aversion—remains central to several other episodes. In "Friday's Child," Kirk finds the Klingons once again meddling in the internal politics of a developing world, instigating tribal unrest on planet Capella IV. As in "A Private Little War," Kirk and Spock must set things right or else ignite an interplanetary war. In "Elaan of Troyius," Kirk spends most of the episode trying to prepare a petulant, uncouth warrior princess for an interspecies marriage that will secure peace between two rival worlds. In "The Savage Curtain," Kirk and Spock (not to mention Abe Lincoln and Surak of Vulcan) battle a quartet of interstellar supervillains (including Genghis Khan and Kahless the Unforgettable, founder of the Klingon Empire), but only after exhausting every possibility of making peace.

On the other hand, in "Errand of Mercy," Kirk seems to be spoiling for a fight. He becomes exasperated with the pacifist Organians' unwillingness to resist when the Klingons invade their planet. Finally, the Organians reveal hidden powers that enable them to repel the invaders—and quash a just-declared war between the Federation and the Empire. After spending most of the episode trying to goad the Organians into action, Kirk is brought up short when they intervene, preventing the humans and Klingons from settling their differences among themselves. "We have a right . . ." he begins. "To wage war, Captain?" asks the Organian elder (John Abbott). "To kill millions of innocent people? To destroy life on a planetary scale? Is that what you're defending?" If it's hard to square Kirk's attitude in "Errand of Mercy" with his actions in other episodes, this is merely indicative of *Star Trek*'s mixed emotions on the subject of war.

## A Balance of Terrors

Another expression of hate—the thirst for revenge—is the subject of several *Star Trek* episodes as well, including "The Doomsday Machine," in which Commodore Matt Decker (William Windom) nearly destroys the *Enterprise* trying to strike back at the giant, planet-eating robot that consumed his crew; "The Conscience of the King," in which a crewman thirsts for vengeance against a war criminal who murdered his parents (and thousands of other civilians); "Obsession," in which Kirk questions his own motivations for delaying a vital, lifesaving mission to attack an alien creature that years earlier killed his mentor; and "The Alternative Factor," which features an alien locked in a perpetual struggle with his alter ego from a parallel universe.

The subjects of vengeance, racism, and war converge in a single narrative with "The Balance of Terror," one of the most brilliantly written and performed of all *Trek* adventures. The *Enterprise* swings into action when a cloaked Romulan war bird devastates several Federation outposts along the Neutral Zone separating Federation and Romulan space. A cat-and-mouse battle ensues, with

Kirk matching wits with a skilled but battle-weary imperial commander (Mark Lenard). The primary theme of the episode is the horrific waste of life brought by war, personified in the death of a young crewman on what was supposed to be his wedding day. Kirk tries desperately to avert war, while his unnamed Romulan counterpart remains glumly resigned to it. "Our gift to the homeland, another war," he muses. "Must it always be so? How many comrades have we lost in this way?"

A subplot involving the *Enterprise*'s navigator, Lieutenant Stiles (Paul Comi), brings both revenge and racism into the story. Stiles's parents, he reveals, were killed in an earlier attack by the Romulans. He wants revenge, but Kirk insists the previous conflict was "their war, Mister Stiles, not yours." Later, when the Romulans are revealed to have Vulcan-like features, Stiles immediately grows suspicious of Spock. Based on the first officer's physical appearance alone, Stiles believes the Vulcan may be a Romulan spy. Again, Kirk forcefully rejects this idea. "Leave any bigotry in your quarters," he says. "There's no room for it on the bridge." (Seated next to Lieutenant Stiles is George Takei, who spent his childhood in a World War II internment camp because many Americans thought like Stiles.) One of this episode's most touching features is the growing respect and admiration between Kirk and the Romulan commander, which the Romulan acknowledges in a transmission to the *Enterprise*. "You and I are of a kind. In a different reality, I could have called you friend."

Friendship: That's the antitoxin for hate prescribed by *Star Trek* in many of these same episodes. Or perhaps it's something greater than simple friendship—fraternity. Having experienced the "Band of Brothers" spirit in action during World War II, Roddenberry envisioned a similar experience for humanity as a whole: People from many backgrounds and of many races joining together in bonds of brotherly love, united in a common cause that elevates everyone involved—making the group stronger than the sum of its parts and bringing out the finest in every person. It may sound corny, but that's the way Starfleet operates, and it's the way Roddenberry believed the world would work—someday.

# What Are Little Girls Made Of?

## The Gender Politics of *Star Trek*

*Worlds may change, galaxies disintegrate, but a woman always remains a woman.*

—*James T. Kirk, "The Conscience of the King"*

Star Trek offered the soaring vision of a future free from prejudice, with men and women of all races and nationalities working side by side in mutual respect for the common good. But the program didn't always live up to its lofty ideals, especially in its treatment of female characters. Although Gene Roddenberry considered himself a feminist, many feminists have questioned his understanding of the term or the sincerity of his commitment to the cause. It's easy to see why. At times the disconnect between the show's guiding principles and its individual teleplays could be glaring. Consider these examples:

- "Spock, the women on your planet are logical," Kirk declares in "Elaan of Troyius. "No other planet in the galaxy can make that claim."
- In "The Changeling," NOMAD describes human females as "a mass of conflicting impulses."
- In "Wolf in the Fold," it's explained that the fear-eating life force known as Redjac preys on females because they frighten more easily than males. (This apparently applies to women of all species and from many planets.)
- "I have never understood the female capacity to avoid a direct answer to any question," Spock complains in "This Side of Paradise."

In these and numerous other moments *Star Trek* seems embarrassingly chauvinistic. Often women are treated more as art objects than flesh-and-blood characters or depicted as emotionally unstable and unfit for command. Clearly, despite Roddenberry's "feminism," the show's gender politics were complex and conflicted.

Although he espoused progressive social and political views consistently throughout his life, and made a concerted effort to portray a racially integrated Starfleet, Roddenberry blew the chance to depict a post-sexism future. In an essay published on the *Sixties City* pop culture website, author J. William Snyder

Spock and Kirk pose alongside "Mudd's Women" (played by, from left to right, Maggie Thrett, Susan Denberg, and Karen Steele) in this press shot.

writes that "*Star Trek*'s portrayal of women was . . . at best, ambivalent—wavering between an implicit belief in women as equals but an unwillingness to exemplify, in a tangible way, what was being professed." This is a keen observation. However, it may not have been a lack of will but rather a lack of vision that prevented the show from better realizing its feminist convictions. Created by a man born in 1921, and written mostly by men of the same generation, *Star Trek* seemed incapable of looking beyond the patriarchal culture of mid-twentieth-century America, the world in which its creators had been raised. As a result, the program reinforced traditional gender roles and social structures. It was a man's galaxy.

## Starfleet's Glass Ceiling

This reflexive reversion to patriarchy was expressed most visibly in *Star Trek*'s dearth of female leaders. In the utopian meritocracy that Starfleet is purported to be, given that the majority of the human population is female, more women should serve as captains and admirals than men, or at least an equal number. Anything less would indicate the persistence of prejudice that humankind has supposedly evolved beyond. Yet, as viewers learn in "Turnabout Intruder," Starfleet has no female commanders at all! Although women serve the Federation as diplomats, scientists, and in other important capacities, there are no female captains.

The only woman ever seen in charge of a Federation starship is First Officer Number One (Majel Barrett) in "The Cage" (and "The Menagerie"), whose icy persona and gender-neutral non-name not only defeminizes her but nearly dehumanizes her. Captain Pike even complains to her (about Yeoman Colt), "I can't get used to having a woman on the bridge. . . . No offense, Lieutenant. You're different, of course." Of course, there are female bridge officers, most notably Lieutenant Uhura, but Kirk never leaves the *Enterprise* under their command. Other than Uhura, the ship's most prominent female crew members were the ever-servile Nurse Christine Chapel and Yeoman Janice Rand, whose primary duty seemed to be delivering food and beverages to Captain Kirk like some interstellar Hooters Girl.

"Turnabout Intruder," the series' final episode, throws these shortcomings into sharp relief. Exo-archeologist Dr. Janice Lester (Sandra Smith), a former lover of Kirk's from his days at the Academy, uses an alien device to switch bodies with the captain. Lester is bent on settling old scores—one with Kirk, who dumped her, and one with Starfleet, who rejected her bid for command. "Your world of starship captains doesn't admit women," Lester seethes. Yet her actions seem to validate the wisdom of Starfleet's glass ceiling. Masquerading as Kirk, Lester's (female) leadership proves so flaky and temperamental that she can't get through a single duty shift without giving herself away. She issues a series of irrational, contradictory orders and snaps at anyone who suggests a more logical course of action, including Spock. After less than a day on the job, she's asked to report to sick bay to have her head examined. McCoy wants to run tests on the captain due to "emotional instability and irrational mental attitudes."

McCoy isn't the only one with doubts. "Doctor, I've seen the captain feverish, sick, drunk, delirious, terrified, overjoyed, boiling mad," Scotty says. "But up to now I have never seen him red-faced with hysteria." Meanwhile, Lester (that is, Kirk-in-Lester's-body) tries to convince Spock, McCoy, and anyone else who will listen that she (he) is the real captain. Finally, Spock, McCoy, and Scotty mount a full-scale mutiny to remove their feminized leader, switch the "life forces" of Lester and Kirk back to their appropriate receptacles, and return a man to the captain's chair.

"Turnabout Intruder" is a substandard episode in most respects—Shatner's amusingly prissy performance as Lester-inhabiting-Kirk, and Smith's dead-on Shatner imitation as Kirk-inhabiting-Lester provide the only points of interest—but the inherent sexism of Herb Wallerstein's teleplay remains its most appalling feature. Unfortunately, however, this wasn't the only *Trek* adventure to cast doubt on female leadership.

The other woman captain depicted on *Star Trek*—the unnamed Romulan commander from "The *Enterprise* Incident"—performs more capably than Janice Lester but ultimately is undone by her feminine nature. With the *Enterprise* held at bay, and Kirk and Spock both captive on her Bird of Prey, the commander has a crowning achievement within her grasp. Yet she allows her infatuation with Spock to distract her and lets down her guard while trying to seduce the Vulcan in her cabin. While she's slipping into something more comfortable, Captain Kirk slips away with her ship's cloaking device. Her behavior could not be more dissimilar to that of the unnamed *male* Romulan commander from "Balance of Terror" whose life is ordered by duty and honor. She temporarily loses her grip on these responsibilities; Spock holds fast to his. "Why would you do this to me? What are you that you could do this?" the humiliated Romulan asks Spock. "First officer of the *Enterprise*," the Vulcan replies. Outfoxed by the wily men of the Federation, she winds up a prisoner on the *Enterprise*.

The women of Sigma Draconis VI, from "Spock's Brain," use "pain bands" to lord over the males of their planet. But they're a bunch of airheads who need Spock's masculine brain to serve as the control matrix for the supercomputer that supports their bizarre, matriarchal-in-name-only civilization. Then there's the Elasian leader Elaan (France Nuyen) from "Elaan of Troyius," a petulant, uncouth, arrogant fire-eater whose impending marriage to a Troyian leader will avert a war between two rival planets. She's a shrew who's only fit to lead once she's been tamed by Captain Kirk. In "The City on the Edge of Forever," Kirk and Spock must prevent crusading missionary Edith Keeler from emerging as a prominent political figure. If Keeler survives, her growing influence will soften America's masculinity, leaving the U.S. too timid and peace-loving, too stereotypically feminine, to effectively combat Nazi aggression. In these and other scenarios, *Star Trek* seemed unable to imagine a culture without the ingrained patriarchal attitudes of 1960s America.

## Of Miniskirts and Mechanical Maidens

Even when Roddenberry placed women on the bridge of the *Enterprise*, he costumed them in miniskirts and go-go boots. The show's female guest stars often wore far less. *Star Trek*'s so-called feminism was never allowed to interfere with costume designer Bill Theiss's genius for cheesecake. After screening several episodes to familiarize himself with the show, Season Three producer Fred Freiberger reportedly remarked, "Oh, I get it. [It's] tits in space."

The show not only put female flesh on display, it allowed male characters to take in the view. Ogling women is an accepted pastime in the "liberated" world of *Star Trek*. Kirk and other male officers often turn their heads to check out a new female crewmate. Every man on board stares at Harry Mudd's chemically enhanced mail-order brides in "Mudd's Women." Captain Pike and a colleague leer at Vena when she appears as an Orion slave girl in "The Menagerie." And Kirk, McCoy, and Scotty gawk at an Argelian belly dancer in "Wolf in the Fold." Even Spock exhibits this behavior in "The Cloud Minders," gaping at the scantily clad Droxine (Dana Ewing). "Extreme feminine beauty is always disturbing," he explains.

In other episodes, women are objectified in more literal ways. No fewer than four installments involve attempts by men to manufacture perfect mates. In "Mudd's Women," Harry Mudd (Roger C. Carmel) convinces three plain-looking old maids to take the forbidden "Venus drug," which grants them unearthly beauty (and makes them acceptable brides). Once transformed, however, they become a commodity that Mudd sells to the highest bidder. That is Mudd's bargain: to become marriage-worthy, the women must relinquish their humanity and become property. (This is moderated to an extent when, deprived of the Venus Drug, the women revert to their original looks and forge more adult and equitable relationships with their husbands/purchasers.) In "I, Mudd," Mudd returns as the ruler of a planet populated entirely by gorgeous female androids of his own design. Both "What Are Little Girls Made Of?" and "Requiem for Methuselah" also involve powerful, intelligent men constructing idealized, robotic brides. These android dream women are beautiful, intelligent, and, perhaps most importantly, perfectly compliant. They are twenty-third-century Stepford Wives.

By far the most egregious misstep in *Star Trek*'s treatment of women comes at the conclusion of "The Enemy Within." Earlier, the Evil Kirk attempted to rape Yeoman Rand. Now, during the show's wrap-up on the bridge, Spock jokes with her about the experience. "The imposter had some . . . interesting qualities, wouldn't you say, Yeoman?" he asks teasingly, apparently inferring that Rand secretly enjoyed the sexual assault. Somehow the line seems even more reprehensible coming from Spock, the show's bastion of logic and intellect. It's an exchange most fans would prefer to forget, but it remains emblematic of the show's unfortunate tendency to treat women as expendable eye candy.

## Dream Girls

*Star Trek*'s attitude toward women also can be observed through the romantic interests of the show's main characters. Over the course of the original seventy-nine episodes, Kirk, Spock, McCoy, and Scotty all fell in love at least once, but

Former Batgirl Yvonne Craig as the homicidal Orion temptress Marta, from "Whom Gods Destroy."

these relationships were seldom equal partnerships. Most placed the man, for one reason or another, into a position of dominance over the woman. And these unions always ended by the close of the episode. None of the show's female love interests became recurring characters (unless you count Nurse Chapel, whose feelings for Spock were unrequited). As Karen Blair writes in *Meaning in Star Trek* (1977), the first book to seriously analyze the appeal of the series, "In almost every episode we have a different female guest star, which usually guarantees that the character she portrays will be alien and disposable."

Captain Kirk romanced dozens of women over the years but seemed to connect most strongly with Miramanee, the native woman he married and with whom he fathered a child while suffering from amnesia in "The Paradise Syndrome," and Edith Keeler from "The City on the Edge of Forever," for whom he's tempted to sacrifice the future of humanity. Miramanee remains blatantly subservient to Kirk—she literally worships the "god" known as "Kirok." The captain's relationship with Edith takes place on more even footing, but Kirk secretly possesses centuries more knowledge (her dream of the future is his past), giving him a secret, mental upper hand and a comforting feeling of superiority.

When McCoy falls in love, it's with Natrina (Katherine Woodville), high priestess of the Oracle from "For the World Is Hollow and I Have Touched the Sky." While she displays exemplary moral fiber and leadership skills, Natrina remains only a few steps ahead of Miramanee in her primitive understanding of the world around her. McCoy submits to her religious leadership in order to become her mate but soon disobeys her because he knows what's best for her people better than Natrina does.

Scotty, in "The Lights of Zetar," falls for Lieutenant Mira Romaine (Jan Shutan), a brilliant scientist who is (at least) his intellectual equal. But she's a young woman making her first deep space voyage and leans on the older, more seasoned Scotty for support and guidance. The engineer's attitude toward Romaine is remarkably paternal—doting and protective.

Of all *Star Trek*'s romances, Spock's relationships with Leila Kalomi (Jill Ireland) from "This Side of Paradise" and Zarabeth (Mariette Hartley) from "All Our Yesterdays" come the closest to being true partnerships between equals. But in both cases Spock is out of his mind, and he breaks off the relationship when he comes to his senses.

While it doesn't involve a primary character, the "romance" between Zefram Cochrane (Glenn Corbett) and the gaslike, electromagnetic entity known as the Companion from "Metamorphosis" also proves illuminating. The superhuman Companion rescues Cochrane from a disintegrating spacecraft and nurses him to health. She protects and feeds him, restores him to youth and prevents him from aging, taking care of all his worldly needs for 150 years. When he complains of loneliness, the Companion immobilizes a shuttlecraft and pulls it to her tiny planetoid home, where Kirk, Spock, McCoy, and the critically ill Commissioner Nancy Hedford (Elinor Donahue) are to remain as distractions for Cochrane. Despite all the affection she has shown him during their century and a half together, Cochrane rejects the Companion once he realizes her interest in him is romantic. He's only willing to embrace the Companion's love once she forsakes her nearly limitless power and joins with the mortal form of Commissioner Hedford. To become acceptable to Cochrane, the Companion literally disempowers herself. Plus, Commissioner Hedford (who we learn has "never known love") abandons her high-ranking career—in the middle of delicate negotiations to avert an interplanetary war, no less. Two powerful females essentially give up their jobs to get married, surrendering a galaxy full of possibilities to spend the rest of their lives on the outer space equivalent of a desert island as a housewife.

This seems to be the *Star Trek* feminine ideal. Certainly the relationship between Spock's parents, Sarek (Mark Lenard) and Amanda (Jane Wyatt), follows this traditional pattern. Kang (Michael Ansara) and Mara (Susan Howard)—the husband-and-wife Klingon warriors from "The Day of the Dove"— have one of the show's more enlightened relationships, but Mara serves under Kang's command. On the other hand, women who challenge the masculine power structure—like Janice Lester from "Turnabout Intruder" or Marta, the mad, man-killing Orion woman from "Whom Gods Destroy"—are portrayed as villains and monsters.

If *Star Trek* often failed to live up to its stated ideals of equality, perhaps we shouldn't judge Roddenberry and his writers too harshly. After all, in 1776, Thomas Jefferson wrote that "all men are created equal" and "endowed by their Creator with certain unalienable Rights." Yet when the Founding Fathers adopted the U.S. Constitution in 1787, they approved a government that kept millions of African Americans in slavery and denied women the right to vote. Sometimes these things take time.

Later *Star Trek* movies and series strived to correct the franchise's troubling sexism. In 1986, *Star Trek IV: The Voyage Home* depicted (for the first time) a female Starfleet captain—the unnamed commander of the USS *Saratoga*, played by Madge Sinclair. Later, Kathryn Janeway (Kate Mulgrew) commanded the starship *Voyager* for seven seasons. And the prequel series *Star Trek: Enterprise* tried to retrofit female leadership into the *Star Trek* universe by introducing Captain Erika Hernandez (Ada Maris) of the pre-Federation Starfleet.

Just as importantly, the later series often presented strong female officers who exercised sound judgment and showed strong leadership skills. Without being defeminized like Number One, characters such as Lieutenant Tasha Yar (Denise Crosby) from *The Next Generation*, Chief Engineer B'Elanna Torres (Roxann Dawson) and Seven of Nine (Jeri Ryan) from *Voyager*, and Colonel Kira Nerys (Nana Visitor) from *Deep Space Nine* were capable of pulling their weight no matter what the situation demanded, up to and including a firefight or a donnybrook. Characters like these compensated in large measure for the deficits of the classic *Trek* series, moving *Star Trek* toward the future it talked about but at first seemed unable to visualize.

# That Which Survives

*Star Trek* in the 1970s

# 35

# Obsession

## Syndication and the Power of Fandom

In the fall of 1969 *Star Trek* was dead.

Production of the series wrapped for good on January 9. By the time the final episode, "Turnabout Intruder," aired on June 3, the cast and crew had moved on to new assignments. Costumes had been mothballed and sets disassembled and packed off to the scene dock. NBC used the program as summer replacement fodder, airing reruns until the network's new shows premiered in September. But now it was over, gone, finished. Nearly everyone—even creator-producer Gene Roddenberry—assumed that, while *Star Trek* might be fondly remembered by its small but loyal audience, the program would quietly fade away. That's what cancelled shows did.

Or that's what *most* cancelled shows did. A few—usually the most successful series, perennial hits like *I Love Lucy*—continued to play in syndication, with repeats turning tidy profits thanks to their ongoing popularity. Unfortunately, *Star Trek*'s syndication prospects seemed dubious. Conventional wisdom dictated that a series needed to compile at least one hundred episodes to become a viable candidate for syndication; *Star Trek* had a meager seventy-nine. Besides, *Trek* was never very popular when it was new. Who would bother to watch its reruns?

But no one reckoned with the extraordinary devotion and fervor of the show's fans, who over the course of the next decade would resurrect *Star Trek*, turning the "failed" series into a cultural touchstone and a revenue-generating machine. *Trek*'s near-miraculous return from the grave was unprecedented, and it remains one of the most amazing stories in entertainment history. That tale begins not with Roddenberry, and certainly not with the suits at Paramount, but with the fans themselves.

### Rise of the "Trekkies"

DAW Books editor Arthur Sasha coined the term "Trekkie" during an interview with *TV Guide*'s Peter Hamill at the 1967 WorldCon in New York City. Sasha used the word to refer to the enthusiastic *Star Trek* fans that helped the show win Best Dramatic Presentation at that year's Hugo Awards. Hamill repeated the term in his article, and the word stuck. Eventually devotees would disassociate themselves from the "Trekkie" label or modify it to the less juvenile-sounding "Trekker."

By any name, however, *Star Trek* fans were a breed apart. Although many other movies, TV shows, and entertainers had inspired legions of energetic followers (Beatlemania springs to mind), no other fan base held such a sense of ownership for their object of adoration, or exerted such influence on its development. Thanks in no small measure to the two triumphant "Save *Star Trek*" letter-writing campaigns mounted following the series' first and second seasons, fans felt an intimate connection with the program. *Star Trek* belonged to them because they believed their efforts had rescued it. And with the Roddenberrian optimism of the show itself, many believed that somehow, some way, they could save *Star Trek* yet again.

Backing this staunch faith was a depth of emotional, intellectual, and financial investment that outstripped anything previously engendered by a television show. Many fans were profoundly inspired by *Star Trek*'s vision of a near-utopian future for the human race and refused to surrender the dream to the whims of network programmers. Some were spurred to activism, volunteering in community programs or in support of progressive political causes, with an eye toward building the future Roddenberry had imagined. With no new episodes—and, at the very beginning, no episodes at all—to watch, fans began writing their own *Star Trek* stories and then publishing their own magazines to share these stories. Fans also voted with their wallets, buying *Star Trek* products of all sorts as they appeared, quickly turning a trickle of books, models, toys, and other memorabilia into a veritable flood of merchandise. (For more on this, see Chapters 41 and 42, "The Damn Books" and "A Piece of the Action.") They formed clubs and held conventions. But the most important thing they did was simple: Once *Star Trek* made its unlikely return to television, they tuned in.

## Vindication Through Syndication

In 1958, the Henry J. Kaiser Corporation, a U.S. conglomerate that included Kaiser Aluminum and other heavy industrial ventures, acquired independent KULA-TV in Honolulu and launched Kaiser Broadcasting. By the mid-1960s, Kaiser Broadcasting had acquired or started a chain of eight independent stations across the U.S.—including WKGB in Boston, WFLD in Chicago, and KBSC in Los Angeles—and was competing aggressively with network affiliates in major markets. Kaiser executives, who thought *Star Trek* might serve as effective counter-programming against network stations' local and national newscasts, began negotiating for syndication rights while the series was still on the air. Kaiser programmers knew that *Star Trek* had an intensely loyal, mostly young audience and that young viewers seldom watched the news. In late 1969, WKBS in Philadelphia became the first station to air syndicated reruns of *Star Trek*. Running at 6 p.m., the show exceeded all expectations, earning far better ratings than it ever had for NBC.

Encouraged, Kaiser rolled out the series to the rest of its stations in 1970 and even hired former cast members to record voice-over plugs for the show.

For instance, station WKBF in Cleveland ran a plug in which Leonard Nimoy intoned, "This is Mr. Spock of the starship *Enterprise*. Logic would dictate that if you are a fan of fast-moving adventure, you'll stay tuned for *Star Trek* . . . coming up next on Channel 61." Soon, *Trek* was trouncing local newscasts in the ratings in cities like Boston, Detroit, and, with an assist from Mr. Spock, Cleveland. Kaiser's success vindicated Gene Roddenberry, who had argued with NBC executives throughout *Star Trek*'s three network seasons that all his series needed to become a hit was a more favorable time slot.

Owner-operators of independent stations in other markets noted Kaiser's success and quickly moved to duplicate it, purchasing *Star Trek* and running it during the dinner hour. In cities without independent stations, many network affiliates purchased the show and ran it at other times of day. Ratings were so good that stations began editing the episodes, removing or shortening minor scenes to free up two or three additional minutes of advertising space. As a result, until the dawn of the home video era,

In the 1970s, many stations, including WGN in Chicago, ran *Star Trek* reruns five nights a week.

it became difficult to see *Star Trek* in its original uncut form. In many markets, the show was "stripped," running five days a week, Monday through Friday. With only seventy-nine episodes, this meant that stations cycled through the repeats quickly, but fans didn't seem to mind. Even as episodes reran for the third and fourth time, ratings continued to climb in most locations. "Instead of getting bored, fans of *Star Trek* actually seemed to enjoy watching repeats of our repeats, studying every episode to the point where they not only knew each storyline but most of the dialogue as well," William Shatner wrote in his book *Star Trek Movie Memories*. By 1972, *Star Trek* was running in more than one hundred cities across the U.S. and in fifty-five foreign countries, from Argentina to Zambia.

## A Raft of Cons

*Star Trek*'s previously unimaginable popular resurgence attracted the attention of the mainstream media, who began referring to *Trek* as "the Show That Wouldn't Die." Reporters from the *New York Times*, the Los Angeles Times News Service, and the Associated Press seemed baffled by the series' belated success. "Nothing fades faster than a canceled television series they say," wrote AP reporter Jerry Buck in a March 1972 feature. "So how come *Star Trek* won't go away?"

The answer was simple: *Star Trek* became the Show That Wouldn't Die because it had the Fans Who Wouldn't Quit. What's more, those devotees were uncommonly well organized, thanks in part to mailing lists and other infrastructure created for the letter-writing campaigns of 1967 and '68. As the show gained popularity in syndication, the old "Save *Star Trek*" rallying cry morphed into a new mantra: "*Star Trek* Lives!"

Despite the largely erroneous stereotype of "Trekkies" as wallflowers and misfits, the shows' fans have always been highly social creatures, and scores of *Star Trek* fan clubs formed while the series remained in production. In the early 1970s, those groups found many eager new members, and many additional clubs were founded. There is no way to compile a comprehensive tally of all these small, grassroots organizations, but Gerry Turnbull's 1979 book *A Star Trek Catalog* provided names and mailing addresses for 279 fan clubs across the U.S, twenty-one Canadian organizations, and twenty other groups scattered from Great Britain to Japan.

In 1971, a small group of New York fans (including Joan Winston, who later coauthored the book *Star Trek Lives* and wrote *The Making of the Trek Conventions*) pooled their resources, rented space at the Statler Hilton Hotel in Manhattan and launched the first widely publicized *Star Trek* convention. Organizers lined up Gene Roddenberry, Majel Barrett, Dorothy Fontana, and science fiction author Isaac Asimov to appear at the event and assembled a display of real-life space

Flyer for the 1975 International *Star Trek* Convention in New York City.

artifacts provided by NASA. Roddenberry agreed to preside over screenings of the series' original pilot, "The Cage," and the soon-to-be-famous *Trek* blooper reel. The convention, which also featured a costume contest, a fan art show, and a room full of dealers selling *Trek* souvenirs, was expected to draw 500 patrons. More than 3,000 showed up, overwhelming the Statler Hilton from January 21 through 23, 1972.

*Star Trek* clubs across the U.S. moved quickly to pull together their own gatherings. Over the course of the next six years, conventions (or "cons," in fan parlance) were held in Boston, Philadelphia, the District of Columbia, Huntsville, Houston, Dallas, Kansas City, and many other locations, with attendance far exceeding expectations at most events. The New York convention became an annual affair, moving to larger venues (and overfilling them) each year for the first half of the decade. It attracted 6,000 fans in 1973 and 15,000 in 1974. Sixteen thousand fans turned out when the entire cast reunited for the first time for a convention at the Hilton Hotel in Chicago, August 22–24, 1975. The following year, twenty-five *Star Trek* conventions were held across the U.S. and Canada. Glendale, California–based Creation Entertainment began producing *Star Trek* conventions at various sites in the early 1970s. (Creation is now the licensed host of the Official Star Trek Convention, held annually in Las Vegas, which attracts over 15,000 fans annually, as well as several smaller events scattered across the country.)

These events helped fans connect with one another in that bygone era prior to Facebook, Twitter, or even e-mail. They helped foster the growing market for *Star Trek* memorabilia and ephemera. And they provided a steady source of income for former cast members, many of whom fell on hard times in the 1970s. (For more on this, see Chapter 38, "Shore Leave.") The cons also gave actors such as James Doohan, George Takei, Walter Koenig, and Nichelle Nichols, who earned little recognition while the show was on the air, the chance to bask in the glow of adoring fans.

## The Fanzine Phenomenon

One of the hottest-selling items in the dealer's rooms at the *Star Trek* cons of the early 1970s were fanzines, fan-written publications with imaginative titles such as *Warped Space, Beyond Antares*, and *Saurian Brandy Digest*. The very first *Trek* zine ever created, *Spockanalia*, was a one-shot sold at the 1967 Science Fiction WorldCon, where the word "Trekkie" was coined. Four years later, when the first *Star Trek* convention was held in New York, more than one hundred *Trek* fanzines were in operation.

These zines varied widely both in appearance—from amateurish, mimeographed booklets with crude black-and-white fan-drawn cover art to professional-looking, custom-printed efforts with full-color cover photos—and in content. Some included interviews with the cast and crew (often transcribed from convention appearances), in-depth reviews of individual episodes, analysis of the show's philosophical and ethical themes, or explanations of various Treknological devices. However, most of the zines existed solely to publish fan-written fiction. The popularity of this peculiar literary form owed a great deal to simple need: If you were looking for original *Star Trek* stories in the early '70s, the fanzines were the only game in town. Writers of fan fiction, according to the authors of *Star Trek Lives!* (1975), "have become so entranced with that world that they simply cannot bear to let it die and will recreate it themselves if they have to—or given half a chance."

Like the zines themselves, these stories also varied widely in their quality and nature. A few were worthy of professional publication (and a handful eventually *were* published in Pocket Books' *Star Trek: The New Voyages* anthologies in the late 1970s), but most were clumsy and rough-hewn. Some writers attempted to recreate the kind of idea-driven yet action-packed tales that were the hallmark of *Star Trek*, delving into characters and concepts introduced but not fully explored in various episodes. Most fan fiction was penned by women and often reflected the romantic fantasies of the author. So-called "Mary Sue" stories, in which the writer introduced a female character (usually a thinly veiled stand-in for the author herself) to serve as a romantic interest for one of the show's cast members (usually Spock or Kirk) quickly became a fan fiction cliché.

The most controversial tales to emerge from the fanzines were those commonly referred to as "Kirk/Spock," "K/S," or simply "slash" fiction, which depicts a homosexual relationship between Captain Kirk and his first officer. Many of these stories employ the Vulcan mating cycle as a plot device, with Kirk and Spock trapped alone on a remote planet (or a similar locale) and Spock suddenly going into *pon farr*; to save the life of his friend, Kirk must have sex with Spock. Initially, "slash" fiction and other sexually explicit stories were relatively rare, but a hefty percentage of fan fiction written today is sexual in nature, often homo- or sado-erotic.

According to Joan Marie Verba's self-published *Boldly Writing: A Trekker Fan and Zine History, 1967–1987*, a meticulously researched history of nonprofessional *Trek* publications, there were 176 zines in print in 1973. By 1977, the number had grown to 458 publications. Gene Roddenberry tolerated and even encouraged the fan press, despite the fact that every issue represented a blatant violation of his cherished *Star Trek* copyright. Surprisingly, Paramount also took (and continues to take) a laissez-faire attitude, permitting fans to publish zines, produce artwork, recordings, and even semipro movies as long as these works were produced on a not-for-profit basis. As a result, fan fiction continues to flourish. Although fanzines have faded into memory (most folded in the 1990s), numerous websites now compile and publish fan-written *Trek* tales free of charge.

Clubs, conventions and zines helped keep fans in contact with one another, and provided a platform for united action toward the primary goal of Trekkers everywhere: the return of *Star Trek*.

In 1971, the same year as the first *Trek* convention, the Star Trek Association for Revival (STAR) was formed. Over the course of the next four years, STAR organized various efforts aimed at pressuring Paramount and/or NBC into reviving *Star Trek* as a TV series or feature film. In its first newsletter, published in May 1972, STAR took a page from the old "Save *Star Trek*" playbook and urged true believers to write Paramount and NBC to demand the return of *Trek*. "How often should you write? Would it be difficult for anyone to write one letter a week?" asked the newsletter (reprinted in *Boldly Writing*). "Then get your friends, cousins, fellow workers, school mates, etc., to write, too. The more letters the better. Let us keep burying Paramount in an avalanche of letters." Eventually, STAR claimed 160 local chapters and compiled a mailing list with more than 25,000 names and addresses of *Star Trek* fans across the U.S. But the organization grew too large for its volunteer leadership to manage and disintegrated in late 1975.

By then, however, Paramount had gotten the message, and *Star Trek* was on its way back. But the voyage home would prove to be long and troubled.

An amusing assortment of vintage 1970s bumper stickers.

# 36

# Amok Time

## Post-*Trek* Projects by Gene Roddenberry, 1970–77

D uring the years that elapsed between the cancellation of *Star Trek* and the franchise's big-screen revival, the restlessly creative Gene Roddenberry developed more than a dozen concepts for movies and TV shows. Most of those ideas went nowhere, and the handful eventually produced met with far less success than *Trek*—or even *The Lieutenant.* Yet all these projects—a big-screen sex comedy, three failed sci-fi TV pilots, and an unsold horror series pilot—remain fascinating for the clues they provide to future *Star Trek* series and for what they reveal about Roddenberry's personality and artistic impulses.

### Pretty Maids All in a Row (1971)

Disillusioned by the cancellation of *Star Trek*, and with no inkling yet of the popular resurgence the program would soon enjoy, Roddenberry turned his back on television and, as the 1960s drew to a close, shifted his focus to motion pictures. A bitter and financially punishing divorce from his first wife, the former Eileen Rexroat, placed Roddenberry in a short-term monetary bind. Fortunately for the erstwhile Great Bird of the Galaxy, an old friend threw Roddenberry a financial and creative lifeline. Herb Solow, who, as Executive in Charge of Production at Desilu, had been instrumental in the sale of *Star Trek* to NBC, was now working as a vice president at Metro-Goldwyn-Mayer Studios. When *Trek* folded, Solow hired Roddenberry to create and develop feature film concepts for MGM. Roddenberry's first idea—a racy Tarzan movie—never progressed beyond the outline stage. On a trip to Japan in August 1969 to scout locations for another unrealized project, Roddenberry married his longtime mistress, Majel Barrett, in a Shinto-Buddhist ceremony.

Then in 1970, Solow assigned Roddenberry to develop a screenplay based on Francis Pollini's salacious 1968 novel *Pretty Maids All in a Row*, a dark comedy about a high school guidance counselor/football coach who seduces female students and then murders some of them (the ones who fall in love and ask him to leave his wife and daughter). Roddenberry's screenplay transformed Coach Michael "Tiger" McDrew into an exaggerated reflection of the Great

Bird himself, a decorated WWII veteran who espouses progressive sociopolitical theories and who possesses an apparently unquenchable thirst for sex.

The project received a green light from Solow, with Roddenberry attached as both producer and screenwriter. Roddenberry hired *Star Trek* veterans for key posts, including costume designer Bill Theiss and actors James Doohan and Bill Campbell (the Squire of Gothos himself), who appear in minor roles as police officers. MGM stacked the cast list with major stars—including Rock Hudson as Tiger McDrew, joined by Angie Dickinson as a teacher and Telly Savalas as an FBI agent—and hired Frenchman Roger Vadim, maker of saucy hits like *And God Created Woman* (1956) and *Barbarella* (1968), to direct. But Roddenberry and Vadim, who was shooting his first Hollywood-made feature, immediately clashed. Appalled by what he considered Vadim's mistreatment of his script, Roddenberry learned the hard way that, while writers and producers hold sway in the world of television, motion pictures are a director's medium. When the studio backed Vadim, the incensed Roddenberry stormed off to an undisclosed location (a hotel in La Costa, California), where he remained hidden until the shoot was nearly complete, occasionally sending his secretary to the set for a report on the proceedings. This behavior did not sit well with Solow, who phoned the set daily in search of his missing producer.

During postproduction, Roddenberry oversaw extensive reediting of Vadim's director's cut. The result was a muddled film that clearly reflected the vision of neither its director nor its producer. *Pretty Maids All in a Row* was one of the first major studio films to feature extensive nudity, and MGM took the unprecedented step of promoting it with a spread in the April 1971 issue of *Playboy* magazine, featuring an article about the picture by Vadim and nude photos of the eight ingénues billed as "the Pretty Maids." Perhaps as a result, although Roddenberry disdained the movie and MGM execs were less than elated with it, *Pretty Maids* turned a tidy profit.

## Genesis II (1973) and Planet Earth (1974)

Bruised by his first encounter with feature filmmaking, Roddenberry returned to television, the medium of his greatest triumphs. In May 1972, while *Star Trek* was defying all odds to emerge as a ratings sensation in syndication, Warner Brothers hired Roddenberry to create a new science fiction TV franchise, hoping he could duplicate the lighting-in-a-bottle genius of *Trek*. But the prospective series, *Genesis II*, fell far short of those lofty expectations.

The seventy-four-minute pilot episode (which aired as a Movie of the Week on March 23, 1973) follows the adventures of Dylan Hunt, a NASA scientist awakened in the year 2133 after a suspended animation experiment gone haywire. (Hunt can be revived either by drugs or, in a quintessentially Roddenberrian flourish, by sexual arousal.) During his 154-year hibernation, Earth was devastated by a nuclear war. Now Pax, a group of scientifically advanced, do-gooding pacifists, are attempting to bring progress and prosperity to the scattered, battered peoples of the world. But Pax is opposed by a city-state full of war-mongering mutants bent on global domination.

Roddenberry wanted Lloyd Bridges to star as Hunt, but network executives forced him to accept B-movie regular Alex Cord instead. Roddenberry cast Mariette Hartley and Ted ("Lurch") Cassidy, both of whom had guest starred on *Trek*, in key supporting roles. Majel Barrett, who would appear in all of Roddenberry's TV projects of the 1970s, also played a minor character. Roddenberry engaged the services of cinematographer Gerry Finnerman, who shot sixty of the seventy-nine original *Trek* episodes, and *Trek* costume designer Bill Theiss, who helped lend the new series a far darker, more savage look and feel than *Star Trek*. Unfortunately, Roddenberry's *Genesis II* teleplay recreated the primary shortcomings of his script for *Trek*'s initial pilot, "The Cage"—too little action and a tendency to bog down in pseudointellectual discussions. (It also suffered from some uncharacteristically clunky dialogue and a few hackneyed plot devices.) *Genesis II* was developed in conjunction with CBS, but the network ultimately rejected the series in favor of *Planet of the Apes*, a similarly postapocalyptic program spun off from the popular feature film franchise. Although it must have seemed like the safer bet, *Planet of the Apes* was cancelled in midseason after just fourteen episodes.

Roddenberry was loath to abandon *Genesis II*, for which he had developed an elaborate proposal, complete with character outlines and thumbnail sketches for more than a dozen projected episodes. He would rework some of this material for future projects, including a story called "Robot's Return" that eventually became the basis for *Star Trek: The Motion Picture* (1979). But in the meantime, Roddenberry took another proposed *Genesis II* episode, "The Poodle Shop," and expanded it to serve as a revised pilot telefilm. ABC was intrigued enough to provide production funds, and the project moved forward under the new title *Planet Earth*. John Saxon replaced Cord as the reawakened Dylan Hunt, who this time falls prisoner to a tyrannical matriarchy ("women's lib gone mad," according to Hunt) where men are kept drugged and docile to serve as manual laborers and sex slaves.

In Saxon, who was among those originally considered for the captaincy of the starship *Enterprise*, *Planet Earth* boasted a more appealing leading man than *Genesis II*, and its screenplay was far livelier and action oriented. The cast again featured Cassidy and Barrett, this time joined by Diana Muldaur, who had guest starred in two classic *Trek* episodes and would appear as Dr. Pulaski during the second season of *The Next Generation*. Cinematographer Archie Dalzell and art director Robert Kinoshita gave *Planet Earth* a gleaming, futuristic look (in contrast to the ramshackle dystopia of *Genesis II*), and Theiss designed snazzy body suits for Pax team members not dissimilar to the uniforms later worn by Starfleet officers on *Next Gen*, *Deep Space Nine*, and *Voyager*. Even though *Planet Earth* corrected many of the failings of *Genesis II*, ABC ultimately rejected the series. The pilot ran as a Movie of the Week on April 23, 1974.

The cast of Gene Roddenberry's failed pilot *Planet Earth* featured (from left to right) Ted Cassidy, John Saxon, Janet Margolin, and Christopher Cary.

After this setback, Roddenberry was ready to move on, but Warner Brothers—who owned the rights to the property—created a third pilot without Roddenberry's participation (or even a credit). Titled *Strange New World*, this version starred Saxon as Captain Anthony Vico, one of three astronauts who return to a postapocalyptic Earth after spending 180 years in suspended animation. Like its two predecessors, *Strange New World* failed to sell. It aired as a Movie of the Week on July 13, 1975. Additionally, some of Roddenberry's *Genesis II/Planet Earth* material resurfaced posthumously, incorporated into Robert Hewis Wolfe's Canadian series *Andromeda*, which ran five seasons, from 2000 to 2005, coproduced by Wolfe and Majel Barrett-Roddenberry. *Andromeda*, set in the distant future, starred Kevin ("Hercules") Sorbo as Captain Dylan Hunt, who awakens after spending 300 years frozen in time to help restore the Commonwealth, an intergalactic, interspecies coalition that has fallen into decline during his long absence.

## The Questor Tapes (1974)

Developed simultaneously with *Planet Earth*, *The Questor Tapes* was perhaps the most promising of all Roddenberry's 1970s pilots, and certainly the one of greatest interest to *Star Trek* historians.

Technician Jerry Robinson (Mike Farrell), working from plans and components created by Nobel Prize–winning scientist Dr. Emil Vaslovic, assembles a fantastically advanced, superhuman android code-named Questor (Robert Foxworth). Then Questor takes off on his own in search of Vaslovic, who has mysteriously disappeared. The android takes Robinson along as an at-first reluctant guide. Robinson's boss, Dr. Geoff Darrow (John Vernon), believes Robinson has stolen Questor and launches an international manhunt (and robot hunt) to find the duo. Ultimately, Vlasovic is revealed to be an android himself; now near death, Vlasovic informs Questor that he is the last in a series of extraterrestrial robots that have covertly assisted mankind over the millennia. However, due to Darrow's clumsy attempts to decipher Vlasovic's programming, Questor has lost the ability to feel love and other emotions. To fulfill his mission, he must partner with Robinson, who will serve as Jiminy Cricket to Questor's superpowered Pinocchio.

Roddenberry adored this concept, developed at Universal for NBC, which he believed had the potential to be even more successful than *Star Trek*. The show's Spock-like, emotionless title character gave the Great Bird a platform for wry commentary on the foibles of the human species. *The Questor Tapes* stands as Roddenberry's most overtly philosophical/theological teleplay. When Robinson suggests Vaslovic might be insane, Questor replies, "One's creator insane? Interesting question. How would you answer that query in your own case?"

Aside from Barrett and Walter Koenig, who have cameos playing lab techs, the only ex-*Trek* regular who worked on *Questor* was Gene Coon, who coauthored the teleplay with Roddenberry. But this wasn't the original plan. Roddenberry had conceived the show, originally titled *Mister Q*, as a vehicle for Leonard Nimoy. The already strained relationship between Roddenberry and Nimoy further deteriorated when (by network edict) Foxworth was cast in the title role—and Nimoy learned of his ouster from director Richard Colla, *not* from Roddenberry. NBC paired Foxworth with costar Farrell, who would soon gain fame as Captain B. J. Hunnicut on *M*A*S*H*.

Initially, the network seemed satisfied with *The Questor Tapes*—pleased enough with the pilot to order a half-season's worth of episodes and schedule the series for 10 o'clock Fridays, immediately following another promising rookie series, *The Rockford Files*. But while Roddenberry assembled his creative team and began preproduction, NBC executives had second thoughts about the concept and demanded wholesale changes to the scenario. The network wanted the Jerry Robinson character written out, and the business about extraterrestrials aiding humankind eliminated, in order to reshape *The Questor Tapes* as an action-adventure show with a lone robot on the run from the military and law enforcement, a science fictional variation on the theme of *The Fugitive*. CBS would later score a hit with a similar concept—*The Incredible Hulk*, featuring a superhero on the lam. But Roddenberry would have none of it. Rather than surrender what he considered the heart and soul of the program, he shut down the entire project. No episodes were produced, although the pilot appeared as a Movie of the Week on January 23, 1974.

Readers by now will have recognized Questor as the forerunner of Data, the android science officer whose popularity would help make *The Next Generation* an astounding success more than a decade later. (At one point, Questor informs a human female that he is "fully functional.") The idea of an alien race working secretly for the benefit of mankind also recalls Roddenberry's proposed *Trek* spin-off starring the character Gary Seven (from the episode "Assignment: Earth"). In 2003, writer-producer Herbert J. Wright (creator of the Ferengi for *Next Gen*) announced plans to reboot *The Questor Tapes*, but Wright was stricken by illness the following year and passed away in 2005 at age fifty-seven. Rod Roddenberry, Gene and Majel's son (who was born thirteen days after the initial

Mike Farrell and Robert Foxworth (on table) starred in Roddenberry's *The Questor Tapes.*

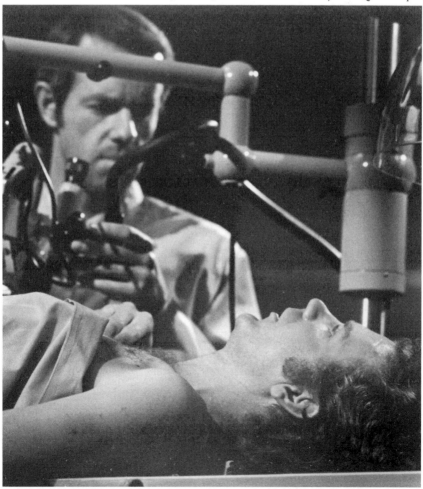

broadcast of *The Questor Tapes*), announced in early 2010 that Roddenberry Productions would partner with producer-director Ron Howard's Imagine Television to create a new *Questor* pilot. As of late 2011, however, no further reports on the project had appeared.

## Spectre (1977)

The most offbeat of Roddenberry's 1970s pilots, *Spectre* costarred Robert Culp and Gig Young as a Holmes-and-Watson-like pair of criminologists who solve paranormal cases involving witchcraft, demon-conjuring, and other supernatural phenomena. In the pilot film, William Sebastian (Culp) and his sidekick "Ham" Hamilton (Young) become embroiled in the mysterious goings on at the estate of a wealthy Englishman who may have accidentally unleashed an ancient demon—Asmodeus, who corrupts human souls through lust and debauchery (and looks a lot like the Gorn). *Spectre*'s basic premise was intriguing, its script—cowritten with Samuel A. Peeples, who had penned "Where No Man Has Gone Before"—was solid, and its leads were likeable. The project also offered Barrett a plum supporting role as Sebastian's enigmatic assistant Lilith, a "good witch" who casts a spell to cure Ham's alcoholism. The pilot was shot in Herefordshire, England, with a mostly British crew and cast, including featured players Gordon Jackson (best remembered from the BBC's *Upstairs, Downstairs*)

Roddenberry mailed this flyer to his Lincoln Enterprises memorabilia customers, urging them to write NBC in support of his horror series pilot *Spectre.*

# SPECTRE
## IS COMING
### NBC — May 21st, 1977 — 9:00-11:00 P.M.
#### Classic horror-SUPERNATURAL DRAMA

Gene Roddenberry, creator of the highly successful "Star Trek" series, which has become an international cult, went to England for the first time as a movie producer to make "Spectre," 20th Century-Fox Television's two-hour horror-supernatural drama for NBC-TV. Roddenberry also wrote the screenplay for "Spectre" with Sam Peeples.

"As much as I like science fiction, I wanted to get away from being completely locked into it," said Roddenberry. "It was my wife (actress Majel Barrett) who suggested my investigating the power of supernatural forces which could be present in today's society. In "Spectre" I am attempting to trace the possible influence on international crime."

"Spectre" stars Robert Culp ("I Spy" television series is one of his best known) and Gig Young (who turned in an Academy Award-winning role in "They Shoot Horses, Don't They?").

Two of Britain's best-known actors are co-starred — Gordon Jackson, who plays the butler in "Upstairs, Downstairs" on television, and John Hurt, who won an award for "The Naked Civil Servant." James Villiers and Ann Bell head a strong supporting British cast. Miss Barrett also plays a top key role. Award-winning Clive Donner ("The Caretaker") directed.

"Spectre" — which is aimed as a possible series next season on NBC-TV — is set mainly in and around a magnificent country mansion, part of an Abbey built 400 years ago in the countryside of Hertfordshire, England. Having been expanded over the years it is now known as All Saints Pastoral Center. Its fine Gothic architecture provided the correct huge and sometimes awesome setting for the film.

and John Hurt (before his breakout roles in *Alien* in 1979 and *The Elephant Man* in 1980). But *Spectre*, developed for 20th Century-Fox Television in partnership with NBC, was undone by budget constraints and production problems. Cinematographer Arthur Ibbetson shot *Spectre* in the flat, overlit style of most 1970s British teleplays, devoid of the shadowy, spooky ambiance a show of this type demanded. And the story's orgiastic human sacrifice finale was rendered laughable by cut-rate visual effects and shoddy sets and costumes.

The network passed on the series but ran the pilot as a Movie of the Week on May 21, 1977. Roddenberry, who frequently appeared at conventions during the 1970s, both to pad his purse with appearance fees and to promote his new projects, did his best to drum up interest in *Spectre* prior to its initial broadcast. In a last ditch effort, he sent a mailer to customers of his Lincoln Enterprises memorabilia business, urging fans to write the network. "NBC *may* consider it as a weekly series *if* enough show interest in *Spectre*," the pamphlet suggested. But this gambit, fashioned after the Save *Star Trek* letter-writing campaigns of the 1960s, failed. *Spectre* also received a theatrical release in England, with topless footage cut into the picture's climactic black mass sequence.

In addition to these projects, the energetic Roddenberry cranked out a fistful of other orphaned television concepts during the 1970s, including *Magna I*, another dystopian scenario (with peace-loving sea-dwellers pitted against warlike land-lubbers), and the alien invasion epic *Battleground: Earth*, both of which were briefly attached to 20th Century-Fox Television. Neither project advanced beyond preliminary development during Roddenberry's lifetime. But *Battleground: Earth*, which foresaw similar series such as NBC's hit *V* (1983–85), was eventually retitled *Gene Roddenberry's Earth: Final Conflict* and produced posthumously for Canadian television, where it ran for five seasons from 1997 to 2002. Majel Barrett-Roddenberry served as executive producer for the show and appeared in a few first-season episodes as Dr. Julianne Belman. Ironically, of all Roddenberry's 1970s endeavors, the project that enjoyed the most success at the time was the one in which Roddenberry was least involved, and which he later disowned: The *Star Trek* animated series, which ran for two seasons Saturday mornings on NBC and won an Emmy.

# 37

# Shore Leave

## Non-*Trek* Projects for the *Enterprise* Crew, 1969–78

F or the former crew of the starship *Enterprise, Star Trek*'s resurgent popularity during the early 1970s created more problems than it solved. During the show's initial network run, only stars William Shatner and Leonard Nimoy had become famous enough to be readily associated with their twenty-third-century alter egos. But as *Trek* became a pop culture phenomenon in syndication, DeForest Kelley, James Doohan, Nichelle Nichols, George Takei, and Walter Koenig became synonymous with McCoy, Scotty, Uhura, Sulu, and Chekov, with lamentable consequences for future employment. Doohan, for instance, was a master of many accents who had played a wide variety of character roles prior to *Trek*. Suddenly, however, he found himself typecast as a flinty Scotsman (and constantly pestered by fans to speak in Scotty's burr). Worse yet, Doohan and friends weren't receiving any compensation for the reruns that were choking the life out of their careers. Under the Screen Actors Guild contracts of the era, actors were compensated only for the first five repeats of any given TV episode. By the early 1970s, those first five reruns (and the skimpy residual checks they generated) were long gone, leaving most ex-*Trek* cast members up Unemployment Creek without a paddle. To survive, some were forced to explore new endeavors.

### William Shatner

Predictably, Shatner weathered this stormy era best. As the lone *Star Trek* regular previously recognizable to many viewers (thanks to the short-lived *For the People* and his frequent guest roles on other series), he was not as rigidly defined by Captain Kirk as the rest of the cast were by their *Trek* characters. Producers and casting directors remained enamored of Shatner's charisma and work ethic, and the actor capitalized accordingly, resuming the hectic schedule he had maintained during the early 1960s.

Between the cancellation of *Star Trek* in 1969 and the release of *Star Trek: The Motion Picture* in 1979, Shatner racked up fifty-five appearances on various television shows, miniseries and made-for-TV movies, including *The Andersonville Trial* (1970). A prestigious PBS production directed by George C. Scott, this picture starred Shatner as an army lawyer prosecuting the former commandant of a

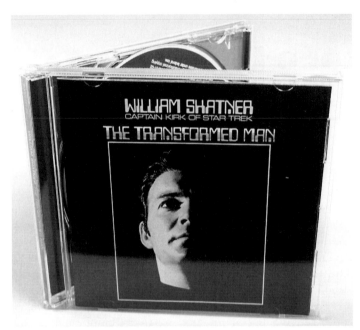

Rykodisc reissued William Shatner's 1968 album *The Transformed Man* on CD, to perplex and amuse a new generation of listeners.

hellish Confederate POW camp for war crimes. His sterling performance earned the actor some of the best reviews of his career. Shatner also landed the starring role in another series—the short-lived *Barbary Coast* (1975–76), a period adventure show with Shatner as a special agent on a secret mission from the governor of California to root out criminals in 1870s San Francisco. He also made five theatrical features. These included *The Devil's Rain* (1975), which pitted Shatner against a coven of devil-worshippers who use magic to melt their victims into goo. This film remains notable for its bizarre cast, which featured Ernest Borgnine, Ida Lupino, Eddie Albert, Keenan Wynn, Tom Skerritt, a young John Travolta, and Anton Sandor LaVey, the real-life founder of the Church of Satan, in addition to Shatner. The former captain of the *Enterprise* also starred in the low-budget *Kingdom of the Spiders* (1977). And as if that were insufficient, the workaholic performer appeared on stage in numerous regional theatrical productions and did voice work on the *Star Trek* animated series.

But of all Shatner's projects of the early 1970s, the one that had the greatest long-term impact on his career was his recording debut, *The Transformed Man* (1970), an LP's worth of Shakespearean monologues that segued into popular songs such as "Lucy in the Sky with Diamonds," "Mr. Tambourine Man," and "It Was a Very Good Year." Shatner didn't exactly sing these numbers; he talked through them, rendering them in the same halting, over-emotive manner with which he delivered soliloquies from *Hamlet* and *Henry the Fifth*. Saccharine strings and bombastic brass arrangements sent the record over-the-top. The result was an astonishingly awful but undeniably hilarious album that left listeners puzzled: Was Shatner really this rotten, or was he putting them on?

Upon its initial release, *The Transformed Man* was an unqualified debacle. Yet, over the years, it gained currency as a (probably unintentional) comedy classic. Based on the growing cult popularity of the record, Shatner was asked to perform Elton John's "Rocket Man" at the 1978 Science Fiction Film Awards. Shatner's vocal stylings reached a wider audience when Rhino Records included his "Lucy in the Sky" and "Tambourine Man" in its 1988 collection *Golden Throats: The Great Celebrity Sing-Off!*, which also featured a pair of tracks by Leonard Nimoy, not to mention Jack Webb crooning "Try a Little Tenderness" and Mae West belting out "Twist and Shout."

By the time *Golden Throats* appeared, Shatner's latest series, the crime drama *T. J. Hooker* (which ran on ABC and then on CBS from 1982 to 1986) had folded, leaving Shatner once again without a steady paycheck. A few years later, Shatner appeared as a lounge singer–like pitchman for Priceline.com, talk-singing his way through a succession of TV spots that enumerated the virtues of the online bargaining website. (Ernest Lupinacci, the advertising copywriter who dreamed up this campaign, was a confessed fan of *The Transformed Man.*) The commercials were a hit, and Shatner's career enjoyed a comedy-driven renaissance, including numerous guest appearances; a gig hosting *Saturday Night Live*; a recurring role on the sci-fi farce *3rd Rock from the Sun* (1999–2001) as John Lithgow's boss, "the Big Giant Head"; and a costarring part on the seriocomic *Boston Legal* (2004–2008). These comedic parts brought Shatner the critical recognition that had mostly eluded him in the past. For his work as the vain, crass, ethically ambiguous, yet endearing attorney Denny Crane on *Boston Legal*, Shatner won an Emmy in 2005 and earned four later nominations. Shatner has been a ubiquitous presence on TV ever since. In 2004, alt-rock singer-songwriter Ben Folds produced *Has Been*, Shatner's once-unthinkable second album. It earned mostly rave reviews.

## Leonard Nimoy

Of all the former *Enterprise* crew, the one who seemed best positioned for post-*Trek* success was Leonard Nimoy, who moved seamlessly from a low-rated show to a much more successful one. Just weeks after receiving official notice of *Star Trek*'s cancellation, Nimoy joined the cast of *Mission: Impossible*.

Also produced at Desilu, *M:I* had premiered on CBS the same fall as *Trek*, but while Gene Roddenberry's series struggled, producer Bruce Geller's show earned high ratings and won five Emmy Awards, including Best Dramatic Series in 1967 and '68. Nimoy was hired to replace Martin Landau, who, ironically, had been Roddenberry's second choice to play Spock. Landau and his costar/wife, Barbara Bain, both left *M:I* following its third season due to a salary dispute. Nimoy's character, Paris, was a virtual carbon copy of Landau's Rollin Hand—an actor, escape artist, and master of disguise who often appeared under heavy makeup and spoke with various accents.

At first, Nimoy enjoyed the part because it enabled him, in essence, to play a different role every week. But he soon grew bored. *Mission: Impossible* was a plot-driven rather than character-focused show with a rigid format: the self-destructing-tape opening scene (cue iconic theme music); followed by a scene in which Peter Graves (or, during Season One, Steven Hill) explained the mission to his team; then a scene where the team concluded preparations for the mission; and so on. Episodes invariably ended in freeze-frame as soon as the mission was complete, with no epilogue. *M:I*'s all-business team members seemed to have no private lives and seldom interacted with one another except as required by the job. When stars Hill, Bain, and Landau left the show, the loss of their characters was never explained. The show (which continued until 1973, was revived for two seasons from 1988 to 1990 and eventually spawned a feature film franchise) shrugged off even more cast turnover in the years ahead because its characters were considered interchangeable. After two dispiriting seasons, Nimoy quit *Mission: Impossible*. The experience proved so unfulfilling that in his book *I Am Spock* the actor confessed, "There are long periods of time where I forget I ever did the show!"

The cast of *Mission: Impossible* (back row, left to right: Peter Graves, Greg Morris, and Peter Lupus; front row: Nimoy and Dina Merrill) were all smiles in this publicity photo, but Nimoy soon grew disenchanted with his role.

This time around, however, there was no soft landing for Nimoy. Roddenberry had created a new series for the actor, *The Questor Tapes*, about a superhuman android, but NBC executives demanded Robert Foxworth replace Nimoy in the title role. (*Questor* never came to fruition anyway due to further network meddling—see the preceding chapter for details.) A fallow period ensued. Between 1971, when he left *M:I*, and the debut of the first *Trek* movie in 1979, Nimoy made just eight on-screen film and television appearances. In the 1978 remake of *Invasion of the Body Snatchers*, Nimoy delivered a finely nuanced, multilayered performance as a smarmy pop psychologist who may or may not be a Pod Person.

Nimoy also appeared on stage in various regional productions and supplemented his income with voice work. In addition to playing Spock on the *Star Trek* animated series, he narrated *In Search Of* (1976–82), a syndicated documentary series that dealt with paranormal topics such as Bigfoot, the Loch Ness Monster, and the Bermuda Triangle. His recording career ground to a halt following the release of *The New World of Leonard Nimoy* in 1970. (He had released four previous albums—*Mr. Spock's Music from Outer Space*, 1967; *The Way I Feel* and *Two Sides of Leonard Nimoy*, both 1968; and *The Touch of Leonard Nimoy*, 1969—all of which are more grueling listens than Shatner's *The Transformed Man*.) Unable to escape the shadow of Spock, and with opportunities dwindling both on the soundstage and in the recording studio, Nimoy began to explore new creative outlets.

He made his directorial debut with a 1973 episode of *Rod Serling's Night Gallery*, a vampire yarn called "Death on a Barge." It was the start of an enjoyable and remunerative second career. In addition to two profitable *Star Trek* features (*The Search for Spock*, 1984, and *The Voyage Home*, 1986), Nimoy went on to helm the comedy smash *Three Men and a Baby*, the highest-grossing picture of 1987. Around the same time that he began directing, Nimoy published his first book of poetry, *You & I* (1973). Six more collections of Nimoy's poems followed, three of which were published between 1974 and '78.

Not all his literary ventures met with as much success, however. He courted disaster by titling his 1977 memoir *I Am Not Spock*. Those who read the book, which is full of existential ruminations on the actor's complex relationship with his famous Vulcan alter ego, understood what Nimoy was trying to express. But based on the title alone, many fans (and, as he would later discover, producers) leapt to the erroneous conclusion that Nimoy hated Spock, hated *Star Trek*, and wanted to distance himself from the franchise. The ensuing flap damaged Nimoy's relationship with *Trek* and its fans for years. He finally healed the wound by penning a second memoir in 1995, which he titled *I Am Spock*.

## DeForest Kelley

During the late 1950s and early '60s, DeForest Kelley felt conflicted about his success as a Western villain. He disliked the narrow bandwidth of the roles but enjoyed the steady stream of paying jobs. His work on *Star Trek*—with the heroic

Dr. McCoy considered in contrast with his earlier black-hat parts—should have established Kelley as a talented and versatile character player capable of tackling a multitude of parts with skill and professionalism. It didn't. Instead, Kelley found he had merely exchanged one trap for another, far less lucrative one. Suddenly producers and casting directors saw Kelley only as the cantankerous country doctor, a part not in great demand at the time.

In the interregnum between *Star Trek* and *Star Trek: The Motion Picture*, Kelley landed a paltry eight TV guest appearances and a single motion picture credit. His lone film role was a thankless supporting part in the notorious bomb *The Night of the Lepus* (1972), starring Stuart Whitman, Rory Calhoun, Janet Leigh, and a passel of oversized killer bunny rabbits. Coincidentally, the cast also featured Paul Fix, who had played Dr. Piper in "Where No Man Has Gone Before" and was replaced by Kelley. *Night of the Lepus* was produced by A. C. Lyles, the man behind a long-running series of low-budget Westerns made during the 1950s and '60s, including Kelley's *Apache Uprising* (1965). Lyles hired Kelley as a favor to an old friend.

There was no denying the financial crisis facing the actor. Kelley's wife Carolyn, who for more than a decade had devoted herself to tracking her husband's residuals and handling his fan mail, was forced to resume her secretarial career. The Kelleys scraped by on Carolyn's salary, assisted by DeForest's unemployment checks and fees for his occasional appearances at *Star Trek* conventions. Although Kelley enjoyed these events and the opportunity they provided to bask in the adoration of the show's fans, he made fewer convention appearances than most other *Trek* regulars because he hated being away from his cherished L.A. bungalow, nicknamed Greenleaf. Voice work on the animated *Star Trek* series helped a bit, but by July 1974, Kelley was reduced to appearing at a dinner theater in Lubbock, Texas. Although the play went well, Kelley did not pursue similar bookings. For him, the weeks he spent in Texas appearing in the show *Beginner's Luck* had been torturous. As biographer Terry Lee Rioux explains in her book *From Sawdust to Stardust*, Kelley simply hated being away from Greenleaf—and from Carolyn.

## Nichelle Nichols

Even though she had one of the most impressive pre-*Trek* résumés of all the show's cast, with more than two decades of acting, singing, and dancing credits, the entertainment career of Nichelle Nichols nearly ground to a halt after the cancellation of *Star Trek*. Aside from the animated *Trek* series, she made only two television appearances during the 1970s. Her only film role was a supporting part—playing a vindictive hooker named Dorinda—in the blaxploitation picture *Truck Turner* (1974), starring Isaac Hayes. Nichols gained twenty-five pounds for the part, then had difficulty losing the extra weight, which only exacerbated her difficulty finding work. Her identification with Uhura also stunted her singing career. Nichols had recorded an R&B single ("Know What I Mean" b/w "Why

Pressbook ad for *Night of the Lepus*, the notorious killer bunny rabbit movie, which featured DeForest Kelley in a minor role. (He doesn't earn a mention in the ad.)

Don't You Do Right") for Epic Records in 1967, and a year later cut the album *Down to Earth*, which featured a mix of jazz standards (such as "The Lady Is a Tramp") and torch ballads (like "Tenderly"). But after *Trek*, bookings and recording offers dried up.

Along with James Doohan, George Takei, and Walter Koenig, Nichols became a frequent *Star Trek* convention guest. At one such event held in Chicago in 1975, Nichols met and befriended a guest speaker from NASA, Dr. Jesco

von Puttkamer. Through von Puttkamer, Nichols met several other NASA offi-
cials, many of whom were *Star Trek* fans. She frequently bemoaned the dearth
of women and minority trainees in NASA's astronaut corps. In September
1976, Nichols and the rest of the *Trek* cast, as well as creator-producer Gene
Roddenberry, attended a ceremony officially naming the prototype space
shuttle orbiter *Enterprise* after the now-iconic Starfleet flagship. Less than five
months later, John Yardley, who led manned spaceflight operations for NASA,
hired Nichols to lead an effort to recruit female and minority candidates for the
space shuttle program. Within four months, the number of women applying to
NASA for astronaut training increased from fewer than 100 to more than 1,600.
Among the many trainees recruited by Nichols and her team were Sally Ride,
the first American woman in space; Guy Bluford and Fred Gregory, two of the
first African American astronauts; and, sadly, three crew members killed in the
*Challenger* disaster of 1986—Ronald McNair, Ellison Onizuka, and Judy Resnick.

## James Doohan, George Takei, Walter Koenig, and Majel Barrett Roddenberry

Like Nichols, James Doohan, George Takei, and Walter Koenig worked sparingly
during the 1970s. The quartet, which Koenig nicknamed the "Gang of Four,"
probably earned more money from *Star Trek* conventions than from film and
television work. Doohan scraped together a meager five television guest spots
and two feature film roles during this era. Based on his exemplary work on the
animated *Star Trek* series, however, he earned a featured part as Commander
Canarvin on the Saturday morning cartoon show *Jason of Star Command* (1978–
80) and continued to do voice work for the remainder of his career. Takei fared
better, racking up fourteen TV appearances during the era, the most of all the
former *Trek* cast members except Shatner and Nimoy. Unfortunately, many of
these were minor "ethnic" roles, which the actor disliked. Walter Koenig snared
eight television parts, including a walk-on in Roddenberry's *The Questor Tapes*,
and launched a second career as a screenwriter, penning an episode of the *Star
Trek* animated series (even though he was the only regular cast member not to
appear on that show) as well as installments of three live-action series during
the 1970s. As is common for all working screenwriters, Koenig also made money
from treatments and story ideas that were never produced.

Majel Barrett Roddenberry tallied seven television appearances during the
1970s, including four in projects produced by her husband. She also landed
three feature film parts, including a memorable cameo as the robot madam
Miss Carrie in writer-director Michael Crichton's sci-fi thriller *Westworld* (1973).
But Barrett was also heavily involved in the management of Lincoln Enterprises,
the company Roddenberry founded to sell *Star Trek* souvenirs and related merchandise, and in managing the Great Bird of the Galaxy's busy itinerary of *Trek*
conventions and other speaking engagements. Increasingly, her most important
role was as Mrs. Gene Roddenberry, the "First Lady of *Star Trek*."

# 38

# Metamorphosis

## The Animated Adventures

S *tar Trek*'s return to television didn't begin with Gene Roddenberry. It started instead with Lou Scheimer, cofounder of Filmation Associates, which vied with Hanna-Barbera Productions and other animation studios in the mercurial, ultracompetitive Saturday morning cartoon market, where shows usually came and went quickly. In the early 1970s, Filmation was best known as the maker of *Fat Albert and the Cosby Kids* (1972–85), as well as numerous programs based on Archie Comics characters and DC Comics superheroes. Scheimer was always on the lookout for marketable properties with a built-in audience that might work in the half-hour animated format. And he was a *Star Trek* fan. So in 1972 Scheimer approached *Trek* creator-producer Roddenberry with the idea of reviving the series in cartoon form. Roddenberry was intrigued by Scheimer's proposal but dreaded dealing with Paramount Pictures, with whom he shared ownership of the franchise. Predictably, Paramount tried to wrest control of the project away from Roddenberry, but the Great Bird refused, afraid that without his oversight the animated *Star Trek* would become "Archie and Jughead go to the moon."

### Unfinished Business

Ultimately Roddenberry was retained as Executive Consultant (and paid $2,500 per episode), with full creative control over the series, although he delegated day-to-day production chores to his trusted associate Dorothy Fontana, who served as the show's story editor and associate producer. For Fontana, the animated series represented an opportunity to take care of unfinished business. "In 1969 when it [the live-action series] went off the air, we felt unfinished," said Fontana in an interview for a documentary included with the *Star Trek: The Animated Series* DVD collection. "We hadn't had a chance to complete the next voyages we had in mind, and this was one way to do it." The show utilized the same "Bible" as the live-action series, and Roddenberry approved all scripts, sometimes adding touches of his own.

To bring the animated series as close to the original as possible, Scheimer and Fontana brought in most of the cast from the live-action *Star Trek* to supply the voices of their characters. Initially, they planned to save money by hiring only William Shatner, Leonard Nimoy, DeForest Kelley, James Doohan, and

# Drawing Power!

**STAR TREK ANIMATED**
22 Animated Half-Hours in Color

**"THE BRADY KIDS"**
22 Animated Half-Hours in Color

Close-up of a *Variety* ad designed to entice local stations to purchase syndicated reruns of the *Star Trek* animated series and another Filmation cartoon, *The Brady Kids*.

Majel Barrett Roddenberry, who would work with members of Filmation's stable of voice artists. But Nimoy refused to participate unless Nichelle Nichols and George Takei voiced Uhura and Sulu. Doohan, Nichols, and Barrett Roddenberry wound up supplying voices for several other characters as well.

To further enhance the show's *Trek* bona fides, Fontana secured the services of screenwriters who had worked on the live-action program. A 1973 Screen Writers Guild strike worked in her favor. The strike prevented guild members from working on live-action movies and TV shows, but cartoon shows were exempt. So Fontana was able to commission teleplays from *Trek* veterans David Gerrold, Margaret Armen, Samuel Peeples, and Stephen Kandel, and purchase scripts from Joyce Perry, Larry Brody, and Larry Niven, all of whom had submitted scenarios to *Trek* that were never produced due to the show's cancellation. Walter Koenig, the only regular cast member left out of the animated show, also contributed a cartoon teleplay, as did Marc Daniels, who had directed more than a dozen episodes of the classic *Trek* series. Peeples, who wrote the second pilot for the live-action series ("Where No Man Has Gone Before"), wrote the first animated episode, "Beyond the Farthest Star."

Hiring top talent wasn't cheap, however. *Star Trek* became the most expensive Saturday morning cartoon on television, with production costs of $75,000 per episode. Since most of this money went to pay the cast, the writers, and Roddenberry, *Star Trek* didn't look any more impressive than other Saturday morning cartoons. In terms of animation, it met the usual Filmation standard—far below that of, for example, a Walt Disney feature film but on par with the Hanna-Barbera product of the period.

## But Is It *Trek*?

Despite Scheimer and Fontana's painstaking and costly efforts to shore up the show's credentials, however, the animated adventures' status within the *Trek* universe remains a matter of passionate debate. In the late 1980s, Roddenberry disowned the cartoon series, officially "de-canonizing" it in 1988 and declaring that he never would have agreed to make the animated show if he had had any idea the franchise would later return to live-action TV and feature films. Nevertheless, many other *Star Trek* insiders, including Fontana, remain adamant that the animated show is canon-worthy, and several elements introduced through it were later "canonized" by their repetition in later live-action programs. Among other items, Captain James T. Kirk's middle name—Tiberius—was first revealed in the animated installment "Bem" and later confirmed in the sixth feature film, *The Undiscovered Country*. And the holodeck, a concept utilized heavily by most of the later *Star Trek* series, first appeared in the animated adventure "The Practical Joker," where it was referred to as the "recreation room." Garfield and Judith Reeves-Stevens, fans of the cartoon show who served as writers and producers for *Star Trek: Enterprise*, intentionally used concepts from the animated series as often as possible to bring them into the canon.

For the most part, the animated show explored themes, ideas, and character relationships established by its live-action predecessor. But the cartoon introduced new elements as well. Freed from the production limitations of a live-action show, the *Enterprise* crew visited many more alien planets and encountered many more nonhumanoid species. These included two new members of the bridge crew, navigator Arax (voiced by Doohan), a three-armed, three-legged Edosian, and M'Ress (voiced by Barrett), a member of the catlike Caitian species, who served as the ship's backup communications officer. Stories were limited only by screenwriters' imaginations and the show's half-hour, kid-friendly format.

## Outstanding Episodes

**"Yesteryear"**—The most celebrated episode of the series was its second installment, "Yesteryear," written by Fontana. Mr. Spock and Captain Kirk have been conducting time-travel experiments using the Guardian of Forever (the trapezoidal gateway used to transport Kirk and Spock into the past during the classic live-action episode "The City on the Edge of Forever"). When the duo returns to the *Enterprise*, Spock finds that no one other than the captain recognizes him; in his place, the ship employs an Andorian first officer. Somehow, he and

Kirk have altered the timeline, resulting in Spock's death at age seven while undergoing the Vulcan ritual known as the Kahs-wan, in which children validate their maturity by fending for themselves alone in the desert. Spock uses the Guardian to travel into the past and save his own life. In so doing, he meets not only his younger self but also a younger version of his father, Sarek (voiced by Mark Lenard).

Several elements of Fontana's "Yesteryear" scenario were later accepted as canon, including the Vulcan rite of Kahs-wan and city of Shikahr (both of which were later discussed or depicted on *Star Trek: Enterprise*). "Yesteryear" also showed Spock's pet sehlat, a saber-toothed, doglike animal first mentioned in the live-action "Journey to Babel." His sehlat, I-Chaya, is mortally wounded during the adventure, which plays like a Vulcan variation on the theme of *Old Yeller*. Director J. J. Abrams revived the idea of Spock traveling in time to meet a younger version of himself for his 2009 feature film *Star Trek*. Producers submitted this episode to the National Academy of Television Arts and Sciences for consideration in the category of Outstanding Entertainment Children's Series at the First Annual Daytime Emmy Awards. It earned a nomination but failed to win.

**"The Lorelei Signal"**—Written by Margaret Armen, who had penned three live-action episodes, "The Lorelei Signal" stands out as more boldly feminist than any episode of the classic *Trek* series. When the *Enterprise* responds to an interplanetary distress call, the all-male landing party (including Captain Kirk, Mr. Spock, Dr. McCoy, and Engineer Scott) beams down to Taurus II and falls under the hypnotic spell of the planet's residents, a race of curvaceous blondes who turn out to be psychokinetic energy vampires. Lieutenant Uhura is forced to take over command of the ship. Joined by Nurse Chapel and an all-female away team, Uhura beams down to the planet, stuns the alien temptresses, and rescues the men, who are now near death. For obvious reasons, this remains Nichelle Nichols's favorite animated episode. While the gender politics of the *Star Trek* have been hotly debated over the years (see Chapter 36, "What Are Little Girls Made Of?"), this episode's feminism is beyond question. It's significant that even the emotionless (but still male) Spock falls prey to the Taurian temptresses and that Uhura's command skills and Chapel's medical know-how ultimately save the day. The "Lorelei" title refers to a Germanic legend similar to the Greek myth of the siren, about beautiful maidens whose singing lures ships to their destruction. Armen also wrote "The Gamesters of Triskelion," "The Cloud Minders" and "The Paradise Syndrome" for the live-action series, as well as "The Ambergris Element," a far less remarkable animated yarn.

**"More Tribbles, More Troubles"**—While escorting two robot ships full of grain to a colony facing starvation, Kirk saves the pilot of a federation vessel under attack by a Klingon Bird of Prey. Then he discovers that the ship's pilot is troublemaking tribble peddler Cyrano Jones, and his pursuer is Captain Koloth, Kirk's antagonist from "The Trouble with Tribbles." Jones is once again selling tribbles—new, genetically engineered tribbles that no longer multiply. However, the creatures still eat gluttonously and now grow huge, creating an entirely different set of headaches. Meanwhile, the Klingons maintain that Jones must be turned over to them, launching a series of attacks that threaten the *Enterprise*'s humanitarian mission.

A sequel to one of the most enduringly popular of all *Star Trek* episodes, "More Tribbles" remains highly amusing but isn't as sharp as the original, in part because it tries too hard to mirror its predecessor, right down to a closing pun by Scotty ("If we've got to have tribbles, it's best if all our tribbles are little ones"). Also, the animated series' half-hour format made it tougher to develop the same careful balance of humor and political tension found in the sixty-minute live-action original. In fact, "More Tribbles" was originally written for Season Three of the live-action series. David Gerrold, who wrote the original "Trouble with Tribbles," created "More Tribbles" at the request of Gene Roddenberry only to have the story rejected by producer Fred Freiberger, who replaced Roddenberry as line producer during the show's final season and who never liked "The Trouble with Tribbles."

Gerrold's live-action concept introduced ferocious, tribble-eating predators that bred as rapidly as the tribbles themselves; out of control, these creatures began feeding on *Enterprise* crew members. This plot was too violent for a Saturday morning cartoon, so Gerrold undertook a nearly complete overhaul. "More Tribbles" is bolstered by the return of actor Stanley Adams, who reprises his role as Cyrano Jones. William Campbell was approached to voice Koloth but was unavailable. Gerrold wrote one more animated episode, the seriocomic "Bem," which is remembered primarily as the show that revealed Captain Kirk's middle name.

This mid-1970s jigsaw puzzle featured imagery from the animated series. Note the prominence of female crew members and Spock in his flight belt, seen only in the cartoon show.

**"Mudd's Passion"**—The funniest—and one of the best—of the animated adventures, "Mudd's Passion" reunites Kirk with another vexing adversary, Harry Mudd. This time, Kirk apprehends the interstellar shyster for selling an illegal drug—a love potion. Once aboard the *Enterprise*, however, Mudd tempts Nurse Chapel into using the drug on Mr. Spock. When (to Mudd's surprise) the stuff works, Mudd creates havoc by using it on the rest of the crew and escapes in the confusion, taking Chapel as a hostage. Written by Stephen Kandel (who penned "Mudd's Women" and "I, Mudd"), the "Mudd's Passion" teleplay is razor-sharp, full of humorous dialogue and rich in character development. Kandel plays on well-established crew relationships, especially Chapel's unrequited affection for Spock, in ways that are funny yet seem authentic. Roger C. Carmel returns to provide the voice of Harry Mudd and delivers a splendid performance. The show's regulars also contribute spirited work. Nimoy and Shatner are hilarious playing the inexplicably lovelorn Vulcan and his puzzled commander. And, as the potion begins to affect the rest of the crew, each of the other principals enjoys a moment of hilarity. "I've saved just about everybody on this here ship," DeForest Kelley coos as Dr. McCoy romances a young female lieutenant. "If the *Enterprise* had a heart, I'd save her, too. Now, let's talk about *your* heart, my dear."

**"The Survivor"**—While patrolling on the edge of the Romulan Neutral Zone, the *Enterprise* rescues a small spacecraft from a meteor storm. The pilot proves to be (or at least seems to be) Carter Winston, a renowned philanthropist long believed dead. Coincidentally, Winston's former fiancée, Anne, now serves on Captain Kirk's ship. Anne begins to suspect something is amiss when Winston rebuffs her. Eventually it's revealed that the pilot is not Winston but a shapeshifting Vendorian who absorbed the consciousness of the dying philanthropist. The Vendorian is in league with the Romulans and leads the *Enterprise* into a deadly trap. But because he has absorbed so many of Winston's memories, the shape-shifter also loves Anne, and to protect her, he double-crosses the Romulans and helps the humans escape. Written by James Schemerer, "The Survivor" boasts a compelling plot, similar in some aspects to the live-action episode "Metamorphosis," and excellent dialogue, including some barbed repartee between Spock and McCoy, including this closing exchange:

McCoy: "I'm glad to see him [the Vendorian] under guard, Jim. If he'd turned into a second Spock, it would've been too much to take."

Spock: "Perhaps. But then two Dr. McCoys just might bring the level of medical efficiency on this ship up to acceptable levels."

Ted Knight, who would gain fame playing a dim-witted sportscaster on *The Mary Tyler Moore Show*, provides the voice of the Vendorian. "The Survivor" is also notable as the only *Star Trek* episode to mention McCoy's daughter, JoAnna, a character created for, but then written out of, the live-action story "The Way to Eden."

**"The Slaver Weapon"**—Perhaps the most imaginative episode of the animated series, "The Slaver Weapon" remains remarkable for several reasons. Written by Hugo and Nebula Award–winning author Larry Niven (best known for his *Ringworld* novels), this story introduces elements from Niven's "Known Space" series into the *Star Trek* universe, including the warlike, telepathic Kzinti species. The episode also features several other novelties: It was the only *Star Trek* adventure since "The Cage" not to include Captain Kirk (only Spock, Uhura, and Sulu are featured); it's the only animated story not to take place at least in part aboard the *Enterprise*; and it's the only animated episode in which a character is killed. A three-member away team led by Mr. Spock is transporting an ancient "stasis box" to the *Enterprise*. These boxes—remnants from an ancient civilization known as The Slavers that once dominated the galaxy—often contain rare artifacts or fantastically advanced technology. Spock, Uhura, and Sulu are transporting it back to the *Enterprise* for investigation when they are duped and captured by the Kzinti, who open the box and discover a weapon of almost limitless power. Spock and friends must recover the weapon before the Kzinti use it to embark on a war against the Federation. "The Slaver Weapon" was adapted from Niven's novella "The Soft Weapon." Apparently Niven was happy with the episode itself but displeased when—like all the other animated episodes—it was novelized by Alan Dean Foster for publication in the *Star Trek Logs* book series. "So I wound up competing with myself, and I find that annoying," Niven explained in a posting on his website.

**"The Counter-Clock Incident"**—The final animated installment produced, "The Counter-Clock Incident" introduces elderly Commodore Robert April, the "first captain of the *Enterprise*." While transporting April to a retirement gala on the planet Babel, the *Enterprise* attempts to rescue another ship and is accidentally drawn through the heart of a supernova and into a negative universe, where time runs backwards. Everyone aboard the ship begins to regress in age, leaving April and his wife (the ship's former chief medical officer) to save their beloved *Enterprise* a final time, as they temporarily return to youth and vitality. This highly enjoyable episode, written by John Culver (under the pseudonym Fred Bronson), builds on elements of *Trek* history and mythology: Robert April was the name Roddenberry gave the captain of his starship (then called the USS *Yorktown*) in his initial prospectus for *Star Trek*; the negative universe was introduced in the live-action episode "The Alternative Factor"; and the basic scenario (with the crew reverting in age) inverts the plot of the classic *Trek* adventure "The Deadly Years," in which the crew ages rapidly. Also, it's undeniably cute to see pint-sized versions of Kirk, Spock, and friends crawling around the bridge.

Other memorable animated adventures include:

- **"The Time Trap,"** which featured the Klingon Kor (introduced in "Errand of Mercy") as well as cameos by members of several recognizable alien species from the live-action series (a Vulcan, an Orion, an Andorian, a Tellarite, and a Gorn), along with several species first seen on the animated show, including a Kzinti.
- **"Once Upon a Planet,"** a sequel to the live-action episode "Shore Leave."

- **"The Infinite Vulcan,"** written by Walter Koenig, an imaginative but convoluted scenario that integrates the Eugenics Wars backstory from "Space Seed" and "The Conscience of the King."

- **"How Sharper Than a Serpent's Tooth,"** despite a shopworn storyline (a thinly veiled rewrite of "Who Mourns for Adonais?"), won Outstanding Entertainment Children's Series at the Second Annual Daytime Emmy Awards, bringing *Star Trek* its first Emmy win in eighteen nominations (including sixteen, in various categories, for the live-action show and the animated series' previous nomination a season earlier in the same category). "How Sharper Than a Serpent's Tooth"—in which the *Enterprise* encounters Kukulkan, a spacefaring feathered serpent who visited Earth centuries ago and was mistaken for a god by the ancient Mayans—was also the first *Trek* episode to feature a Native American Starfleet officer, Ensign Walking Bear, a Comanche.

- **"Keep America Beautiful" PSA**—Filmation also produced a public service announcement for the nonprofit Keep America Beautiful Inc., in which the *Enterprise* encounters the "Rhombian Pollution Belt." Set on the bridge, the spot features Captain Kirk, Mr. Spock and Lieutenant Sulu voiced by Shatner, Nimoy, and Takei. Arax and Uhura are also shown but have no lines. For reasons unknown, this charming spot was not included with the DVD release of the animated series.

Although today it tends to polarize fans (for many, it's a love it or hate proposition), in its day the animated series offered new stories (albeit sometimes juvenile ones) to a fan base starved for new *Star Trek* adventures after watching the same seventy-nine episodes over and over again in syndication. In an era when few Saturday morning cartoon series lasted more than a single season, *Star Trek* earned a renewal, running on NBC at 10:30 a.m. EST in 1973 and 11:30 a.m. EST in 1974. Sixteen episodes were produced for the first season and another half-dozen for Season Two. While it garnered solid ratings, *Star Trek* failed to attract the young viewers essential to long-term Saturday morning success. "We ended up doing a show that was basically the same as the nighttime show—same writers in many cases, same actors obviously and the same audience, too," Hal Sutherland, who directed most of the animated episodes, said in a DVD interview. "The problem was, the audience was all in their 20s and 30s, and our [Filmation's] normal audience was, like, 8 to 10."

As a result, NBC once again cancelled *Star Trek*, this time after only two seasons. Yet, like its live-action predecessor, the animated series went on to a long and prosperous afterlife in syndication.

# "The Damn Books"

## Early *Star Trek* Novels and Comics

**S**tar Trek's original seventy-nine episodes simply weren't enough. Although fans gobbled up those shows in weekly—or, in some markets, nightly—reruns, they remained ravenous for new adventures starring their beloved characters. Until the late 1970s, however, such stories remained in short supply. And strangely, considering that the program's primary audience ranged in age from the late teens to the early thirties, most of the authorized *Trek* material available was aimed at kids: comics, a children's "chapter book," the Saturday morning cartoon series, and book-and-record sets. To sate their gnawing hunger for stories aimed at grown-ups, fans began writing their own *Trek* tales and publishing them in a multitude of unauthorized, amateur fanzines. The robust black market for these often crude publications indicated a ready audience for official, licensed *Star Trek* fiction. In the final years of the decade, this audience would be served at last.

### Gold Key Comics (1967–79)

The first authorized *Star Trek* fiction arrived in comic book form from Western Publishing's Gold Key imprint. It was a rocky start.

The earliest Gold Key comics, from 1967, were illustrated by Italian artist Alberto Giolitti, who had never seen the show and drew the characters, spacecraft, and props based on publicity photos. Predictably, his likenesses of the characters were poor. The title's first writer, Arnold Drake, had created the offbeat superheroes the Doom Patrol and Deadman for DC Comics. He was talented and imaginative, but his stories often diverged drastically from the tenets of the television show. In the first issue, for instance, Kirk, McCoy, and Yeoman Rand beam down to a world where carnivorous plants are the highest life form; animals of all species are rounded up like cattle to serve as food for the plant beings. After the landing party narrowly escapes, Kirks makes the shocking decision to obliterate all life on the planet before leaving orbit! In addition to this jaw-dropping violation of the Prime Directive (not to mention human decency), the story contains less egregious but still irksome lapses (the characters use improper Treknological jargon, narration states that the *Enterprise* has a crew of "thousands," etc.). Also, in this and other early Gold Key yarns, Spock is left in command of the ship while Kirk leads the landing party, rendering the show's most popular character secondary to the plot.

Fortunately, the quality of the comic books improved dramatically over time, as new writers (including George Kashdan and Len Wein) and a new artist (American Al McWilliams), who were more familiar with the source material, took over. Eventually, the comics began including stories that tied in directly with episodes of the TV series. Issue 49, cover-dated November 1977, included a story called "A Warp in Space." This sequel to "Metamorphosis," written by Kashdan and drawn by McWilliams, involved the Companion and a 200-year-old Zefram Cochrane, kept alive by his extraterrestrial lover. Issue 56, dated October 1978, featured a tale titled "No Time Like the Past." Also by Kashdan and McWilliams, this sequel to "The City on the Edge of Forever" dealt with a deposed twenty-third-century dictator who uses the Guardian of Forever to escape into ancient times and help Hannibal defeat the Roman Empire. Gold Key's *Star Trek* series continued for sixty-one issues until Marvel outbid the company for the rights to the property in 1979. The final Gold Key issue, dated March 1979, included a story involving interstellar con man Harry Mudd. Marvel published only eighteen issues of *Star Trek* before canceling the title in 1981 due to disappointing sales. DC took over the comic book license in 1984, and *Trek* comics have remained active ever since, licensed to several different publishers over the years.

## Mission to Horatius by Mack Reynolds (1968)

Despite the fact that this first *Star Trek* novel targeted young readers, it ranks among the most satisfying of its era, vividly recreating the experience of a classic *Trek* episode—or, rather, a string of episodes. The book was a spin-off from the Gold Key comic book series, issued by Western Publishing under its Whitman Books imprint. Author Mack Reynolds, either upon instruction from creator-producer Gene Roddenberry or by fortuitous coincidence, delivered a story clearly modeled after Jonathan Swift's *Gulliver's Travels*, one of Roddenberry's primary inspirations for *Star Trek*.

The *Enterprise* travels to the fringes of Federation territory to answer a distress call from the distant Horatius system, home to three Class M (Earthlike) planets settled a century earlier by anti-Federation dissidents. Like Gulliver, Captain Kirk and company visit a series of strange lands that parallel (and parody) various political systems and worldviews. Residents of the first planet, settled by colonists with a Luddite antitechnology bent, live in caves like "savages"; the people of the second world, a religious enclave, have been subjugated by a repressive theocracy (whose leaders pacify the masses with LSD!); citizens of the third planet labor under the boot-heel of a Hitlerlike dictator. Undeterred by the Prime Directive, the *Enterprise* crew quickly sets about putting things right on all three Horatian worlds. In addition to its Swiftian overtones, *Mission to Horatius*, the only original *Star Trek* novel published while the program remained in production, contains story elements found in classic episodes such as "Return of the

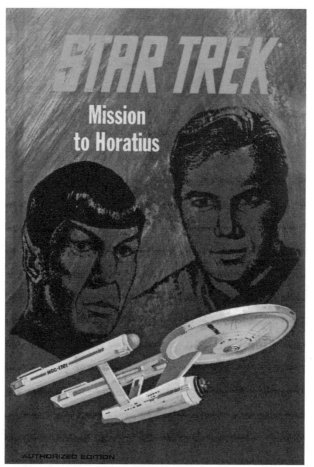

Cover of the 1996 replica edition of Mission to Horatius, the first
Star Trek novel ever published.

Archons," "Bread and Circuses," "Patterns of Force," and "The Tholian Web."
It's a lively pastiche, with characters, settings, and Treknological jargon that ring
true to the TV show. Only the book's poorly rendered illustrations disappoint.

Originally published in hardcover, *Mission to Horatius* went out of print when
*Star Trek* was cancelled in 1969. But in 1996 Pocket Books issued a facsimile edi-
tion, billed as "The Lost *Star Trek* Novel," which remains easily available. Original
Whitman editions of the book are now prized collector's items.

## Spock Must Die! by James Blish (1970)

In 1967, decorated British science fiction author James Blish undertook a long-
running series of paperback adaptations of *Trek* teleplays for Bantam Books.

These paperbacks, published under the generic title *Star Trek* and later reprinted in the four-volume *Star Trek Reader*, together sold millions of copies. Blish was able to retire from other writing and live off the royalties. The author's crisply written novelizations remain of interest to diehard fans because they were based on early scripts rather than the finalized versions and often feature subtle (or sometimes significant) deviations from the aired episodes. Nevertheless, by 1970, after adapting three volumes' worth of *Star Trek* episodes, Blish was growing restless and wanted to try writing an original *Trek* story.

The result was *Spock Must Die!*, the first original *Trek* novel created for grownups. Although Blish's credentials were impeccable (his novel *A Case of Conscience* won a 1959 Hugo Award), his results were disappointing. Surprisingly, given his apparent familiarity with the idiom, the author gets a number of things wrong. Some of the discrepancies, like inaccurate Treknospeak, may be considered minor, but others are more troublesome. Blish struggles to find the voices of Captain Kirk, Dr. McCoy, and Scotty, who simply do not speak or act like themselves in *Spock Must Die!* The book is static and talky, full of protracted philosophical discussions, with a plotline mostly rehashed from Richard Matheson's teleplay "The Enemy Within." In that episode, a transporter accident produces a duplicate Captain Kirk; in *Spock Must Die!*, a similar mishap creates an evil twin of Mr. Spock. The story also functions as a sequel to screenwriter Gene Coon's "Errand of Mercy," with the Klingons mobilizing for a full-scale war against the Federation.

Even though *Spock Must Die!* sold well, Blish never attempted another *Trek* novel. He penned another nine volumes of episode adaptations before dying of throat cancer in 1975. His widow, author Judith Ann Lawrence, completed the final volume in the series and wrote *Mudd's Angels* (1978), which featured novelizations of the two Harry Mudd episodes, along with a new Mudd novella written by Lawrence. She captured the voices of the characters more accurately than her husband in her tale about Mudd's plot to trade android wives for dilithium crystals, cornering the galactic market for this vital commodity. Meanwhile, Alan Dean Foster penned a similar series of adaptations based on animated *Star Trek* episodes, known as the *Star Trek Log* series, which was published by Ballantine Books from 1974 to '78. And in 1977 and '78, Bantam published twelve "Fotonovels"—picture books that told the story of a classic episode through a series of stills laid out in comic book format with dialogue delivered via word balloons.

## Peter Pan Records (1975–79)

Meanwhile, licensees continued to churn out products aimed at kids. Those companies included Peter Pan Records, which specialized in music and spoken-word recordings for children. Peter Pan's most popular products were book-and-record sets that paired a comic book with a 45 rpm record that "read" the story for youngsters, who were prompted to turn the page at the sound of a bell. Narration and character voices were supplied by the company's in-house repertory, billed as The Peter Pan Players. During the 1970s, Peter Pan's Power Records imprint released book-and-record sets, as well as long-playing albums without accompanying storybooks, featuring Marvel and DC Comics super heroes and film and television properties like *The Six Million Dollar Man*, *Planet of the Apes*, *Space: 1999*, and *Star Trek*.

The *Trek* tales were written by sci-fi specialist Alan Dean Foster during the same period when he was writing the *Star Trek Log* novelizations. His audio plays, which ran from twelve to sixteen minutes in length, incorporated elements from both the live-action and animated series. The cast of characters included Ensign Chekov, who had been omitted from the cartoon show. Although Foster's plots were juvenile, a few included amusing elements: In "In Vino Veritas," a diplomatic summit between the Federation and the Klingon and Romulan Empires breaks down when someone spikes the ambassadors' drinks with truth serum; in "Starve a Fleaver," the crew is paralyzed with giddiness after becoming infested with seemingly indestructible flea-like symbiotes that feed off happiness; and in "Dinosaur Planet," Kirk and Spock meet a race of intelligent tyrannosauruses.

Illustrators Neal Adams, Dick Giordano, and Russ Heath drew the accompanying comics. For the most part, the likenesses of the characters were very good, but there were some egregious lapses. In the first four releases, Sulu is depicted as an African American man in a blue tunic and Uhura as a blond Caucasian woman. In a later comic, the Romulans look like green-skinned wood

Sleeve for the first of Peter Pan Records' many Star Trek story albums.

sprites. In all, Peter Pan produced eleven original *Star Trek* audio plays, some of those featured in 45 rpm book-and-record sets, and others available only via the company's LPs, which collected the book-and-record stories and featured additional original content. The company recycled these eleven stories many times in various combinations, issuing a total of twenty-three separate *Star Trek* records.

## Star Trek: The New Voyages Edited by Sondra Marshak and Myrna Culbreath (1976)

After *Spock Must Die!*, no new *Trek* novels appeared for six years, but nonfiction books about *Star Trek* proliferated. Ballantine Books published David Gerrold's *The World of Star Trek* (1973), the first serious evaluation of "The Show the Network Could Not Kill!," along with Gerrold's *The Trouble with Tribbles* (also 1973), a behind-the-scenes account of the making of the classic episode. Other Ballantine books included *The Star Trek Blueprints* and *The Starfleet Technical Manual* (both 1975), and *The Starfleet Medical Reference* (1977), presenting schematics for the *Enterprise* and an "instruction manual" for phasers, tricorders, twenty-third-century medical equipment, and other gadgets; Bjo Trimble's *Star Trek Concordance* (1976), which reprinted the original show "Bible" and offered the first official episode guide; and *Trek or Treat* (1977), which reprinted stills from the TV show with humorous captions and word balloons. *The Making of Star Trek*, written by Stephen E. Whitfield (cocredited with Roddenberry), first published in 1968 while the show was still on the air, also remained in print. And Anima Press published Karen Blair's *Meaning in Star Trek*, the first book to explore the show's philosophical elements. The mania for printable *Trek* material reached a kind of zenith in 1977 with Ballantine's publication of *Letters to Star Trek*. This book was just what it sounds like, a collection of creator-producer Gene Roddenberry's fan mail, assembled by his secretary, Susan Sackett, with commentary (ranging from patient explanations to sarcastic wisecracks) by Sackett and a brief introduction from Roddenberry.

Meanwhile, Bantam kept churning out the Blish episode novelizations and published a nonfiction entry of its own, *Star Trek Lives!* by Jacqueline Lichtenberg, Sondra Marshak, and Joan Winston, the first book to try to explain the cult appeal of the series. Acclaimed science fiction author Frederik Pohl, who would publish his Hugo-winning novel *Gateway* in 1977, was overseeing Bantam's *Star Trek* line. In 1976, Marshak (who knew Pohl from her coauthorship of *Star Trek Lives!*) and friend Myrna Culbreath approached the editor to lobby for the publication of more original *Trek* fiction. To test the waters, they proposed what must have seemed like a radical idea: an authorized, professionally published collection of fan-written *Trek* stories. After careful consideration, Pohl gave Marshak and Culbreath the go-ahead to assemble the collection and talked Roddenberry into writing a forward. Marshak and Culbreath's resulting compilation featured stories that focused on individual members of the *Enterprise* crew—Spock, Kirk, McCoy, Scotty, Uhura, Sulu, and Chapel—with introductions to their character's story from Leonard Nimoy, William Shatner, DeForest Kelley, James Doohan, Nichelle Nichols, George Takei, and Majel Barrett-Roddenberry. A story featuring Chekov, with an intro by Walter Koenig, was cut when the manuscript ran long.

The stories do not read like the work of unpublished amateurs; the best of them are superior to some later *Trek* tales penned by professional authors. This is a tribute to the judicious work of editors Marshak and Culbreath. "We were collecting, editing, and sometimes, at the author's requests, extensively cutting or partly rewriting some stories," the editors told Jeff Ayers in his book *Voyages of Imagination: The Star Trek Fiction Companion.* "Our judgment was vindicated when *Star Trek: The New Voyages* became one of the most beloved books of *Trek* fiction." Released in March 1976, it also became a mass market best-seller and proved definitively that readers craved new *Trek* fiction. A sequel, *Star Trek: The New Voyages 2*, followed in 1978. The fan-created Internet series *Star Trek: New Voyages* was named in honor of Marshak and Culbreath's groundbreaking collection, the first ever professional publication of fan-written fiction.

## The Bantam Novels (1976–81)

Even before the breakout success of *The New Voyages*, Pohl was making tentative plans to launch the *Star Trek* literary franchise in earnest with a series of six original novels. For the most part, Pohl commissioned manuscripts from experienced, bankable sci-fi authors such as Joe Haldeman, whose 1974 novel *The Forever War* won the Hugo and Nebula Awards, and Gordon Eklund, a Nebula laureate in 1975 for his novella "If the Stars Are Gods." But he also purchased a novel by Marshak and Culbreath, who were rapidly becoming fan favorites themselves. The initial wave of six paperbacks—*Spock, Messiah!* (September 1976) by Theodore Cogswell and Charles A. Spano Jr., Marshak and Culbreath's *The Price of the Phoenix* (July 1977), Haldeman's *Planet of Judgment* (August 1977), *Vulcan!* (September 1977) by Kathleen Sky, Eklund's *The Starless World* (November 1978), and Stephen Goldin's *Trek to Madworld* (January 1979)—sold out their initial print runs of up to a quarter-million copies and went into second printings almost immediately.

The quality of these novels varied considerably. The best of the lot was *Planet of Judgment*, which found an *Enterprise* away team trapped on a hostile world where Starfleet technology doesn't work. Haldeman's no-nonsense brand of character-driven military SF perfectly suited *Star Trek*. *The Price of the Phoenix*, in which a shadowy alien offers to return the deceased Captain Kirk to life in exchange for Spock's soul, was an intriguing entry, despite Marshak and Culbreath's tendency to interrupt the narrative for philosophical debates. Cogswell and Spano's *Spock, Messiah!*, on the other hand, seemed like a random science fiction novel with *Trek* characters shoehorned in. Notably, however, this book featured a story element that figured prominently in James Cameron's

First time published
8 original Star Trek stories
never seen on the screen

# STAR TREK: THE NEW VOYAGES

EDITED BY SONDRA MARSHAK AND MYRNA CULBREATH
FOREWORD BY GENE RODDENBERRY
SPECIAL INTRODUCTIONS BY THE CAST OF STAR TREK

Sondra Marshak and Myrna Culbreath's Star Trek: The New Voyages marked a turning point in the emerging literary franchise.

2009 blockbuster *Avatar*. Eklund's *The Starless World* begins well, with the *Enterprise* trapped in a "Dyson sphere" (a giant artificial construct that surrounds a star), but suffers from a groan-inducing, literal deus ex machina finale.

Based on the strong sales of these titles, Bantam released seven more *Star Trek* novels over the next three years, including second efforts from Haldeman (*World Without End*, 1979), Marshak and Culbreath (*The Fate of the Phoenix*, 1979), and Sky (*Death's Angel*, 1981). The later Bantam releases also included *The Galactic Whirlpool* by David Gerrold. Sky's first *Trek* novel, *Vulcan!*, was adapted from a scenario the author had created for the show's never-realized fourth season. The Bantam novels proved so popular—and so profitable—that when the company's license ran out in the early 1980s, Pocket Books (a subsidiary of Paramount Pictures) assumed control of the literary franchise and has published nearly every authorized work of *Star Trek* fiction in the decades since.

Throughout the 1970s and early '80s Roddenberry, preoccupied with numerous other projects, was dismissive of the *Star Trek* comic books and paid little attention to the proliferation of *Trek* novels. That changed in 1985 when Pocket Books published Della Van Hise's novel *Killing Time,* which suggested a homoerotic undercurrent in the relationship between Kirk and Spock. (Stories depicting this idea in a far more graphic manner comprise an entire subgenre of fan fiction.) Roddenberry, tipped off by irate letters from fans, went ballistic (or perhaps went photon?). *Killing Time* was recalled, and a new edition was subsequently printed that contained more than fifty alterations from the original version. From that point on, the Great Bird of the Galaxy (and ultimate arbiter of what was and wasn't *Trek*) began to personally review every new *Star Trek* story, a task he despised. Eventually he hired an assistant, Richard Arnold, to help monitor the novels (which Roddenberry habitually referred to as "the damn books") and other licensed *Trek* tie-ins to make sure they conformed to the established format, characterizations, historical "facts," and guiding philosophy of the franchise. After Roddenberry's death in 1991, final editorial decisions regarding all *Star Trek* literature reverted to executives at Paramount Pictures and Pocket Books.

Since the humble origins of the *Star Trek* literary franchise in the late 1960s, nearly 600 original *Trek* novels and short story collections have been published. These include lines based on all the subsequent sequel and prequel TV series, as well as newly created lines featuring original characters and delving into previously unexplored aspects of the *Trek* universe, such as the *Starfleet Corps of Engineers* series. Additionally, more than 400 issues of *Star Trek* comic books have seen print, as well two as newspaper strips (a British series that ran weekly from 1969 to 1973 and an American strip that ran daily from December 2, 1979, until December 3, 1983). Given the spotty nature of much *Trek* literature, especially during its early years, the canon-worthiness of story elements originating from the novels and comics remains dubious. Occasionally, however, some "facts" established in these stories—such as Lieutenant Sulu's first name, Hikaru, revealed in Vonda McIntyre's 1981 novel *The Entropy Effect*—have been "canonized" by their use in later films and TV shows. In terms of sheer volume, however, the amount of printed *Star Trek* material now outweighs the 725 television episodes and eleven feature films so far produced.

# A Piece of the Action

## Vintage *Star Trek* Merchandising

In 1977, 20th Century-Fox unleashed a blockbuster of previously unimaginable proportions in George Lucas's *Star Wars*, which not only shattered all existing box-office records but also generated hundreds of millions of dollars in ancillary revenue through the sale of toys, T-shirts, posters, soundtrack albums, and other ephemera. Immediately, rival studios began a frantic search for properties with similar merchandising possibilities. Paramount quickly realized that in *Star Trek* it already had one. For years, diehard fans had supported *Trek* not only by watching the show but by spending their money. They had turned an assumed-dead TV series into a merchandising bonanza, snapping up *Trek*-branded toys, model kits, books, trading cards, T-shirts, buttons, posters, bumper stickers, watches, and . . . well, just about everything else in the galaxy. Fans' passion for all things *Trek* played a major role in convincing Paramount Pictures to revive the franchise with a theatrical film.

### Lincoln Enterprises

From the beginning, creator-producer Gene Roddenberry grasped the merchandising potential of *Star Trek*, and in 1967, he set up a mail-order company, Lincoln Enterprises, to capitalize on it. The business was actually owned by Roddenberry's attorney, Leonard Maizlish, who officially turned the company over to Majel Barrett Roddenberry in the early 1980s. Operated by Roddenberry and Barrett, Lincoln began as a mechanism for handling the show's copious fan mail and requests for photographs and other souvenirs. Soon it was selling publicity photos and copies of scripts through mail-order catalogs and at science fiction conventions. Initially, in apparent violation of Writers Guild of America rules, the authors of the teleplays received no compensation from these sales, but Lincoln ironed out a deal with the Guild to continue selling scripts.

Beginning in 1968, Lincoln offered fans the chance to own a piece of their favorite show—literally—when the company began selling 35 mm frames clipped from the program's daily outtakes. This development stoked brewing animosity between Paramount Pictures and Roddenberry, since technically this footage was owned by the studio and not the producer. Also in 1968, another Lincoln endeavor damaged the already strained relationship between Roddenberry

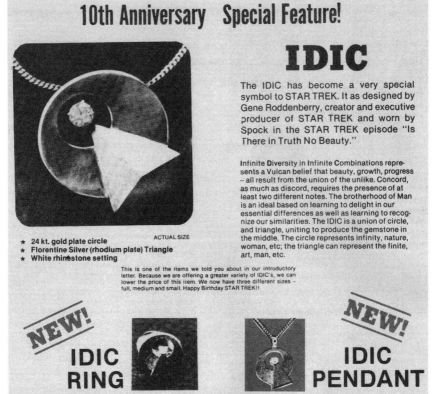
Well into the 1970s, Roddenberry continued to sell IDIC jewelry through his Lincoln Enterprises mail-order business. (This ad ran in a 1978 catalog.)

and Leonard Nimoy. During production of the episode "Is There in Truth No Beauty?," Roddenberry inserted a scene in which Kirk and Spock explain to guest star Diana Muldaur the significance of a stylized medal the Vulcan is wearing—the IDIC, short for "infinite diversity in infinite combinations." This interlude served no function within the framework of the plot; it was created specifically to introduce IDIC pins and medallions, which were about to go on sale from Lincoln Enterprises. Nimoy felt that this ploy cheapened the show and protested vociferously. The sequence was rewritten to minimize the dialogue about the IDIC (which Kirk refers to as "the most revered of all Vulcan symbols"), and Nimoy reluctantly played the scene. In the finished episode, Spock models both an IDIC brooch (which receives a loving close-up) and, later, a large IDIC necklace.

By the late 1970s, Lincoln had grown into a thriving cottage industry, selling T-shirts, patches, iron-on transfers, buttons, bumper stickers, posters, stationary, commemorative coins, and jewelry (including IDICs), as well as 35 mm frames, teleplays, and reprints of the series' writer's guide. Roddenberry also used Lincoln to promote his post-*Trek* productions, selling copies of his scripts for *Pretty Maids All in a Row*, *Genesis II*, *Planet Earth*, *The Questor Tapes*, *Spectre*, and even his unrealized *Tarzan* and *Magna I* projects. The company remains in business, now operated by Rod Roddenberry, whose Roddenberry.com website replaced the old mail-order catalogs.

## AMT Model Kits

Among the earliest and most popular *Trek* tie-ins were plastic model kits manufactured by Troy, Michigan–based AMT, then a leading producer of model cars and trucks. In 1966, during the show's first season, Roddenberry struck a deal with AMT: The company's skilled model makers helped production designer Matt Jefferies create some of the miniatures used in the show's production; in exchange, AMT received an exclusive license to produce and market *Star Trek* model kits. AMT craftsmen also constructed the life-size mock-up of the shuttlecraft *Galileo 7*. A plastic reproduction of the USS *Enterprise*, which first appeared in 1966, marked AMT's first venture beyond automotive models. The *Enterprise* became a top seller and was followed a year later by a Klingon battle cruiser kit. During the show's cash-strapped third season, Jefferies sometimes used AMT models in the background for complex shots involving multiple spacecraft. These models are recognizable by their lack of internal lights.

Eventually, AMT issued several more *Star Trek* kits: a Romulan *Bird of Prey*; the *Galileo 7* shuttlecraft; the *Enterprise* bridge; *Space Station K-7* (from "The Trouble with Tribbles"); and an "Exploration Set" including ¾-scale replicas of a phaser, communicator, and tricorder. The model series outlived the television show, continuing well into the 1970s. AMT (short for Aluminum Model Toys) leased the international *Star Trek* model rights to rival Aurora, a company best known for its figure model kits. In 1976, Aurora introduced a model of Spock, depicted with phaser drawn against what looked like a three-headed space serpent. Through a reciprocal agreement, the Spock model was sold by AMT in the U.S.

AMT went on to release a plethora of models based on other sci-fi properties, including *Star Wars*, *Alien*, and *Space: 1999*, as well as kits featuring spacecraft from the *Star Trek* feature films, *The Next Generation* and *Deep Space Nine*. In 1968, AMT issued a model spaceship designed by Jefferies for *Star Trek* but never actually used on the series—an angular, double-finned craft sold as "The *Leif Ericson* Galaxy Cruiser." This kit included a 45 rpm record of "the sounds of outer space" and a two-page short story ("Danger on an Alien Planet") depicting the adventures of the ship's crew, led by the valiant Captain Walker of the Galactic

AMT's "U.F.O. Mystery Ship" (originally released as the "Leif Ericson Galaxy Cruiser") featured a spacecraft designed by Matt Jefferies for *Star Trek* but never used on the series. (This is one of Round2's reissue kits, struck from the original AMT molds and reproducing the original packaging.)

Expeditionary Force. The *Leif Ericson*'s *Star Trek* origins were never mentioned. In the 1970s, the *Leif Ericson* was recast in glow-in-the-dark plastic and sold as the "Interplanetary UFO Mystery Ship."

AMT was absorbed by Britain's Lesney Products, makers of the Matchbox line of toy cars, in 1978. Ownership of the brand changed hands twice more, winding up with Round 2 LLC, a South Bend, Indiana–based model maker known for reissues of classic models, in 2007. Beginning in the late 2000s, Round 2 began selling new pressings of the classic AMT *Star Trek* models cast from the original molds. Vintage AMT model kits remain treasured collectibles. AMT's original, exclusive *Trek* license expired in 1999, and since then several other companies—including Revell-Monogram, Polar Lights, and Bandai—have also released *Star Trek* models. In addition, many unlicensed, homemade, or semiprofessional "garage kits" have emerged over the years. These models—from makers with names like Warp Models, Federation Models, and Nova Hobbies—often feature lesser known vessels of interest only to hardcore fans, such as the *Botany Bay* from "Space Seed."

## Trading Cards

Chicago-based Leaf Brands (now known as Donruss) issued the first set of *Star Trek* trading cards in 1967. These cards, which were not distributed outside the Midwest, were sold briefly but quickly recalled. This may have been due to a licensing issue or because Roddenberry was displeased with the product, which was far from ideal. The Leaf cards featured grainy black-and-white photos backed by poorly written text that misidentified the picture on the front and "recapped" absurd stories never featured on the show. Card Number 63, for instance, features a publicity still of Spock from "The Cage" but suggests that this shot originates from an episode where the *Enterprise* is "demobilized" and boarded by space pirates. Card 23 backs a picture of McCoy supporting a dazed Spock with this far-fetched explanation: "A weird gas causes Mr. Spock to believe he is a 1967 teeny-bopper. Dr. McCoy attempts to restrain him." And Card 45 recounts a nonexistent episode where Spock ("again the dead center target of an enemy ion fuser") escapes the unnamed enemy by *telling jokes* ("Why do some men wear suspenders?"). Despite—or perhaps because of—these oddities, the ultra-rare Leaf *Star Trek* cards, which originally sold for a nickel per pack, now command a princely $35 or more per card. In pristine condition, a complete set of seventy-two cards can sell for thousands. Even empty wrappers are valuable. An unauthorized reprint series of these cards emerged in 1981.

The next set of *Star Trek* trading cards, from a British maker called A&BC, featured sharp-looking color photos but had other drawbacks. Most importantly, all fifty-five cards in the series originated from a single episode—"What Are Little Girls Made Of?" And once again the text on the back of the cards contained glaring inaccuracies. Among other errors, Spock is identified as "part Martian." These cards were sold only in the U.K. The first set of *Star Trek* trading cards widely available in the U.S. was issued by industry giant Topps in 1976. Although best known for originating the modern baseball card in 1952 (and monopolizing that market for nearly thirty years), Topps was also a pioneer of nonsports trading cards, issuing sets devoted to the space program, the life story of President John F. Kennedy, and the Beatles. In 1962, Topps released its now-legendary (and ultracollectible) *Mars Attacks* cards. The company's 1976 *Star Trek* cards, which sold for ten cents per pack, included eighty-eight cards and twenty-two stickers with color frame enlargements from various episodes on the front and accurate descriptions (in "Captain's Log" format) on the back. In the years since, numerous companies, including Skybox and Rittenhouse Archives, have issued additional trading card series devoted to the *Star Trek* franchise. In 1997, Skybox inserted autographed cards (one signed card per box) into random packs of its *Star Trek: The Original Series - Season One* cards. This gambit was quickly copied by other companies and has become nearly a standard practice for cards based on movies or television shows.

## Mego Action Figures

Mego was a leading manufacturer of action figures in the 1970s, marketing eight-inch poseable dolls with cloth uniforms and plastic accessories based on Marvel and DC Comics superheroes, as well as film and television properties including *Planet of the Apes*, *The Wizard of Oz*, and Universal Studios monsters.

**23**

### TEENY BOPPER

A weird gas causes Mr. Spock to believe he is a 1967 Teeny-Bopper. Dr. McCoy attempts to restrain him. There appears no antidote. Kirk becomes annoyed and shouts at his officer. The sound of authority, spoken like an angry father, jolts Mr. Spock. He rebels at first, then returns slowly to his own personality.

TEENY BOPPER

Front and back of one of the most bizarre (and hilarious) of the 1967 Leaf trading cards, which were quickly withdrawn from circulation. (This image derives from a 1981 reprint edition.)

Mego also issued figures in the likenesses of musicians and celebrities such as Farrah Fawcett, Sonny and Cher, and Kiss. The secret to the company's success was the ingenious design of its plastic figures, which had interchangeable heads. This enabled the company to stockpile standard body types that, by changing only the costume and the head, could be refitted to resemble many different characters.

In 1974, the company issued its first collection of *Star Trek* figures, which included Kirk, Spock, McCoy, Uhura, Scotty, and a generic Klingon (who favored William Campbell's Koloth from "The Trouble with Tribbles"). Not surprisingly, Mego's *Star Trek* toys sold like crazy. The company followed with two waves of *Star Trek Aliens* figures, released in 1975 and '76. These eight dolls varied widely in their fidelity to the characters seen on the show. Mego's Romulan, Andorian, and Cheron were quite faithful, but its Talosian, Gorn, and Mugato looked almost nothing like their on-screen counterparts. And one figure—"The Neptunian," a bipedal lizard with an insectoid head—was a wholly original creation with no origin in *Star Trek* at all. Mego's *Star Trek* line also included a series of "playsets," including the *Enterprise* bridge (complete with a plastic replica of the captain's chair); a transporter room (featuring a spinning "transporter" that made figures seem to disappear); and a pair of "communicator" walkie-talkies. Mego thrived throughout the early and middle 1970s, but its sales declined late in the decade after rival Kenner outbid Mego for the license to produce *Star Wars* action figures. Mego went out of business in 1983.

Although many far more realistic *Star Trek* action figures have been sold in the decades since, the original Mego toys retain a nostalgic value for many fans. Some of them also carry a big-dollar collectible value. Over the years, hobbyists recreated the classic Mego *Trek* figures and expanded the line with "custom" versions of characters like Nurse Chapel and Harry Mudd, with homemade heads and hand-sewn uniforms. Beginning in 2006, EMCE Toys, in conjunction with Diamond Select Toys, began releasing authorized recreations of the original Mego *Trek* figures as well as a newly created Khan figure. Nine of the thirteen classic Mego figures have been reissued so far, and EMCE has announced plans for releases featuring Lieutenant Sulu and Ensign Chekov, whom Mego ignored, and a revised, accurate version of the Gorn.

Scores of other *Trek* products were also produced during this era. Puzzle and trivia books from various publishers, board games, and a Bally pinball machine served as the forerunners of the later, highly lucrative *Star Trek* video game franchise. Fans could also invest in *Star Trek* beach towels, bed linens, belt buckles, dinnerware, lunch boxes, Halloween costumes, paint-by-numbers kits, Frisbees, and freeze pops. In 1970, Primrose Confectionary even sold *Star Trek*–branded candy cigarettes.

About the only thing fans couldn't buy were the shows themselves—at least not officially. Sony's first Betamax home video systems went on sale in the spring of 1975, in the midst of *Trek*'s popular resurgence. The following year, JVC's first Video Home System (VHS) recorders entered the market. While Paramount Pictures and other Hollywood Studios sat out the ensuing format war, *Star Trek* became one of the most-taped programs in the early history of the medium. Bootleggers soon began hawking unauthorized recordings of the program in both formats. Paramount Pictures Home Entertainment didn't begin selling authorized, prerecorded VHS tapes until 1985. However, in 1979, RCA produced licensed editions of *Star Trek* episodes in its proprietary SelectaVision CED format (video discs played with a special needle, like a vinyl record album). In 1982, Pioneer released the series on laser disc.

# Five-Year Mission

## The Long Voyage Back, 1975–79

I n March 1978, Paramount Pictures held a massive press conference, with scores of journalists from around the world, to announce the return of *Star Trek*. Production would soon commence for *Star Trek: The Motion Picture*, a $15 million theatrical feature produced by Gene Roddenberry and directed by Oscar winner Robert Wise, which would reunite the entire cast of the TV series and introduce new characters as well.

Fans were elated, but most had one question: What took so long?

Although few outsiders knew it at the time, the revival of *Star Trek* was a torturously convoluted process that consumed much of the 1970s and left a barge-load of false starts and scuttled projects in its wake. As early as 1972, former story editor Dorothy Fontana revealed that Paramount (which essentially co-owned the franchise with Roddenberry) was considering a *Star Trek* feature film. The following year, a frustrated Roddenberry told reporters that NBC was interested in resurrecting the series but that Paramount refused to move forward because it feared new episodes would deflate the market for *Trek*'s highly profitable syndicated reruns. The *Star Trek* animated series premiered that fall, but this Saturday morning cartoon show did little to quell the pent-up demand for new live-action *Trek* adventures. Over the next five years, Roddenberry and a host of other writers, producers, and directors worked on a myriad of film and television efforts intended to resuscitate the franchise. Most of these led nowhere.

### The God Thing (1975)

Throughout the 1970s, Paramount leadership dithered and vacillated regarding *Star Trek*. The series' success in syndication and merchandising was unprecedented, and executives didn't know what to make of it. Some believed the show's popularity was a fad that would quickly pass. With that possibility in mind, in 1975, the studio hired Roddenberry to develop the screenplay for a low-budget ($2–3 million) theatrical film. The idea was to rush the picture into production and capitalize on the *Trek* craze before its appeal faded. The studio even gave Roddenberry his old office back to write the screenplay. One day, William Shatner—who was on the lot filming his short-lived TV series *Barbary Coast*—found Roddenberry in the old *Star Trek* offices, pounding away on a typewriter. The actor recalls in his book *Star Trek Movie Memories*:

"Hey, Gene!" I called from the doorway. "Didn't anybody tell you? We got cancelled!"

"Whaddya mean?" he said, not looking up but continuing to type. "I'm almost finished revising our 1968 scripts!"

In fact, the erstwhile Great Bird of the Galaxy was writing a screenplay titled *The God Thing*. Although the script itself has never been published, a basic outline of the story can be discerned by piecing together accounts from the published memoirs of Roddenberry, Shatner, Susan Sackett (Roddenberry's secretary), and Water Koenig.

Admiral James T. Kirk hastily reassembles the crew of the starship *Enterprise* and races out to counter a giant alien Object, which has already destroyed the starship *Potemkin* and is now headed toward Earth. The Object claims to be God and demonstrates its powers by restoring the amputated legs of helmsman Sulu (injured in the earlier battle). A shape-shifting emissary from the Object boards the *Enterprise*, appearing in several forms including that of Jesus Christ. Eventually, the Object is revealed to be a malfunctioning interdimensional computer intelligence programmed to relate and interpret interstellar law. During its first visit to Earth, the Object was mistaken for God by the Hebrews of the Old Testament; Christ, it turns out, was one of its mechanical lawgivers. Finally, Kirk convinces the Object to return to its own dimension.

Paramount rejected this scenario as too anti-religious. "Gene had been iconoclastically asking, What if the God of the Old Testament, full of tirades and demands to be worshipped, actually turned out to be Lucifer?" Sackett wrote in

Walter Koenig, seen here reading his fan mail, later novelized Gene Roddenberry's rejected *God Thing* screenplay.

*The Making of Star Trek: The Motion Picture.* "If so, was the serpent's offer of the Fruit of Knowledge actually a gift from the real God? Captain Kirk versus God. This was not the story Paramount had expected!"

Despite the studio's antipathy for this concept, Roddenberry remained fascinated by his *God Thing* story and incorporated many elements from it into the final, approved script for *Star Trek: The Motion Picture.* He also planned to novelize the rejected screenplay, but he never completed the manuscript. In 1976, Walter Koenig collaborated with Roddenberry on a novella-length adaptation of *The God Thing*, but the book was abandoned when Roddenberry received a green light for the TV series *Star Trek: Phase II.* In 1993, *The God Thing* (billed as a "lost *Star Trek* novel by Gene Roddenberry and Michael Jan Friedman") was solicited by Pocket Books, but the title never appeared. Friedman, who had written several *Star Trek* novels, was assigned to expand and revise the Roddenberry-Koenig *God Thing* novella by Pocket Books editor David Stern, but the project was abandoned at the request of the Roddenberry estate.

## *The Billion Year Voyage* and Other Tales from the Scrap Heap (1976)

The studio's rejection of *The God Thing* dimmed the prospects for a quick cash-in on the *Star Trek* "fad," but Paramount decided to give Roddenberry a second chance. He had until the spring of 1976 to develop a usable screenplay. Screenwriter Jon Povill, who worked extensively with Roddenberry during this period, produced a treatment in which Captain Kirk and friends travel into the past to battle a psychic cloud that is driving the people of the planet Vulcan mad. Roddenberry liked the idea but felt Povill's story lacked the scope necessary to carry a feature.

Roddenberry then penned a time-travel yarn of his own. In this tale, a shuttlecraft crewed by Spock, Scotty, and a handful of other officers gets sucked into a black hole, triggering a reaction that temporarily scrambles the molecules of the *Enterprise* and its crew, who eventually coalesce back into existence after an eleven-year absence. But the universe as they knew it is gone. The shuttle was transported into the past (Earth, circa 1937), where Scotty's well-intentioned efforts to avert World War II created a corrupted timeline. Now the Earth is ruled by a benevolent supercomputer. The planet is peaceful, famine and sickness have been wiped out, but human beings have become mere automatons with no ambition or imagination. After wrestling with the pros and cons of the situation—after all, Earth is a near-utopia, and millions of lives have been saved—Kirk decides to travel into the past and restore the original timeline. It's up to the crew of the *Enterprise* to restart the Second World War! While the available details of this story remain sketchy, this seems to be a very promising scenario, reminiscent in key aspects of the treasured "City on the Edge of Forever." Nevertheless, Paramount rejected this concept as well.

Still hoping to exploit *Star Trek*'s surging popularity, Paramount next turned to writers other than Roddenberry in its search for a filmable story. Executives, including Roddenberry, entertained pitches from four writers: John D. F. Black, who had served as story editor during the first half of *Star Trek*'s initial season and penned the key episode "The Naked Time"; Harlan Ellison, the author of "The City on the Edge of Forever"; and fellow esteemed science fiction authors Ray Bradbury and Robert Silverberg.

Black's concept involved a black hole that was being used as an interstellar garbage dump by the inhabitants of a renegade solar system. After consuming centuries of space junk, the black hole explodes and begins consuming whole planets and suns. The *Enterprise* is sent to find some way of preventing the hole from devouring the entire galaxy. Paramount dismissed the idea because, as Black has often repeated in interviews, "it wasn't big enough."

Ellison proposed a story where the *Enterprise* crew travel into the past to combat a race of time-hopping alien reptiles bent on the conquest of Earth. The movie would have begun with a series of unexplained occurrences, including the disappearance of one of the Great Lakes. Then a mysterious, cloaked figure would have been seen kidnapping members of the *Enterprise* crew. The kidnapper would be revealed as Captain Kirk, rounding up his former crew for a secret mission back in time to combat the nefarious lizard people. According to numerous accounts of the meeting (including Ellison's, from his book about the writing of "City on the Edge of Forever"), the author's pitch came to an abrupt end when Paramount executive Barry Trabulus asked if the story could involve Mayans. Trabulus, intrigued by Erich von Daniken's book *Chariots of the Gods* (which postulated that extraterrestrials may have influenced the development of ancient civilizations, including that of the Maya) wanted to shoehorn that concept into Ellison's story. The testy Ellison dismissed Trabulus's suggestion as "a stupid idea." A confrontation resulted, and Ellison stormed out of the meeting.

Details of Bradbury's idea remain elusive, but Silverberg pitched a story called *The Billion Year Voyage* that was more pure science fiction than the typical *Trek* sci-fi action yarn. In it, an *Enterprise* away team would have discovered the ruins of a long-dead but superadvanced civilization known as the Great Ones and battled other alien races for the Great Ones' fantastically powerful relics. This scenario, which shares some common concepts with Larry Niven's excellent animated *Trek* adventure "The Slaver Weapon," was also rejected.

## Planet of the Titans (1976–77)

Paramount's nearly two-year search for an acceptable *Star Trek* story came to an end—or so it seemed—in October 1976 when the studio finally purchased a scenario titled *Planet of the Titans* from British screenwriters Chris Bryant and Allan Scott.

The Federation and the Klingon Empire both lay claim to a recently discovered planet that may be the home world of the near-mythical Titans, an ancient, long-extinct, superadvanced race. The possible treasures awaiting discovery on the planet could tip the balance of power in the galaxy, but the world is about to be consumed by a black hole. The *Enterprise* arrives and discovers a second opponent even more formidable than the Klingons—the mysterious Cygnans, who effected the disappearance of the Titans eons ago. In order to defeat the Cygnans, Kirk is forced to fly the *Enterprise* into the black hole, which catapults the starship through time and space to prehistoric Earth. There, Kirk and his crew aid the primitive humans of the era and suddenly realize that they themselves are the legendary Titans.

Curiously, this story plays like Silverberg's discarded *Billion Year Voyage* mashed up with pieces and parts from many of the other rejected tales, plus a dash of *Chariots of the Gods* at the end. Story elements from *The God Thing* were also present—including an opening scene depicting the destruction of a Federation vessel (here named the *Da Vinci*) and Spock studying on Vulcan to purge the last vestiges of his humanity. Bryant and Scott's yarn featured several spectacular action sequences, including the separation of the *Enterprise*'s saucer section from the rest of the ship during a battle with the Klingons.

Paramount assigned *Planet of the Titans* a budget of $7.5 million and hired writer-director Philip Kaufman, who would later helm such successful films as *Invasion of the Body Snatchers* (1978), *The Right Stuff* (1983), and *The Unbearable Lightness of Being* (1988), to oversee the production. To devise the look of the picture, the studio engaged production designer Ken Adam, renowned for his work on the James Bond films and Stanley Kubrick's *Dr. Strangelove*, along with conceptual artist Ralph McQuarrie, who had served a similar function on George Lucas's *Star Wars* and Steven Spielberg's *Close Encounters of the Third Kind*. *Planet of the Titans* was scheduled to shoot in England beginning in late 1977.

Bryant and Scott expanded their treatment into a full screenplay, which they delivered in March 1977. Kaufman, a gifted writer who penned (among other things) the story for Spielberg's *Raiders of the Lost Ark* (1981), immediately began revising the script. His version more prominently featured Spock and a Klingon commander he hoped would be played by Japanese screen legend Toshiro Mifune. But Kaufman clashed with Roddenberry, who felt the director's alterations were turning the movie into something that wasn't *Star Trek*. Paramount chief Barry Diller shared Roddenberry's trepidation about the script and was alarmed by the production's rising costs. By this point the budget had ballooned to $10 million, and shooting was still months away. In early May, before Kaufman had completed his rewrite, Diller abruptly cancelled *Planet of the Titans*.

Just a few weeks later, *Star Wars* premiered.

## Star Trek: Phase II (1977)

Diller, who had taken over as CEO of Paramount in 1974 and moved up to chairman in 1976, had an ulterior motive for shutting down *Planet of the Titans*. He dreamed of starting a fourth television network and saw *Star Trek* as the anchor for this venture, a highly desirable property with a young, relatively affluent built-in audience. The original *Trek* series was being broadcast on 137 stations across the U.S. at the time. Diller's plan, announced on June 10 (about a month after *Planet of the Titans* was scrapped), was for the new Paramount network to begin modestly, with one night of programming per week: *Star Trek: Phase II*, an all-new weekly series, at 8 p.m. Saturdays, followed by a made-for-TV movie at 9. (Diller, as a programming VP at ABC in the 1960s, had pioneered the weekly telefilm concept with that network's long-running ABC Movie of the Week.) The Paramount network was slated to debut in February 1978.

Roddenberry promptly corralled Paramount executive Robert Goodwin to serve as line producer for *Phase II*, brought in screenwriter Harold Livingston to serve as coproducer/story editor, and tried to hire his old friend Matt Jefferies away from the hit series *Little House on the Prairie* to return as production designer. Jefferies demurred but recommended Joe Jennings, who Roddenberry hired as art director. Roddenberry also brought back *Trek* veteran William Ware Theiss to design costumes for the new show.

Most of the original cast was soon brought on board as well. The glaring exception was Leonard Nimoy, who was embroiled in a lawsuit against Paramount over royalties from the sale of merchandise featuring his (Spock's) likeness. He had also filed a Screen Actors Guild complaint against Roddenberry due to the producer's unauthorized use of the *Star Trek* blooper reel at speaking engagements. Although Roddenberry hoped to woo Nimoy into making guest appearances on *Phase II*, the producer hired actor David Gautreaux to portray Xon, the *Enterprise*'s new, young, full-Vulcan science officer. (Spock would be off teaching at the Vulcan Science Academy.) Roddenberry also planned to introduce two new characters: Commander Will Decker (the son of Commodore Matt Decker from "The Doomsday Machine"), envisioned as a younger version of Kirk who would serve as the ship's second-in-command; and Ilia, an exotically beautiful, bald female Deltan, a telepathic species known for its brazen sexuality.

*Planet of the Titans'* $10 million-plus budget made the project impractical for television, sending Roddenberry back to the drawing board in search of a screenplay for the *Star Trek: Phase II* pilot telefilm. He dusted off "Robot's Return," an episode concept from his failed *Genesis II* TV series that was highly reminiscent of both his previously jettisoned *God Thing* screenplay and John Meredith Lucas's classic *Trek* episode "The Changeling." He handed off the story outline and other materials to Alan Dean Foster, a best-selling science fiction author who had novelized the teleplays of the *Star Trek* animated series. Foster cooked up an expanded version of the story titled "In Thy Image," which was quickly selected to serve as *Phase II*'s feature-length pilot episode. The concept was favored by both Roddenberry and Michael Eisner, who had succeeded Diller as Paramount CEO. Livingston expanded the yarn into a full-length teleplay.

Roddenberry, hoping to avert the teleplay gap that plagued the original *Star Trek* during its first season, solicited additional stories from many different writers. A few of these were later developed into treatments or even full-length scripts. Foster submitted a story where the *Enterprise* discovers a parallel Earth akin to the American South of the early 1800s, only with whites enslaved by blacks. Shimon Wincelberg, John Meredith Lucas, and Margaret Armen, all of whom wrote for the original *Star Trek*, sold stories to *Phase II*. Roddenberry bought a half-dozen scenarios from sci-fi author Jerome Bixby, who had written four classic episodes including "Mirror, Mirror" and "Day of the Dove." In all, eighteen scenarios were purchased, including:

- "The Child" by Jon Povill and Jaron Summers, in which Ilia is impregnated by a noncorporeal alien life force. This scenario was later revived for *The Next Generation*.
- "To Attain the All" by Norman Spinrad (who had penned "The Doomsday Machine"), about a superadvanced, noncorporeal alien race who offers the gift of immortality and other wonders in exchange for the temporary use of human bodies to move about the galaxy. Although similar to the Season Two episode "Return to Tomorrow," Spinrad's story took a very different direction, with the aliens remaining benevolent but their gifts proving too dangerous.
- "The Prisoner" by James Menzies, in which someone who looks like Albert Einstein claims to have been abducted by aliens during the twentieth century and kept prisoner on a distant planet.
- "Tomorrow and the Stars" by Larry Alexander, in which a transporter accident sends Kirk back in time to Pearl Harbor just prior to the 1941 Japanese attack
- And "Devil's Due" by William Lansford, designed as a science fiction update of "The Devil and Daniel Webster," with Kirk in the role of the defense attorney.

Within a few months, Paramount's plans for a fourth television network fell apart. The studio couldn't prebook enough advertising to make the operation profitable. Despite this setback, Diller retained his dream of founding a fourth network and realized that goal after jumping from Paramount to Fox in 1984. Along with owner Rupert Murdoch, Diller launched the Fox Broadcasting Company in 1986. Nine years later, Paramount belatedly premiered its UPN Network, which lasted until 2006, when it merged with the Warner's failed WB Network to form the CW Television Network.

Even though Paramount's 1977 network plans were sunk, the studio continued preproduction on *Phase II* in hopes of selling the series directly to syndication, as it would *Star Trek: The Next Generation* a decade later. At the same time, however, Paramount executives found themselves under increasing pressure to respond to *Star Wars*, which was smashing box-office records and raking in hundreds of millions of dollars in merchandising revenue. It soon became clear that the studio's best chance at a similar bonanza was *Star Trek*. That meant pulling the plug on *Phase II* and converting the project back into a feature film. The "In Thy Image" screenplay was retained as the basis for the movie but would undergo a new round of rewrites. Director Robert Collins, who had been hired to helm *Phase II*'s pilot episode, was discharged and replaced by Oscar winner Robert Wise. Although the official announcement wouldn't arrive until the spring of 1978, by December 1977 (when gossip columnist Rona Barrett broke the story), *Star Trek: Phase II* had morphed into *Star Trek: The Motion Picture*.

With a potential blockbuster hanging in the balance, Paramount settled its suit with Nimoy, and Spock rejoined the crew of the *Enterprise*. (Gautreaux's Xon character was promptly eliminated.) Expectations soared. Fans were jubilant over the mouth-watering prospect of a big-budget, big-screen *Star Trek* movie directed by the great Wise (who in 1951 had made *The Day the Earth Stood Still*). How could it fail? A *Star Trek* movie with such sterling credentials was *guaranteed* to be at least as wonderful as *Star Wars*, right? "Industry insiders hint that if the movie is successful, *as it is sure to be*, more features will be made" (italics added for emphasis), author Gerry Turnbull wrote in his 1979 book *A Star Trek Catalog*, published as fans breathlessly awaited *Trek*'s silver screen debut. "With more time, a bigger budget and some of the recent new frontiers crossed in the studio special effects field, the new *Star Trek* promises to be even more exciting [than the series]."

Unfortunately, *Star Trek: The Motion Picture* didn't turn out quite the way fans dreamed. The production was beleaguered from the start, plagued by perpetual rewrites, cost overruns, and personality clashes between Roddenberry and Wise, among other problems. The movie finally debuted December 6, 1979, nearly five years after Paramount first commissioned a *Trek* screenplay from Roddenberry. But this lackluster effort squandered much of the fan loyalty *Star Trek* had built over the course of the past decade, and cost Roddenberry his previously unassailable position as master of his twenty-third-century universe. To survive, the franchise would have to make a second remarkable comeback.

For that story, tune in to *Star Trek FAQ 2.0: Everything Left to Know About the Feature Films, the Next Generation, and Beyond*, coming in 2013.

# On the Edge of Forever

## The Legacy of *Star Trek*

# Personal Log

## Spouses, Children, and Private Lives

S*tar Trek* has many legacies. It forecast technological innovations, altered the course of both television and science fiction, and inspired countless scientists, engineers, physicians, and writers, to name only a few of its aftereffects. But for those who helped create it, the series left a different sort of mark, taking an emotional (and in some cases physical) toll on the personal lives of its cast and crew.

Marriages collapsed and addictions formed. Nichelle Nichols, badly injured in a car accident on her first day of shooting, was patched up at a hospital and reported to the set anyway, working until she finally collapsed at Lieutenant Uhura's communication console late in the day. William Shatner suffered tinnitus (permanent ringing in the ears) when a flash pod rigged with too much explosive blew up near him during production of "The Apple." Midway through Season One, exhausted associate producer Bob Justman crumpled to the floor one morning and was forced to take an unscheduled week off before he could return to work. By the show's second season, Leonard Nimoy had become an alcoholic.

Of course, *Star Trek* also brought its makers fame and (eventually) fortune, along with the pride of helping launch a legendary entertainment franchise and the simple yet profound satisfaction of producing high-quality work. But for better or worse, the show forever changed the lives of its creator and cast, and their families.

### Gene Roddenberry and Majel Barrett

During the first season of *Star Trek*, Majel Barrett took up residence in an apartment located near the Desilu studio, where Gene Roddenberry was a frequent overnight guest. Nevertheless, Roddenberry remained married to the former **Eileen Rexroat** until the summer of 1969, when the pair finally divorced after 27 mostly troubled years. It was an acrimonious and, for Roddenberry, financially punishing split, which left lingering bitterness on both sides. Less than a week after his divorce was final, on August 6, 1969, Roddenberry and Barrett were married in a traditional Shinto-Buddhist ceremony in Japan, where Roddenberry was scouting locations for a film project that never materialized.

Gene and Eileen had two daughters, who were age twenty-one and sixteen at the time of the divorce. **Darleen Anita Roddenberry-Bacha** (born April 4, 1948) is the eldest of the two. She and her younger sister were among several *Star Trek* kids who made uncredited guest appearances as orphaned children in the episode "Miri." (She's a dirty-faced brunette girl in a flower-print dress.) It was her only acting role. She was killed in a car crash on October 29, 1995, at age forty-seven, and is survived by her husband and two children. **Dawn Allison Roddenberry Compton** (born August 31, 1953) also made an uncredited appearance in "Miri." (She's a teenager with straight blonde hair wearing a striped frock.) She made another uncredited appearance in her father's first feature film, *Pretty Maids All in a Row* (1971) but did not pursue an acting career. She married entrepreneur Richard H. Compton in 1977. She also garnered headlines with a pair of unsuccessful lawsuits. Following her father's death in 1991, she filed a challenge to his will that cost her her inheritance. She had been granted a half-million dollars, as well as one-quarter of all family profits from the *Star Trek* franchise, but wanted a larger cut. However, the will also contained a clause stipulating that any heir who challenged its stated bequests would be denied any portion of the estate. The California courts upheld the will, including the disinheritance clause. She also filed, but later withdrew, a suit alleging that Majel Barrett Roddenberry mismanaged her father's financial affairs prior to his death.

Dawn Roddenberry Compton's stepson, **Richard Compton Jr.,** caused a stir in 1996 by signing a petition from an organization known as the Voyager Visibility Project demanding the introduction of an openly gay character to the cast of *Star Trek: Voyager*. Compton, who is gay, claimed that prior to his death Gene Roddenberry pledged to feature a homosexual character in a future *Star Trek* series.

Roddenberry and Barrett remained together until Roddenberry's death and from all reports had a happy life together, even though Roddenberry continued to have romantic dalliances with other women. (Gene's longtime secretary, Susan Sackett, claimed in her 2002 memoir *Inside Trek* that she was sexually involved with her boss for more than a decade.) Majel Barrett Roddenberry held the financial reigns of the Roddenberry *Star Trek* empire until her death from cancer in 2008. During that period, she also fought off legal action from Roddenberry's first wife.

In her divorce settlement, Eileen Rexroat Roddenberry was awarded a half-interest in all future profits from *Star Trek* realized by Norway Corp., an independent production company Roddenberry set up to create the series in conjunction with Desilu. In 1987, Roddenberry's ex-wife filed suit against Norway and her former husband, claiming that she had been defrauded of royalties. She also demanded a half-interest in profits from the *Star Trek* feature films and *The Next Generation* series. By the time the California Supreme Court settled the matter in April 1996, Roddenberry had been dead for nearly five years. Eileen was awarded overdue profits from merchandising and other revenue related to the original series (along with a $900,000 punitive judgment) but denied any profit interest in the later films and TV series. On balance, it was a multimillion-dollar victory for Roddenberry's estate, administered by Majel Barrett Roddenberry.

**Eugene Wesley Roddenberry Jr.** (born February 5, 1974) was the only child born to Barrett and Roddenberry. The family interest in the *Star Trek* franchise passed to him following his mother's death. Known as "Rod" Roddenberry, he operates Kirschner/Roddenberry Production and Lincoln Enterprises, the memorabilia company created by his parents, which now functions through his Roddenberry.com website. Roddenberry has tinkered on the edges of show business—serving as a production assistant on an episode of *The Next Generation*, writing an episode of *Earth: Final Conflict*, and financing and narrating *Trek Nation*, a 2006 documentary about the franchise and its fans. But he has devoted most of his energy to promoting space exploration and ecological causes in cooperation with NASA, the Planetary Society, and X Prize Project, among other organizations. In 2011, the X Prize Project, a philanthropic enterprise that grants lucrative cash awards to individuals and corporations who "bring about radical breakthroughs for the benefit of humanity," announced a $10 million Tricorder Competition. The contest will reward the development of a handheld medical examination tool similar in function to those used by Dr. McCoy on *Star Trek*. Rod Roddenberry, an avid scuba diver, also founded the Roddenberry Dive Team, which promotes environmentally conscious diving and ocean preservation. According to its mission statement, the organization is dedicated to "incorporating the philanthropic ideals embedded in *Star Trek* into real world experiences . . . We are committed to carrying on the legacy of vision and optimism that was handed down by Gene Roddenberry."

## William Shatner

William Shatner endured a pair of painful losses during *Star Trek*'s broadcast run—first the death of his father and then the dissolution of his marriage. Joseph Shatner died during production of "The Devil in the Dark." The shooting schedule was rearranged to allow Shatner to travel to Florida, where his father had passed away, and transport the body home to Montreal. Shatner soldiered on, returning to Los Angeles to complete the episode just a day later. During *Trek*'s final season, Shatner's wife of thirteen years, actress **Gloria Rand,** filed for divorce. In his autobiography, *Up Till Now*, Shatner blames the breakup on his own personal failings, but the grueling schedule of *Star Trek*, along with what Shatner describes as a stream of "new and beautiful—and seemingly available— women . . . on the set," helped splinter the couple's already brittle relationship. Shatner and Rand had three daughters, who were eleven, eight, and five years old at the time of the divorce.

**Leslie Carol Shatner** (born August 31, 1958), the eldest of Shatner's three daughters, also made an uncredited appearance in the episode "Miri" as a nameless orphan girl. Lieutenant Leslie, a background character played by Shatner's stunt double, Eddie Paskey, was named for her. Unlike her two younger sisters, Leslie never pursued a show business career. She operates a web design business and is involved in various other entrepreneurial ventures. She also maintains the Shatner Family Blog, which updates fans on the goings-on of her sisters and father. On the website she posts that "I've been married for a long time and I have two wonderful sons. I'm also very proud of my Dad." **Lisabeth Mary Shatner** (born June 6, 1961) also appeared in "Miri." She is the little orphan girl who Shatner holds in his arms while delivering Captain Kirk's climactic speech. Lisabeth also appeared in an episode of her father's series *T. J. Hooker* and in an installment of the short-lived *TekWar* TV series, which her father starred in and produced. In the *TekWar* episode "Betrayal" (1996), she worked alongside her younger sister Melanie. Lisabeth Shatner also cowrote with her father the book *Captain's Log*, about the making of the ill-fated *Star Trek V: The Final Frontier*. She is married to makeup effects artist Andy Clement, who worked on the later *Star Trek* series *Voyager* and *Enterprise*, and on J. J. Abrams's 2009 feature film *Star Trek*, among many other movies and TV shows. **Melanie Shatner** (born August 1, 1964) didn't appear in "Miri" but later played a small role as Captain Kirk's yeoman in *The Final Frontier*, which her father directed and cowrote. Melanie enjoyed the greatest show business success of Shatner's progeny, racking up nearly twenty film and television appearances from 1989 through 1998. Then she gave up acting to start Dari, a posh Ventura Boulevard fashion boutique in Studio City, California. She is married to actor Joel Gretsch, and the couple has two daughters, Kaya and Willow. Shatner's Lemli Productions Inc. is named for his three daughters (taking letters from each of their first names). Contrary to erroneous information included in some Internet biographies, Shatner does *not* have a son named Daniel.

In 1973, around the time of the *Star Trek* animated series, Shatner married actress **Marcy Lafferty,** who he met during the production of the PBS TV movie *The Andersonville Trial*. That union lasted until 1994, when Lafferty divorced Shatner. In *Up Till Now*, Shatner wrote that the two were driven apart by their radically uneven careers. While Shatner regularly earned starring roles, Lafferty played a smattering of bit parts, including small roles in *Star Trek: The Motion Picture* (1979) as well as in Shatner's film *Kingdom of the Spiders* (1977) and four guest appearances on *T. J. Hooker*. Shatner married again in 1997, to model **Nerine Kidd,** an alcoholic who died in a pool accident in 1999. His tempestuous marriage to Kidd, ironically, deepened Shatner's friendship with costar Leonard Nimoy. A recovering alcoholic himself, Nimoy offered advice to Shatner and tried to help Kidd get sober. "Leonard Nimoy's personal experience of alcoholism now came to play a central role in my life and it helped us bond together in a way I never could have imagined in the early days of *Star Trek*," Shatner wrote in *Up Till Now*. Since 2001 Shatner, an avid horseman, has been married to **Elizabeth Martin,** an acquaintance from the equestrian community who claimed to have never watched *Star Trek*.

## Leonard Nimoy

Leonard Nimoy also suffered personal problems during the production of *Star Trek*, becoming an alcoholic as he struggled to cope with his demanding work schedule and sudden fame. Celebrity came as a shock to Nimoy, who wrote in both of his memoirs that he was ill-equipped emotionally to deal with the demands and security concerns his fame created. Before *Star Trek* premiered, he didn't even bother to switch his home telephone to an unlisted number! At first he tried to sign every autograph and reply to every letter, tasks that quickly became impossible. He sought solace in alcohol. Although he never drank during the workday, according to his memoir *I Am Spock*, he often began drinking after work and didn't stop until he passed out. "I started drinking regularly, ritually, during the second or third year of our series," Nimoy told a reporter from the London newspaper *The Telegraph* in an October 2001 interview. "The minute we finished the last shot I would have a drink. Then it became a series of drinks, little by little." At least initially, however, Nimoy's marriage was not a casualty of his addiction. Nimoy had married actress Sandra Zober in 1954; the couple stayed together until 1987, when Nimoy left her. A year later, he married actress Susan Bay, a cousin of director Michael Bay. With Susan's help, Nimoy finally gained sobriety in the late 1980s. Nimoy and Bay remain married.

Nimoy and Zober had two children. Unlike Shatner and Roddenberry, Nimoy refused to allow his children to appear in "Miri" and tried to keep them out of show business. That effort met with mixed results. **Julie Ellen Nimoy**

Leonard Nimoy, surrounded by his family (son Adam, daughter Judy, and first wife Sandi Zober) and his ever-present fan mail.

**Schwartz** (born March 21, 1955) is a chef, a graduate of the California School of Culinary Arts and Le Cordon Bleu Culinary School in Pasadena. She operates the J.E.N. catering company in Sherman Oaks, California. In 1984, she married Gregory Schwartz, with whom she has three children (sons Alex and Spencer and daughter Dani). **Adam Brett Nimoy** (born August 9, 1956) earned a J.D. and worked as an attorney for a while but gave up the legal profession for television. Beginning in the 1990s, he has directed dozens of TV episodes, including two installments of *Star Trek: The Next Generation* and a *Babylon 5*. In 1995, he directed the "I, Robot" remake, starring his father, for Showtime's revamped *Outer Limits* series. (Leonard Nimoy played a different role in the original *Outer Limits* "I, Robot" episode back in 1964.) Adam Nimoy also teaches at the New York Film Academy's campus in Los Angeles and is the author of the memoir *My Incredibly Wonderful, Miserable Life.*

## DeForest Kelley

DeForest and Carolyn Kelley remained blissfully married for nearly fifty-five years until the actor's death in 1999. The couple had no children.

## Nichelle Nichols

Along with Shatner and Nimoy (not to mention the quickly fired Grace Lee Whitney), the cast member who endured the most personal difficulties during *Star Trek*'s production was Nichelle Nichols. She was unhappy with the development of her character (or lack thereof). In her 1994 autobiography *Beyond Uhura*, Nichols reports being subjected to racial slurs by Desilu employees and complains that the studio withheld most of her fan mail so that the actress wouldn't realize the extent of her character's popularity and demand more money. She became so fed up with the situation that she decided to leave the show after its first season, only to have Dr. Martin Luther King Jr. talk her out of it when he met her at a party. King, as Nichols has said and written many times over the years, impressed on her the importance of Uhura as a role model for African American women.

Nichols has been married twice and has had a few other long-term relationships. Her first marriage, to dancer **Foster Johnson** when she was eighteen years old, lasted only a year but produced a child. Like his mother, **Kyle Johnson** (born August 14, 1951) is an actor and musician, best known for playing the lead in Gordon Parks's 1969 film *The Learning Tree.* He made more than a dozen other film and television appearances in the 1960s and '70s, including a small role in Roddenberry's film *Pretty Maids All in a Row* (1971). In the early 2000s, he hosted a radio talk show on KNFT in Silver City, New Mexico.

In 1968, as *Star Trek*'s final season was winding down, Nichols married songwriter Duke Mondy. Although the couple remained together until 1972, the relationship quickly deteriorated. In *Beyond Uhura*, the actress describes her second marriage as "a mistake." Since becoming involved with recruiting for NASA in the 1970s, Nichols has remained a vocal supporter of the space program. Her younger brother Thomas died in the mass suicide of the Heaven's Gate cult in 1997. Thomas, who was fifty-nine, and thirty-eight other cult members, took their own lives at the community's compound in Rancho Santa Fe, California.

## James Doohan

At the time of his death in 2005, James Doohan had tallied three marriages, seven children, nine grandchildren, and one great-grandchild.

When he signed on to play chief engineer Montgomery Scott, Doohan was recently divorced from his first wife, the former **Janet Young,** with whom he was married from 1949 to 1964. He was Catholic, she was Protestant, and from the start their marriage was riven by both personality conflicts and religion-based family tensions. In his 1996 autobiography *Beam Me Up, Scotty,* Doohan wrote that taking part in the D-Day assault on Normandy "was a hell of a lot easier" than his first marriage. Doohan and Young's troubled union produced four children: **Larkin** (born in 1954), **Deirdre** (born in 1957), and twins **Christopher** and **Montgomery** (born in 1959). In 1967, during *Star Trek*'s second season, Doohan married **Anita Yagel,** the young woman Gene Roddenberry had hired as an executive assistant when his former secretary, Dorothy Fontana, took over as the show's story editor. Doohan's marriage to Yagel lasted until 1972 but produced no children.

In October 1974, he married **Wende Braunberger,** a seventeen-year-old *Star Trek* fan the fifty-four-year-old actor met following a theatrical appearance. Old friend (and former Squire of Gothos) William Campbell attended as Best Man. James and Wende Doohan remained devoted to one another until the actor's death at age eighty-five. Doohan's final marriage produced three offspring: **Eric, Thomas,** and **Sarah,** who was born April 11, 2000, when her father was eighty. Christopher Doohan and his twin brother Montgomery worked as extras on *Star Trek: The Motion Picture,* but of all Doohan's children, only Christopher has undertaken a show business career. A group of *Star Trek* fans lobbied director J. J. Abrams to cast Christopher Doohan as Scotty in his 2009 *Star Trek* feature film. That role went to actor Simon Pegg, but Christopher landed a small part as a red-shirted transporter operator. Christopher Doohan is primarily a singer, the lead vocalist of the Los Angeles–based blues-rock band the Mudflaps. In the mid-2000s, the group was occasionally featured on the VH1 channel reality series *Breaking Bonaduce,* about the life of former child star and L.A. disc jockey Danny Bonaduce.

## George Takei

Throughout his life, George Takei has worked for various philanthropic and political causes. He mounted an unsuccessful run for Los Angeles City Council in 1973. During the campaign, L.A.'s KNBC-TV stopped airing *Star Trek* reruns and delayed the broadcast of the first installment of the *Trek* animated series to remain in compliance with the FCC's "Equal Time" regulation, which requires that stations that give free airtime to one candidate must provide the same benefit to that candidate's opponent. Later, Takei served on the board of directors for the Southern California Rapid Transit District. He was called away from production of *Star Trek: The Motion Picture* to cast the deciding vote to create the Los Angeles subway system.

Since coming out of the closet (which he did, publicly, after appearing as himself in an episode of the sitcom *Will & Grace* in 2006), Takei has continually promoted gay rights. He and his longtime partner, **Brad Altman,** were married in September 2008 during a brief period when California law permitted same-sex marriage. Walter Koenig and Nichelle Nichols served as Best Man and Matron of Honor at the ceremony. Takei lobbied against California's Proposition 8, which banned gay marriage beginning in November 2008. He and Altman later became the first gay couple to appear on TV's *The Newlywed Game*, where they won $10,000 for the Japanese American National Museum in L.A, which Takei cofounded.

Takei currently serves on the Human Rights Campaign's Coming Out Project. In May 2011, in response to a bill passed by the Tennessee state legislature that prohibited elementary and middle school teachers from referring to homosexuality in any way (the so-called "Don't Say Gay" bill), Takei released a public service announcement suggesting that Tennesseans substitute his last name for the word "gay." "You could safely proclaim you support Takei marriage," he says in the spot. "If you're in a more festive mood, you can march in a Takei Pride Parade. Even homophobic slurs don't seem as harmful if you say, 'That's so Takei!'"

## Walter Koenig

Walter Koenig married actress **Judy Levitt** in 1965, two years prior to his debut as Ensign Pavel Chekov. The couple, which remains together, had two children. **Joshua Andrew Koenig** (born August 17, 1968) was an actor, director, writer and editor who had a recurring role on the sitcom *Growing Pains* from 1985 to 1989. He appeared in a 1993 episode of *Deep Space Nine* and played the Joker in the well-known fan film *Batman: Dead End* (2003). He committed suicide in 2010 at age forty-one. **Danielle Beth Koenig (born February 5, 1973)** is also an actress and writer, although she has earned only sporadic film and television credits. She is married to stand-up comic Jimmy Pardo, and the couple has one child. Water Koenig has always lived a guarded private life, rarely speaking about his wife or children in public. In his 1997 memoir *Warped Factors*, Koenig wrote, "I have made a very conscious decision in the writing of this book to exclude my family life from its pages."

# "Beam Me Up, Scotty"

## The Quotable (and Misquotable) *Star Trek*

In the early 1970s, as *Star Trek* moved from failed TV series to pop culture phenomenon, quotes—and sometimes misquotes—gained currency as idiomatic expressions. Captain Kirk's illusory "Beam me up, Scotty" and Mr. Spock's stately "Live long and prosper" were so often repeated that they quickly became the subject of parody by the mass media. For better or worse, a handful of these catchphrases became emblematic of the series.

### "Beam Me Up, Scotty"

This is a phantom phrase along the lines of Humphrey Bogart's fictitious "Play it again, Sam," which is *not* heard in *Casablanca,* and Sherlock Holmes's "Elementary, my dear Watson," which appears nowhere in the canon of Sir Arthur Conan Doyle. Although Captain Kirk approached the line on several occasions—coming closest in the animated episodes "The Lorelei Signal" and "The Infinite Vulcan," when he said "Beam us up, Scotty"—he never actually uttered the complete phrase, nor was it spoken by any other character during any *Star Trek* episode or film. Rather, it originated with a popular bumper sticker from the early 1970s, which read: "Beam me up, Scotty. There's no intelligent life here." Regardless of its inaccuracy, "Beam me up, Scotty" emerged as *the* symbolic catchphrase for *Star Trek,* and has been co-opted (usually as a punch line) in countless later films and television shows. Scott Bakula, later to star as Captain Jonathan Archer on the series *Star Trek: Enterprise,* employed the line for comedic effect on a 1992 episode of his series *Quantum Leap.* James Doohan even titled his autobiography *Beam Me Up, Scotty.* "I've had 'Beam me up, Scotty' hollered to me from across four lanes of freeway at 70 miles an hour," Doohan wrote in the book's introduction.

### "Live Long and Prosper"

Mr. Spock's elegant valedictory was written by science fiction legend Theodore Sturgeon for his teleplay "Amok Time." The phrase was repeated by Spock in numerous other episodes and feature films, and has been employed by other

Vulcans, and sometimes humans, in every subsequent *Star Trek* series. It can also be found emblazoned on T-shirts, bumper stickers, coffee mugs and all sorts of other *Trek* merchandise.

## "He's dead, Jim" and "I'm a doctor, not a . . ."

The irrepressible Dr. McCoy contributed two catchphrases to the *Star Trek* lexicon. The first of these, "He's dead, Jim," was spoken in its entirety or with minor variations twenty times. On other occasions, the doctor used other words (i.e., "The man is dead!") to announce a character's demise. Actor DeForest Kelley grew to despise this particular phrase and refused to say it following Spock's death near the conclusion of *Star Trek II: The Wrath of Khan*. Instead, a similar line was given to Engineer Scott (James Doohan). Nevertheless "He's dead, Jim" became so linked with McCoy that DeForest Kelley once joked that the words would be carved on his tombstone.

Kelley was much happier with McCoy's famous "I'm a doctor, not a . . ."

Star Trek catchphrases have emblazoned T-shirts, coffee mugs, bumper stickers, and just about everything else in the galaxy.

expressions, such as "I'm a doctor, not a bricklayer" (from "The Devil in the Dark") and "I'm a doctor, not a coal miner" (from "The Empath"). McCoy clarified his vocation nineteen times during the course of the seventy-nine live-action episodes and twenty-two animated adventures. During an appearance on *Rowan & Martin's Laugh-In*, DeForest Kelley parodied the catchphrase, saying, "I'm not a doctor, I'm a convicted murderer." In tribute to McCoy (and Kelley), variations on the line were written for Dr. Julian Bashir (Alexander Siddig) on *Star Trek: Deep Space Nine*, the Doctor (Robert Picardo) on *Star Trek: Voyager*, and Dr. Phlox (John Billingsley) on *Star Trek: Enterprise*. And in J. J. Abrams's 2009 *Star Trek* feature film, Dr. McCoy (Karl Urban) says, "I'm a doctor, not a physicist."

## "Space, the final frontier . . ."

After the series received the green light from NBC, associate producer

Bob Justman hit on the idea of running a voice-over during the opening credits (a device not employed for either of the show's two pilots). This narration would introduce newcomers to the basic concept of the show and set the proper heroic tone. Creator-producer Gene Roddenberry collaborated with associate producers John D. F. Black and Justman to pen this narration. The short speech improved dramatically as it went through multiple rewrites. Roddenberry's clunky first draft read:

> This is the story of the United Space Ship Enterprise. Assigned a five year patrol of our galaxy, this giant starship visits Earth colonies, regulates commerce and explores strange new worlds and civilizations. These are its voyages . . . and its adventures.

Black contributed an alternate version, eliminated that business about regulating commerce, introduced the opening words "Space, the final frontier," and incorporated screenwriter Sam Peeples's phrase "where no man has gone before" (from the title of the second *Trek* pilot). Justman came up with a third draft, combining and revising elements from the Roddenberry and Black scripts. Then Roddenberry polished Justman's revision to come up with the now-famous opening:

> Space, the final frontier. These are the voyages of the starship Enterprise. Its five-year mission: to explore strange new worlds, to seek out new life and new civilizations, to boldly go where no man has gone before.

## More Quotes

As these catchphrases gained traction in the American vernacular, diehard *Trek* fans watched the show's original seventy-nine installments over and over again in syndication. Many came to know their favorite episodes by heart, and the most ardent could recite scenes back and forth to one another, line by line. Forty years later, *Star Trek* remains one of television's most eminently quotable series. Here's a topically grouped sampling of the show's wit and wisdom:

### On Leadership and Diplomacy

"Risk is our business! That's what the starship is all about! That's why we're aboard her!"

—Kirk, "Return to Tomorrow"

"One of the advantages of being a captain, doctor, is being able to ask for advice without necessarily having to take it."

—Kirk, "Dagger of the Mind"

"Intuition, however illogical, Mister Spock, is recognized as a command prerogative."

—Kirk, "Obsession"

"Command and compassion is a fool's mixture."
        —Gary Mitchell (played by Gary Lockwood), "Where No Man Has Gone
Before"

"The chain of command is often a noose."
        —McCoy, "The Conscience of the King"

"The commander is responsible for the lives of his crew, and for their deaths. Well, I should have died with mine."
        —Commodore Decker (William Windom), "The Doomsday Machine"

"I got the biggest [territory] in the world. You know, there's one thing wrong with having the biggest. There's always some punk trying to cut you out."
        —Bela Okmyx (Anthony Caruso), "A Piece of the Action"

"The best defense is a strong offense, and I intend to start offending right now."
        —Kirk, "The Empath"

"Maybe you're a soldier so often that you forget you're also trained to be a diplomat. Why not try a carrot instead of a stick?"
        —McCoy, "Metamorphosis"

"I'm a soldier, not a diplomat. I can only tell you the truth."
        —Kirk, "Errand of Mercy"

"Diplomats and bureaucrats may function differently, but they achieve exactly the same results."
        —Spock, "The Mark of Gideon"

"The best diplomat I know is a fully activated phaser bank."
        —Scotty, "A Taste of Armageddon"

## On Gender Politics

"The idea of male and female are universal constants."
        —Kirk, "Metamorphosis"

"Men will always be men no matter where they are."
        —Harry Mudd (Roger C. Carmel), "Mudd's Women"

"The sound of male ego. You travel halfway across the galaxy and it's still the same song."
        —Eve McHuron (Karen Steele) in "Mudd's Women"

"Worlds may change, galaxies disintegrate, but a woman always remains a woman."

—Kirk, "The Conscience of the King"

"But is not that the nature of men and women? That the pleasure is in the learning of each other?"

—Natira (Katherine Woodville),
"For the World Is Hollow and I Have Touched the Sky"

"Spock, the women on your planet are logical. No other planet in the galaxy can make that claim."

—Kirk, "Elaan of Troyius"

Kirk: "That unit is a woman."
NOMAD: "A mass of conflicting impulses."

—"The Changeling"

"I have never understood the female capacity to avoid a direct answer to any question."

—Spock, "This Side of Paradise"

"There's no right way to hit a woman."

—Kirk, "Charlie X"

"The imposter had some . . . interesting qualities, wouldn't you say, Yeoman?"
—Spock (infamously), after the Evil Kirk has attempted to rape Yeoman Rand
in "The Enemy Within"

"Believe me, it's better to be dead than to live alone in the body of a woman."
—Janice Lester (Sandra Smith), "Turnabout Intruder"

## On Romance

"I've already got a female to worry about. Her name's the *Enterprise*."

—Captain Kirk, "The Corbomite Maneuver"

"Extreme feminine beauty is always disturbing, madam."

—Spock, "The Cloud Minders"

"When I see you, I feel like I'm hungry all over. Hungry. Do you know how that feels?"

—Charlie Evans (Robert Walker Jr.) to Yeoman Rand, "Charlie X"

"And this ship. All this power. Surging and throbbing, yet under control. Are you like that, captain?"

—Lenore (Barbara Anderson), "The Conscience of the King"

"If I touch you again, Your Glory, it'll be to administer an ancient Earth custom called a spanking . . ."

—Kirk, "Elaan of Troyius"

"All a girl needs is Don Juan."

—Tonia Barrows (Emily Banks), "Shore Leave"

"This business of love. You have devoted much literature to it. Why do you build such a mystique around a simple biological function?"

—Kelinda (Barbara Bouchet), "By Any Other Name"

"Too much of anything, Lieutenant, even love, isn't necessarily a good thing."

—Uhura, "The Trouble with Tribbles"

"You may find that having is not so pleasing a thing as wanting. It is not logical, but it is often true."

—Spock, "Amok Time"

"My dear girl, I am a doctor. When I peek, it's in the line of duty."

—McCoy, "Shore Leave"

## On the Human (and Vulcan) Condition

"To be human is to be complex. You can't avoid a little ugliness from within and from without."

—Kirk, "Requiem for Methuselah"

"We all have our darker side. We need it! It's half of what we are. It's not really ugly. It's human."

—McCoy, "The Enemy Within"

"Where there is no emotion, there is no motive for violence."

—Spock, "Dagger of the Mind"

"The heart is not a logical organ."

—Janet Wallace (Sarah Marshall), "The Deadly Years"

"Sometimes pain can drive a man harder than pleasure."

—Kirk, "The Alternative Factor"

"The more complex the mind, the greater the need for the simplicity of play."

—Kirk, "Shore Leave"

"Blood thins. The body fails. One is finally grateful for a failing memory."

—Anton Karidian (Arnold Moss), "The Conscience of the King"

"Immortality consists largely of boredom."

—Zefram Cochrane (Glenn Corbett), "Metamorphosis"

"Every life comes to an end when time demands it. Loss of life is to be mourned only if the life was wasted."

—Spock, "Yesteryear" (animated episode)

"There are a million things in this universe you can have, and there are a million things you can't have."

—Kirk, "Charlie X"

"Man stagnates if he has no ambition, no desire to be more than he is."

—Kirk, "This Side of Paradise"

"Change is the essential process of all existence."

—Spock, "Let That Be Your Last Battlefield"

"Monsters come in many forms. You know the greatest monster of them all, Jim? Guilt."

—McCoy, "Obsession"

"Self-pity's a terrible first course. Why don't you try the soup instead?"

—Nurse Chapel, "Obsession"

"Compassion. That's the one thing no machine ever had. Maybe it's the one thing that keeps men ahead of them."

—McCoy, "The Ultimate Computer"

"Humans do have an amazing capacity for believing what they choose and excluding that which is painful."

—Spock, "And the Children Shall Lead"

"In critical moments, men sometimes see exactly what they wish to see."

—Spock, "The Tholian Web"

## On Ethics

"Spock, I've found that evil usually triumphs . . . unless good is very, very careful."

—McCoy, "The Omega Glory"

"Without followers, evil cannot spread."

—Spock, "And the Children Shall Lead"

"Leave any bigotry in your quarters. There's no room for it on the bridge."

—Kirk, "Balance of Terror"

"I, too, felt a brief surge of racial bigotry. Most distasteful."

—Spock, "Day of the Dove"

"Alexander, where I come from, size, shape or color makes no difference,"

—Kirk, "Plato's Stepchildren"

"This troubled planet is a place of the most violent contrasts. Those who receive the rewards are totally separated from those who shoulder the burdens. It is not a wise leadership."

—Spock, "The Cloud Minders"

"I speak of rights. A machine has none. A man must!"

—Samuel Cogley (Elisha Cook Jr.), "Court Martial"

"Liberty and freedom have to be more than just words."

—Kirk, "The Omega Glory"

"Without freedom of choice, there is no creativity. Without creativity, there is no life."

—Kirk, "The Return of the Archons"

"Uncontrolled, power will turn even saints into savages. And we can all be counted upon to live down to our lowest impulses."

—Parmen, "Plato's Stepchildren"

"In every revolution, there is one man with a vision."

—Kirk, "Mirror, Mirror"

"'Let me help.' A hundred years or so from now, I believe, a famous novelist will write a classic using that theme. He'll recommend those three words over 'I love you.'"

—Kirk, "The City on the Edge of Forever"

"Knowledge is freedom."

—Kirk, "The Magicks of Megas-Tu" (animated episode)

## On Violence

"Do you know that you're one of the few predator species that preys even on itself?"

—Trelaine (William Campbell), "The Squire of Gothos"

"You find it easier to understand the death of one than the death of a million. You speak about the objective hardness of the Vulcan heart, yet how little room there seems to be in yours."

—Spock, "The Immunity Syndrome"

"You [humans] are still half savage. But there is hope."

—Metron, "The Arena"

Petri: "We cannot make peace with people we detest."
Kirk: "Stop trying to kill each other. Then worry about being friendly."
—"Elaan of Troyius"

"In the strict scientific sense, Doctor, we all feed on death. Even vegetarians."
—Spock, "Wolf in the Fold"

Sulu: "What a terrible way to die."
Kirk: "There are no good ways, Sulu."
—"That Which Survives"

"No one may kill a man. Not for any purpose. It cannot be condoned."
—Kirk, "Spock's Brain"

"Murder is contrary to the laws of man and God."
—M-5 Computer, "The Ultimate Computer"

Kirk: "War. We didn't want it, but we've got it."
Spock: "Curious how often you humans manage to obtain that which you do not want."
—"Errand of Mercy"

"There's no honorable way to kill, no gentle way to destroy. There is nothing good in war except its ending."
—Abraham Lincoln (Lee Bergere), "The Savage Curtain"

"You Earth people glorify organized violence for forty centuries, but you imprison those who employ it privately."
—Spock, "Dagger of the Mind"

Kirk: "Your Surak is a brave man."
Spock: "Men of peace usually are, Captain."
—"The Savage Curtain"

## On the Divine

"Mankind has no need for gods. We find the one quite adequate."
—Kirk, "Who Mourns for Adonais?"

"Maybe we weren't meant for paradise."
—Kirk, "This Side of Paradise"

"The glory of creation is in its infinite diversity."
—Miranda Jones (Diana Muldaur), "Is There in Truth No Beauty?"

## On the Final Frontier

"May the Great Bird of the Galaxy bless your planet."

—Yeoman Rand, "The Man Trap"

"Space still contains infinite unknowns."

—Spock, "The Naked Time"

## On the Crew's Interpersonal Dynamics

"I can't change the law of physics!"

—Scotty, "The Naked Time"

"Mr. Scott, there are always alternatives."

—Spock, "The Galileo Seven"

"This is a mystery, and I don't like mysteries. They give me a bellyache, and I've got a beauty right now."

—Kirk, "The Man Trap"

"By golly, Jim! I'm beginning to think I can cure a rainy day!"

—McCoy, "The Devil in the Dark"

"You could hardly claim to be an angel with those pointed ears, Mr. Spock. But say you landed someplace with a pitchfork . . ."

—McCoy, "Bread and Circuses"

Kirk: "Now you're sounding like Spock."
McCoy: "If you're going to get nasty, I'm going to leave."

—"Tomorrow Is Yesterday"

Kirk: "I suspect you're becoming more and more human all the time."
Spock: "Captain, I see no reason to stand here and be insulted."

—"The Devil in the Dark"

"Shut up, Spock! We're rescuing you!"

—McCoy, "The Immunity Syndrome"

"Well, this is an *Enterprise* first! Dr. McCoy, Mr. Spock and Engineer Scott find themselves in complete agreement! Can I stand the strain?"

—Kirk, "The Lights of Zetar"

# Highly Illogical

## Notable and Notorious *Star Trek* Parodies

Imitation, they say, is the sincerest form of flattery. By the same token, parody may be the truest measure of cultural significance.

The extent to which a film, television series, or other work of art has been absorbed into the popular consciousness can be gauged by the frequency with which it is lampooned. After all, you won't win many laughs poking fun at a show no one has seen. By this yardstick, the multitude of *Star Trek* spoofs can be considered a sort of cockeyed testimonial. Over the years, cartoonists, filmmakers, animators, stand-up comics, disc jockeys, and even pornographers have mocked *Trek*, with skits, strips, and movies ranging from witty and insightful to crass and puerile. An exhaustive accounting of these parodies would fill this book many times over, but the following notable (and notorious) spoofs serve as a representative sampling.

### *Mad* Magazine (December 1967 and October 1976)

One of the earliest *Star Trek* parodies arrived in the pages of *Mad* magazine's December 1967 issue. The five-page spoof "Star Blecch" by artist Mort Drucker and writer Dick De Bartolo follows Captain Kook and Mr. Spook of the Starship *Booby-Prize* as they beam down to planet Rama IV to rescue Fob, sole survivor of a planet devastated by disease and pollution. Kook and Spook bring him aboard the *Booby-Prize*, until Dr. BeCoy determines that Fob is contagious; then Kirk (er, Kook) tries to shove the Raman out the nearest airlock. "Star Blecch" includes caricatures of Nichelle Nichols and James Doohan as well as those of William Shatner, Leonard Nimoy, and DeForest Kelley. It's satire of the typically sophomoric *Mad* variety, but it has its moments—working in a joke about the apparent lack of restrooms on the starship *Enterprise* and some not-so-subtle commentary on L.A. smog and other environmental issues.

This was one of the few *Star Trek* spoofs created while the show was still in production. Publicity photos show Nimoy and Shatner yukking it up as they read "Star Blecch" during location shooting for "A Private Little War." While the *Mad* parody was on newsstands, Nimoy appeared on *The Carol Burnett Show* in a skit titled "Mrs. Invisible Man." Burnett played a confused young mother in search of parenting advice who mistakenly calls in *Mr.* Spock (Nimoy, in full makeup and costume) rather than famed pediatrician *Dr.* Spock.

Tellingly, however, the real flood of *Star Trek* parodies began in the 1970s, after the show became a syndication sensation. The rising tide of *Trek* spoofs included "Keep on Trekkin'—the *Mad Star Trek* Musical," from *Mad*'s October 1976 issue. Its cover featured a painting of Kirk and Spock dancing with Alfred E. Neuman. The seven-page parody, written largely in verse (to the tune of popular songs and show tunes) lampoons the lack of post-*Trek* success among the show's cast ("None of the engines are workin' and neither am I," the Doohan caricature croons to the tune of "Send in the Clowns"). It also toys with various *Star Trek* clichés, including the short life expectancy of red-shirted extras. "Keep on Trekkin'" not only includes caricatures of the show's entire regular cast, including Majel Barrett and George Takei, who were omitted in "Star Blecch," but gives every character at least one solo "vocal." By and large, it's a very clever and well-observed piece, although it misses the mark at the end, in which the cast refuses to reunite and return to TV because they are making easy money from the sale of *Star Trek* toys and other merchandise. Actually, cast members saw very little of this revenue; Nimoy sued Paramount over this issue.

## Saturday Night Live, 1976 and 1986

*Saturday Night Live*, which has targeted *Star Trek* numerous times over the years, scored a bull's-eye with "The Last Voyage of the Starship Enterprise" on May 29, 1976 (toward the end of *SNL*'s first season). The frequently copied idea behind the sketch was that *Star Trek*'s stars have lost touch with reality. Completely consumed by their characters and the twenty-third-century sets and props, they have forgotten it's all just a TV show. John Belushi stars as Captain Kirk, with Chevy Chase as Mr. Spock and Dan Aykroyd as Dr. McCoy. As the skit begins, the *Enterprise* is pursued through space by a 1968 Chrysler Imperial. Out of the car steps an NBC executive played by host Elliott Gould, arriving to break the news that the show has been cancelled due to low Nielsen ratings. Spock attempts to stun the executive, but since his phaser is just a prop, nothing happens. "Most peculiar, captain," says a puzzled-looking Chase. "I can only assume that they possess some sort of weapons deactivator." Gould nonchalantly collects the phaser and then plucks the ears off "Nimoy's" head. As workmen dismantle the bridge set around him, Belushi delivers a final Captain's Log entry: "We have tried to explore strange new worlds, to seek out new civilizations, to boldly go where no man has gone before, and except for one television network, we have found intelligence everywhere in the galaxy."

When Shatner himself hosted *SNL* ten years later, the show inevitably included another *Trek* parody, titled "Star Trek V: The Restaurant Enterprise." In this spoof, the *Enterprise* is purchased by Marriott and turned into a hotel. Shatner, naturally, starred as Captain Kirk, with Kevin Nealon as Spock and Phil Hartman as Dr. McCoy. Dana Carvey appeared as Khan, who attempts to gain revenge by bringing a health inspector to the restaurant. Kirk defuses the threat by bribing the inspector. The skit's funniest moment belongs to Hartman. Told that a customer needs medical attention, he replies, "Dammit, Jim, I'm a doctor, not a—oh, sure."

"The Restaurant Enterprise," while amusing, was eclipsed by the episode's other *Star Trek*-themed sketch, which lampooned *Trek* conventions. Shatner appeared as himself, railing at "Trekkies" played by Nealon and Carvey, to "get a life!" When Shatner reminds them that *Star Trek* was only a TV show, Carvey asks, "Are you saying we should pay more attention to the movies?" Many Trekkers didn't appreciate being the subject of such lacerating satire and believed the sketch reflected Shatner's real feelings toward *Star Trek* fans. The actor insisted it was only a skit, but the fallout inspired Shatner to write his 1999 book *Get a Life!* about his sometimes strained relationship with fandom and experiences at *Star Trek* conventions.

## Trek or Treat, 1977

Authors Terry Flannagan and Eleanor Ehrhardt published this slim paperback book, which provided humorous captions to freeze-frames from various *Star Trek* episodes. The cover of the book illustrates the formula. It's a shot of Spock (wearing the IDIC medallion from "Is There in Truth No Beauty?") flashing the Vulcan hand sign. But instead of "Live long and prosper," he's saying, "Same to you, fella!" Most of the humor in *Trek or Treat* functions on this level, and many of the jokes are badly dated (with references to *The Waltons*, citizens band radios,

Eleanor Ehrhardt and Terry Flanagan's 1977 paperback *Trek or Treat* featured *Star Trek* photos with satirical captions.

and other 1970s fads). But its publication by a major publisher (Ballantine Books) speaks to the era's insatiable appetite for all things *Trek*.

## The Muppet Show, 1977–81

Three episodes into its second season, producer-puppeteer Jim Henson's *The Muppet Show* premiered a new recurring sketch: "Pigs in Space," which spoofed science fiction in general but *Star Trek* and *Flash Gordon* most directly. Set on the bridge of the starship *Swinetrek*, "Pigs in Space" starred the preening Captain Link Hogthrob, insubordinate First Mate Miss Piggy, and the bumbling Dr. Julius Strangepork. It quickly became one of the program's most popular recurring bits. In all, *The Muppet Show* aired thirty-two "Pigs in Space" adventures over the course of its final three seasons, although some of those installments parodied movies and programs other than *Star Trek*. (In 1980, for instance, an extended *Star Wars*-themed "Pigs in Space" consumed nearly half an episode. It featured host Mark Hamill, along with R2-D2, C-3PO, and Chewbacca.) The recurring skit grew so popular that "Pigs in Space" posters, T-shirts, lunch boxes, storybooks, and even an Atari video game, among other products, were issued. Henson's short-lived prime-time series *Muppets Tonight* (which ran on ABC in 1997) revived the sketch as "Pigs in Space: Deep Dish Nine (The Next Generation of Pigs in Space)," which (as the title suggests) parodied *Star Trek*'s sequel series. Leonard Nimoy made a cameo appearance in this skit.

## In Living Color, 1990 and 1992

*Saturday Night Live* was hardly the only sketch comedy series to fire a shot at *Star Trek*; in fact, virtually every such program has taken a whack at it. Keenan and Damon Wayans's *In Living Color* took their turn in 1990 with "The Wrath of Farrakhan," which simultaneously satirized both *Star Trek* and controversial Nation of Islam leader Louis Farrakhan. The skit featured Jim Carrey (doing an extremely exaggerated William Shatner impression) as Captain Kirk and Damon Wayans as Farrakhan. Farrakhan boards the *Enterprise* to free the "enslaved" minorities aboard the vessel, including Sulu and Spock but beginning with Lieutenant Uhura. When Kirk asks Uhura to contact Starfleet Command, Farrakhan interrupts: "My Nubian princess, how long have you placed his calls? I watch this show every week, and all I see is the back of your nappy wig."

Two years later the program served up a second spoof, "Star Trek VII: The Really Last Voyage," which poked fun at the aging of the classic *Trek* cast. "We just left the Romulan galaxy and we are approaching . . . senility," reports Carrey (again playing Kirk) in an opening Captain's Log entry. He moves around the bridge with the assistance of a walker, and applies a defibrillator to Sulu when the geriatric lieutenant collapses at the helm. In a knowing nod to "slash" fan fiction, Spock (David Allan Grier) reminds Kirk that as a Vulcan he must mate every seven years. "I only have two days left and you're looking pretty good to me," Grier says. At the conclusion of the skit, a nurse and two orderlies arrive to fetch the crew back to the Sunnyside Retirement Colony.

## MADtv, 1997

Not to be outdone, in 1997 *MADtv* aired "The Kirk and Spock Variety Hour," which parodied both *Star Trek* and 1970s variety shows. Kirk (Will Sasso) and Spock (Pat Kilbane) cohost a *Laugh-In*-like comedy-variety program featuring (intentionally) lame comedy routines and awkward musical numbers. Special guests include McCoy (guest star Tim Conlon) , Uhura (Debra Wilson), Sammy Davis, Jr. (Phil LaMarr), Phyllis Diller (herself), the June Taylor Tribbles (dancers in giant, puffy tribble costumes), and a go-go dancing Orion slave girl. Sasso attempts to mock Shatner's notorious performances of "Rocket Man" and "Lucy in the Sky with Diamonds," but fails to recapture their astounding weirdness and hilarity. Midway through the sketch, Diller opines, "Beam me up, Scotty. This show sucks!" In a later episode, Sasso and Kilbane reprised their roles as Kirk and Spock in "Estrella Viaje!" a *Trek* spoof performed entirely in Spanish and based on Hispanic stereotypes. During *MADtv*'s long run (from 1995 to 2009), the program also lampooned *The Next Generation*, *Deep Space Nine* and *Voyager*, with mixed results.

## Galaxy Quest, 1999

Director Dean Parisot's delightful *Galaxy Quest* (1999) parodied both *Star Trek* and its fans without condescending to either.

The washed-up stars of *Galaxy Quest*, a *Trek*-ish cancelled TV series with a cultish fan base, are abducted by the Thermians, aliens from a distant planet who want the Questers to help them defeat an interplanetary warlord. The Thermians have modeled their entire culture after *Galaxy Quest*, developing all the sci-fi gadgetry used on the show (which they don't realize was a work of fiction). The *Galaxy Quest* stars—played by Tim Allen, Sigourney Weaver, Alan Rickman, Sam Rockwell, and Tony Shalhoub—gamely offer to help, but don't know how to work the gizmos from their own program. As a result, they're forced to rely on their obsessive fans, who have memorized every minute detail of the "imaginary" technology.

Clever and keenly observed, with a rare combination of sweetness and directness, *Galaxy Quest* was a surprise hit, earning more than $90 million worldwide and scoring mostly glowing reviews. It was enthusiastically embraced by *Star Trek* fans and actors including William Shatner and George Takei, both of whom went on record as *Galaxy Quest* devotees. "I was rolling in the aisles," Takei told a Sci Fi Channel interviewer. "And Tim Allen had that Shatner-esque swagger down pat."

Interestingly, the producers of *Deep Space Nine* considered a story idea very similar to the plot of *Galaxy Quest*. The idea was to send Captain Sisko to planet Sigma Iota II, last seen in the classic yarn "A Piece of the Action," in which the highly imitative Iotians have built up an entire culture based on Chicago gangs of the 1920s. Sisko would have discovered that, following their encounter with Kirk, Spock and McCoy, the Iotians have now developed a culture imitating Starfleet of the twenty-third century. The concept was intended as a playful jibe at fandom, but given the reaction to Shatner's "Get a Life!" *SNL* sketch, the idea was abandoned. Instead, producers developed "Trials and Tribble-ations," which transported Sisko and his crew back into the classic episode "The Trouble with Tribbles."

## Futurama, 2002

*Futurama*, an animated comedy sci-fi series created by *The Simpsons*' Matt Groening, was often replete with inside jokes derived from *Star Trek*. In 2002, however, *Futurama* created what may be the ultimate spoof/tribute with "Where No Fan Has Gone Before." The episode reunited *Star Trek*'s entire surviving cast (except for James Doohan, who declined to participate) and also featured a cameo by Jonathan Frakes of *The Next Generation*. Shatner, Nimoy, Nichols, George Takei, and Walter Koenig played themselves—or, rather, they played their living disembodied heads, sustained in glass jars.

The series' protagonist was Philip J. Fry (Billy West), a twentieth-century pizza delivery boy accidentally placed in a cryogenic deep-freeze and thawed out in the year 3000. In "Where No Fan Has Gone Before," Fry discovers that *Star Trek* has been banned for 800 years after the show's ardent fan following grew into a full-blown religious cult. A flashback shows the Church of Star Trek, where a priest reads from "scripture": "And Scotty beamed them to the Klingon ship, where they would be no tribble at all." To which the congregation chants, "All power to the engines!" To quell the growing power of the cult, Fry learns, *Star Trek* was banned and the last surviving copies of the seventy-nine original episodes and six movies "along with that blooper reel where the door doesn't close all the way," were shipped to the forbidden planet Omega III. To save *Star Trek*, Fry convinces his friends to travel to Omega III, which they discover houses a cloudlike noncorporeal alien intelligence named Melllvar (yes, with three "l's"). Melllvar gathers the preserved heads of the show's cast and, after creating new bodies for them, forces them to hold a *Star Trek* convention that will last until the end of time. (At the convention, Shatner talk-sings a version of rapper Eminem's "The Real Slim Shady.") Fry vows to rescue the *Trek* cast from Omega III but is forced into an "Arena"-like hand-to-hand battle with the actors.

All this plays just as fast and furious (and funny) as it reads. More so, in fact. "Where No Fan Has Gone Before" was written by *Trek* buff David A. Goodman, who labored meticulously to ensure that its nonstop stream of *Star Trek* references (to dozens of episodes) were all accurate. The episode also makes clever use of original *Trek* musical cues and sound effects. It not only lampoons the show itself, but the excesses of fandom and the strained relationships between some of the show's former cast members. (At one point Shatner asks, "Wasn't there an episode where I threw my shoe at the enemy?" To which Nimoy replies, "You mean Doohan?") While the satire remains barbed, "Where No Fan Has Gone Before" also includes a moment of affectionate tribute to *Star Trek* as well. While trying to explain the appeal of the show, Fry says that *Trek* "taught me so much. Like how you should accept people, whether they be black, white, Klingon or even female. But most importantly, when I didn't have any friends, it made me feel like maybe I did."

Because of that moment, for its persnickety accuracy, and because it's roll-on-the-floor, gasping-for-breath funny, "Where No Fan Has Gone Before" quickly became one of the *Star Trek* parodies most widely beloved by *Star Trek* fans. The producers of *Star Trek: Enterprise* were so impressed that they invited Goodman to write for their series. He wound up penning four episodes.

## More Parodies (of Dubious Quality and Questionable Taste)

On the other end of the spectrum, *Star Trek* has been the butt of many dunder-headed, lowbrow spoofs, too. For instance, **Airplane II: The Sequel** (1982) wasn't so much a follow-up to the original *Airplane!* (1980) as a wide-ranging lampoon of numerous sci-fi movies and TV shows, including *Star Trek*. It included many (mostly lame) *Trek*-themed jokes and even featured William Shatner as Commander Buck Murdock of the Starship *Mayflower*. Writer-producer Mel Brooks's scattershot **Spaceballs**(1987) took a similar approach, and generated almost as few laughs. But for truly inept satire, *Trek* fans should seek out **Turist Ömer Uzay Yolunda** (1973), a Turkish film that must be You Tubed to be believed. The film, whose title translates as "Ömer the Tourist in Star Trek," was part of a series of comedies starring unfunny funnyman Sadri Alisik as the bumbling traveler Omer, who continually finds himself in one scrape after another. In this adventure he's beamed aboard a cut-rate copy of the *Enterprise,* led by a remarkably swishy Captain Kirk, and becomes embroiled in a scenario similar to "The Man Trap." The movie's title theme and spaceship footage are lifted directly from actual *Star Trek* episodes, which only makes everything else seem even cheesier.

*Turist Ömer Uzay Yolunda* would be the nadir of *Star Trek* spoofery, were it not for **Sex Trek.** From 1991 to 1999, Moonlight Entertainment issued a series of seven (!) pornographic parodies, and Platinum Blue Productions revived the *Sex Trek* franchise with two more entries in 2006. These pictures lampooned specific original series

William Shatner seems amused by Mad Magazine's parody "Star Blecch," Leonard Nimoy less so. This shot was taken during location shooting for "A Private Little War."

episodes, primarily those with romantic or sexual themes, such as "Charlie X," "Amok Time," "Mudd's Women," "The Cage," and "Turnabout Intruder." Lest *Next Gen* fans feel left out, Moonlight also issued *Sex Trek: The Next Penetration*, along with four sequels set in *Trek*'s twenty-fourth century milieu. Hustler Entertainment released the appropriately titled *This Ain't Star Trek XXX* in 2009, in the wake of director J. J. Abrams's blockbuster *Star Trek* reboot.

And, finally, we have (whether we want it or not) **"Star Trek: The Lost Episode,"** a notorious, raunchy audio collage created anonymously in the late 1980s. After airing on the *Dr. Demento* radio show in the early 1990s, it was replayed many times by "shock jock" comedians on stations across the country. "The Lost Episode" is a patchwork of sound bites, music, and sound effects from several classic *Trek* episodes reassembled to form a new narrative in which Kirk and Spock engage in a graphic sexual encounter. When two disc jockeys played this bit for James Doohan during a visit to Norfolk, Virginia, rock radio station WNOR, Doohan became enraged and threatened to leave unless they stopped the tape immediately.

# Starfleet Commendations

## Awards Won (and Lost), 1966–75

*Palm Leaf of Axanar Peace Mission, Grankite Order of Tactics, Prentares Ribbon of Commendation (Classes First and Second), Award for Valor, Medal of Honor, Silver Palm with Cluster, Starfleet Citation for Conspicuous Gallantry, Karagite Order of Heroism . . .*

That's the list of Captain Kirk's medals and commendations, as rattled off by the Starfleet Computer in the episode "Court Martial" before attorney Cogley (Elisha Cook Jr.) decides the court has heard enough and halts the recitation. *Star Trek* wasn't quite as decorated as the captain of the *Enterprise*. Here's a complete rundown of honors bestowed on *Star Trek* and its animated successor.

### Emmy Awards

The Emmy Awards, bestowed annually since 1949 by the Academy of Television Arts & Sciences, remain the industry's most prestigious honor. During its three-year run, *Star Trek* earned a total of thirteen nominations but failed to bring home a trophy. Later *Star Trek* series earned more nominations (142 in all) and sometimes won Emmys (thirty-three altogether) but rarely received recognition in the major categories. The original *Trek* was nominated as Outstanding Dramatic Series following each of its first two seasons. The only other *Trek* series to be so honored was *The Next Generation*, which earned a similar nomination in its final season. Leonard Nimoy, nominated as Outstanding Supporting Actor, remains the only cast member to earn an Emmy nomination for his work on a *Star Trek* program.

In 1967, following its first season, *Star Trek* was nominated for five Emmy Awards but lost in every category. The nominations:

- Outstanding Dramatic Series, which *Star Trek* lost to *Mission: Impossible.*
- Outstanding Performance by an Actor in a Supporting Role in a Drama (Leonard Nimoy). Eli Wallach won for his work in the TV movie *The Poppy*

*Is Also a Flower.* (At the time, supporting performers in TV movies and series competed in the same category.)

- Individual Achievements in Art Direction and Allied Crafts (to Jim Rugg for mechanical special effects). The Emmy went to the CBS special *Mark Twain Tonight.*
- Individual Achievements in Cinematography (to Darrell Anderson, Linwood Dunn, and Joseph Westheimer for special visual effects). The stodgy Western *Bonanza* took home the award in this category. This was arguably *Star Trek's* most galling defeat.
- Individual Achievements in Film and Sound Editing (to Douglas Grindstaff, sound editor). *Star Trek* lost to Irwin Allen's *Voyage to the Bottom of the Sea.* (But at least it wasn't *Lost in Space!*)

A year later, *Star Trek* was nominated in four categories:

- Outstanding Dramatic Series, which it again lost to *Mission: Impossible.*
- Outstanding Performance by an Actor in a Supporting Role in a Drama (Leonard Nimoy), who this time lost to Milburn Stone—"Doc" from *Gunsmoke.*
- Outstanding Achievement in Film Editing (Donald R. Rode, editor). This Emmy went to NBC's *Bell Telephone Hour.*
- Special Classification of Individual Achievements (the Westheimer Company, for Special Photographic Effects). This was a strange, catch-all category for outstanding work that didn't fit conveniently under any other category. Multiple nominees were named from various disciplines. In 1968, there were seven nominees and two Emmys awarded, both to actors: Art Carney of *The Jackie Gleason Show* and Pat Paulsen of *The Smothers Brothers Comedy Hour.*

In 1969, following its final campaign, the show earned four more nominations:

- Outstanding Continued Performance by an Actor in a Series (Leonard Nimoy). This category was for lead actors, not supporting ones—which is where Nimoy should have been nominated in the first place. Nevertheless, he lost again, this time to Don Adams of *Get Smart.*
- Outstanding Achievement in Art Direction and Scenic Design (John Dyer, set decorator, and Walter M. Jefferies). Matt Jefferies finally received an overdue nomination but lost to *Mission: Impossible.*
- Outstanding Achievement in Film Editing (Donald R. Rode, editor). The award went to *Judd for the Defense*, one of the few shows *Star Trek* outperformed in the Nielsen ratings.
- Special Classification Achievements (Howard A. Anderson Company, The Westheimer Company, Van der Veer Photo Effects, and Cinema Research for special photographic effects). Almost inconceivably, the show's visual effects never won an Emmy. This year there were nine nominees for Special

Leonard Nimoy earned three consecutive Emmy nominations but lost three years in a row.

Classification Achievements and four Emmys issued. They went to actors Harvey Korman for *The Carol Burnett Show* and Arte Johnson for *Rowan & Martin's Laugh-In,* and producers Don Meier for *Mutual of Omaha's Wild Kingdom* and Warren Steibel for *Firing Line with William F. Buckley.*

*Star Trek* finally won an Emmy in 1975 when the animated series was named Outstanding Entertainment Children's Series at the Second Annual Daytime Emmy Awards. The award went to Filmation founder/president Lou Scheimer. The previous year, the series had earned a nomination in the same category but lost to the PBS show *Zoom.*

## Hugo Awards

The Hugo Awards, handed out annually at the World Science Fiction Convention and based on attendee's votes, were initiated in 1953 and remain one of the genre's most distinguished honors. The award is named for legendary *Amazing Stories* publisher Hugo Gernsback, who coined the term "science fiction." Although the Hugos were created to honor literary sci-fi, in 1960, a category was added for Best Dramatic Presentation. Over the years, nominees in this category have included movies, TV shows, record albums, and other disciplines. However, television programs have rarely won Hugo Awards. There are just two

The entire cast assembled on the transporter pads for this publicity still. (If they all beam out, who's going to run the ship?)

exceptions: Rod Serling's *The Twilight Zone*, which claimed the first three Hugos awarded in the category, and *Star Trek*.

In 1967, "The Menagerie, Parts I and II" won the Hugo for Best Dramatic Presentation. That year, two other *Trek* episodes were nominated in the same category ("The Naked Time" and "The Corbomite Maneuver"). In 1968, all five Hugo nominees in the category were *Star Trek* episodes—"The Trouble with Tribbles," "Mirror, Mirror," "The Doomsday Machine," "Amok Time," and the award-winning "City on the Edge of Forever"—a singular achievement on par with the Beatles holding all five spots on the Billboard pop chart simultaneously. It is unlikely ever to be equaled. In 1969, following its beleaguered third season, *Star Trek* failed to earn a single Hugo nomination.

Following *Star Trek*'s dominance in 1968, no TV show won a Hugo for the next twenty-five years, when *The Next Generation* won a Hugo for the episode "The Inner Light." In all, *Next Gen* earned three Hugo nominations and won twice. *Deep Space Nine* and *Star Trek: Enterprise* earned two Hugo nominations apiece but never won. All the *Star Trek* feature films except *The Final Frontier* and *Nemesis* were Hugo-nominated, but no *Trek* movie has ever won the award.

## Writers Guild of America Awards

The Writers Guild of America Awards, voted on by members of the professional organization for screenwriters, has held two ceremonies per year since 1933, one for East Coast Guild members and one for West Coast Guild members. In 1968, two *Star Trek* teleplays earned Writers Guild nominations—John T. Dugan's "Return to Tomorrow" and Harlan Ellison's "The City on the Edge of Forever." Ellison's screenplay won, which created a minor controversy because the writer submitted his original, first draft of the screenplay rather than the heavily rewritten version that was actually produced. Gene Roddenberry submitted the broadcast version of "City on the Edge" for Hugo consideration, where it also won. Ironically, both awards went to Ellison.

## NAACP Image Awards

*Star Trek* also received one of the first Image Awards from the NAACP in 1967. That year, the NAACP launched its annual awards ceremony to honor achievement by people of color in film, television, music, and literature. Nichelle Nichols, for her inspiring portrayal of Lieutenant Uhura, was the first television performer to win the award.

## Contemporary Honors and Awards

Over the years, countless polls—taken by magazines and cable TV channels or over the Internet—have asked fans and/or critics to name the best science fiction TV series of all time. *Star Trek* regularly finishes at or near the top of these lists, especially when voting is left up to fans. *Trek*'s stiffest competition usually comes from classic programs like *The Outer Limits* and *The Twilight Zone*, newer shows such as *The X-Files*, *Babylon 5*, the new *Battlestar Galactica*, and its own progeny, especially *The Next Generation*.

In recent years, *Star Trek* also has been honored through television specials and magazine articles, achievements that compensate in part for the glaring disconnect between the show's enduring cultural impact and its many Emmy defeats.

***TV Guide***—When this venerable weekly named its 50 Greatest TV Shows of All Time in 2002, the original *Star Trek* series failed to make the cut, even though *The Next Generation* finished No. 46. However, when *TV Guide* published its survey of the Top Cult Shows Ever in 2004, the classic *Star Trek* finished No. 1—and was the only *Trek* series to make the twenty-five-show list.

***TV Land* Awards**—The TV Land cable network honored *Star Trek* with its Pop Culture Award during the initial broadcast of its annual TV Land Awards in 2003.

***Time***—TIME magazine placed *Star Trek* on its list of the 100 Best TV Shows of All-TIME in 2007. The list was unranked and alphabetical. Critic James Poniewozik wrote: "Though the sci-fi show was colored by its troubled times, it also had a genuine postwar optimism, believing that technology, science and cooperation could actually lead humanity to unity and progress. Dated as the original *Trek* can look—with Kirk chasing galactic babes and space hippies—its first-rate sci-fi plots still hold up, as does the hope that hundreds of years from now we might be still boldly going."

# Keep On Trekkin'

## Famous and Influential Fans

Star Trek fans have endured decades of ridicule and abuse. The image of the socially awkward, obsessive-compulsive, possibly delusional "Trekkie" became fixed in the public mind, even among many who loved Star Trek. Millions of viewers flocked to blockbuster movies like Star Trek II: The Wrath of Khan (1982) and Star Trek IV: The Voyage Home (1986), and made Star Trek and its sequel series the most profitable syndicated TV franchise of all time. Yet somehow, many in the audience failed to count themselves as fans, in part because the series' most ardent devotees had become stigmatized, an easy punch line for stand-up comics and snarky critics. Even William Shatner famously exhorted fans to "get a life" in a 1986 Saturday Night Live skit. "Move out of your parents' basements . . . and grow the hell up!"

There's no denying that extremists exist, and have always existed, in the community of Trek fandom. These are the people who tried to rip Shatner's clothes off during a 1968 public appearance, the ones who creator-producer Gene Roddenberry said "scare the hell out of me" in a 1976 interview with the Associated Press. Despite the stereotype, however, most Star Trek fans have always led perfectly normal lives. Rather than hanging out in Mom's basement, many have been inspired by the program to take action—volunteering with food banks or literacy programs, or lobbying for progressive political causes—and to pursue their own dreams. They have become scientists, engineers, physicians, actors, writers, directors, titans of industry, even president of the United States. Not bad for a bunch of dweebs.

### Tom Hanks

Two-time Oscar-winning actor Tom Hanks frequently has professed his admiration for Star Trek. He was ten years old when the program premiered, and the series helped foster a childhood aspiration to join the space program. That didn't work out, but he played astronaut Jim Lovell in the 1995 film Apollo 13, coproduced the HBO miniseries From Earth to the Moon (1998) about the Apollo program, and coproduced, cowrote, and narrated the IMAX documentary Magnificent Desolation: Walking on the Moon 3D (2005). Hanks was offered the role of Zefram Cochrane in the motion picture Star Trek: First Contact (1996) but had to decline because he was working on his directorial debut, That Thing

*You Do!* (also 1996). Instead, James Cromwell played Cochrane in *First Contact*. Hanks also expressed interest in making a cameo appearance in J. J. Abrams's 2009 *Star Trek* film. According to Patrick Stewart, Hanks boasts that he can name every episode of *The Next Generation*.

## Ben Stiller

Actor-writer-director Ben Stiller, who attended his first *Star Trek* convention at age eleven, works *Trek* inside jokes into nearly all his films. In his 2001 movie *Zoolander*, Stiller named the villain "Mugatu" in tribute to the Mugato, the horn-headed white gorilla creature seen in "A Private Little War." The 1996 comedy *The Cable Guy*, directed by Stiller, used composer Gerald Fried's "Ritual/Ancient Battle" suite (written for Captain Kirk's clash with Spock during "Amok Time" and reused frequently in later episodes) to score the climactic fight between Steven Kovacs (Matthew Broderick) and his demented cable television installer (Jim Carrey). Stiller also gave William Shatner a cameo in his 2004 film *Dodgeball*. Even the name of Stiller's production company, Red Hour Films, is a *Star Trek* reference. The Red Hour is the time when denizens of planet Beta III run amok in the episode "The Return of the Archons."

## Whoopi Goldberg

Whoopi Goldberg (born Caryn Elaine Johnson in 1955 in New York City) was eleven years old when *Star Trek* debuted. She was inspired to pursue a career in acting by Nichelle Nichols's portrayal of Lieutenant Uhura. By the time *Star Trek: The Next Generation* premiered in 1987, Goldberg had established herself as a popular stand-up comedian and had proven her dramatic skills with an Oscar-nominated appearance in director Steven Spielberg's *The Color Purple* (1985). She also won a Golden Globe and an NAACP Image Award for her work in that film. Then, at the pinnacle of her career, Goldberg approached creator-producer Gene Roddenberry and asked to join the cast of *Next Gen*. Roddenberry, once he realized Goldberg was serious, created the recurring character of Guinan especially for her. The actress appeared in twenty-nine episodes scattered throughout the show's final six seasons and had cameos in the *Star Trek* feature films *Generations* (1994) and *Nemesis* (2002). According to Nichelle Nichols's autobiography, *Beyond Uhura*, Goldberg was irked when she realized that her girlhood idol would not appear in *Generations*. "Where the hell is Nichelle?" complained Goldberg, who hoped that Uhura and Guinan would share a scene together.

## Other Actors and Entertainers

**Jason Alexander,** of *Seinfeld* fame, is a self-identified "Trekkie" who guest starred (in alien makeup, no less) in the 1999 *Voyager* episode "Think Tank." He also appeared, wearing Spock ears and a "Beam Me Up" T-Shirt, in country singer Brad Paisley's 2007 music video "On-Line," which also featured William Shatner. **Kelsey Grammer,** star of *Cheers* and *Frasier,* is a diehard *Trek* fan who spoke Klingon in the *Frasier* episode "Star Mitzvah" (2002). Grammer guest starred in the 1992 *Next Generation* episode "Cause and Effect"; Patrick Stewart and Brent Spiner returned the favor by making guest appearances on *Frasier.* Actor **Robin Williams,** who became a household name playing an extraterrestrial on *Mork & Mindy* (1978–82), visited the set of *Star Trek: The Motion Picture* in 1979. He was offered the role of time-traveling con man Berlinghoff Rasmussen in the *Next Gen* episode "A Matter of Time" (1991) but had to decline due to conflicts with the shooting schedule of *Hook* (1991). Instead, the role went to Matt Frewer, best remembered as TV's "Max Headroom."

Actor **Christian Slater,** who had a cameo in *Star Trek VI: The Undiscovered Country* (1991), is another *Trek* devotee. So is Academy Award-winning actress **Mira Sorvino,** whose father, Paul Sorvino, played Worf's adoptive father in the *Next Gen* episode "Homeward" (1994). Actress **Angelina Jolie** told *The Daily Show's* Jon Stewart that she had an adolescent crush on Leonard Nimoy's Mr. Spock.

Writer-producer **Seth MacFarlane** often peppers episodes of his popular animated shows (*Family Guy, American Dad*) with *Star Trek* references and inside jokes. He also appeared in the *Star Trek: Enterprise* episodes "The Forgotten" (2004) and "Affliction" (2005). Writer-producer **David A. Goodman,** who worked with MacFarlane on *Family Guy,* also penned an episode-length *Trek* parody for *Futurama* ("Where No Fan Has Gone Before') and wrote four teleplays for *Star Trek: Enterprise.* Director **Bryan Singer,** who helmed *The Usual Suspects* (1995) and the first two *X-Men* movies, is another avowed *Trek* fan who made a cameo in *Star Trek: Nemesis.*

Drummer **Mick Fleetwood,** a founding member of the rock group Fleetwood Mac, is another confessed "Trekkie"; he had a cameo in the *Next Generation* episode "Manhunt" (1989). Guitarist **Tom Morello,** formerly of alt-rock band Rage Against the Machine, appeared in the *Star Trek: Voyager* episode "Good Shepherd" (2000). Country music superstar **Brad Paisley** asked William Shatner to appear in his 2007 music video "On-Line" and performed on Shatner's 2004 album *Has Been.* When one of Paisley's fans won a contest to spend a day with the singer in Las Vegas, Paisley took the lucky winner to *Star Trek: The Experience* at the Las Vegas Hilton. Singer-songwriter **Jimmy Buffett** included allusions to *Star Trek* in the lyrics of several songs. Even the Chairman of the Board himself, **Frank Sinatra,** was a fan. Reportedly, he watched *The Next Generation* religiously. As a tribute, Brent Spiner recorded an album titled *Ol' Yellow Eyes Is Back,* comprised of standards popularized by Sinatra.

## Martin Cooper, Inventor of the Cell Phone

Martin Cooper, while an employee of Motorola in 1973, led the team that developed the first functional cordless cellular phone—a twenty-eight-ounce

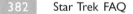 

unit nicknamed "the brick." His first call was to AT&T's Bell Labs, where engineers were simultaneously working to create a similar device. Cooper phoned to inform them they had lost the race. Cooper admits that the now-ubiquitous cell phone was inspired by the flip-top communicators used on *Star Trek*. In the 2006 Discovery Channel documentary *How William Shatner Changed the World*, Cooper says of the communicator: "That was not a fantasy to us. . . . That was an objective."

## NASA Scientists

A photo taken on October 19, 1967 (the night before the broadcast debut of "The Doomsday Machine") shows a control room full of technicians from NASA's Jet Propulsion Laboratory in Pasadena wearing "Spock ears" as they monitor the Mariner 5 probe's flyby of Venus. The space agency has been a hotbed of *Trek* fandom ever since. The original prototype space shuttle was named *Enterprise* in honor of the Starfleet flagship.

Tom Hanks may never have become an astronaut, but many other fans of the show did. Some of those were recruited by Lieutenant Uhura herself, Nichelle Nichols, who became an advocate for the space program in the 1970s and led an effort to attract minority candidates for the astronaut corps. Among the many trainees recruited by Nichols were Sally Ride, the first American woman in space; Guy Bluford and Fred Gregory, two of the first African American astronauts; and three crew members killed in the *Challenger* disaster of 1986.

Also, NASA scientists have often used *Star Trek* lingo and metaphors to explain their work. For example, in July 2011, NASA announced plans for an ambitious new mission to send astronauts to explore an asteroid within fifteen years, a project with daunting technical and logistical challenges. Scientists aren't sure yet how this will be done. Since asteroids have minimal gravity, you can't walk on one without floating away. NASA is exploring the use of jetpacks and tethers, or even nets and harpoons, to allow explorers to float near the surface of the asteroid while attached to a tiny, shuttle pod–like ship that would launch from a larger spacecraft. The same technology could be used to divert an asteroid on a collision course with Earth. "This is the big step. This is out into the universe, away from Earth's gravity completely," Kent Joosten, of the Human Exploration Team at Johnson Space Center in Houston, told the Associated Press in a July 23, 2011, interview. "This is really where you are doing the *Star Trek* kind of thing." Indeed, two classic *Trek* episodes—"Paradise Syndrome" and "For the World Is Hollow and I Have Touched the Sky"—have plots that hinge on preventing an asteroid from colliding with a populated planet.

## IBM Computer Programmers

Telecommunication and space exploration are hardly the only fields where innovators have been influenced by *Star Trek*. Entire books have been written about scientific breakthroughs inspired by the show. But at least one more advance deserves mention: IBM's development of a voice-activated, interactive computer, nicknamed Watson, to compete on the TV quiz show *Jeopardy!* in February 2011. In a two-episode challenge, Watson mopped up the floor with the show's two highest-earning human champions, racking up $77,147 to Ken Jennings's $24,000 and Brad Rutter's $21,600. *Jeopardy!* awarded the winner a $1 million prize, which IBM donated to charity. In subsequent interviews, IBM programmers compared Watson to the *Enterprise* computer, voiced by Majel Barrett. In an interview available on the company's website, IBM researcher David Ferrucci stated flatly that "the computer on *Star Trek*" is an appropriate comparison for Watson:

> A powerful and fluent conversational agent, like the *Star Trek* computer, is a driving vision for this work. . . . When you think about the *Star Trek* series, Captain Picard or Captain Kirk just speaking to the computer and the computer immediately has a sense of what's the context, what is he asking me about, what are my follow-up questions, how to behave as an information-seeking tool that helps this person get at what they need rapidly through a natural language dialogue in their terms.

## Stephen Hawking

The world's most famous living scientist, author of *A Brief History of Time* and other books that have helped laypeople better understand the mind-boggling realms of physics and cosmology, is also a *Star Trek* fan. Stephen Hawking played himself (or, rather, a holodeck recreation of himself) in the 1993 *Next Generation* adventure "Descent." In this installment, Commander Data plays cards with Hawking, Albert Einstein, and Sir Isaac Newton. Hawking has the distinction of being the only person to appear as himself on *Star Trek*. During the shoot, he asked to visit the *Enterprise* engine room set. Nodding at the warp drive engine, the wheelchair-bound Hawking reportedly quipped, "I am working on that." Hawking also penned the foreword to physicist Lawrence M. Krauss's book *The Physics of Star Trek*. In this foreword, Hawking wrote that "Science fiction like *Star Trek* is not only good fun but it also serves a serious purpose, that of expanding the human imagination."

## Randy Pausch

Professor Randy Pausch, a computer scientist diagnosed with terminal pancreatic cancer, delivered a lecture titled "Really Achieving Your Childhood Dreams" to his students at Carnegie-Mellon University in Pittsburgh September 18, 2007. His upbeat speech was videotaped and soon became a YouTube sensation. Pausch suddenly found himself in demand for interviews and speaking engagements, including an appearance before Congress to appeal for pancreatic cancer research and a guest spot on *Oprah*. He expanded his well-loved speech into a short book, *The Last Lecture*, which became a posthumous bestseller in October 2008. All this attention helped Pausch achieve a childhood dream of his own: joining Starfleet. In interviews, the professor sometimes mentioned his long-standing admiration for *Star Trek*. According to a May 8, 2009, *New York Times* story, director J. J. Abrams was inspired by Pausch's message and e-mailed the professor about appearing in the 2009 *Star Trek* movie: "I just wanted to put the invitation out there—that if you had any desire to be in the film . . . it would be my honor and pleasure." Pausch is glimpsed briefly in the picture's opening scene, playing a bridge officer on the Starship *Kelvin*. He has one line ("Captain, we have visual"). Sadly, Pausch died July 25, 2008, before *The Last Lecture* reached bookshelves or Abrams's *Star Trek* made it to theaters.

## Sir Richard Branson

Sir Richard Branson, the British billionaire owner of hundreds of businesses, including Virgin Records, Virgin Atlantic Airways, and Virgin Galactic (the first space tourism company), is a confessed *Star Trek* devotee. The names of Virgin Galactic's first two spacecraft are a dead giveaway: VSS *Enterprise* and VSS *Voyager*.

## Political Leaders

U.S. President **Barack Obama**'s affection for *Star Trek* also is well known. He ran J. J. Abrams's 2009 *Star Trek* film at the White House and later gave interviewer Jon Meacham from *Newsweek* a capsule review (thumbs up). "You know, *Star Trek* was ahead of its time," Obama said of the classic series in the May 15, 2009, interview. "The storylines were always evocative, you know. There was a little commentary and a little pop philosophy for a 10-year-old to absorb." Obama also flashed Meacham the Vulcan salute. The president's affection for *Star Trek*

In 2008, Barack Obama became the 44th president of the United States—and the first Trekker in Chief.

has inspired ribbing from humorists, especially the irreverent staff of Internet news parody site the Onion.

But Obama is hardly the only *Star Trek* fan among the world's political elite. Others include:

- King Abdullah II of Jordan, who appeared as an extra in the 1996 *Voyager* episode "Investigations."
- Canadian Prime Minister Stephen Harper.
- Former secretary of state Colin Powell, who visited the set of *Star Trek: The Next Generation* during his tenure as Chairman of the Joint Chiefs of Staff.
- Former vice president of the U.S. and Nobel Peace Prize winner Al Gore, who often skipped class to watch *Star Trek* reruns (according to his former Harvard College roommate, actor Tommy Lee Jones).
- And President Ronald Reagan, who screened *Star Trek III: The Search for Spock* at the White House in 1984 and later gave interviewers a capsule review (thumbs down). In 1991, then ex-president Reagan visited the set of *Star Trek: The Next Generation* during the filming of the episode "Redemption." He reportedly quipped that he liked the Klingons because "they remind me of Congress."

# Bibliography

## Books

Alexander, David. *Star Trek Creator: The Authorized Biography of Gene Roddenberry.* Penguin, New York: 1994.

Asherman, Allen. *The Star Trek Compendium.* Pocket. New York: 1989.

Ayers, Jeff. *Star Trek: Voyages of Imagination—The Star Trek Fiction Companion.* Pocket. New York: 2006.

Blair, Karen. *Meaning in Star Trek.* Warner. New York: 1977.

Blish, James. *Spock Must Die!* Bantam. New York: 1970.

Blish, James. *Star Trek.* Bantam. New York: 1967.

Block, Paula M. with Terry J. Erdman. *Star Trek: The Original Series 365.* Abrams. New York: 2010.

Bond, Jeff. *The Music of Star Trek.* Lone Eagle. Hollywood, CA: 1999.

Brooks, Tim and Earle Marsh. *The Complete Directory to Prime Time Network and Cable TV Shows 1946–Present* (7th ed.). Ballantine. New York: 1999.

Brunas, Michael and John and Tom Weaver. *Universal Horrors: The Studio's Classic Films, 1931–1946.* McFarland. Jefferson, NC: 1990.

Cogswell, Theodore R. and Charles A. Spano Jr. *Spock, Messiah!* Bantam. New York: 1977.

Doctorow, Cory and Karl Schroeder. *The Complete Idiot's Guide to Publishing Science Fiction.* Alpha. Indianapolis: 2000.

Doohan, James with Peter David. *Beam Me Up, Scotty: Star Trek's "Scotty" in His Own Words.* Pocket. New York: 1996.

Eklund, Gordon. *The Starless World.* Bantam. New York: 1978.

Ellison, Harlan. *Harlan Ellison's The City on the Edge of Forever: The Original Teleplay That Became the Classic Star Trek Episode.* White Wolf. Clarkston, GA: 1995.

Engel, Joel. *Gene Roddenberry: The Myth and the Man Behind Star Trek.* Hyperion. New York: 1994.

Farraland, Phil. *The Nitpicker's Guide for Classic Trekkers.* Dell. New York: 1994.

Fern, Yvonne. *Gene Roddenberry: The Last Conversation.* Pocket. New York: 1994.

Gerrold, David. *The Trouble with Tribbles: The Complete Story of One of Star Trek's Most Popular Episodes.* Ballantine. New York: 1973.

Gerrold, David. *The World of Star Trek.* Ballantine. New York: 1973.

Goldin, Stephen. *Trek to Madworld.* Bantam. New York: 1979.

Gross, Edward. *Trek: The Lost Years.* Pioneer. Las Vegas, NV: 1989.

Gross, Edward and Mark Altman. *Captain's Logs: The Unauthorized Complete Trek Voyages.* Little, Brown. New York: 1995.

Gross, Edward and Mark Altman. *Great Birds of the Galaxy: Gene Roddenberry and the Creators of Star Trek*. Image. New York: 1992.

Haldeman, Joe. *Planet of Judgment*. Bantam. New York: 1977.

Joseph, Franz. *The Starfleet Technical Manual*. Ballantine. New York: 1975.

Joseph, Franz. *Star Trek Blueprints*. Ballantine. New York: 1976.

Kelley, Steve. *Star Trek: The Collectibles*. Krause. Iola, WI: 2008.

Koenig, Walter. *Warped Factors: A Neurotic's Guide to the Universe*. Taylor. Dallas: 1997.

Krauss, Lawrence M. *The Physics of Star Trek* (2nd ed.). Basic. New York: 2007.

Lawrence, J. A. *Mudd's Angels*. Bantam. New York: 1978.

Lichtenberg, Jacqueline, Sondra Murshak, and Joan Winston. *Star Trek Lives!* Bantam. New York: 1975.

Marshak, Sondra and Myrna Culbreath. *The Price of the Phoenix*. Bantam. New York: 1977.

Marshak, Sondra and Myrna Culbreath (Eds.). *Star Trek: The New Voyages*. Bantam. New York: 1976.

McNeil, Alex. *Total Television: The Complete Guide to Programming from 1948 to the Present* (4th ed.) Penguin. New York: 1996.

Meyer, Nicholas. *The View from the Bridge: Memories of Star Trek and a Life in Hollywood*. Viking. New York: 2009.

Nichols, Nichelle. *Beyond Uhura: Star Trek and Other Memories*. Boulevard. New York: 1994.

Nimoy, Leonard. *I Am Not Spock*. Buccaneer. Cutchogue: 1976.

Nimoy, Leonard. *I Am Spock*. Hyperion. New York: 1995.

Okuda, Michael and Denise and Debbie Mirek. *The Star Trek Encyclopedia*. Pocket. New York: 1999.

Palestine, Eileen. *Star Trek: Starfleet Medical Reference Manual*. Ballantine: New York: 1977.

Phillips, Mark and Frank Garcia. *Science Fiction Television Series: Episode Guides, Histories, and Casts and Credits for 62 Prime-Time Shows, 1959–1989*. McFarland. Jefferson, NC: 2006.

Reynolds, Mack. *Mission to Horatius* (Replica ed.). Pocket. New York: 1996.

Rioux, Terry Lee. *From Sawdust to Stardust: The Biography of DeForest Kelley, Star Trek's Dr. McCoy*. Pocket. New York: 2005.

Sackett, Susan. *Inside Trek: My Secret Life with Star Trek Creator Gene Roddenberry*. Hawk. Tulsa, OK: 2002.

Sackett, Susan. *Letters to Star Trek*. Ballantine. New York: 1977.

Sackett, Susan and Gene Roddenberry. *The Making of Star Trek: The Motion Picture*. Pocket. New York: 1980.

Shatner, William and Chris Kreski. *Star Trek Memories*. HarperCollins. New York: 1993.

Shatner, William and Chris Kreski. *Star Trek Movie Memories*. HarperCollins. New York: 1994.

Shatner, William with David Fisher. *Up Till Now*. St. Martin's. New York: 2008.

Sky, Kathleen. *Vulcan!* Bantam. New York: 1978.

Smith, Christine. *DeForest Kelley—A Harvest of Memories: My Life and Times with a Remarkable Gentleman Actor.* Self-Published: 2001.

Solow, Herbert F. and Robert Justman. *Inside Star Trek: The Real Story.* Pocket. New York: 1996.

Takei, George. *To the Stars: The Autobiography of George Takei, Star Trek's Mr. Sulu.* Pocket, New York:1995.

Trimble, Bjo (Ed.). *The Star Trek Concordance.* Ballantine. New York: 1976.

Turnbull, Douglas (Ed.). *A Star Trek Catalog.* New York: 1979.

Whitfield, Stephen E. and Gene Roddenberry. *Star Trek: The Making of the TV Series* (Revised ed.). Titan Books. London: 1991.

Whitney, Grace Lee with Jim Denney. *The Longest Trek: My Tour of the Galaxy* (2nd ed.). Quill Driver. Sanger, CA: 2007.

Winston, Joan. *The Making of the Trek Conventions or, How to Throw a Party for 12,000 of Your Most Intimate Friends.* Doubleday. New York: 1977.

## Publications

"Believing in Captain Kirk." Barrie Hale. *Calgary Herald.* April 26, 1975. p. 10.

"Cult Fans, Reruns Give Star Trek an Out of This World Popularity." Doug Shult (Los Angeles Times News Service). *Milwaukee Journal.* July 3, 1972.

Lincoln Enterprises Mail Order Catalog. (Lincoln Enterprises). 1977.

*Roddenberry v. Roddenberry* (opinion). Hon. John Zebrowski, et. al., California Court of Appeal, 1996.

"Roddenberry Would Like to Leave Star Trek Behind." Bob Thomas. *Williamson Daily News.* May 25, 1976. p. 14.

"Star Trek Engenders Cult in U.S., England." Jerry Buck (Associated Press). *Youngstown Vindicator.* March 14, 1972. p. 18.

"Star Trek Fandom as a Religious Phenomenon." Michael Jindra. *Sociology of Religion* Vol. 55 #55, 1994. pp. 27–51.

"Star Trek's Familiar Face." Tara Parker-Pope. *New York Times.* May 8, 2009.

"Where is the Welcome Mat?" *TV Guide.* August 24, 1968.

## Websites

http://abcnews.go.com/Technology/wireStory?id=14142219

http://home.comcast.net/~cjh5801a/Flash.htm

http://ctva.biz/US/TV-Ratings/CTVA_NielsenRatings.htm

http://www.fastcopyinc.com/orionpress/articles/startrekmyths2.htm

http://www.ftlpublications.com/bwebook.pdf

http://www-03.ibm.com/innovation/us/watson/index.html

http://www.imdb.com/

http://www.insidetrek.com/quotes/quoteweeklog.html

http://www.isfdb.org/

http://www.jklm.net/atn/oldcard.html
http://www.magicdragon.com/UltimateSF/emain.html
http://www.megomuseum.com/
http://en.memory-alpha.org/wiki/Portal:Main
http://www.nielsen.com/us/en.html
https://www.netflix.com/
http://www.ottens.co.uk/forgottentrek/
http://round2models.com/
http://www.shemadeit.org/meet/biography.aspx?m=112
http://www.sixtiescity.com/startrek/sttosmain2.htm
http://www.startrek.com/
http://www.telegraph.co.uk/news/worldnews/northamerica/usa/1361090/
    Star-Trek-drove-me-to-drink-says-Spock.html
http://www.thedailybeast.com/newsweek/2009/05/15/a-highly-logical-
    approach.html
http://www.trekplace.com/article19.html
http://www.wikipedia.org/
http://www.wired.com/dangerroom/2009/05/look-out-spock-pentagon-works-
    on-real-life-phasers/
http://www.wixiban.com/trading-cards/tos-76topps.htm
http://www.youtube.com/

## DVDs

*Airplane II: The Sequel.* Paramount, 2000.
*The Beach Girls and the Monster.* Image, 2002.
*The Brain Eaters.* Direct Video, 2003.
*Classic Sci-Fi TV—150 Episodes.* Mill Creek, 2009.
*Combat! The Complete Series.* Image, 2005.
*Futurama: The Complete Collection.* Fox, 2009.
*Galaxy Quest.* Dreamworks, 2000. *Genesis II.* Warner Archives, 2009.
*Gunfight at the O.K. Corral.* Paramount, 2003.
*How William Shatner Changed the World.* Allumination, 2005.
*Incubus.* Winstar, 2001.
*The Intruder (Special Edition).* Buena Vista, 2007.
*Invasion of the Body Snatchers* (1978). MGM, 1998.
*Judgment at Nuremberg.* MGM, 2004.
*Kid Monk Baroni.* Image, 2007.
*M Squad: The Complete Series.* Timeless Media, 2008.
*Mind Meld—Secrets Behind the Voyage of a Lifetime.* Goldhill, 2002.
*Mission: Impossible—The Fourth Season.* Paramount, 2008.
*Mission: Impossible—The Fifth Season.* Paramount, 2008.
*The Man from U.N.C.L.E: The Complete Series.* Warner, 2008.
*Night of the Lepus.* Warner, 2005.

*The Outer Limits—The Original Series, Season 1.* MGM, 2002.

*The Outer Limits—The Original Series, Season 2.* MGM, 2003.

*Planet Earth.* Warner Archives, 2009.

*Pretty Maids All in a Row.* Warner Archives, 2010.

*The Questor Tapes* (1974). Private copy.

*Saturday Night Live—The Complete First Season, 1975–76.* Universal, 2010.

*Spaceballs.* MGM, 2000.

*Spectre* (1977). Private copy.

*Star Trek: The Animated Series—The Animated Adventures of Gene Roddenberry's Star Trek.* Paramount, 2006.

*Star Trek: The Complete Comic Book Collection* (DVD-Rom). Graphic Imaging Technology Inc., 2008.

*Star Trek: The Motion Picture (The Director's Edition).* Paramount, 2001.

*Star Trek: The Original Series—The Complete First Season.* Paramount, 2004.

*Star Trek: The Original Series—The Complete Second Season.* Paramount, 2004.

*Star Trek: The Original Series—The Complete Third Season.* Paramount, 2004.

*Star Trek: The Original Series—Season* (Blu-ray). Paramount, 2009.

*3rd Rock from the Sun—Season 4.* Starz/Anchor Bay, 2006.

*Thriller: The Complete Series.* Universal, 2010.

*The Twilight Zone: The Complete Definitive Collection.* Image, 2006.

*Warlock.* Fox, 2005.

*Zombies of the Stratosphere* (1952). Private copy.

The *Star Trek* saga continues in *Star Trek FAQ 2.0: Everything Left to Know About the Feature Films, The Next Generation, and Beyond,* coming in 2013.

# Index

# THE FAQ SERIES

## Lucille Ball FAQ
*by James Sheridan and Barry Monush*
Applause Books
978-1-61774-082-4
$19.99

## The Beach Boys FAQ
*by Jon Stebbins*
Backbeat Books
978-0-87930-987-9
$19.99

## Black Sabbath FAQ
*by Martin Popoff*
Backbeat Books
978-0-87930-957-2
$19.99

## The Doors FAQ
*by Rich Weidman*
Backbeat Books
978-1-61713-017-5
$19.99

## Fab Four FAQ
*by Stuart Shea and Robert Rodriguez*
Hal Leonard Books
978-1-4234-2138-2
$19.99

## Fab Four FAQ 2.0
*by Robert Rodriguez*
Hal Leonard Books
978-0-87930-968-8
$19.99

## Led Zeppelin FAQ
*by George Case*
Backbeat Books
978-1-61713-025-0
$19.99

## Pink Floyd FAQ
*by Stuart Shea*
Backbeat Books
978-0-87930-950-3
$19.99

## Star Trek FAQ
*by Mark Clark*
Applause Books
978-1-55783-792-9
$19.99

## Three Stooges FAQ
*by David J. Hogan*
Applause Books
978-1-55783-788-2
$19.99

## U2 FAQ
*by John D. Luerssen*
Backbeat Books
978-0-87930-997-8
$19.99

## Neil Young FAQ
*by Glen Boyd*
Backbeat Books
978-1-61713-037-3
$19.99

# HAL•LEONARD®
## PERFORMING ARTS
## PUBLISHING GROUP

**FAQ.halleonardbooks.com**